THE STATE IN GLOBAL PERSPECTIVE

The State in Global Perspective

Edited by
ALI KAZANCIGIL

Gower/Unesco

First published in 1986 by
the United Nations Educational Scientific and Cultural Organization,
7 Place de Fontenoy, 75700 Paris, France
and

Gower Publishing Company Limited
Gower House, Croft Road
Aldershot, Hants GU11 3HR
England

Gower Publishing Company
Old Post Road, Brookfield
Vermont 05036
USA

British Library Cataloguing in Publication Data
The State in global perspective.
    1. Political sociology   2. State, The
    I. Kazancigil, Ali
    306'.2   JA76

Library of Congress Cataloguing-in-Publication Data
Kazancigil, Ali.
    The state in global perspective.

    Bibliography: p.
    Includes index.
    1. State, The – Addresses, essays, lectures.
    2. Comparative government – Addresses, essays, lectures.
    I. Title.
JC325.K39 1986   320.1   85–31741

Unesco ISBN 92-3-102283-0
Gower ISBN 0 566 05160 5

Printed in Great Britain by
Blackmore Press, Shaftesbury, Dorset

Contents

PART II Structures and Functions **143**

Notes on contributors

Bertrand Badie is professor of political science at the Faculty of Law and Political Science, Clermont-Ferrand, and associate professor at the Institut d'études politiques, Paris, France.

Pierre Birnbaum is professor of political sociology at the University of Paris I, Sorbonne, and at the Institut d'études politiques, Paris, France.

V.E. Chirkin is professor at the Institute of the State and Law of the Academy of Sciences of the USSR, Moscow, USSR.

S.N. Eisenstadt is professor of sociology at the Hebrew University of Jerusalem and at the Truman Research Centre of that University.

Maurice Godelier is director of the sciences of man and society at the Centre national de recherche scientifique (CNRS) and director of studies (anthropology) at the Ecole des hautes études en sciences sociales, Paris.

Marcos Kaplan is professor of political science at the Instituto de Investigaciones Jurídicas of the National Autonomous University of Mexico (UNAM).

Ali Kazancigil is the editor of the *International Social Science Journal*, Unesco, Paris.

Ali A. Mazrui is professor of political science at the University of Michigan, Ann Arbor and at the University of Lagos, Nigeria.

Philip Resnick is professor of political science at the University of British Columbia, Vancouver, Canada.

M.G. Smith is professor of anthropology at the University of Yale, Connecticut, USA.

Romila Thapar is professor of anthropology at the Jawaharlal Nehru University, New Delhi, India.

Göran Therborn is lecturer in political sciences at the Catholic University, Nijmegen, Netherlands and at the University of Manchester, Manchester, UK.

Immanuel Wallerstein is professor of sociology and director of the Fernand Braudel Center for the Study of Economies, Historical Systems and Civilizations, at the State University of New York at Binghampton NY, USA.

Aristide R. Zolberg is professor of political science at the New School for Social Research in New York, USA.

Introduction

Ali Kazancigil

The pervasiveness of the state

The state has seen an unprecedented expansion in the twentieth century. But the fascination, mingled with fear, that it exerts is very old, and this 'monstrous progeny of power and law', as Paul Valéry called it, has produced throughout the ages a number of metaphors evoking mythical monsters, and deities such as Leviathan and Moloch. For the present time, the Mexican poet, Octavio Paz, has given us the metaphor of the 'philanthropic ogre', which exactly conveys the contradictory feelings aroused by the modern state, seen as a dominating force with totalitarian ambitions, but also as a guardian, which protects and regulates society.

Fernand Braudel has noted that '[n]owadays the state is rated very highly', and that, unlike the structures of the past, it fills 'the entire social space'.[1] Indeed, the pervasiveness of the state is one of the inescapable realities of our time, both for the industrialised countries, whether capitalist or socialist, and for the developing ones. 'Living without the state'[2] would not be an alternative for societies that are part of the world system or that wish to be. And for many stateless people, state building is the *sine qua non* for independence and development. The growing role of the state is a profound historical trend, at the very centre of the world's dominant political and economic processes.[3]

Historically, industrial civilisation and capitalism developed with the active participation of the state. In this volume, Philip Resnick refers to 'Wagner's law' concerning the continuous growth of state expenditure, formulated at the end of the nineteenth century by the conservative German economist, Adolph Wagner, and implying a relation between the rise of capitalism and the growth of the state. The current trends largely confirm this 'law'. The forms, modalities and degrees of state intervention vary from one country to another, but its reality is undeniable.

The growth of the state in industrialised capitalist societies can be quantitatively measured in areas such as the level of state expenditures as a percentage of GNP, the level of taxation, state control over the national economy, or the number of public agencies, officials and legislation.[4] This phenomenon is observable even in countries where anti-statism is widespread. For example, in the United States, under the Reagan administration, public spending grew as a percentage of national income and Federal taxes went up from 27.8 per cent of the national income in 1981 to 31.6 per cent in 1983. In the United Kingdom, the Thatcher government, elected on a programme of the state 'disengagement', did not prevent the growth of public expenditure from 39 per cent of GDP in 1979–80, to 43.5 per cent in 1981–2.[5] For the OECD as a whole, state expenditure grew from 29.3 per cent of GDP in 1961 to 43 per cent in 1983.[6]

Beyond its traditional functions of internal and external security, justice and sovereignty, the state makes itself felt in all societal spheres, in economic, social, ideological and cultural processes, and even in the private lives of citizens.[7] The hypertrophy of the state, which provokes legitimate resistance and protest, is not circumstantial. It corresponds to long-term structural phenomena, linked to major historical processes which have been shaping the world for nearly four centuries.

This development, which began in Western societies, has spread to the socialist countries and the Third World, where the state is often omnipresent. In socialist countries, where the pervasiveness of the state and its control over society are greater than elsewhere, it is important to note its exclusive role in achieving an accelerated economic, educational and cultural accumulation in the initial phase of the development of these societies. The current problems of socialist societies are quite different from those of the initial phase, and raise a number of questions as regards the future evolution of socialist states.

In the Third World countries the state leads the formation of nations and national economies, but here it is handicapped by a rather limited external autonomy, and its capacity to control society is much more restricted than that of the industrialised states in the East or in the West.

Study of the state

Systematic and rigorous study of the state belongs traditionally to political philosophy and, more recently, to the social sciences. Questions of power, authority or domination, all of which concern the nature of the state, have always been at the centre of political thinking produced by the Chinese, Indian, Greco-Roman, Judaeo-Christian and Islamic civilisations. The philosophers of the Renaissance and the Enlightenment, as well as Hegel, shaped the thinking on the state, before social scientists took up the subject in the nineteenth century, particularly the political economists, Marx and his disciples, and the German historical sociologists, whose great figures were Max Weber and Otto Hintze. However, this great intellectual tradition[8] has not always been followed up, and until the Second World War the study of the state was influenced too exclusively, both in Western Europe and in the United States, by legal and constitutionalist approaches.[9] While the latter continued to dominate the study of the state in a number of Western European countries after the War, in the United States the social sciences, and more particularly sociology and political science, in which behaviourism and empiricism then prevailed, considered the state to be too broad a conceptual category to be subjected to empirical analysis. The proponents of functionalism and systems analysis preferred to study political processes and the behaviour of individuals and groups. Political regimes were analysed from the point of view of developmentalism and modernisation, excluding not only the state but also the relations of domination and dependence, at both the internal and the international levels.[10]

The reaction to this ahistorical trend came from several quarters. In the Third World during the 1970s, the question of the state became one of the major concerns of researchers, the initial impetus having been provided in the 1960s by the Latin American theoreticians of *dependencia*.[11] In the West, the renewal of political economy,[12] historical sociology and political anthropology contributed to the advance of studies on the state, while Marxist research, which had never neglected the question, though without always producing an original analysis of it, was improved through the neo-Marxist schools in the United States, the United Kingdom, the German Federal Republic, Scandinavia and France. In some socialist countries, such as Yugoslavia, Hungary and Poland, several interesting analyses were produced, which went beyond the limits set by strictly orthodox ideology. At present, the state is a central concern in social science research in all regions, disciplines and paradigms, even in the United States, in spite of traditional American reticence about the state as an analytical category.[13]

Aim of this volume

The essays presented here reflect this renewal of state studies and attempt to provide elements of response to some of the major questions on the state, through the contributions of political economy, anthropology, sociology, political science and history.[14] The international, multi-disciplinary and pluralist perspective of this volume reflects the diversity of the state itself around the world. We are not concerned here either with making professions of faith in anti-statism or with indulging in 'statolatry',[15] but with studying the state as rigorously as possible, trying to distinguish between what comes from reasoned analysis and what is based on ethics. Naturally, this does not imply that the state is a category that stands beyond axiological considerations, nor that one should not try to measure it, particularly with regard to its totalitarian practices, with the yardstick of ethics.

The state has had many definitions since Machiavelli used the word in its modern sense. The two most widely quoted definitions in social science are the Weberian and the Marxian. Max Weber defines the state as a human community which, within the limits of a determined territory, successfully reserves to its own use the monopoly of legitimate physical violence.[16] Marx, who takes the state in its relations with society, sees it as an organisation of class domination, as the creation of an order which legalises and strengthens class oppression, by acting as moderator in the class struggle.[17] Beyond these two major references, other definitions are found which vary according to theoretical or disciplinary perspectives.

The essays in this volume do not aim primarily to define the state. On the whole, it is analysis rather than description that is at the centre of their concern, and definition belongs more to the latter than the former. They raise such questions as: why does the state exist? Why do people obey it? Is the state part of the substance of society, of the whole complex of social, economic and political processes, or is it a separate reality, derived from society but situated autonomously above it? What is meant by state autonomy, and what are the relations between the state and the social classes? How does it intervene in societal processes, and how far does this intervention go? Is it a legal concept (of sovereignty and public order) or, from a sociological point of view, a space where social forces confront each other? Or again, is it a mediation between internal and external spheres and between the political and the economic? Can all forms of political domination without distinction be classified under this concept, ranging from the chieftainships of primitive societies to the modern state, including the city-state, the tribal confederations, feudalism, the historic empires and the absolutist state?

One can characterise these texts in several ways. First, they combine the genetic approach with the functional approach. The phenomenon of the state and its nature, as well as the identification of many layers of meaning within it, are explained by analysing its origin and growth as both a universal and a specific mode of domination, together with its forms and functions. Second, they offer various disciplinary perspectives: anthropology (Godelier and Smith), history (Thapar and Mazrui), historical sociology (Eisenstadt and Zolberg), political and cultural sociology (Birnbaum, Badie and Therborn), international relations and political economy (Kaplan, Kazancigil, Resnick, Chirkin and Wallerstein) — while each of them combines several disciplinary approaches as well. They also differ according to their underlying theories or schools of thought: Marxian or neo-Marxian (Godelier, Kaplan, Chirkin and Therborn), functionalist (Eisenstadt, Smith), Weberian approaches (Badie, Zolberg, Mazrui), analyses situated implicitly and explicitly between Marx and Weber (Wallerstein, Kazancigil), or between Marx and Pareto, so as to establish a correlation between the type of state and the organisation and ideology of social groups (Birnbaum).

A number of themes emerging from these essays cut across the boundaries both of the disciplines and of the major Marxian, Weberian or structural-functional paradigms. One such theme concerns the place to be given to the endogenous and exogenous determinations of the state. Should the status of independent variable be accorded to internal economic, social, political and cultural processes and structures, or to external and global processes? Some authors, such as Godelier, Eisenstadt, Smith and Birnbaum, opt for the primacy of endogenous processes. Wallerstein, on the other hand, sees the global system as the primordial factor, rather than the modern state considered only in its relations with internal processes and structures. Others, like Zolberg or Kaplan, take a less radical position on this question, and do not offer a verdict on the hierarchy of state functions. Zolberg's analysis bears on the space where the internal and external facets of the state meet, which he calls the 'interface'. His study, which sheds light on the role of political and strategic factors in the formation of the modern state, is complementary to that of Wallerstein, for whom this important dimension of the formation of the inter-state system is less primordial.[18]

Another debate, which is a corollary to the preceding one, concerns the relation of the economic to the political and the weight of these two variables in explaining the state. First there are those for whom the state is not a simple reflection of the interests of classes or dominant groups. These writers accord to it considerable autonomy[19] as manifested by its structure, which is clearly differentiated from that of society, and by its capacity to formulate and pursue its own objectives, which deeply influence a number of processes within the civil society. Theoretical studies in this direction have increased considerably in recent years, along with the increasing role played by the state. This is also connected to the abundant literature devoted to the corporatist state and to neo-corporatism, both in industrialised capitalist countries and in the Third World.[20] Resnick criticises this concept, which concerns the articulation between the interest groups within the society and the decision-making mechanisms of the state; his preference would go to the concept of organised capitalism. Therborn is also very critical of corporatism, as a theory aiming at explaining the welfare state. In this respect he finds equally unsatisfactory the pluralist or liberal, statist as well as the earlier versions of neo-Marxist theories. In formulating hypotheses about the development patterns, structures and socio-economic implications of the welfare state, he proposes to use a class power theory, which he characterises as historical and empirical.

Authors such as Wallerstein see the state, or the political, as the dependent variable and the economic as the independent one. For Wallerstein the state responds to production processes and class forces, which are constituted objectively at the world-economy level and subjectively at the state level, the latter being a product of the capitalist world-economy, rather than a primordial instance. Other authors, such as Kaplan, Kazancigil or Therborn, recognise the increased importance of the economic, while according a certain degree of autonomy to the political variable. Chirkin's analysis of the socialist state follows the classical approach of the Soviet school of 'the science of the state'. Distinguishing between the essence, the substance and the form of the state (the latter may differ from country to country), he describes how the socialist state evolves from the dictatorship of the proletariat to the socialist state of all the people (the only current example of which being, according to him, the Soviet Union). He sees this as the evolutionary path that must be followed by all socialist societies before the final phase of communism is reached.

For the analysts who favour the autonomy of the political variable, the specific form taken by the modern state in a given country depends less on this country's relations with the market economy than on its own history with its particular socio-cultural and religious context. This is how Birnbaum raises the question of the relation of the state to culture and ideology, which in his opinion explains the fact that societies with comparable economic structures and levels of development can have quite different states. Deriving its distinctive character from the culture of the society within which it developed, the state in its turn conditions the ideologies and social movements that spread within that society.

This analysis, through the role it gives to culture, implies that the modern state, as it has evolved in Western Europe since the close of the Middle Ages, is radically different from all other state forms preceding it in history, and is thus not replicable in other socio-cultural contexts.[21]

Such is precisely the thesis advanced by Badie, who puts the concept of state in quotation marks in his analysis of legitimacy and protest in Islamic culture. Badie maintains that, in the context of Islam, which functions simultaneously as a culture, a religion and an ideology, the political sphere is driven apart from the rationality which presides over the state.

The privileged role assigned to culture in the formation of the state is also found in Eisenstadt, who uses the perspective of comparative sociology to examine the cultural codes, symbols of collective identity and modes of legitimisation which condition the institutionalisation process of the state in different historical and civilisational contexts. This is also shown by Mazrui, who analyses African, Islamic and European cultural heritages which have influenced the formation of the post-colonial states in Africa.

Another approach which combines cultural traits with social structure is that of Smith, who offers a typology, in a heuristic perspective, aiming at generating new research. This typology shows the relations between plural, segmentary or hierarchical societies and the different types of state, according to a number of criteria by which they can be categorised. He also analyses the relations between types of society, state structure and collective violence.

Analysis of peripheral state formations is the subject of the articles by Kaplan and Kazancigil, who do not underestimate its autonomy but stress the importance of explicating the state by its modes of insertion into the international system. Thus they try to take into account in their analyses the exogenous and endogenous variables, as well as the economic and political variables.

Kaplan is interested in a theory that accounts for the specificities of relations between the state, civil society and the social classes in the Third World. Kazancigil analyses the emergence of the modern state in the periphery, not as a result of the desire of élites in the South to imitate the North — though this is by no means a negligible factor — but as a global process corresponding on the one hand to the demands of sovereignty, economic accumulation, the formation of a civil society and of a nation, and on the other hand to the realities of the world system as it functions today. Thus his analysis is distinct from both evolutionism and diffusionism as explanations of the formation of the modern state in the Third World.

The refusal to see the state as a mere appendix to the world system is characteristic of many scholars of the state in the Third World. Although it may be dependent and excessively authoritarian and denounced as such, the state is still seen as the only instrument of sovereignty and autonomy that can bring about economic liberation. For these authors, the state is a crucial factor in the dialectic of dependence and autonomy in which it is simultaneously and to changing degrees a relay in the dependence–domination process, as well as a space within which objectives of freedom and sovereignty can possibly be achieved. According to this viewpoint, in the present world system, only the state can organise the struggle against domination, structure civil society, provide a basis for autonomous accumulation and thus eventually make it possible for free and democratic societies to exist in the Third World.

However, the states of the Third World are still in gestation. They are incomplete and little differentiated from civil society, the formation of which depends on the action of the state. This aspect of the question is stressed by Kazancigil, who maintains that the formation of states is complicated by the disarticulating impact of domination exercised by the centre of the world system on its periphery. Countries of the Third World do not have the advantage of the historical circumstances enjoyed by Western Europe between the sixteenth and the twentieth centuries, when the modern state was formed simultaneously with the world capitalist system.

Godelier and Thapar analyse, from an anthropological and historical perspective, the initial endogenous processes which are at the origin of the state. Thapar identifies a complex set of factors in ancient India, such as the transition from kinship to stratified communities, the relations between castes and economic interests, the characteristics of peasant economy and trade with the urban centres. In passing, she casts doubt on the applicability of concepts like the Asiatic mode of production and oriental despotism to India. Godelier and Kazancigil also refer to such concepts, in view of the important controversies they have caused about the evolution of the state in the Third World.

Godelier studies the mechanisms by which collective representations are constituted, legitimising the consent of the majority to the domination of a minority. He sees such representations, together with ideology and religion, not as a mere reflection, which legitimises in a *post hoc* manner relations of domination created without their participation, but as one of the conditions for the formation of such relations. They are part of the foundation on which rest the relations of production and exploitation. Godelier's arguments also concern the basis of the differentiation of social functions and the formation of hierarchies, such as orders, castes and classes, which marked the transition from stateless to state societies. They shed light on the origins of a number of processes observed in contemporary complex societies.

Resnick approaches the state from its economic, political and legitimisation functions. After reviewing the different theories of the state, he concludes that 'the state, as the modern form of political power, is here to stay into the indefinite future . . . The real question then becomes, what limits can be placed on its repressive qualities, and how much power can in fact be devolved back to its citizens.'

The various problematics that emerge from this volume do not obviously cover all the questions about the state that could be asked. Particularly, the question of the limitation of state power and its restitution to the citizens is not addressed here, except incidentally. And yet, this is one of the major difficulties with the state in the West, and even more so in the East: its democratisation at the grassroots level, through participation and self-management, while preserving the representative democracy, which safeguards freedoms. In the Third World countries, this problem is even harder to resolve, first because of the weakness of the society *vis-à-vis* the state, secondly because of the relations of dependence which dislocate peripheral social formations, and finally because of the need to discover forms of democracy and state that are in harmony with their histories and cultures.

Other questions, which have not received here the attention they deserve, concern the extent to which the modern state is actually capable of performing the tasks assigned to it. This 'crisis of governance' is due to several factors, such as the contradictions between conservative economic and fiscal policies aimed at accumulating capital, and social or redistributive measures, through which the Welfare State, approached here by Therborn from a theoretical perspective, tries to alleviate the consequences of such policies, or the transnational dimensions of major problems (inflation, financial crises, international trade, energy, and so on) in the face of which individual states are powerless. The state, to use Daniel Bell's aphorism, seems to have become too big for little problems, and too small for big ones.

When all is said and done, perhaps the main justification of this collection of essays is to report, through the very diversity of approaches it contains, on the complexity of the phenomenon of the state and its irreducibility to simplistic formulas.

Notes

1   Fernand Braudel, *Civilisation matérielle, économie et capitalisme, XVe–XVIIIe siècle*, Vol. 3: *Le temps du monde*, Paris, Armand Colin, 1979, p. 39.

2   Jean-William Lapierre, *Vivre sans Etat? Essai sur le pouvoir politique et l'innovation sociale*, Paris, Le Seuil, 1977.

3   Pierre Souyri, *La dynamique du capitalisme au XXe siècle*, Paris, Payot, 1983, especially pp. 9–41.

4   Klaus von Beyme, 'The Role of the State and the Growth of Government', *International Political Science Review*, vol. 6, no. 1, 1985, pp. 11–34.

5   Figures quoted in *Le Monde:* for the United States, 14 November 1984, p. 13; and for the United Kingdom, 30 January 1985, p. 36. See also Jacqueline Grapin, *Forteresse America*, Paris, Grasset, 1984, who shows that in spite of the myth of Reaganism, the United States practises a modern form of *dirigisme*, with the President and the Pentagon controlling the military-industrial complex, and the Federal Reserve controlling credit and money.

6   OECD figures, quoted in 'World Economy Survey', *The Economist*, 24 September 1983, p. 29.

7   A theoretical explanation of this phenomenon is offered by Jacques Attali, who shows the fluctuating relations between the state and the 'market order' *(ordre marchand)*; the crisis of the latter leads the state to support the extension of the market order at the expense of non-market systems, intervening further and further beyond the public sphere, into the private life and the most intimate areas of activity. See Attali, *La figure de Fraser*, Paris, Fayard, 1984.

8   A questionable aspect of this intellectual tradition should be noted, which contrasts the 'civilised' political systems of the West with the 'despotic' ones of the East. This has been a recurrent theme, from Aristotle to Marx, via Machiavelli and Montesquieu. It still characterises a good deal of current scholarship on the non-Western states, displaying Manichaean and ethnocentric forms. For a psychoanalytical critique of this approach, as a fantasy generated by the classical Western imagination, see the remarkable study by Alain Grosrichard, *Structure du sérail*, Paris, Le Seuil, 1978.

9   See Harry Eckstein, 'On the "Science" of the State', *Daedalus*, vol. 108, no. 4, Autumn 1979, pp. 1–20, and the article on 'State' in the *International Encyclopaedia of the Social Sciences*, 1968, vol. 15, pp. 143–57.

10   For example, one looks in vain for the concept of state in the series of volumes on comparative politics (such as G. Almond and J. Coleman (eds), *The Politics of the Developing Areas*; L. Pye (ed.), *Communications and Political Development*; J. La Palombara (ed.), *Bureaucracy and Political Development*; R. Ward and D. Rustow (eds), *Political Modernization in Japan and Turkey*; L. Pye and S. Verba (eds), *Political Culture and Political Development*; L. Binder *et al.*, *Crises and*

Sequences in Political Development) published during the 1960s in the United States under the auspices of the Committee on Comparative Politics of the Social Science Research Council and which exercised considerable influence on several generations of students and scholars.

11 For a description of this paradigm, see Pedro Henriquez, 'Beyond Dependency Theory', *International Social Science Journal*, no. 96, 1983, pp. 391–400.

12 Elizabeth Crump Hanson, 'International Political Economy as a New Field of Instruction in the United States', *International Social Science Journal*, vol. 30, no. 3, 1978, pp. 666–77.

13 Theda Skocpol, 'Bringing the State Back In', *Items*, vol. 36, nos. 1 and 2, June 1982, pp. 1–8.

14 The essays by Badie, Chirkin, Mazrui, Kaplan, Kazancigil, Resnick, Smith and Therborn have not been previously published in English. Those of Birnbaum, Godelier, Eisenstadt, Thapar, Wallerstein and Zolberg appeared in the *International Social Science Journal*, vol. 32, no. 4, 1980. The majority of these texts were prepared as part of Unesco's international research project on 'The State and Society in the World' and discussed at a symposium in February 1981 in Wolfenbüttel (FRG), organised jointly by the University of Hanover and Unesco, with the support of the Volkswagen Foundation. Badie's text was presented at the ECPR Workshop on 'The Entry of Socially Subordinate Groups in Political Arena' in Salzburg in April 1984. Kazancigil and Therborn's essays are versions of papers presented at the Thirteenth World Congress of IPSA in Paris in July 1985 and Resnick's is a version of a paper presented at the Twelfth World Congress of IPSA in Moscow in August 1979.

15 Eric Weil, *Philosophie politique*, 3rd edn, Paris, J. Vrin, 1971, p. 135.

16 Max Weber, *Economy and Society* (ed. G. Roth and C.W. Wittich), Vol. 1, Berkeley, University of California Press, 1968, p. 56.

17 Tom Bottomore *et al.* (eds), *A Dictionary of Marxist Thought*, Oxford, Blackwell, 1983, p. 464.

18 See Aristide R. Zolberg, 'Origins of the Modern World System: A Missing Link', *World Politics*, vol. 33, January 1981, pp. 253–81, for a critical analysis of Wallerstein's approach.

19 The autonomy of the state, the relative existence of which was recognised by Marx — cf. Karl Marx, 'The 18 Brumaire of Louis Bonaparte' in L. Feuer (ed.), *Basic Writings on Politics and Philosophy*, Garden City, Doubleday, 1959 — and which has always been minimised by the orthodox Marxist tradition, is given a better treatment by the neo-Marxist analyses. See for example Nikos Poulantzas, *State, Power, Socialism*, London, New Left Books, 1978. Another recent analysis which highlights state autonomy is that of Theda Skocpol, *States and Social Revolutions: A Comparative Analysis of France, Russia and China*, Cambridge, Mass., Cambridge University Press, 1979.

20 See, for example, Philip Schmitter and Gerhard Lehmbruch (eds), *Trends Towards Corporatist Intermediation*, London, Sage, 1979; Leo Panitch, 'Recent Theorizations of Corporatism: Reflections on a

Growth Industry', *British Journal of Sociology*, vol. 30, no. 2, June 1980, and Alfred Stepan, *The State and Society: Peru in Comparative Perspective*, Princeton, NJ, Princeton University Press, 1978.

21   Bertrand Badie and Pierre Birnbaum, *The Sociology of the State*, Chicago, University of Chicago Press, 1983, p. 97.

Part I
Origins and Formation

1 Processes of state formation

Maurice Godelier

Differentiation and domination

Traditionally, a distinction is drawn between two processes which govern the formation of the state, one exogenous to society, the other endogenous. The term 'exogenous' is used when one society conquers another and the conquered people are subjected to permanent domination by their conquerors; the term 'endogenous' when one part of a society gradually establishes its predominance over the other members.

This essay will be devoted mainly to an abstract analysis of the conditions which render possible the development, within a society, of one dominating and several dominated groups. I have adopted, for this purpose, a method which might be regarded as formal and applicable to any kind of division of society into two groups, one dominating and the other dominated. What I have in fact done is to pose in abstract terms the general question of what constitutes the power to dominate.

Any power to dominate, I consider, always has two components which are indissolubly linked and which give both strength and efficacy: violence and consent. It is my view that, of these two components of power, the stronger is not the violence of the faction which establishes its domination, but the consent of those who are dominated. If this is the case, it will be appropriate, in order to understand the processes of the formation of relations of domination

3

and state power in archaic societies, to operate on the theory that, in order for one part of society to establish and perpetuate its domination over another, i.e. to maintain its position at the centre and summit of society, repression is less important than agreement, physical violence and psychological pressure less important than ideological conviction, leading to the consent and acceptance, if not actually the 'co-operation' of the dominated section of the society. In this abstract form, this hypothesis applies not only to the formation of relations of domination of the order, caste and class type, but equally to relations between the sexes and the domination of women by men.

A theoretical point of fundamental importance is therefore to decide how certain concepts of the social and cosmic order can be shared by groups having, to some extent, opposing interests. It is this question of the sharing of concepts that constitutes the theoretical problem to be solved.

Let me make myself quite clear, so as to leave no room for idle or insincere objections. Domination is never established without violence, though the latter may sometimes be only latent. There is all the difference in the world between passive acceptance and active consent. Moreover, active consent is never 'spontaneous', but the result of cultural background and individual education. Moreover consent, even passive, will never come about on the part of all the members or all the groups in a society, and never without reservations and contradictions.

As I see it, the violence/consent relationship is not static. In certain circumstances — but the problem is which ones — consent changes into passive resistance; in others, passive resistance turns into active resistance and sometimes into rebellion against the social order. Then again, rebellion may sometimes be transformed into revolution, seeking to change the structure of society. Or again, but more rarely, a revolution may succeed. Yet these changes in the relations between violence and consent are the outcome not of chance circumstances, but of a particular accumulation of all the opposing forces that divide society and set one part of it against the others. Divisions and antagonisms affect the whole character of a society, and not merely its symbols and people's images of their fellow men. They permeate the whole of the everyday life of society, which is at once their strength and their weakness. In view of this, I shall not approach the subject from the standpoint of formal philosophical theory, so as to avoid sterile juggling with opposites, violence and consent. That is not the crux of the matter: it is that, essentially, violence and consent are not mutually exclusive. In order to endure, any power of domination — and this is true in particular of power born of the brute force of conquest and war — must include and reconcile these two prerequisites. The proportions will vary according to circumstances and to the strength of the resistance, but, even when domination is the least contested, there is always the potential threat of recourse to violence the moment consent is weakened or gives rise first to refusal, and then to resistance.

The purpose of the foregoing is to forestall misunderstanding, whether theoretical or political. I am attempting a theoretical understanding of the fact that dominated groups can spontaneously 'consent' to being dominated. My hypothesis is that, for this to be possible, the dominators must appear to be rendering some sort of service. It is only in these conditions that the power of the dominating group can be regarded as 'legitimate', so that it becomes the 'duty' of the people dominated to serve those who are serving them. It is thus essential that dominators and dominated should share the same concepts, for there to be consent based on recognition of the 'need' for society to be divided into several groups, and for one of them to dominate the others.

In my view, the problem of the formation of the state refers back to that of the formation of an aristocracy in archaic societies; and also to the concentration of social power in the hands of certain individuals who come to personify the general interest.

Let me give an example. The So are an agricultural people living in Uganda, on the slopes of Mount Kadam and Mount Moroto. They live on sorghum, stock-raising and a little hunting, but their situation is precarious. Their agriculture is threatened periodically by drought or disease attacking their crops. Their cattle are constantly being stolen by the various groups of Karimojong shepherds living on the plains. The forest is shrinking as a result of burn-baiting, and nearly all the game has disappeared. These people number about 5,000, divided into widely dispersed patrilineal clans. In this society the men dominate the women, and the older members dominate the younger. But there is, among the elders, each of which represents his lineage or clan, a small minority of men who dominate the rest of the society: those who are initiated in *kenisan*, who have the power to communicate with the ancestors (*emet*) and to obtain from their benevolence everything that makes life happy — good harvests, peace, health, and so on. The ancestors themselves communicate with a remote god (*belgen*). When a man dies his soul (*buku*) becomes one of the ancestors and the elders of all the groups recall the names of their ancestors, but only the *kenisan* initiates can call them by their names and speak to them face to face. Any non-initiate who dared to do this would be struck at once by madness, begin to devour his own excrement, and 'climb the trees like a baboon' — behave like an animal, in fact — and die. This threat hanging over the population puts a hedge of 'potential violence'

5

around the persons and the acts of the *kenisan* initiates, who carry out their rites in a sacred place concealed from the public and close to the 'house of *belgen*', the god.

What then are the functions of these elder-initiates, of whom there are approximately fifty out of a total of 5,000 people? One of their main tasks is to bury important dead, both men and women, and to ensure the transition of the soul of the deceased to the condition of *emet*, ancestor. They also take action whenever society is threatened by serious drought, epidemics, enemies from without or internal conflicts. In the last case, they set up a kind of court of justice, which names the culprits after consulting the ancestors. Their skill in witchcraft is such that they are even feared by their enemies, the Karimojong, who raid their territory. When their harvest is laid waste by drought, insects, worms or mildew, they carry out ceremonies to 'bring rain' or 'bless the sorghum'. A goat is sacrificed to the ancestors, part of the meat is placed on the altar and the rest consumed by the *kenisan*. The sacred site and the rites for bringing rain belong to a few clans only, of which only one has the power of making rain fall for the whole of the tribe, for which only the *kenisan* perform the rites.

We see thus that this group of a few men derive their power from the fact that they have special access to the ancestors and the god, who have the capacity to reproduce every form of life, to bring prosperity, justice and peace, and to triumph over enemies and adversity. They thus hold, as it were, a monopoly for influencing the conditions (to us imaginary) governing the reproduction of society. By exercising their powers and making sacrifices to the ancestors, they serve the common interest and are identified, in the eyes of the living and the dead, with the interests of all the members of the society — men, women, elders, rich and poor. They personify and embody their society. Naturally, 'in exchange' for their services, they enjoy the greatest prestige, authority and also some material advantages.

This is an example of domination by a group of elders organised on the basis of a secret society of initiates. It does not constitute an aristocracy in the true sense of the word, but only the extension of the domination of the elders over the younger members of the group, of the men over the women.

Let us now take a second example, that of the Pawnee Indians of North America who lived, before the arrival of the Europeans, in large sedentary villages along the valley of the Mississippi, cultivating maize and engaging in seasonal hunting of the bison. This society had an aristocracy composed of hereditary chieftains and hereditary priests. The chieftain inherited from his maternal ancestors a magic package, to be found today in many museums in America, consisting of an antelope skin containing a few teeth and other sacred objects. The

Pawnee Indians believed that this package had the power of ensuring the fertility of the land and the annual return of the bisons in the summer. Thus the chieftain's family owned the means for ensuring the intervention of supernatural powers for the general welfare of the community and for their prosperity, both material (good crops, successful hunting) and social. The tradition was that if, as a result of war, the magic package was stolen or destroyed, the whole tribe would disintegrate, split up and cease to exist as a society, in which case each family would have to go off and merge with other tribes. We have here an example of religious concepts serving to justify the dependence of the common people on a hereditary aristocracy of chieftains and priests. Religion provides the ideal milieu for a domination relationship and, it might be said, a source of violence without violence.

Here again, this power of domination appears to stem from the monopolisation by a group of society of conditions which we in our civilisation today regard as imaginary, conditions governing the reproduction of life. The point at issue is whether the religious beliefs are only a representational system putting the stamp of legitimacy on an existing relationship of domination which would have been established without those beliefs, or whether, on the contrary, they constitute one of the conditions responsible for development of this domination relationship and are an integral component of it.

Let us now take a final example, that of the Incas whose civilisation, unlike the other two described above, was a state society, the state being personified by the Inca, the son of the Sun, a living god. In the garden of the Temple of the Sun, at Cuzco, was an offering to the gods consisting of numerous models, in gold, of all the plants and animals of the Tawantinsuyu, the Empire of the Four Quarters, including first and foremost ears of Indian corn and statuettes of llamas and shepherds. Every year, the Inca and members of his family, in another garden, themselves sowed, watered and harvested the Indian corn destined for the great festival of the Sun-god. The fact that, to us in the present day, the services rendered by the Inca appear to be 'imaginary' whereas the forced labour done in the fields of the Inca or his father, the Sun, and on the construction of roads, temples, towns and granaries seems to us both very real and a form of extortion, oppression and exploitation, is an indication of at least two points: first, that this 'imaginary' service, since it was not regarded by the Indians as different from or opposed to reality, was not illusory at all; and, second, that the monopoly exercised by the Inca and his family over the 'imaginary' conditions governing the reproduction of life was one of the main foundations from which his right to appropriate part of the land and of the labour of the village communities was derived.

If this is true, religion is seen to be not only a reflection of social relations but also a factor which governs the development of these relations and becomes a part of the internal structure of the production and exploitation system. The difference between the Pawnee and the Inca aristocracy is that the former continues to be a group of men superior in kind because they are closer to the gods to whom they have special access, exercising a sort of monopoly, whereas the Inca, on the contrary, is no longer a man, but a god. Like the Pharaoh in Egypt, he is a god living among men. It will be noted that the material basis of the Pawnee aristocracy was a combination of agriculture and hunting, whereas the material basis of the Inca empire consisted of a combination of intensive agriculture and stock-breeding. Conditions for the production of surplus labour-time in the two cases were very different. In the former, there was an aristocracy, but there was no separate institution, distinct from family groups, to ensure the domination of one group over the others; in the latter, there was a specialised instrument and apparatus — the politico-religious bureaucracy — for the exercise of power, and the state existed as an institution, distinct from the kinship system though based on the structure of that system.

Between these two examples there is a qualitative difference due to the emergence of a certain type of state resulting from the attribution of a divine character to the social authorities and a section of the society.

I therefore put forward the following hypothesis: that in order to take shape and reproduce itself on a continuing basis, a relationship of domination and exploitation must take the form of an exchange, and an exchange of services; it is this that enlists the consent, either passive or active, of those on whom it is imposed. I make the further hypothesis that one of the main factors responsible for the internal differentiation of social functions and social groups and thus for the formation, over varying periods of time, of new hierarchies based not on kinship but on new types of division (orders, castes, classes) is that the services provided by the dominant group should be related to reality and to invisible forces seeming to control the reproduction of the universe. This must have played an essential part since, in the balance between the services 'exchanged' those rendered by the dominant group appeared all the more fundamental for being 'imaginary', while those rendered by the dominated appeared all the more trivial for being more visible, more material, and concerned only with means available to all for influencing the reproduction of society.

I believe, however, that for the development of the movement resulting in the formation of the new divisions, orders, castes and classes, it was essential that not all the services rendered by the dominant group should be 'illusory' or even 'invisible'. Returning to the example of the Pharaoh who, in Ancient Egypt, was regarded as a living god, son of the Nile, lord of the land and waters, sole source of all life force, both that of his subjects and that of all the creatures of nature, we can see that this power and this image of a benevolent god, lord of life, was more than just a symbol. Did men not require royalty, and the reunification of the two kingdoms of Upper and Lower Egypt, to dam the flow of the Nile which every year brought the fertile river deposits, the rich 'black' earth hemmed round on every side by the sterile 'red' earth of the desert? And as for the Inca, was he not responsible for the construction of the vast embankments thanks to which many mountain slopes, previously barren, could be sown with Indian corn? It is true, of course, that the Inca was, by this means, encouraging the development of a crop which was easy to stock and transport to the town, the palace, for the use of the Inca, the army, the priests and the administration. And Indian corn was also used traditionally for sacrifices to the gods and ritual ceremonies. But not all the maize planted went to the Inca and the dominating group, nor was it stored by the Inca for his own needs: he used to throw open the state granaries periodically to the poor, and, in the event of catastrophe, he made the stocks available to all those in need of succour.

Thus more than religion is needed for religion to dominate men's minds and the life of society. It is only under certain historical conditions that it can provide a basis for the formation of hierarchical relations and give a minority sovereign power over society. What is required, therefore, in collaboration with archaeologists and pre-historians, is a study of the processes which have led, all over the world, to the emergence of new types of status and power hierarchies in social groups previously based on kinship links within the same global social unit (which we vaguely call a tribe). Archaeology shows that these processes began with the sedentarisation of certain groups of hunter-gatherers having vast natural resources available in their vicinity. But these processes spread and, above all, diversified only with the development of agriculture and stock-breeding. I think that the development of new material relations between man and nature and among men created new possibilities for the emergence of differentiated and even opposing group interests. It also created the need for ritual and direct control over nature, which was steadily becoming less wild and more domesticated, without which man was unable to reproduce himself, and which in turn, was experiencing growing difficulty in reproducing itself without man (animal and plant species found in agriculture and stock-breeding). I think that these new material conditions and distinct new interests gave rise to divisions which seemed at first to be advantageous for everyone, as differences serving the interests of all and, to that extent, legitimate.

9

It is therefore with the paradoxical statement that the process of the formation of castes and dominating classes and the emergence of the state were, in a way, legitimate, that I propose to conclude this brief view of the problem.

Thus labour devoted towards community ends (*travail-en-plus*), which exists in every classless society, gradually became transformed into surplus labour (*sur-travail*), a form of exploitation of man by man. The term 'surplus labour' is used to denote all forms of material activity which are designed to reproduce a community as such, as opposed to the individuals and families that make it up. In many so-called primitive societies, the work designed for the reproduction of the individual and his family is done separately. There are, on the other hand, forms of collective work, performed by all or a majority of the families in a society, and designed to produce the material means for the reproduction of the community as such — celebration of rites, sacrifices, preparation for war, and so on.

Thus the function and nature of the labour normally done by families for the reproduction of the community to which they belong change when this work is designed to reproduce the conditions for the existence of those who alone henceforth represent the community and embody its common interests. Surplus labour can gradually be transformed into surplus labour-time in the form of exploitation.

To complete this analysis, it might be useful to investigate how, in situations of domination born of violence and conquest, mechanisms conducive to pseudo-consent are set up, for the purpose of stabilising this power. The ceremonies for the enthronement of a new king by the Mossi of Yatenga provide a striking example. The Mossi are descended from horsemen from Ghana, to the south, who, about the middle of the fifteenth century, conquered the Volta basin. They subjugated the native agricultural peoples, who are known today as the 'people of the land' or the 'sons of the land'. The latter have retained all their ritual power over the land and agricultural production. When a Mossi king dies, a new king is chosen from among the sons of the deceased sovereign. Only Mossi descended from the former conquerors may designate the new king. He then sets off alone and poorly clad on the long enthronement journey which brings him back after some fifty days, to the gate of his capital, where he makes his triumphal entry on horseback as king. His journey takes him through the conquered villages, where the 'masters of the land' reside, and where he is invited to take part in rites addressed to the ancestors of the peoples subjugated, and to the powers of the land. As M. Izard writes:

The new chief of the foreigners appears alone, humbly, before the representatives of the oldest occupants of the country, to ask them to accept his authority and accord him the legitimacy that only the land can confer. He offers or promises them presents. A play is enacted between the king and the 'sons of the land': he is humiliated, kept waiting and mocked, nothing is done to provide him with food or lodging.[1]

Thus, by including him in their rites, the priests and chiefs of the indigenous clans have the king recognised by their ancestors and by the earth as one of their own people, so giving his power a legitimacy that conquest prevented him from possessing fully. This recognition of the king is, of course, at the same time, a recognition by the king of the legitimacy of the power of the indigenous people; and this mutual recognition is sealed by the exchange of royal protection for their labour and a share of the produce of the land.

In this way the kingship, established by force of arms, is transformed into a sacred institution. The king alone unites in his person the community of the conquerors and the community of the conquered; he alone personifies the unity of the two communities, albeit opposed to one another. He thus represents at a higher level the whole of society, and he alone constitutes the state. His person, when he is king, becomes sacred, which accounts for the taboos applying both to him and to all those approaching him.

Even power established by conquest must, in order to become stabilised, seek the means of enlisting a degree of consent.

In attempting a comprehensive view of the development of social relations that has transformed the social divisions existing between kinship groups in primitive societies, three types of process might be identified. First of all, there is a minority group which gradually comes to represent the whole of the community, reaping the benefit of the surplus labour normally intended to ensure the reproduction of the community, and so having privileged access to the product of social labour. Secondly, this minority, representing the community *vis-à-vis* the outside world, becomes capable of controlling the exchange of goods and services between communities, thereby assuming control of valuable goods used for reciprocal gifts or the exchanges through which the relations between communities are reproduced. And lastly, this minority can gain mastery of the use of the common resources of the land, gradually controlling them completely, though community ownership of these resources is not actually abolished. There are thus instituted processes which may, in the long run, result in the community's material conditions of production being expropriated by a minority representing it. This leads to a separation of the producers from their material means of existence, and dependence of a new type,

11

material this time and not social or ideological, of the majority of the members of society on the minority dominating it.

It is these transformations in various forms that have produced the hierarchies of orders, castes and classes which, in the course of history, have succeeded the earlier forms of social life represented by tribal or inter-tribal communities.

Orders and classes

Orders, castes and classes are forms of social hierarchy often associated with distinct forms of state. Orders, in the ancient world, are associated with the city-state. Castes, in India, combined to form the social and territorial units constituting the kingdoms of India, for the sub-continent was formerly divided into a hundred or so local kingdoms at the summit of whose hierarchy were the Brahmins and the king. As to classes, this appears to be a modern form of social hierarchy and exploitation of man by man, a product of the disintegration of an order society, the feudal system, and of the development of the mode of production of capitalist society.

The distinction between orders and classes, in Western thinking, crystallised in the eighteenth century. From the works of the early economists it may be noted that both Quesnay and Adam Smith use the concept of class to describe the social groups composing the economic system of modern society. Quesnay, who was physician to the King of France and thus uniquely versed in the vocabulary of ancient feudal society, with its divisions into 'estates' — nobility, clergy, third estate — chose to base his *Tableau économique de la France* (1759) on classes and the relations between the 'productive class' and the 'unproductive class'. He shows how the annual product of a modern 'agricultural' nation circulates among three 'classes' — the class of farmers and agricultural workers, which is the only productive one, the landowner class and the 'industrial or unproductive class'. A generation later Adam Smith, in his *Inquiry into the Nature and Causes of the Wealth of Nations* (1776), maintains, on the contrary, that of the three classes into which every 'civilised' society is divided, only the landowning class is indolent and unproductive, whereas those of the farmers and the capitalists serve the general interest of society. Subsequently, Ricardo (1813) and Marx (1857) continued to analyse modern capitalist society in terms of classes. Thus it seems that the eighteenth century saw the development of new social relations different in type from the orders and social levels bequeathed by the Middle Ages.

This concept of classes designates social groups occupying the same place in the production process, regardless of their membership of a social order. Thus a bourgeois owning land and a landowning noble-man are both classified as landowners, occupying a similar place in the production process, although occupying different places in the order hierarchy.

It would therefore appear that the concept of 'classes' was intro-duced after the development, in society, of production relations entirely divorced from the old social institutions — family, political and religious hierarchies. At the same time, the concept of classes refers to a historical situation in which the old relations of dependence, personal, individual and collective, have disappeared or are dis-appearing, and there is increasing legal equality among the members of society. Outside the industrial production process, where the workers are subordinated to the owners of money and the means of production, individuals, in theory, enjoy the same rights. In theory, differences of sex, race, religion and opinion no longer directly affect the place individuals occupy in the production process and the work process. Comparing this situation with that existing in antiquity, we note that the fact of being born a citizen of Athens conferred the right to the use of a part of the land of the city, which the citizen could either cultivate himself, or have cultivated by slaves. Citizenship, or membership of a local community in the form of a city, gave privileged access to the land, which was the basis of the economy in ancient times. On the other hand, a free man coming from another neighbouring city had no right to own and cultivate a plot of land in Athens. The result of this was to confine 'foreigners' to other occupations, such as crafts or trade.

Here, as we see, production relations are not based on the division of labour but are, on the contrary, the basis of it: individuals occupying the same place in the division of labour do not occupy the same place in the production process. It is essential to draw a distinction between the labour process and the production process. If a free man exercised the same manual trade as a slave, he occupied the same place in the labour process, but a different place in the production process. For a slave had no rights over his production which, like his person, belonged to his master. Whereas, on the contrary, the status of a free man, because he was free, gave him a different position in regard to his labour and the product of his labour. It is clear from this that membership of a city-state, i.e. citizenship, constituted, in the Greek city, the original form of production relations. In a sense 'politics' here constitutes a 'production relation', an infrastructure. As opposed to the situation in the capitalist production system, there is here no division between economic activities and the institutions in which they take place (enterprises, etc.), on the one hand, and non-economic

13

social, political and religious activities, on the other.

Thus orders are not the same as classes, though they are, like classes, forms of domination and of exploitation of man by man. Marx, in *The German Ideology* (1845–6), draws a very clear distinction between order and class. Making a brief outline of the evolution of feudal society, he describes how the bourgeoisie is slowly transformed from an order into a class. Originally a local group, inhabiting small towns and cities, with only local interests and influence, the bourgeoisie came gradually to form a social group with national interests and influence. With the development of market production, the new role of money, colonial expansion, international trade, etc., the bourgeoisie, originally a specific fraction of the feudal order — the third estate — changed its character.

It was in order to define this change that Marx introduced the distinction between class 'in itself' and class 'for itself'. The bourgeoisie, although it had become a national force, none the less continued for a long time to behave like an order subordinated to the nobility, without either challenging the culture and values of the nobility or laying claim to even a share of the political power. According to Marx the bourgeoisie still continued to behave like an order, although it was already a class 'in itself'. It was only later, in the seventeenth and eighteenth centuries, that the bourgeoisie, from being a class 'in itself' became a class 'for itself', and conscious of its new and separate identity, claimed its share of the exercise of power.

However, the works of Marx do present one difficulty, since, in the *Communist Manifesto* (1848), he uses the word 'class' to designate the orders of the society of the ancient world or of feudal society. The celebrated phrase at the beginning of the Manifesto is: 'The history of all hitherto existing society is the history of class struggles.' What Marx meant to say, in my view, was that orders, like the classes of modern society, were forms of exploitation of man by man at a certain stage in the development of productive forces. He used this term, which he knew to be relatively inappropriate and anachronistic, in order to suggest that the time had come for a different view to be taken of 'orders', a view different from that of the actors taking part in that period of history. In other words, Marx means that these 'orders' were social divisions, based on and implying the exploitation of man by man, and not, as they were officially represented as being, a perfectly harmonious relationship between groups performing complementary functions.

It is therefore, a mistake, I consider, to attempt to see in the orders of antiquity classes visible only to modern historians of Marxist leanings. Marx seeks not so much to discern something else beneath the appearances as to put a different interpretation on what appeared, to see it from the viewpoint of the modern era which, by separating economic activities from the other social relations, made it possible for the first time to discern more clearly the part played by economics in the formation of social relations and the course of history.

If asked to explain the development of the social orders in antiquity, I should say that these orders represent relations of domination and exploitation born of the partial disintegration of earlier community-production relations. These relations resulted from forms of labour and ownership that developed gradually, becoming distinct from the earlier community forms, which they contradicted without being able to abolish completely. Reverting to the example of the landed-property system in a city like Athens, we see that the paradox, the contradiction of the form of private ownership practised there, was that it could only exist and be maintained by being subordinated to the communal ownership of part of the city land by the city and the state. The paradox was that, in order to own and cultivate a plot of land marked off from the community land, the citizen was obliged, in a way, to produce and reproduce the community to which he belonged.

The notions of the Asiatic mode of production and state in Marx

This context of the development of new forms of labour and ownership, differing from and opposed to the early community forms, provides the basis for an analysis of what Marx calls the 'Asiatic', the 'ancient' and the 'Germanic' modes of production.

These, according to him, were the three oldest forms of property and production, which he sometimes calls the tribal mode of production. In this tribal mode of production, the land belongs to the community as such. But this communal land is divided into two parts; one of which the community owns directly, the other which it lets to individual families for their temporary use. This arrangement corresponds to an evolution of the forms of production, as a result of which certain groups (families, clans) are able gradually to satisfy their main material needs separately, by their own efforts. Collective labour continues to exist, and is performed by various families and clans, but it is designed not so much for their benefit as to produce the means for the reproduction of the community as a whole (religious sacrifices, warfare activities, and so on). Under these conditions, according to Marx, several transformations may occur. One such transformation leads to the development of the Asiatic mode of production. The content of social relations changes without any radical modification of their forms. The land, owned directly by the community, may in certain conditions be expropriated by a higher community. The

15

individual families composing the community as a whole continue, when this occurs, to work the land which now belongs to another community. Now as before, these families and individuals hold and use the land, but do not own it. The surplus labour which they normally contributed to the reproduction of their community serves henceforth to reproduce a higher community which exploits them and might be personified by a king or a god.

There is thus a change of content but not of form and, paradoxically, this line of evolution goes on reproducing archaic communal forms of property and production which henceforth constitute the basis of state power. According to Marx, this mode of production and these types of state and oppression seriously hampered the emergence of private property and of development bases distinct from and opposed to the archaic forms of property and production. It is for this reason that Marx tended to regard the Asiatic line of evolution as a historical development which led, more often than other lines of evolution, to stagnation and 'dead-end' societies. However, he subsequently went back on this view when, writing to Vera Zazulich in 1881, he admitted that the continued existence of these local village communities was a dynamic force serving as a support for these forms of class and state structure.

Marx contrasts this line of evolution with what he termed the ancient mode of production and the Germanic mode. The ancient mode likewise originated in the tribal mode of production and community forms of property. But it was distinguished by the development, alongside community property, of a private-property system subordinated to it; also by the fact that the community takes the form of a state, and that community property is state property. Marx does not explain how, in the case of the Greeks, a tribal community became a state, and a state having its centre in a city. He talked about several tribes assembling on a certain territory, but this does not explain the form their association assumed, which was that of a community of citizens.

It should be remembered that, in antiquity, private property was regarded as being 'cut off' or 'separated from' the common property (*privatus* in Latin means cut from the *ager publicus*). It was on the basis of this form of citizens' private property that the social differences between rich and poor, etc., developed, which gave rise to the major political and social conflicts in Greek cities such as Athens. When the private ownership of land was combined with the private use of slaves in production, the impulse towards the unequal accumulation of wealth reached its zenith in the ancient world. But it must be remembered that in Sparta, in the same area, land continued to be the property of the state, even when parts of it were distributed to citizens

16

for their use, to be cultivated by families of helots who were also the property of the community, of the state. In Sparta slaves were not privately owned, and neither was the land.

The third line of evolution Marx mentioned was that which led to the formation of the late Germanic community. According to him, at the time of Tacitus, after the intense Romanisation of certain Germanic tribes, there existed communities formed by the association of families or clans, each owning their own plots of farming land, but sharing common land for cattle-grazing, forests for gathering berries, etc. Marx stressed that this form of community differed from the others, in that in this case, in his view, the private ownership of farming land became the starting-point for community property, which served as an appendage to private property, its complement for the organisation of stock breeding and other economic activities. The community, instead of being a 'substantial' unit like the ancient tribal community, the Asiatic community or, to a certain degree, the city in antiquity, was an association of owners linked by kinship, working in co-operation.

Marx's theories as regards the idea of the Germanic community evolved in the course of his life. The works of Maurer, Haxthausen, Grimm and others gradually made him realise that this type of community, composed of private owners, was in fact the delayed result of the disintegration of a far older type of Germanic community in which there was no private ownership of the land, but only a right to the use of plots of land redistributed periodically among families. The very fact of plots of land being allocated for varying periods of time indicates that the land continues to be the property of the community as such. What Marx learned from the works of Haxthausen and others was that there had existed an ancient Germanic property system very similar to the one still surviving in nineteenth-century Russia, where the *mir* sometimes still redistributed land among families. Marx regarded the *mir* as the basis of Asiatic forms of state, which had also existed in Russia. In view of this, it is not surprising to find Engels, in 1881, when writing about the Mark and the early forms of Germanic communities, advancing the hypothesis that, in other circumstances, the Germanic communities might have constituted the basis, in Europe, for Asiatic-type states. But Romanisation changed the course of development and produced, between the time of Caesar and that of Tacitus, the new type of Germanic community which was to give rise to the development of the feudal mode of production. The feudal mode of production, however, according to Marx and other nineteenth-century writers, had more than one base; it was the product of two opposing lines of evolution nevertheless moving in the same direction: first, the gradual disappearance of the slave system in

17

production, to be replaced by forms of dependence which, though still personal, did not make the individual the property of a master (Roman colonate, etc.); and, second, the gradual enslavement of the 'free' German peasants. If asked to draw a conclusion from this brief summary of Marx's theories — which are exceedingly complex and enlightening despite the fact that they betray the limitations of the information available at his time — I would stress that there appear to exist as many types of state as there are types of social hierarchy and modes of production supporting them. The Asiatic form of state is totally different from that of an ancient city-state which, in its turn, has little in common with the feudal hierarchy composed of vassals and suzerain. Many problems have today to be posed in different terms. It is increasingly clear that the development of a complex caste system in India was the outcome of the evolution of ancient tribal and inter-tribal structures, a form of evolution no more primitive than that which led to the differentiation of orders in the ancient city. In both cases, orders and castes are combined within forms of states, of which they constitute the supports. But despite the work of Louis Dumont and many others, the relation between the caste system and the state is still not very clear, and it will probably be necessary, here again, to make a very thorough analysis of the significance of the king and kingship in India.

Finally — and this is fundamental — the emergence of one form of state does not follow automatically from the existence of a hierarchy of orders and classes. To illustrate this, let us take an example from anthropology. There existed in the nineteenth century in the Niger a group of nomad Touareg societies dominating the African farmers. These societies were organised in a hierarchy of groups with, at its summit, a tribal aristocracy which wielded political power and dominated nomad tribes which supplied it with cattle, labour and armed forces. Lastly, subordinated to the stock-breeders, were African farmers who paid tribute. The domination of the aristocracy was exercised without the existence of a state structure. Thus we have here a society composed of orders/classes without a state. When the territory was colonised by the French, a mutation occurred amongst certain of the Touareg groups, including in particular the Kel Gress, studied by Pierre Bonte. What happened was that one of the aristo-cratic families attempted to rise above the others, laying claim to part of the tribute which the others levied from their dependants for the defence of their common interests against the European colonisers. This meant that the other aristocratic families would have had to renounce some of their power, privileges and material goods. The attempt failed, but the example is a very important one, since it signifies at least two things. The first is that the formation of a coherent state system is not necessary in cases where the dominant group is a warrior aristocracy with a permanent supply of arms and means of destruction. The second, that the formation of a state may, for a certain period, constitute a regression, a diminution of the powers of the dominating class. Its power is concentrated, as it were, in a part of this class, and it may not have been easy to recognise in this case that this partial loss suffered by each section of the aristocracy in fact redounded to the benefit of the aristocracy as a whole.

Note

1   Michel Izard, 'Le royaume de Yatenga' in R. Cresswell (ed.), *Eléments d'ethnologie,* Paris, A. Colin, vol. 2, p. 234, 1975 (Collection 11).

References

Balandier, G. (1969). *Anthropologie politique.* Paris, Presses Universitaires de France.

Claessen, H. and Skalnik, P. (1978). *The Early State.* The Hague, Mouton.

Engels, F. (1977). *Origins of the Family, Private Property and the State.* Moscow, Progress Publishers.

Fortes, M. and Evans-Pritchard, E.E. (1940). *African Political Systems.* Oxford, Oxford University Press.

Fried, M. (1957). *The Evolution of Political Society.* New York, Random House.

Godelier, M. (1978). 'La part idéelle du réel', *L'Homme,* vol. 18, nos. 3–4, July–December, pp. 155–88.

Godelier, M. (1970). 'Introduction' in *Sur les sociétés précapitalistes.* Paris, Editions Sociales, pp. 13–142.

Krader, L. (1968). *Formation of the State.* Englewood Cliffs, NJ, Prentice-Hall.

Krader, L. (1975). *The Asiatic Mode of Production.* Assen, Van Gorum, 1975.

Marx, K. (1953). *Epochen Ökonomischer Gesellschaftsformation in Grundrisse der Politischen Ökonomie.* Berlin, Dietz Verlag, pp. 373–413.

2 Comparative analysis of the state in historical contexts

S.N. Eisenstadt

Towards a new analytical approach

Our approach to the analysis of the state in general and the modern state in particular has emerged above all from the reanalysis of the concept of tradition, itself arising from the reappraisal of studies of modernisation and the idea of convergence of industrial societies.

The single most important element of the new perspective is the recognition that, in the shaping of the institutional dynamics of societies, two aspects seem to be of special importance: first, their cultural traditions, and second, their politico-ecological settings in general and their place in the international system or systems in which they participate in particular.

Tradition, which figured in many works initially as a sort of general residual category to cover major aspects of institutional structures which could not be explained in terms of the original model of modernisation, became defined in a more specific way. The various aspects of tradition were differentiated and their relations to concrete institutional patterns specified.

It was broadly shown that tradition is perhaps best viewed as the process — or at least part of the process — by which different aspects of reality are culturally and socially constructed and transmitted in society, i.e. as the reservoir of the most central social and cultural experience of a society or civilisation. This reservoir is not, however, some sort of general, undifferentiated 'store'; rather it has several components, the relations between which are complex and often paradoxical.

There are three major components: the first one consists of certain generalised modes or orientations of perception and evaluation of social reality, of the cosmic and of the socio-political order, which, for convenience, we shall call cultural 'codes'; second, there are the symbols of collective identity; and, third, the major modes of legitimation of the social and political order.

One of the most important findings of our research was that these different aspects of tradition can change at different tempos. It was found, paradoxically enough, that the different cultural orientations tend to be more continuous than the symbols and 'content' of collective identity, even if the latter are often seen as more stable and continuous.

Further, this analysis has indicated how these codes influence and shape some very basic components of the social structure. We were able to formulate in a systematic way, going beyond the rather vague indications found in the earlier literature on traditions or in sociological analysis, those aspects of the institutional structure that cannot be fully explained in terms of levels of technological development or of structural differentiation and specialisation, which are influenced by such codes. The most important among these — of direct relevance to the analysis of the state — are: (a) the structure of authority and conceptions of justice; (b) the structure of power and of political struggle; (c) principles of social hierarchisation; and (d) the definition of membership within different communities all of which greatly influence the major policies adopted in any society, and the perception of social problems within it.

As a result, such conceptions also greatly influence the modes of integration — moral, legal or communicative — of the societies in which they are prevalent, and the major patterns of their legitimation.

Moreover, these conceptions — and their institutional derivatives — are 'carried' by special social actors and mechanisms, especially by several types of cultural, educational and political élites and frameworks and may cut across different societies. They also exhibit dynamics of their own.

Our research has equally indicated that many of these institutional aspects seem to be continuous across different historical settings; they span levels of technological development and are closely related to continuities in certain basic social and cultural orientations and to the construction of traditions, even in modern settings.

The research has also indicated that the very institutionalisation of cultural orientations systematically generates potential for tensions,

21

conflicts and change. This potential is rooted, first, in the contradictions arising within the systems or sets of codes themselves; second, in their application to broad institutional complexes; and third, in the clash between various complexes of codes and various types of institutions and interests. Hence, conflicts and protest are inherent in human societies and influence organisational and symbolic dimensions of social change. This appears in different patterns of rebellion, social conflict and heterodoxies, the constellations of which vary greatly between societies and strongly influence their specific historical experience and dynamics.

In practice, these tendencies occur in different politico-ecological settings, two aspects being specially important. Very strongly stressed in recent research is the importance of international political and economic systems and of the place of different societies within them, particularly relations of hegemony and dependency. There is also the more general recognition of the great variety of different politico-ecological settings of societies, such as small and large societies, dependence on internal and external markets, and the like.

In our work on comparative civilisation we have distinguished between several types of political regimes, each characterised by a certain constellation of structural features closely related to characteristics of élites, cultural orientations and processes of change. The major types we have analysed are the imperial, imperial-feudal, patrimonial and 'exceptional' city-states.

Imperial and imperial-feudal societies

The major characteristics of centre–periphery relations (Shils, 1975, chaps. 1 and 3) in the imperial — and to a large extent also in the imperial-feudal societies — were a high level of distinctiveness of their centres; the perception of the centre as a distinct symbolic and organisational unit, and sustained attempts by the centres not only to extract resources from the periphery but also to permeate and reconstruct it according to the centre's premises. The political, and to some degree, cultural-religious centres in these societies were conceived as autonomous foci of the charismatic elements of the socio-political, and often also of the cosmic-cultural order. These centres — political, religious and cultural — were the foci and loci of the various great traditions that developed in these societies, distinct from local traditions not only in content but also in the symbolic and organisational structural characteristics. The permeation of the periphery by the centres was discernible in the development of widespread channels of communication which emphasised their symbolic and structural difference, and in the attempts of these

22

centres, even if only to a limited degree, to break through the ascriptive ties of the groups at the periphery.

Closely connected to such centre–periphery relations is strong articulation — especially among the higher strata — of symbols of social hierarchies and stratification, of country-wide strata-consciousness and of tendencies to some political articulation and the expression of such consciousness, as well as a high degree of ideological symbolisation and mutual orientations among the major religious, political and even ethnic and national communities. Although such communities tended to attain a relatively high degree of autonomy as well as distinct boundaries, yet in most of these civilisations, they also tended to constitute mutual referents of each other (i.e. being a good 'Hellene' was identified with citizenship in the Byzantine state, and vice versa) (Eisenstadt, 1969, 1978).

This strong symbolic articulation and the distinctiveness of the major institutional patterns is, in these imperial and imperial-feudal societies, closely related, to certain cultural orientations.

Most of these empires developed in close relation to some of the great civilisations or traditions in the history of mankind, such as the special Chinese blend of Confucianism, Taoism and Buddhism; the Christian tradition in all its variants and the Islamic one; all of them constructed civilisational frameworks distinct, both symbolically and organisationally, from the political, ethnic and national ones.

Most shared several basic cultural orientations or codes which set them off from some of the other civilisations which emerged in the same so-called axial age (the first millennium BC) (*Daedalus*, 1975; Voegelin, 1954). They were characterised by a great autonomy and the dissociation of the cosmic (religious) from the mundane order; and also, because of their mutual relevance and impingement, by strong emphasis on the need to bridge the transcendental sphere and the mundane order. While they shared emphasis on the tension between the cosmic and mundane worlds with other civilisations — such as the Hindu and Buddhist — unlike these, they exercised some kind of this-worldly activity, above all in the political, military and cultural, but (especially in the European case) also in the economic spheres, as a bridge between the transcendental-cosmic and the mundane world (in Weber's terminology, as a 'focus of salvation').

Further, there developed a strong emphasis on the commitment of the different population groups to the cosmic and social orders, and relatively autonomous access of at least some groups to the major attributes of these orders.

Such cultural orientations, the structure of centres and of centre–periphery relations, were very closely related to differences between the major élites and institutional entrepreneurs.

Most of the élites or institutional entrepreneurs (Barth, 1963; Eisenstadt, 1971*b*) in imperial and imperial-feudal societies — and above all the articulators of models of cultural and social order, political élites and (to a lesser degree) representatives of different collectivities and economic élites — possessed autonomous resource bases and potentially independent access to the centre and to each other. Moreover, there arose a multiplicity of secondary élites. These, by their impingement on the centres and the periphery shaped various movements of protest, political activities and the struggle within them. Each élite — whether 'primary' or 'secondary' — could be at the origin of certain movements of protest or of a political struggle with a higher level of organisational and symbolic articulation and of certain potential orientations and linkages among themselves and to the centre.

Patrimonial societies

The major patrimonial societies were characterised by a relative absence of the symbolic and structural distinction between centre and periphery; they possessed a higher degree of status segregation but a lower degree of country-wide 'class' consciousness and of symbolic articulation of the major collectivities (Eisenstadt, 1973*b*; Schrieke, 1957); relatively little symbolic and institutional distinction between centre and periphery; a strong tendency to narrow status association; and low autonomy of the major élites. The predominant cultural orientations are either an emphasis on a low or a high level of distinction and tension between the transcendental and the mundane orders, the focus of resolution being other-worldly; weak commitment to the socio-political and even to the cultural order and a tendency to accept it as given.

These societies were also characterised by relatively weak symbolic articulation of different communities and of major élites (whether functional (political and economic) or articulators of cultural models and of the solidarity of different communities) and by the embedding of such élites within ascriptive groups.

Exceptional city-states and tribal federations

The societies in which the second pattern of change developed — the Greek (and Roman), the city-states of antiquity and the Near-Eastern, above all Israelite and Islamic tribal federations (Eisenstadt, 1971*a*, chap. 6) — were characterised by a somewhat different pattern.

The cultural orientations prevalent within them were also those of a perception of some degree of tension between transcendental and mundane orders; some strong this-worldly conception of the appropriate resolution of this tension as well as a relatively high level of commitment to the cultural and social order.

The centre–periphery relations were characterised by a growing symbolic and structural (but not so much organisational) differentiation between the centre and the periphery and by their mutual impingement, thus being rather similar to the imperial regimes, as were some of the basic characteristics of their élites.

But the structural difference between the centre and periphery was not, in both these types of societies, fully institutionalised. This was shown by the fact that, while their central symbols and the officials who dealt with internal and external problems were distinguished from the periphery, yet most citizens could also participate in the centre. Even when many could do so only to a limited extent, this was not dissimilar from the social distinctions made at the periphery.

The most important outcomes of a structurally and symbolically distinct centre, and of overlapping membership between the centre and the periphery, were the relatively weak identity (beyond embryonic nuclei) of the ruling class, as well as of other élites, as autonomous social formations, organisationally — not only symbolically — distinct from the leaders of different social groups and divisions.

Variations in patrimonial societies — Buddhist and Hindu civilisations

Within each of these social types, however, there develop far-reaching variations along three dimensions. First of all there existed variations within cultural orientations, in the 'locus' of the resolution of tensions between the transcendental and the mundane orders (or for salvation), especially in the emphasis placed on this-worldly and other-worldly orientations; in their interweaving; in the delineation of the institutional loci of resolution and in the extent to which basic ascriptive groups were seen as bearers of certain attributes.

Second, there existed important differences of structure in the loci of the activity and internal autonomy of the major élites and institutional entrepreneurs; in the extent to which different élite activities were undertaken through identical roles and in their organisational settings; and in solidarity between different entrepreneurs and between them and the broader strata of the society.

Third, there existed far-reaching variations in the politico-ecological settings of these societies — especially with respect to the existence of relatively compact political regimes (such as empires or patrimonial kingdoms, not tribal federations or feudal regimes) and to size. The most important variants arose within those patrimonial city-state and tribal regimes that were related to religions or traditions connected to the great traditions emphasising strong other-worldly conceptions of salvation, such as Buddhism (Tambiah, 1976) and Hinduism.

These great traditions and their local versions were carried by relatively autonomous, often international élites, such as the Buddhist Sangha (and to a smaller degree the Zoroastrian clergy) the likes of which could not be found among the little traditions of most other regimes under which patterns of relatively non-coalescent change occurred. These élites created centres that, in the religious sphere, were distinct from their own periphery as well as special interlinking networks between these centres and the periphery — between the great and little traditions.

But, given the strong other-worldly emphasis of these great traditions, these cultural orientations did not generate corresponding distinctiveness in the political centres and in the relations between these centres and their periphery, nor did they tend to produce far-reaching restructuring of other institutional spheres. True, autonomous cultural-religious groups, especially the Sangha in Buddhist societies, often participated in political life, the basis of which was their organisational dependence on the rules, and the rulers' quest for legitimation. But such participation occurred mostly within the frameworks of the various patrimonial regimes under which these élites often became politically very powerful.

The situation in the Hindu civilisation of India was rather different. Like Buddhism, which started as a heterodox sect within Hinduism, the latter was an other-worldly great civilisation; yet its negation of the mundane world was not as total as that of Buddhism (Biardeau, 1972; Dumont, 1970b).

Hinduism, as most fully articulated in Brahmanic ideology and symbolism, strongly emphasised the tension between the transcendent and the mundane order — tension derived from the perception that the mundane order is polluted in cosmic terms. This pollution can be overcome either through total renunciation or through ascriptive ritual activities and adherence to the arrangement of social activity in a very complicated hierarchical order reflecting individual standing in the cosmic order and emphasising the differentiated ritual standing of basic primordial kinship and territorial social units (the *jatis*). In all these ways it has a much more direct relation to worldly activities than Buddhism (Cohn, 1971; Dumont, 1970b; Heesterman, 1964; Mandelbaum, 1970; Singer and Cohn, 1968; Thapar, 1978, pp. 40–63).

The cultural-religious centre — the ideological core of which was the Brahmanic ideology and symbolism that developed in India — consisted of a series of networks and organisational-ritual sub-centres (pilgrimages, temples, sects, schools) spreading throughout the sub-continent, often cutting across political boundaries (Cohn, 1971; Singer and Cohn, 1968).

The religious centre or centres became very closely associated with the broad, ethnic Hindu identity (even more closely associated than the religious symbols and those of political community in Buddhist societies). The vague, general, yet resilient boundaries of Hindu ethnic identity constituted the broadest ascriptive framework within which the Brahmanic ideology was worked out.

At the same time, however, as in different other-worldly religions, the major centre of Hinduism was not political. Although there arose in India small and large states and semi-imperial centres, no single state emerged with which the cultural tradition was identified (Heesterman, 1971). Accordingly, centre–periphery relations in most Indian principalities and kingdoms did not differ greatly from such relations in other patrimonial regimes, city-states, or tribal federations. These political centres, although organisationally more compact than the ritual centres, were not continuous — regimes and kingdoms arose and fell — nor did they serve as major foci of Indian cultural identity. This gave Indian civilisation its internal strength and explained its capacity to survive under alien rule (Fox, 1971; Heesterman, 1957, 1964, 1971).

The relative dependence of the cultural traditions, centres, and symbols of identity from the political centre was paralleled by the relative autonomy of the social structure, the complex of castes and villages and the networks of cultural communication (Beteille, 1965; Ishwaran, 1970; Mandelbaum, 1970).

It was these groupings and networks that bred the major types of institutional entrepreneurs and élites, political and economic entrepreneurs on the one hand and articulators of models of cultural order and of the solidarity of different ascriptive groups on the other. Their entrepreneurial activities were structured by two fundamental aspects of Indian social life. First of all, they were rooted in, and defined by, the combination of ascriptive primordial and ritual characteristics; second, such definitions contained very strong emphasis on the proper performance of mundane activities (Neale, 1969; Rudolph, Rudolph and Singh, 1975).

Islamic civilisation

A rather special pattern of relations among cultural orientations, centre–periphery relations, and institutional entrepreneurs crystallised in the realm of Islamic civilisation (Gibb, 1962; Von Grunebaum, 1946, 1954; Hodgson, 1974; Holt, Lambton and Lewis, 1970; Lewis, 1950, 1973; Turner, 1974).

The most important cultural orientations were the distinction between the 'cosmic', transcendental realm and the mundane one and the stress on overcoming the tension inherent in this distinction by total submission to God and by this-worldly — above all, political and military — activity; the strong universalistic element in the definition of the Islamic community; the, in principle, autonomous access to all members of the community to the attributes of the transcendental order (to salvation) through submission to God; the ideal of the *ummah* (the politico-religious community of all believers distinct from any ascriptive, primordial collectivity); and the ideal of the ruler as the upholder of the ideal of Islam, of the purity of the *ummah*, and of the life of the community (Gibb, 1962; Von Grunebaum, 1954).

In the Islamic realm the original vision of the *ummah* assumed complete convergence between the socio-political and the religious communities. The original Islamic state developed out of conquest, motivated by a new universal religion and borne by conquering tribes. In this initial state of conquest the identity between polity and religion was initially very close. Similarly, many of the later caliphs (such as the Abbasides and Fatimides) came to power on the crest of religious movements, legitimised themselves in religious terms, and sought to retain popular support by stressing the religious aspect of their authority and by courting the religious leaders and sentiments of the community. Political problems (e.g., the determination of legitimate succession and the scope of the political community) originally constituted the main theological problems of Islam. But, owing to widespread Muslim conquest, to the tensions between tribal conquerors and conquered peoples, to the emphasis on total submission to God, as well as to the strong ideological dissociation between the universal Islamic community and primordial local or ethnic communities, after the initial attempts of the first caliphs and the beginning of the Abbaside caliphate, the ideal of a common political and religious community was never realised. Accordingly, there developed in Islamic politics a growing dissociation between the political and the religious élites, and the various local communities and institutional spheres, albeit with a strong latent religio-ideological orientation towards the unification of these spheres (Gibb, 1962, pp. 3–33; Turner, 1974).

The identity of the religious community was forged and upheld mainly by the Holy Law (*Sharia*) as annunciated and elaborated by the religious leaders, the *ulema*, and enforced by the rulers. Between the *ulema* and the rulers a very peculiar relation was forged in which the *ulema* became politically passive or subjugated to the rulers even though relatively autonomous in the performance of their legal-religious functions (Schacht, 1970).

This combination gave rise to the very high degree of symbolic and organisational autonomy of the political élites; to the relatively great symbolic autonomy — but only a minimal organisational one — of the religious élites; and to a growing separation of the two. The religious leadership depended heavily on the rulers and did not develop into a broad, independent and cohesive organisation. Religious groups and functionaries were not organised as a separate entity; nor did they constitute a tightly organised body except, as in the Ottoman Empire, when organised by the state (Gibb and Bowen, 1957, chaps. 8–12).

The strong ideological dissociation of the universal Islamic community and the different primordial communities generated weak solidarity between its carriers and the political or religious articulators of the cultural model of Islam.

The combination of religious orientations, the structure of élites, and relations between élites and local ascriptive communities gave rise, in imperial and patrimonial Islamic systems alike, to certain unique types of ruling groups — especially to the military-religious rulers who emerged from tribal and sectarian elements, and to the system of military slavery which created special channels of mobility such as the *qul* system in general, the Mameluke system and Ottoman *devshrirme* in particular, through which the ruling group could be recruited from alien elements (Ayalon, 1951; Itzkowitz, 1972; Miller, 1941).

Similarly, except in the case of so-called missionary orders which established new regimes, few structural linkages were forged between the political élites and the articulators of cultural models and economic entrepreneurs (though often there were close family relations among some of them).

Variations in imperial and imperial-feudal societies

The Chinese Empire China's Confucian–Taoist–Buddhist–legalist tradition, by contrast to monotheistic religions, was characterised by a somewhat weaker stress on the tension between the transcendental and the mundane order; a very weak conception of a historical-transcendental time dimension; a strong this-worldly focus for overcoming this tension; relative openness in formulation as well as in its accessibility or flexibility to broader strata (Balazs, 1964; Elwin, 1973; Reischauer and Fairbank, 1960, chaps. 2–10).

This ideology was very closely tied to the political framework of the Chinese Empire. The empire was legitimised by the Confucian symbols, while the Confucian symbols and the ethical orientation found their natural place and framework, their major referent, in the Empire.

The Chinese was probably the most this-worldly of all the great traditions. The thrust of the official Confucian–legalist framework was the cultivation of the socio-political and cultural orders as the major focus of cosmic harmony. It emphasised this-worldly duties and activities within the existing social frameworks — the family, broader kin groups, and imperial service — and stressed the connection between the proper performance of these duties and ultimate criteria of individual responsibility.

Of course, the tradition also emphasised individual responsibility along with a strongly transcendental orientation, but this responsibility was couched largely in terms of the importance of the political and familial dimensions of human existence.

Chinese tradition also stressed a basic affinity between the symbols of the centre and the status identities of the peripheral groups. Orientation to the centre and to participation in it constituted an essential component of the collective identity of many local and occupational groups.

All these orientations greatly influenced the structure of the Chinese centre and of the major élites and strata in Chinese society. The Chinese centre was an absolutist one in terms both of political and cultural orientations. The imperial centre, with its strong Confucian orientation and legitimation, was the sole distributor of macro-societal prestige and honour. Social groups or strata did not develop independent status orientations except on a purely local level; the major (almost the only) wider orientations were bound to the politico-religious centre (Balazs, 1964; Eisenstadt, 1971b; Lapidus, 1975a; Michael, 1955).

Of crucial importance in the linkage between the centre and the periphery in general, and to the process of strata-formation in particular, was the structure of the major groups linking the imperial centre to the broader society — the literati, i.e. all those who took the Confucian examinations or studied for them (Balazs, 1964; Ho, 1962; Kracke, 1953). This élite was a relatively cohesive congeries of individuals and quasi-groups sharing a cultural background enhanced by the examination system and by adherence to Confucian classical teachings and rituals.

The literati constituted the source of recruitment to the bureaucracy and combined the activities of political élites, and of articulators of models of cultural order, enjoying close relations with the articulators of the solidarity of collectivities (the heads of family and of wider kinship groups), and they exercised almost a monopoly over access to the centre. The organisational framework was nearly identical to that of the state bureaucracy (which recruited 10 to 20 per cent of all the literati), and except for some schools and academies it had no organisation of its own. This élite, which was relatively widespread, was in principle recruited from all strata, even from the peasantry, though in fact more literati were recruited from the gentry. Thus, unlike in Russia, it maintained relatively close solidarity relations with most groups within society.

The Russian and Byzantine empires A different constellation of cultural orientations, structure of élites and structure of centres and centre–periphery relations developed in the Russian and Byzantine empires (and in the Abbasside, Fatimide and Ottoman empires).

Within the late (post-Mongol) variant of Christian civilisation (Muscovite) (Pipes, 1975; Seton-Watson, 1952) the centre succeeded in imposing a relatively high degree of subordination of the cultural order to the political order, and a relatively low degree of autonomous access of the major strata to the principal attributes of the social and political orders. The political sphere became the monopoly of the rulers; the economic sphere became less central, and economic activities were left, in so far as they did not impinge directly on the centre, to their own devices.

The broader strata were granted autonomy in other mundane, primarily economic, activities, without being permitted to imbue them to any large extent with wider meanings in terms of the basic parameters of the cultural-religious spheres.

To this end, the centre vigorously segregated access to the attributes of the cosmic order (salvation) (which was extended to all groups with only comparatively weak mediation by the Church) from access to the attributes of the political and social orders which, after the post-Mongol period were almost totally monopolised by the political centre.

Religious heterodoxies became either other-worldly or dissociated from the political sphere. However, sometimes, as in the case of the True Believers, they impinged to a degree on the economic sphere (Gerschenkron, 1970).

The major mechanism through which the centre attained its goals was forced segregation between the political power élites (which were also the articulators of the cultural order especially in its political dimensions), the economic and educational élites and the articulators of the solidarity of the major ascriptive collectivities (Eisenstadt, 1971*b*, chap. 6; Raeff, 1966).

The Byzantine Empire did not experience a trauma like the Mongolian conquest which in Russia paved the way to the weakening of the autonomous orientations and structures of the major active strata. Hence, the Byzantine centre was never able to segregate this-worldly and other-worldly orientations of different groups, strata or élites to the same extent as the Russian centre, though such attempts were often made; and the religious supremacy of the Emperor over the Patriarch was the official doctrine of the Byzantine Empire and Church (Hussey, 1937; Ostrogorsky, 1956).

Cultural-religious orientations did not become as totally subjugated to the political sphere as in Russia, and the Church, oriented as it was towards other-worldly activities, never became politically as fully controlled as the Russian one. Similarly, different strata, such as the aristocracy and the peasantry, had relatively more autonomous access to the centre. Similarly, Byzantine society was characterised by great autonomy of secondary élites and of linkages among them and the broader strata (Charanis, 1940–41, 1951a, b).

Western European civilisation A still different set of relations developed in the imperial and imperial-feudal structure of medieval and early modern (Western and Central) Europe (Beloff, 1964; Bloch, 1961; Hintze, 1975; Lindsay, 1957).

European civilisation was characterised by a very high number of cross-cutting cultural orientations and structural settings. The symbolic pluralism, or heterogeneity, of European society was evident in the multiplicity of traditions — the Judaeo-Christian, the Greek, the Roman, and the various tribal ones — out of which its own cultural tradition crystallised. The most important among Europe's cultural orientations were an emphasis on the autonomy of the cosmic, cultural and social orders and their interrelatedness, which was defined in terms of the tension between the transcendental and the mundane order; and an emphasis on ways of resolving this tension through a combination of this-worldly (political and economic) and other-worldly activities (O'Dea, O'Dea and Adams, 1975; Troeltsch, 1931).

These symbolic orientations became connected with a very special type of structural-organisational pluralism, which differed greatly from what can be found, for instance, in the compact Byzantine (or Russian) Empire, though it shared many aspects of cultural models with Western Europe. In the Byzantine Empire, this pluralism was manifest in a relatively high degree of structural differentiation within a relatively unified socio-political framework in which different social functions were apportioned to different social categories. The structural pluralism developed in Europe was characterised, above all, by a combination of steadily increasing levels of structural differentiation, on the one hand, and constantly changing boundaries of collectivities, units and frameworks, on the other hand.

Among these collectivities and units there was no clear-cut division of labour. Rather, there was constant rivalry between them over their standing with respect to the attributes of the social and cultural orders; over the performance of the major societal functions — whether economic, political or cultural — as well as over the very definition of the boundaries of ascriptive communities.

The combination of these cultural orientations and structural conditions generated several basic institutional characteristics in Europe (Bloch, 1930, 1961; Brunner, 1968; Prawer and Eisenstadt, 1968); the most important being: the multiplicity of centres; a deep permeation of the periphery by the centres and impingement of the periphery on the centres; relatively little overlap of the boundaries and restructuring of class, ethnic, religious and political entities; a comparatively high degree of autonomy of groups and strata and of their access to the centres of society; much overlap between various status units, together with a high level of country-wide status (class) consciousness and political activity; a multiplicity of cultural and functional (economic or professional) élites enjoying relatively great autonomy; much cross-cutting, and a close relationship with the broader, more ascriptive strata; a relatively great autonomy of the legal system with regard to other integrative systems — above all, the political and religious spheres; and great autonomy of cities as independent centres for social and structural creativity and identity formation (Brunner, 1968, pp. 213–41).

Patterns of change and transformation

We shall now consider the major patterns of change in the historical societies described; proceed then to the analysis of the cultural orientations and institutional patterns that existed within them; and finally analyse the connections between the patterns of change on the one hand and the cultural orientations, institutional patterns and politico-ecological settings on the other.

The pattern of coalescent change

A closer look at the historical evidence indicates that several major patterns of change — each with some very important sub-variants — can be identified.

One such pattern, characterised by a relatively high degree of coalescence both in the outcomes of change in major institutional spheres, as well as in its processes, can be identified above all in the Chinese Empire (Balazs, 1964; Elwin, 1973; Reischauer and Fairbank, 1960, chaps. 2–10), in the Byzantine and Russian empires (Pipes, 1975; Ostrogorsky, 1956; Seton-Watson, 1952), in some, but only some, of the Islamic states (Gibb, 1962; Lewis, 1950; Turner, 1974) —

especially the Abbasside and to a lesser extent the Ottoman empires (Inalcik, 1973; Itzkowitz, 1972; Wittek, 1963), and in medieval and early modern Western and Central Europe (Beloff, 1964; Bloch, 1961; Hintze, 1975; Lindsay, 1957).

The outstanding feature of the patterns of change in these societies was that, first, modifications and restructuring of the major collectivities — political, religious and national — and of institutional frameworks — the economic, religious and that of social stratification — tended to go rather frequently hand in hand with radical restructuring of the political system itself.

Second, there tended also to develop strong connections between changes in the bases of access to power and its symbols and those in the group bases and criteria of structuring social hierarchies and between the various movements of protest and central political struggle, as well as a very high level of organisation and ideological articulation of the issues of this struggle.

True enough, even within these generally imperial and imperial-feudal societies, the most frequent types of change were dynastic ones, sometimes affecting the boundaries of the polity, and often failing to produce far-reaching modifications in their political structures. But beyond this, although sometimes in close relation, other patterns developed with a far greater degree of coalescence between the restructuring of the political regimes and other institutional domains. Thus, dynastic changes were often connected with the rise, growth and strengthening, or the decline and weakening, of professional, cultural and religious élites and institutions as against more ascriptive groups; with shifts in the strength of the monarch versus the aristocracy and of the aristocracy versus the urban groups and the free peasantry, or with shifts in the strength and independence of the bureaucracy.

These changes were also often connected with shifts in the principles of the political articulation of such groups, especially with the broadening and narrowing of their autonomous access to the centre (Eistenstadt, 1969, 1978, chap. 4).

A similar picture emerges with respect to the relation between the continuity of the economic frameworks and that of the political boundaries of the empires. Here, more than in other types of traditional societies, changes in the scope and structural principles of the economic systems or of strata formation tended to impinge directly on the political centres; at the same time as far-reaching changes in the political regimes could affect the functioning of economic institutions and the structuring of social hierarchies.

Within these political systems there also developed tendencies towards coalescence or linkage between the major types of movements of protest and conflict, i.e. between rebellions and heresies; between these and institution-building (primarily in the economic and cultural spheres by secondary élites); and between each of these and the more central political struggles and processes. Some of these connections became more than merely *ad hoc* coalitions, and gave rise to closer organisational and symbolic 'merging' of these movements, often generating new symbolic and institutional patterns. This last tendency was closely related to the high level of symbolic and ideological articulation of the political struggle that tended to occur in these societies.

Within this broad pattern there were several important sub-variants which can be distinguished, first, according to the degree of coalescence between changes in the major institutional domains of a society, and in the major movements of protest and conflict; second, according to the continuity of any given political regime and, in cases of discontinuity, the nature of the 'outcome' — above all whether it entailed a breakdown or a transformation (with different degrees of violence) of a regime.

The Chinese, Russian, Byzantine and Islamic empires The Chinese and the Russian empires were characterised by the lowest degree of coalescence, with the Chinese evincing a very long and the Russian a much shorter continuity, in both cases the outcome of discontinuity being violent revolutionary transformation.

The major types of protest and political conflict that occurred in the Chinese Empire — rebellions and the emergence of provincial governors as relatively semi-autonomous warlords, as well as conquests by foreign dynasties — did not usually exhibit a distinctly new level of political articulation. Most rebellions provided only secondary interpretations of the prevailing value structure and did not create any radically new orientations. The political orientations of the military governors and warlords were likewise set within the existing value and political frameworks. Although they strove for greater independence from, or seizure of, the central government, they rarely envisaged the establishment of a new type of political system (Dardess, 1973; Eisenstadt, 1969).

Similarly, the major heterodoxies — Taoism, Buddhism, and especially the secondary Confucian schools — worked within the prevailing social framework, or tended towards withdrawal from it. The only close relations between ideological struggles and changes in the central élite groups and the actual policies of the centre arose in some of the orthodox Confucian controversies among the central élites. However, these changes were usually limited to the centre, the upper echelons of the bureaucracy and the literati (Dubs, 1939; Liu, 1959).

The closest relation between changes in political regime and strata formation in the Chinese Empire was the one common to all imperial societies — namely those political changes connected with shifts in the relative strength and standing of free peasants against would-be aristocratic elements. But even this connection manifested itself in China, in contrast, for instance, to the Byzantine Empire, more at the level of rulers' policies than at that of political articulation of these strata. Similarly, the great urban and commercial developments under the Sung, while associated with alterations in the policies of the government, were not correlated with changes in the mode of impingement of these groups on the centre.

In imperial Russia (Pipes, 1975; Seton-Watson, 1952) the centre was able for a relatively long period to maintain a very strict segregation between local rebellions, religious movements and events and conflicts at the centre itself.

This centre which, from at least the period of Peter the Great, was strongly modernising, generated widespread processes of economic and social change, but tried to control it and minimise the emergence of any autonomous political expression and organisation which might arise.

The major mechanisms of control were the autonomous access of the various groups to the centre; conversion of economic into political resources; and segregation of the major strata and institutional entrepreneurs.

The Byzantine Empire was characterised by a relatively high degree of coalescence of change, of internal restructuring and transformability, especially with respect to shifts in the strength of imperial and aristocratic rulers and the free peasantry. But the very intensity of this struggle was among the causes of the ultimate demise of this empire (Ostrogorsky, 1956).

Among the imperial systems within the Islamic realm, the Abbaside and Fatimide empires (Lewis, 1950) evinced a pattern rather close to the Byzantine, while the Ottoman is closer to its direct predecessor, the Byzantine — except that its breakdown was connected with a (relatively non-violent) revolutionary transformation.

Western and Central Europe Within the European — and especially the Western and Central European — societies (Beloff, 1964; Bloch, 1961; Hintze, 1975; Lindsay, 1957) there developed a high degree of coalescence of change and restructuring of political regimes and other institutional domains, as well as coalescence of movements of protest, religious heterodoxies and political struggle and their mutual restructuring.

Thus, changes within any institutional domain often impinged on others, and most significantly on the political sphere. These changes gave rise to the continual mutual restructuring of these spheres which did not, however, necessarily coalesce into a unified political or cultural framework.

There was also a close connection between movements of rebellion, heterodoxies and political struggle, concomitant tendencies on the part of various élites and the broader social strata to support centre-formation and the combination of such activities with institution-building in the economic, cultural and educational spheres.

As compared with the pure imperial systems, the imperial-feudal Western societies were characterised by much lesser stability of regimes, by constant changes in regime and collectivity and by continual restructuring of centres. At the same time, they evinced a much greater capacity for institutional innovation cutting across different political and national boundaries and centres, ultimately leading, in appropriate economic and entrenched settings, to the Great Western Revolution.

Partially coalescent and non-coalescent patterns of change

A second pattern of change in historical societies, and which was prevalent above all in some (especially Greek and Roman) city-states of antiquity and in Near-Eastern, especially ancient Israelite and Islamic, tribal federations was characterised by a high level of coalescence between the processes of change, i.e. between rebellion, religious or intellectual heterodoxies and central political struggle, but connected with a far more short-lived institutionalisation of coalescent changes in the major institutional spheres (Ehrenberg, 1960; Eisenstadt, 1971*a*, chap. 6; Fuks, 1974).

A third pattern of change, to be found above all in the ancient Near Eastern (Moscati, 1962) or early South-West Asian (Steinberg, 1971) and in most Islamic (Turner, 1974) societies was characterised by a relatively low level of coalescence both in the institutionalisation of change in the major domains, as well as in the processes of change.

In most of these societies, even the more dramatic or widespread changes in the principles and boundaries of regimes and of other collectivities and institutions, despite obvious mutual impingement, did not tend, on the whole, to coalesce; each tended to change in relative isolation or conversely each might evince relative continuity while important alterations took place in the others. Similarly, there developed a relatively loose connection between changes in political regimes, on the one hand, and the restructuring of principles of access to political power by the economic and social spheres, on the other.

Far-reaching changes in these political regimes were usually combined with personal or dynastic changes, with shifts in the relative hierarchical standing of different families, ethnic groups or regions, in the boundaries of the different polities; in the content of symbols of legitimation which upheld the special virtue of the rulers; or in the policy orientations of the rulers, such as coercive, manipulative or solitary modes.

Such changes were also often connected with the emergence of new economic or religious groups, which, however, rarely gave rise to, or were directly connected with, the restructuring of the principles of access to political power. At most, they were connected with shifts in the policies of the rulers.

The kingdoms, tribal organisations and city-states were also compatible with the development of relatively extensive economic systems, based on interstate commerce and even agricultural markets, which cut across political boundaries and survived the demise of regimes. Accordingly, deep modifications in technological or economic activities and in institution-building, or 'modes of production', though often contributing indirectly to the crises of different patrimonial regimes, did not always necessarily coalesce with such changes.

This pattern was very closely related to a relatively low level of connection or coalescence, or a high level of segregation between different movements of protest and conflict, i.e. between rebellions and heterodoxies, between them and the central political struggle, as well as between these processes and those of institutional innovation, above all in the economic and cultural spheres. Concomitantly, this pattern was also closely connected with loose ideological articulation of issues of political struggle and activities.

Buddhist and Hindu societies Within this broad pattern several variants can be distinguished, according to the degree of the differentiation or complexity of the various societies and according to whether they were embedded in relatively 'archaic', 'local' frameworks and culture or, on the contrary, were connected with 'high civilisations', above all other-worldly religions, such as Hinduism and Buddhism (Biardeau, 1972; Dumont, 1970*a, b*; Tambiah, 1976) or to some degree Zoroastrianism.

In the relatively 'simple', less differentiated regimes, such as some of the earlier Near-Eastern or early South-Asian societies, the demise of a political regime could also entail the disappearance of whole 'peoples', as well as of their religion. At the same time, the connection between changes in certain broader ethnic, linguistic and chiefly economic systems and those in the political field, was in many cases, very weak.

In the more complex and differentiated regimes, especially in so far as they were connected with the higher civilisations, there usually developed greater distinctiveness of 'ethnic', national, cultural and above all religious collectivities and institutions, and of economic frameworks, as well as of frameworks of social stratification. These tended to persist or change without direct connection to shifts in political regimes.

At the same time, some connections appeared between changes in the religious and civilisational frameworks and the political and economic institutions even if these connections were much weaker than those to be found in societies in which the more coalescent type of change predominated.

Several versions of such (weak) connections can be discerned in the development. In the (Theravada) Buddhist realm (Tambiah, 1976), rebellions tended to have relatively well-articulated millenarian orientations, sometimes connected with political groups. This often gave rise to the construction of new symbols and dimensions in the definition of the local political community, adding a higher level of symbolic articulation, a broader orientation which sometimes served as the basis and framework for the crystallisation of symbols and national boundaries. Such 'nations' often evinced much greater continuity than the political regimes, as did the religious traditions.

But these movements did not generate distinctiveness of the political centres or in the relations between these centres and their peripheries; nor did they redefine the criteria of access to political power or profoundly restructure other institutional spheres.

In India, within the framework of the Hindu civilisation, certain more complex movements of change occurred, linked to relations between rebellion and heterodoxy and broader institutional change. Many of India's movements of change were related to broad caste categories and groups, and they generated modifications in those institutional spheres in which such caste groups were especially active. Throughout Indian history these characteristics encouraged a strong propensity to piecemeal innovation within different institutional spheres, i.e. the redefinition of political boundaries, changes in technology and in levels of social differentiation and some restructuring of the economic sphere, and transformations in social and economic polities as well as in the religious sphere, as manifest primarily in the appearance of new movements and sects (Dumont, 1970a; Kolff, 1971; Singer and Cohn, 1968; Thapar, 1978).

These religious movements often became closely connected with major structural components of change, particularly, with the processes of regional and caste change and caste mobility, with the crystallisation of new caste groups, and continual restructuring of caste activities and political boundaries. Yet these processes were only rarely connected with the restructuring of the political systems or the relations between the political and economic spheres. In general, traditional Indian civilisation exhibited great heterogeneity in the structural-organisational aspects of its institutional spheres, together with continuity in its other parameters.

Sunni Islam A special pattern of connection between movements of change and modifications in different institutional spheres also arose within most of the Islamic (Sunni) societies (Lewis, 1973, pp. 217–60), which, on the whole, were characterised by a relatively low level of coalescence between movements and processes of change, despite the strong ideological emphasis inherent in Islam on the merging of the political and religious realms.

Various religious sects and popular movements frequently emerged but the religious check on political authority was weak in stable regimes since there was no machinery for enforcement other than revolt. Hence numerous sects and movements were aimed at the destruction of the existing regime and the establishment of a new, religiously pure and true one, or they were politically passive.

And yet, because of the tendency towards coalescence inherent in the ideology of Islam, there developed, at least in the geographical heart of Islam, a dynamic change that went beyond the typical segregative pattern and tended more towards coalescent patterns of change, and which was manifest in attempts to re-establish the Islamic ideal of the pure religious-political community — the *ummah*. This tendency was strongest during the establishment of new political regimes, like imperial systems (the last and most enduring of which was the Ottoman Empire), semi-tribal ones, like those in the Maghreb (Gellner, 1969) or even lately among the Swat (Ahmed, 1976) and it tended to subside after the establishment of a new regime.

Accordingly, we witness in Islamic history — principally in the heartland of Islam — a constant swing between the upsurge of quasi-totalistic politico-religious movements which aimed at the complete transformation of the political regime through such illegitimate means as assassination and rebellion, and the strong other-worldly attitude and political passivity that helped to maintain the despotic character of existing regimes.

Analytical and comparative conclusions

The preceding analysis indicates that a high level of articulation of political struggle and the coalescence of movements and patterns of change is strongly related to a great symbolic and institutional distinctiveness of the centre from the periphery, of articulation of strata-consciousness, a multiplicity of autonomous élites in general and secondary élites in particular, and to the prevalence of high tension between the transcendental and the mundane order, a relatively strong this-worldly conception of the resolution of this tension or a close commitment to the cosmic and social order.

The key to the understanding of this correlation lies in the fact that there exists a close relation or parallelism between the degree of symbolic articulation or 'problematisation' (akin to Geertz, 1973, p. 171) in the different cultural contexts of certain major problems of human existence, on the one hand, and a high degree of symbolic and institutional distinctiveness of the major aspects of the institutional order, on the other.

Our analysis has pointed to some of the institutional mechanisms and social actors connecting such symbolic problematisation and articulation in the symbolic-cognitive and institutional spheres, by contrast to the pure structuralists such as Lévi-Strauss (1963), who have often been accused of simple emanation (Gluckman, 1974; Rossi, 1974).

The major élites and institutional entrepreneurs constitute the main linkage, between the cultural orientations and the symbolic articulation of the principal institutional spheres as also between all these and processes of social change. These entrepreneurs are the active carriers of diverse cultural orientations, while coalitions between them ensure the structural and symbolic articulation of the principal institutional spheres, as well as different collective actions, organisations and movements, and of the linkages between them.

The most important mechanisms by which such élites shape the major elements of the institutional order are, first, the availability of 'free' resources or activities not entirely embedded in ascriptive units, such as families, communities and guilds. These can serve as the bases of new institutional centres, hierarchies and collectivities. Second, there is the simultaneous development of broad markets which cut across such units; and thirdly, alternative conceptions of the social, political or cultural order which differ from the existing pattern not only in the sense of a reversal of the status quo (Gluckman, 1963, chap. 3) but also of possibly going beyond it.

41

Symbolic articulation and 'problematisation'

Our analysis indicates that the articulation of the problem of human existence is greater when there is a perception of tensions between the transcendental and the mundane order, close commitment to such orders; or when they are not accepted as given.

In so far as such orientations become institutionalised they tend to generate strong tendencies towards freeing resources, relatively wide markets, alternative conceptions of the social order, as well as the autonomous crystallisation of major élites and institutional entre-preneurs.

The more autonomous institutional entrepreneurs often serve as activators of alternative conceptions of the social order and as organisers of free resources, linking such resources and activities drawn from different spheres, and potentially crystallising them along new directions.

Accordingly, they favour the emergence of close symbolic articula-tion of the major components of the institutional order; autonomous access of élites and collectivities to each other, intimate mutual linkage between them and their common convergence on the centres, as well as the ability of entrepreneurs to organise collective action (rebellions and political struggle in particular), in relatively 'autonomous' formations.

In such cases, other things being equal, close connections tend also to grow between the different types of rebellions, heterodoxy, and political struggle, as well as coalescence in the rates of change in different institutional spheres.

By contrast, a weak perception of tension between the transcen-dental and mundane order tends to minimise the problematisation of human existence, and hence does not favour close symbolic articula-tion of the major institutional spheres, free resources and autonomous élites not embedded in ascriptive collectivities.

Other-worldly orientations

But even within those civilisations where a perception of a tension between the transcendental and the mundane order is prevalent and institutionalised, many differences exist in institutional contours and in processes of change. These are also strongly influenced by varied cultural orientations and the concomitant characteristics of major élites.

Our preceding analysis stressed two variables of special importance. One is the distinction between, and relative emphasis on, this-worldly and other-worldly resolution of the tension between the transcendental and the mundane orders (or of salvation). The second, cutting across the first, are the relations between the attributes or foci of the resolution of this tension, the attributes of salvation, and the attributes of the major primordial ascriptive collectivities.

Thus, first of all, the level of generalisation of resources, the scope of different markets, and the symbolisation of institutional spheres, as well as the emergence of alternative conceptions of social order, tend to be least developed when the focus of salvation is on other-worldly activities, or on a combination of other-worldly and this-worldly activities.

Similarly, the opportunity of linking the free resources generated either by such conceptions or by the prevailing technological and structural conditions and directing them into new institutional channels is greater where a close relation among the attributes of salvation, and those of the major ascriptive ('ethnic' or 'national') communities exist.

An emphasis on other-worldly resolution of the tension between the transcendental and the mundane order tends to generate broad markets and distinctive religious centres, but not of other institutional spheres, and only very weak connections between such resources as may become available through technological forces in other spheres and those that develop in the religious sphere.

Here the articulators of the models of cultural order, while autonomous in their religious activities, are, from the institutional viewpoint, embedded in broader ascriptive collectivities (as are the political and economic élites). Hence, they do not undertake many autonomous activities or orientations or possess the ability to create new institutional complexes.

The segregation of the internal dynamics of these mundane spheres from the dynamics of the cultural and religious centres is greater when the foci of the other-worldly resolution of the tension between the cosmic and the mundane order is dissociated, as in Buddhism, from the major ascriptive, primordial communities.

In these cases, other-worldly resolution of such tension may combine with the main attributes and symbols of the collectivities, but not with restructuring the major institutional spheres and of centre–periphery relations.

When the other-worldly resolution of the tension between the transcendental and the mundane orders is based, as in Hinduism, on a closer relation between the other-worldly attributes of salvation and the major attributes of the basic ascriptive groups, certain free resources become available and wide markets are created beyond the purely religious sphere. These resources may be directed into various secondary channels, though ultimate control over their conversion is also vested in the religious sphere.

Such orientations tend to generate, reinforce, and be carried by élites that combine, on one hand, a certain autonomy in their function (political, economic, etc.) and some internal differentiation among these functions, while, on the other, they are strongly embedded in solidarity groups and there exists predominance of the articulators of the models of the cultural order, who are the carriers and models of other-worldly salvation.

While here the conception of alternative orders is, as in Buddhism, very limited and on the whole other-worldly, it has become connected to defined activities in institutional spheres.

The ideal of renunciation, a major aspect of Hinduism (Biardeau, 1972; Thapar, 1978, pp. 63–105), while setting up a new focus of commitment, did not lead to upgrading the secondary limitations or to linking them to the ultimate level of socio-cultural reality and identity. This ideal did not generate new motivations or orientations that could tie activities in these non-religious spheres to the fundamental parameters of Indian cultural identity. None of India's movements produced new linkages between the mundane and the religious spheres, or gave rise to fundamental changes in the meaning and structure of different institutional spheres (Thapar, 1978, pp. 63–105).

Foci of salvation

A high tension between the transcendental and the mundane order, along with some emphasis on this-worldly activities, tends to generate plentiful free resources, wide markets, close articulation of institutional spheres, and a large variety of alternative conceptions of the social and political order.

The perception of this tension gives rise to, or at least is associated with or carried by, autonomous élites whether articulators of the models of the cultural order, political élites or articulators of the solidarity of different collectivities. Accordingly, societies in which these orientations are prevalent tend to develop multiple coalitions of such élites, which may be able to mobilise free resources as well as to channel them in new directions. Given the potentially mutual orientations of such institutional entrepreneurs, the directions of change may coalesce.

Within this pattern there may be several varieties according to the content and constellations of these orientations. These constellations may vary according to the interweaving or segregation of this-worldly and other-worldly foci of salvation (a problem inherent in most high civilisations and religions), the institutional spread of the foci of

44

this-worldly resolution of the tension between the transcendental and the mundane orders, and the relations between the major attributes or foci of the resolution of the tension and the basic attributes of the principal ascriptive collectivities.

The weaker the emphasis on the other-worldly realm (as in China) the sharper the focus of salvation on the this-worldly, and the more this-worldly salvation is focused on a single institutional area (as in both China and Islam), the stronger the tendency for potentially autonomous élites — especially articulators of models of cultural and social order and political élites — to be brought together within a single social framework or category exhibiting little internal differentiation, as best illustrated by the Chinese literati. Such a structure gives only limited scope for free resources and markets even if the symbolisation of the dominant institutional spheres is relatively strong. The flow of resources among markets is relatively restricted: most of the free resources are directed towards the centre. Concomitantly, in such situations élites will find very weak bases for the autonomous mobilisation of resources and hence the potential for internal transformation tends to be relatively restricted.

The stress on a single institutional focus of this-worldly salvation was common to China and Islam (in Islam the focus was politico-military) and resulted in a similar structure of entrepreneurs and to limits to the society's transformative capacities. But in Islam there also existed a very strong other-worldly emphasis (segregated from the this-worldly one) that generated a relatively strong conception of an alternative social and political order and the special sectarian political dynamics characteristic of that civilisation.

The more institutionally segregated the relations between symbolically tightly interwoven this-worldly and other-worldly foci of salvation (as was the case in Russia), the stronger the trend towards a situation in which the different élites, instead of merging, are increasingly segregated. However, they retain powerful mutual orientations as to the centre. Hence such situations are characterised by wider markets, the free flow of resources, albeit under stricter control, from the centre, and stronger tendencies towards institution-building as well as impingement on the centre, which can be checked only by coercive measures.

At the same time, the close symbolic interweaving of the foci of salvation creates a potent and potentially articulate conception of alternative social orders. Low coalescence and segregation between different movements of protest and élites, which yet retain some mutual orientations, tend to assure relative longevity of regimes. When these can no longer be maintained, very violent upheaval occurs, carried by certain (especially secondary) élites recognised in revolutionary movements.

By contrast to all the foregoing cases, in so far as there develop, as in Western Europe, both a tight interweaving of this-worldly and other-worldly foci of salvation and a relative multiplicity of this-worldly arenas serving as the loci of such conceptions, the potentialities of transformability of the social order are highest. These orientations generated a rich variety of conceptions of alternative social orders, and of their attainment, as well as different autonomous élites (articulators of models of social order, functional élites, even articulators of the solidarity of ascriptive collectivities), and coalitions between them. Hence, there developed many points of crystallisation of free resources and of linkages among them.

The comparison between Europe and Islam underlines the importance of the second dimension mentioned above, namely, the degree of association between the attributes of salvation and the attributes of the basic ascriptive collectivities, an association that was very weak in Islam and very strong in Europe. The closer such association, the more channels of resources and the stronger the bases of solidarity between entrepreneurs.

Ecology and change

Ecological settings above all influence the availability of resources for institutional restructuring and the capacity to institutionalise the potential for change that may be contained in any society. Ecological settings also influence the availability of resources in different markets by determining the relative importance of domestic and external markets.

The comparison between the Byzantine and the Russian empires on the one hand, and Western European imperial-feudal patterns and the Islamic and Hindu civilisations, on the other, shows that, under imperial systems there developed relatively unified frameworks of the major compact markets, while in the Western European and the Islamic cases (as well as the Indian one) cross-cutting markets were established.

The relative predominance of 'internal' markets — whether compact or cross-cutting — generates, in all these cases, great reservoirs of resources which can be channelled in different directions. Hence they enhance the institution-building and transformative capacity of societies — and in all these societies access to the markets and the flow of resources within them were structured by the major dominant élites. In imperial (and patrimonial) societies such activities were ultimately controlled by the political élites. In the imperial-feudal and different decentralised systems, the structure of the cross-cutting

46

markets and the linkages between them were greatly influenced by the multiplicity of élites which often cut across political boundaries. In all societies the nature of such linkages depended heavily on certain characteristics of élites, as analysed above.

Thus, in the realm of Islam, linkages were provided mostly by the *ulemas* and the various orders. Given their dissociation from the political élite and the official disregard in the Islamic tradition of the major 'local' ascriptive collectivities, these élites did not usually develop very strong solidarity linkages with such collectivities. This lack of solidarity linkages between the *ulemas*, the political rulers, and broader ascriptive collectivities, minimised their effectiveness in the structuring of broad markets, in mobilising resources and in directing them into new coalescent channels. But, given their basic orientations, tendencies arose, at least in extreme situations, to coalescence between political and religious change. In Europe, solidarity linkages, maximised the tendency to the mobilisation of resources in many directions and a high degree of coalescence of changes.

The Western European and Islamic civilisations, from the point of view of their ecological settings, seem to be close to the Hindu one. But given that in the Hindu case it was only or mainly the ascriptive-ritual networks and caste organisation that constituted major linkages — with but little this-worldly emphasis on political or economic activities — the connection between religious movements and political systems was much weaker than either in Islam or in Europe. It chiefly gave rise to patrimonial formations with only modest transformative capacities in the political realm.

The institutionalisation of potentialities of change does vary not only according to the cultural orientations and solidary relations of élites but also as between societies in which compact, as opposed to cross-cutting markets, predominate. In societies with compact markets, the central controlling mechanism constitutes an easy target for the processes of change, thus often creating an all-or-nothing struggle where the chances of a breakdown of regimes inevitably increases. Cross-cutting markets create greater opportunities of finding various ways of restructuring the different institutional spheres.

High dependence on external markets (as can be seen from the analysis of the exceptional city-states and tribal federations) minimises the opportunity of institutionalising change, even if it is characterised by a relatively close coalescence of rebellions, heterodoxies and the central political struggle, and by the development within them of transformative tendencies. The intensification of political struggle has, we have seen, more often led to the demise of these systems and their incorporation in various ways into other societies.

The explanation lies in the fact that certain societies attempted to maintain, in their particular international settings, institutional activities more appropriate to 'bigger' societies with wide internal markets (Eisenstadt, 1977). Hence these societies tended to specialise in working for different external markets while maintaining a much lower level of domestic specialisation. This, as we have seen, is manifested in the minimal, embryonic development of specialised activities, ruling groups and institutional frameworks. The combination of the available resources with the relatively low organisational capacities of the élites explains the difficulties experienced in the institutionalisation of potential capacities over the long run.

International settings

Yet these institutional constellations in general, and the structures of élites and processes of change in particular, are greatly influenced by the international system in which different societies develop.

There exists a sort of feedback effect between the place of a society within an international system and the structure of its élites. A hegemonic society tends, on the whole, to foster or reinforce more autonomous élites while a state of dependence tends rather to foster or reinforce less autonomous ones, with all the structural and institutional consequences this implies.

Two additional processes or factors are significant. One is the 'original' structure of élites as related to the cultural orientations in different societies. In so far as these are relatively non-autonomous, as was the case in Spain, their very hegemony tends to reinforce relatively non-autonomous tendencies, both in the hegemonic centre and in the dependencies.

However, as in the case of Japan, such élites do evince sufficient autonomy for them to attempt to forge a relatively hegemonic position, or at least an independent niche in the international system. Their ability to do this also depends on the structure of the international system.

The most important variables in such situations are: the rigidity or flexibility of the organisational and symbolic structure of the hegemonic society and of the dependent societies; the parallelism or similarity between the structures of the imperial centre and its dependencies; permeation of the dependencies by the hegemonic systems, economic, social, political 'imperialisms', are identical or organised in a common framework; the uniformity of the different links and mechanisms of dependency; the prevalent type of dependency, whether it is direct (direct rule, conquest, etc.) or indirect; the keenness of competition between different hegemonic powers operating within an international orbit and the extent to which secondary powers also develop within each such an orbit.

The more prevalent the heterogeneity within an international system and the greater the distance and difference between its component units, the greater is the opportunity for transformation and changes from within. Thus the relatively low transformability noted in the Chinese and Byzantine cases seems connected to their setting in international systems characterised by relative rigidity and monolithic tendencies in social and symbolic structures; parallelism or similarity between the structure of the imperial centre and of the peripheries; heavily direct dependency (conquest or geographical contiguity between the imperial centre and its territories); and relatively common frameworks of the prevalent international systems, political, cultural and economic.

The higher transformability in the other cases seems to be related, first, to the internal structure of the hegemonic power, which was more pluralistic or heterogeneous. Within the various economic, political and cultural international systems, which were not organised under one framework, there were certain autonomous and contradictory developments. An especially important contradiction arose out of the premise of the cultural and political international systems, which often undermined the power structure of a particular imperial system. In most of these cases, too, dependence was multiple and rather indirect. There was, further, no close parallel between the social structure of the hegemonic and the dependent units. Finally, multiple sub-centres of power tended to emerge, representing autochthonous generators of change.

Much structural and cultural autonomy (as well as the other aspects of flexibility, noted above) facilitated various transformations, i.e. changes in the internal structure and regimes of the imperial centres and their dependencies, shifts of power in the relations between the 'core' of such systems and its dependencies, as well as developments within the hegemonic power, the secondary power and the dependencies. These in turn often favoured new cultural orientations and élites, which tended to transform the restructuring of relations between centre and periphery, between conquerors and conquered.

References

Ahmed, A.S. (1976) *Millennium and Charisma among Pathans, A Critical Essay in Social Anthropology*. London, Routledge & Kegan Paul.

Ayalon, D. (1951) *L'Esclavage du Mameluk*. Jerusalem, Israel Oriental Society.

Balazs, E. (1964) *Chinese Civilization and Bureaucracy: Variations on a Theme*. New Haven, Conn., Yale University Press.

Barth, I. (1963) *The Role of Entrepreneur in Social Change in Northern Norway*. Bergen, Artok.

Beloff, M. (1964) *The Age of Absolutism*. London, Hutchinson.

Bendix, R. (1960) *Max Weber: An Intellectual Portrait*. New York, Doubleday.

Bendix, R. and Roth, G. (1971) *Scholarship and Partisanship: Essays on Max Weber*. Berkeley, University of California Press.

Beteille, A. (1965) *Caste, Class and Power: Changing Patterns of Stratification in a Tanjore Village*. Berkeley, University of California Press.

Biardeau, M. (1972) *Clefs pour la pensée hindoue*. Paris, Editions Seghers.

Bloch, M. (1930) 'Feudalism — European' in E.R.A. Seligman (ed.), *Encyclopaedia of the Social Sciences*. Vol. 6, pp. 203–10. New York, Macmillan.

Bloch, M. (1961) *Feudal Society*. Chicago and London, University of Chicago Press.

Brunner, O. (1968) *Neue Wege der Sozialgeschichte*. Göttingen, Vandenhoeck & Ruprecht.

Charanis, P. (1940–1) 'Internal Strife at Byzantium in the Fourteenth Century', *Byzantian*, vol. 15, pp. 208–30.

Charanis, P. (1951a) 'On the Social Structure and Economic Organization of the Byzantine Empire in the Thirteenth Century', *Byzantinoslavica*, vol. 12, pp. 94–153.

Charanis, P. (1951b) 'The Aristocracy of Byzantian in the Thirteenth Century' in P.R. Coleman-Norton (ed.), *Studies in Roman Economic and Social History in Honor of A.C. Johnson*. Princeton, NJ, Princeton University Press, pp. 336–56.

Cohn, B.S. (1971) *India: The Social Anthropology of a Civilization*. Englewood Cliffs, NJ, Prentice-Hall.

Daedalus (1975) 'Wisdom, Revelation and Uncertainty', spring issue.

Dahrendorf, R. (1959) *Class and Class Conflict in Industrial Society*. Stanford, Calif., Stanford University Press.

Dardess, J.W. (1973) *Conquerors and Confucians: Aspects of Political Change in Late Yuan China*. New York, Columbia University Press.

Dubs, H.H. (1939) 'Wang Mang and his Economic Reforms', *T'oung Pao*, vol. 35, pp. 263–5.

Dumont, L. (1970a) *Homo Hierarchicus: The Caste System and its Implications* (ed. Mark Sainsbury). London, Weidenfeld & Nicolson.

Dumont, L. (1970b) *Religion, Politics and History in India: Collected Papers in Indian Sociology*. Paris and The Hague, Mouton.

Ehrenberg, V. (1960) *The Greek City-State*. Oxford, Basil Blackwell.

Eisenstadt, S.N. (1969) *The Political Systems of Empires*. New York, Free Press of Glencoe.

Eisenstadt, S.N. (1971a) *Political Sociology: A Reader*. New York, Basic Books.

Eisenstadt, S.N. (1971b) *Social Differentiation and Stratification*. Glenview, Scott Foresman.

Eisenstadt, S.N. (1971c) 'Societal Goals, Systematic Needs, Social Interaction and Individual Behavior: Some Tentative Explanation' in H.

Turk and R.R. Simpson (eds.), *Institution and Social Exchange. The Sociologies of Talcott Parsons and George C. Homans.* Indianapolis, Ind., Bobbs-Merrill, pp. 36–56.

Eisenstadt, S.N. (1973*a*) *Tradition, Change and Modernity.* New York, Wiley.

Eisenstadt, S.N. (1973*b*) *Traditional Patrimonialism and Modern Neo-Patrimonialism.* (Research Papers in the Social Sciences, Beverly Hills, Calif., Sage. (Studies in Comparative Modernization); No. 90–033.)

Eisenstadt, S.N. (1977) 'Sociological Characteristics and Problems of Small States', *Journal of International Relations* (Jerusalem), vol. 2, pp. 35–60.

Eisenstadt, S.N. (1978) *Revolutions and the Transformation of Societies.* New York, The Free Press.

Eisenstadt, S.N. and Curelaru, M. (1976) *The Form of Sociology — Paradigms and Crises.* New York, Wiley.

Eisenstadt, S.N. and Curelaru, M. (1977) 'Macro-Sociology — Theory Analysis and Comparative Studies', *Current Sociology*, vol. 25, no. 2.

Elwin, M. (1973) *The Pattern of the Chinese Past.* London, Eyre & Methuen.

Forster, R. and Green, J.D. (eds.) (1970) *Preconditions of Revolution in Early Modern Europe.* Baltimore, Md., Johns Hopkins.

Fox, R.G. (1971) *Kin, Clan, Raja and Rule, State–Hinterland Relations in Pre-Industrial India.* Berkeley, University of California Press.

Fuks, A. (1974) 'Pattern and Types of Social Economic Revolution in Greece from the Fourth to the Second Century BC', *Ancient Society*, vol. 5, pp. 51–81.

Geertz, C. (1973) *The Interpretation of Cultures.* New York, Basic Books.

Gellner, E. (1969) 'A Pendulum Swing Theory of Islam' in R. Robertson (ed.), *Sociology of Religion.* Harmondsworth, Penguin, pp. 127–41.

Gerschenkron, A. (1970) *Europe in the Russian Mirror: Four Lectures in Economic History.* Cambridge, Cambridge University Press.

Gibb, H.A.R. (1962) *Studies on the Civilization of Islam.* Boston, Mass., Beacon Press.

Gibb, H.A.R. and Bowen, H. (1957) *Islamic Society and the West, Islamic Society in the Eighteenth Century.* London, Oxford University Press.

Gluckman, M. (1963) *Order and Rebellion in Tribal Africa.* New York, Free Press.

Gluckman, M. (1974) *Structuralist Analysis in Contemporary Social Thought.* London, Routledge & Kegan Paul.

Heesterman, J.C. (1957) *The Ancient Indian Royal Consecration, the Rajsuya Described according to the Yajus.* The Hague, Mouton.

Heesterman, J.C. (1964) 'Brahmin, Ritual and Renouncer', *Wiener Zeitschrift für die Kunde Süd- und Ostasiens*, vol. 8.

Heesterman, J.C. (1971) 'Kautalya and the Ancient Indian State', *Wiener Zeitschrift für die Kunde Süd- und Ostasiens*, vol. 5.

Heuss, A. (1973) 'Das Revolutions Problem in Spiegel der Antiken Geschichte', *Historische Zeitschrift*, vol. 216, no. 1, pp. 1–72.

Hintze, O. (1975) *The Historical Essays of Otto Hintze* (ed. F. Gelbert). New York, Oxford University Press.

Ho, Ping-Ti. (1962) *The Ladder of Success in Imperial China, Aspects of Social Mobility 1368–1911*. New York, Columbia University Press.

Hodgson, M.G.S. (1974) *The Venture of Islam — Conscience and History in a World Civilization*. Vol. I, *The Classical Age of Islam*. Chicago, University of Chicago Press.

Holt, P.M., Lambton, A.K.S. and Lewis, B. (1970) *The Cambridge History of Islam*. Cambridge, Cambridge University Press.

Hucker, C.O. (ed.) (1969) *Chinese Government in Ming Times, Seven Studies*. New York, Columbia University Press.

Hussey, J.M. (1937) *Church and Learning in the Byzantine Empire (867–1185)*. London, Oxford University Press.

Inalcik, H. (1973) *The Ottoman Empire, The Classical Age 1300–1600*. London, Weidenfeld & Nicolson.

Ishwaran, K. (ed.) (1970) *Continuity and Change in India's Villages*. New York, Columbia University Press.

Itzkowitz, N. (1972) *Ottoman Empire and Islamic Tradition*. New York, Knopf.

Kolff, D.H.A. (1971) 'Sannyasi Trader-Soldiers', *The Indian Economic and Social History Review*, vol. 8, pp. 214–20.

Kracke, E.A. (1953) *Civil Service in Early Sung (960–1067)*. Cambridge, Mass., Harvard University Press.

Kracke, E.A. (1955) 'Sung Society: Change within Traditions', *Far Eastern Quarterly*, vol. 14, pp. 479–89.

Kracke, E.A. (1957) 'Religion, Family and Individual in the Chinese Examination System' in J.K. Fairbank (ed.), *Chinese Thought and Institutions*. Chicago, University of Chicago Press, pp. 251–68.

Laoust, H. (1965) *Les Schismes dans l'Islam, introduction à une étude de la religion musulmane*. Paris, Payot.

Lapidus, I.M. (1975*a*) 'Hierarchies and Networks: A Comparison of Chinese and Islamic Societies' in F. Wakeman and C. Grant (eds.), *Conflict and Control in Late Imperial China*. Berkeley, University of California Press.

Lapidus, I.M. (1975*b*) 'The Separation of State and Religion in the Development of Early Islamic Society', *International Journal of Middle East Studies*, vol. 6, pp. 363–85.

Legoff, J. (1968) *Hérésies et sociétés dans l'Europe pré-industrielle*. Paris, Mouton.

Lévi-Strauss, C. (1963) *Structural Anthropology* (trans. C. Jacobson and B.G. Schoepf). New York, Basic Books.

Lewis, B. (1950) *The Arabs in History*. London, Hutchinson.

Lewis, B. (1973) 'The Significance of Heresy in Islam' in *Islam in History: Ideas, Men and Events in the Middle East*. London, Alcove Press, pp. 217–36.

Lindsay, J.O. (ed.) (1957) *New Cambridge Modern History*. Vol. VII: *The Old Regime, 1713–63*. Cambridge, Cambridge University Press.

Liu, J.T.C. (1959) *Reforming Sung China: Wang An-Shih (1021–86) and His New Policies*. Cambridge, Mass., Harvard University Press.

Mandelbaum, D.G. (1970) *Society in India*. Vol. I: *Continuity and Change*. Vol. II: *Change and Continuity*. Berkeley, University of California Press.

Michael, F.H. (1955) 'State and Society in Nineteenth-century China', *World Politics*, vol. 7, pp. 414–33.

Michael, F.H. (1965) *The Origin of Manchu Rule in China: Frontier and Bureaucracy as Interacting Forces in the Chinese Empire*. New York, Octagon.

Miller, B. (1941) *The Palace School of Mohammed the Conqueror*. Cambridge, Mass., Harvard University Press.

Mommsen, W. (1974) *Max Weber — Gesellschaft Politik und Geschichte*. Frankfurt am Main, Suhrkamp.

Moscati, S. (1962) *The Face of the Ancient Orient*. New York, Doubleday.

Nakamura, H. (1964) *Ways of Thinking of Eastern Peoples: India–China–Tibet–Japan*. Honolulu, East–West Center Press.

Nakane, C. (1970) *Japanese Society*. London, Weidenfeld & Nicolson.

Neale, W.C. (1969) 'Land is to Rule' in R.E. Frykenberg (ed.), *Land Control and Social Structure in Indian History*, pp. 3–16. Madison, University of Wisconsin Press.

O'Dea, J., O'Dea, J. and Adams, C. (1975) *Religion and Man: Judaism, Christianity and Islam*. New York, Harper & Row.

Ostrogorsky, G. (1956) *History of the Byzantine State*. Oxford, Basil Blackwell.

Pipes, R. (1975) *Russia under the Old Regime*. London, Weidenfeld & Nicolson.

Prawer, J. and Eisenstadt, S.N. (1968) 'Feudalism' in D.L. Sills (ed.), *International Encyclopedia of the Social Sciences*. Vol. V, pp. 393–403. New York, Macmillan/Free Press.

Raeff, M. (1966) *Origins of the Russian Intelligentsia: The Eighteenth-century Nobility*. New York, Harcourt, Brace & World.

Reischauer, E.O. and Fairbank, J.K. (1960) *East Asia, The Great Tradition, A History of East-Asian Civilization*. Vol. I. Boston, Houghton Mifflin.

Resink, G.I. (1966) *Indonesia's History between the Myths. Essays in Legal History and Historical Theory*. The Hague, W. van Hoeve.

Riggs, F.W. (1966) *Thailand: The Modernization of a Bureaucratic Polity*. Honolulu, East–West Center Press.

Rossi, I. (ed.) (1974) *The Unconscious in Culture: The Structuralism of Claude Lévi-Strauss in Perspective*. New York, Dutton.

Rudolph, S.M., Rudolph, L.I. and Singh, M. (1975) 'A Bureaucratic Lineage in Princely India: Elite Formation and Conflict in a Patrimonial System', *Journal of Asian Studies*, vol. 34, pp. 717–54.

Sarkisyanz, E. (1965) *Buddhist Backgrounds of the Burmese Revolution*. The Hague, M. Nijhoff.

Schacht, J. (1970) 'Law and Justice' in P.M. Holt, A.K.S. Lamblen and B. Lewis (eds.), *The Cambridge History of Islam*. Vol. II, pp. 539–68. Cambridge, Cambridge University Press.

Schrieke, B.J. (1957) *Ruler and Realm in Early Java: Selected Writings of B. Schrieke*, Indonesian Sociological Studies. The Hague, W. van Hoeve.

Seton-Watson, H. (1952) *The Decline of Imperial Russia 1855–1914*. London, Methuen.

Shils, E. (1975) *Center and Periphery*. Chicago, University of Chicago Press.

Singer, M. and Cohn, B.S. (eds.) (1968) *Structure and Change in Indian Society*. Chicago, Aldine.

Sourdel, D. (1970) 'The Abbasid Caliphate' in D.M. Holt, A.K.S. Lamblen and B. Lewis (eds.), *The Cambridge History of Islam*. Vol. I, pp. 104–40. Cambridge, Cambridge University Press.

Spuler, E. (1970) 'The Disintegration of the Caliphate in the East' in P.M. Holt, A.K.S. Lamblen and B. Lewis (eds.), *The Cambridge History of Islam*. Vol. I, pp. 143–74. Cambridge, Cambridge University Press.

Srinivas, M.N. (1966) *Social Change in Modern India*. Berkeley, University of California Press.

Steinberg, D.J. (ed.) (1971) *In Search of Southeast Asia. A Modern History*. New York, Praeger.

Tambiah, S.J. (1976) *World Conqueror and World Renouncer*. London, Cambridge University Press.

Thapar, R. (1978) *Ancient Indian Social History*. Delhi, Orient Longman.

Tilly, C. (ed.) (1975) *The Formation of National States in Western Europe*. Princeton, Princeton University Press.

Troeltsch, E. (1931) *The Social Teaching of the Christian Churches*. New York, Macmillan.

Turner, B.S. (1974) *Weber and Islam: A Critical Study*. London, Routledge & Kegan Paul.

Voegelin, E. (1954–5) *Order and History*. Vols. I–III. Baton Rouge, Louisiana State University Press.

Von Grunebaum, G.E. (1946) *Medieval Islam: A Study in Cultural Orientation*. Chicago, University of Chicago Press.

Von Grunebaum, G.E. (ed.) (1954) *Studies in Islamic Cultural History*. (American Anthropologist, Memoir, 76.)

Wittek, P. (1963) *The Rise of the Ottoman Empire*. London.

3 State formation in early India

Romila Thapar

Theories on the earliest formation of states in India remain generally rather simplistic. There is none of the richness of concepts, which has entered the discussion of state formation in Africa or Meso-America. This poverty of theory derives, in part, from an abiding obsession with one image of the early Indian state, that of oriental despotism. Projected initially by nineteenth-century British administrators and historians,[1] it did not even find its counterpoint, as did many other images from the same source, in the more radical writings of this century. The equally obsessive and generalised Marxist concern with the 'Asiatic mode of production', despite contrary empirical evidence, continued to be enthusiastically projected and the labours of Indian Marxists[2] who tried to show its inapplicability have often been brushed aside.

The emphasis on the nature of the Asian state was given such weight that the preliminary question of the process of state formation tended to be neglected. Some tentative suggestions grew in the main out to two possible explanations; the first hung on the conquest theory, where it was argued that the Aryans conquered the indigenous population in the first millennium BC, and this was the initial step in what ultimately resulted in the creation of the state. The other argued for internal stratification, that the emergence of castes was an indication of the coming of the state. In the light of more recent research, both these theories are subject to substantial qualification. In the first case, there is considerable doubt now as to whether there was an

Aryan race which conquered systematically throughout the Indian sub-continent. Instead it is being suggested that 'Aryan' should be seen as a cultural and linguistic concept, its diffusion relating more to migration and technological links, rather than to conquest. In the second case, the equation of caste stratification with class stratification is being questioned. Perhaps the best way of re-examining the question would seem to be to analyse afresh the process of state formation to the earliest historical period and ascertain the major changes which took place in the transition from a non-state to a state society.

A state is generally associated with political authority which functions within a territorial limit, delegates its powers to functionaries, is financed by revenue collected from those who contribute regularly on an impersonal basis to its maintenance and acts as an instrument for integrating social segments identified, not merely by ritual roles but also by economic functions.[3] The state, therefore, is different from government and is in turn different from society.

The emergence of such a system, historically attested for the first time in India, occurred in the middle of the first millennium BC, and had as its geographical focus the central Ganges valley (Figure 3.1). Earlier, at the start of the first millennium BC, there is evidence from Vedic texts and archaeology of a society located in the western Ganges valley which appeared to be on the edge of state formation but was different from the subsequent society to its east, which clearly shows evidence of the existence of a state. The evidence gathered from the various Vedic texts and other related literature suggests a range of stratified societies. The chiefships of the Rig-Vedic times, such as that of the Bharatas, moved gradually towards a monoarchica system in the western Ganges valley of which the Kuru and the Pañcála were typical. The chiefships of the central Ganges valley, among which the most famous was that of the Vrijjis, survived for a longer period, and in the view of some historians had evolved into states before they fell prey to the powerful monarchies of the area.

The analysis of these early forms is particularly relevant in the Indian context, since the process of state formation was a continuing process in the sub-continent throughout the centuries, with the new areas being brought into state systems. It has been said that there was a pathological fear of anarchy in India, defined as the absence of a king or a state; it can be equally well argued that it was not the fear of anarchy but the justification for this continual process of state formation which was being emphasised in the sources. The emergence of the state in any of the larger regions of the Indian sub-continent was not a uniform change affecting the entire region; more often it was initially limited to small nuclei. This tended to make the change all the more dramatic. A study of the earliest forms therefore may provide a

56

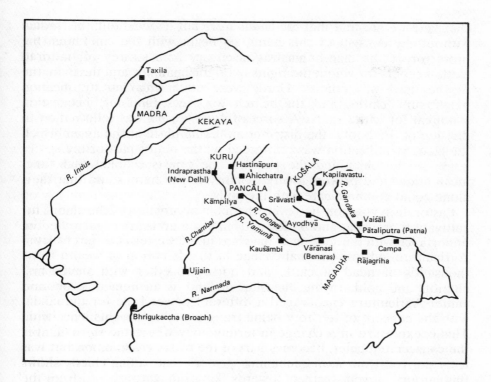

Figure 3.1 The Ganges Valley

pattern, which was either repeated or modified or reorganised in later periods, but of which the constituents would remain substantially the same.

In the western Ganges valley, the transition from chiefship to kingship resulted in a condition which might be called arrested development of the state.[4] Certain trends inclined towards the emergence of a state, but others remained impediments. Vedic society of the earlier half of the first millennium BC can be characterised as a lineage-based society. The unit was the clan, and this formed the essential structure at many levels. There was a consciousness of territory and an identity with territory expressed through the clan name being bestowed on the territory claimed. Thus, the territories of Gandhàra, Madra, Kekeya, Kuru, Pañcála, Matsya, were all named after the clan which claimed sovereignty over them. Such territories were termed the *janapada*, literally 'the area where the *jana* tribe placed its foot'.

The clan consisted of the families of the chiefs (*rājanya*) and the rest of the clan (the *viś*). Land was originally owned in the name of the

57

clan, and we are told that the chiefs were not allowed to give it away without the consent of the clan.[5] To begin with the chief was the protector of the clan. This was necessary in a society of pastoral cattle-keepers for whom the rights over grazing lands and the increase of the herd was crucial. Herds were often enlarged by stealing neighbours' cattle, and the search for cows (*gāviṣṭhi*) became a synonym for cattle raids. A successful cattle raid was followed by a division of the booty, the distribution taking place at the assembly of the clan. Stratification was reinforced by the major part of the spoils going to the chief and the priests. The priests claimed that their incantations and prayers assured victory to the heroes and that they alone could communicate with the gods.

Pastoralism was not, however, the main occupation of the clan. The cultivation of wheat and barley and, in some areas, rice, increased in importance with the settling of the clans in the western Ganges valley.[6] Agriculture led to a gradual change in the definition of wealth from thousands of head of cattle and horses together with slave-girls, chariots and gold, to the inclusion of land as an item of economic value. Agriculture encouraged a different power base for the chief, with the concept of territory being transformed into rights over land. This is expressed in a change in terminology where the *rājanya*, still the consecrated chief, becomes part of the wider group of *kṣatriyas*, a term derived from *kṣatra* meaning 'power'. The ruling chiefs within this group moved further towards kingship through a series of elaborate sacrificial rituals. These involved assertions of association with divinity. The rituals were performed for the chiefs by the brahmins who thus become the legitimisers of the new status, and incidentally, thereby also improved their own status and claimed the pre-eminent position in the social hierarchy. The gradual concentration of power in the hands of the *kṣatriya rāja* increased his effective control, but, at the same time, lesser chiefs were not his appointees and held the position in their own right. There was a minimal delegation of authority. The power of the king was further weakened by the separation of sacred and temporal functions. The office of the king drew heavily on religious sanction, as is evident from the association of kingship with fecundity and prosperity. This association is often symbolised by the king being regarded as a 'rain-maker'. It is repeatedly stated that unrighteous kings are responsible for drought. Many stories refer to the coming of the rains after twelve years of drought, when the throne is restored to the rightful incumbent.

The support for the office came from occasional tribute and prestations. The words used for such tribute, *bali*, *bhāga* and *śulka*, were subsequently to become the regular terms for periodic taxation. This has led to some controversy as to whether they should not be interpreted as taxes in this early period as well.[7] But in the context in which they occur they seem to connote tribute rather than tax, since they are not periodic nor of a stipulated amount nor are they collected from designated categories of persons.

The providers of prestations and tribute were of course the lesser members of the clan and the texts speak of the *kṣatra* eating the clan in the same way as deer eat corn.[8] The *viś* or clan had itself undergone a change with the *grihapati*, the head of the household gradually emerging as a distinct social entity. Significantly in the subsequent period, the *grihapati* is often described as the *vaiśya* (derived from *viś*) and the functions of the *vaiśya* are precisely those performed by the *grihapati* in the earlier period, namely, cattle rearing, agriculture and trade.[9] The *grihapatis* may originally have been the junior members of the ruling lineages or the wealthier members of the clan. Their emergence suggests the existence of what might be termed 'a house-holding economy' in which each patrilineal household was the unit. Cultivated land owned by the *grihapati* was worked by the family and, if necessary, by hired labourers and slaves as well. Minimum handicrafts required for servicing the household were also produced by such employees, an activity, which, when it increased, became the basis for exchange and trade. The identity of the labourers and slaves is not clearly indicated but they are referred to as *śūdras* and *dāsas*. Both terms have unknown etymologies. They occur earlier as the names of tribes in north-western India and may therefore reflect the subordination of alien groups.[10] *Dāsa* was later to become the technical term for slave.

The theory of varṇa

Society was by now sufficiently stratified to require a theoretical structure of explanation and this is expressed in the theory of *varṇa*, often translated as 'caste'. It has been argued that this was a system of ritual ranking in which the purest, the brahmin, was ranked the highest.[11] The others, in degrees of impurity, took lower positions with the lowest being that of the untouchable, whose emergence belongs to the later post-Vedic period. An alternative hypothesis maintains that the establishment of the *varṇas* indicates a class stratification which points to the existence of the state, even though the other elements of the state remain elusive at this time.[12] What has not been recognised in these theories is that the main criterion in differentiating each *varṇa* in the initial stage is precisely that which links it most closely with lineage and relates to different patterns of marriage systems. Three distinct patterns are discernible. The first is that of the brahmins observing the *gotra* subdivisions in which exogamy is crucial and marriage within the subdivision is not allowed. A special dispensation had to be given to the brahmins of the south for them to break this rule and marry the mother's brother's daughter. The second pattern is that of the *kṣatriya* and the *vaiśya* who more often than not marry endogamously within the *vaṃśa* or lineage. The third pattern of the *śūdra* system is totally different and is based on the notion that the parentage is of 'mixed castes' (*sankīrṇa jāti*). The rank of the *śūdra* is determined by the particular inter-caste combination of his parentage.[13] The reconstruction of the origins of the *śūdra* castes is in any case an exercise in theory, since the possible permutations are infinite and the *śūdra* lists in the texts do not necessarily agree.

Food taboos associated with each *varṇa* strengthen the notion of ritual ranking,[14] as does the fact that the non-brahmin Buddhist and Jaina literature reserves the ranking of the first two castes and the *kṣatriyas* are placed higher than the brahmins. In so far therefore as it was a ritual ranking it only applied to areas dominated by brahminical values. The co-relation with economic status is also not invariable for there are impoverished brahmins and wealthy *śūdras*.

The unity of society and internal harmony was sought to be established through the *varṇa* structure. There were no formal procedures for legal action and the redressing of wrong was linked to social pressures and expiatory rituals. External protection was highlighted in the office of the *rājā* or chief. Indirect attempts to sanction his control over physical force can be seen in the close association of the *senāni* (commander) with his immediate retinue, as well as in the tradition of leadership in battle being a prerequisite for the office of the chief. There were multiple prestations and gifts to support elaborate rituals maintaining the status of both the chief and of sacred authority, but there was no systematic method of collecting an income to finance the institutions of a state. Most of the wealth was consumed in any case in prestigious rituals. The vast sacrificial ceremonies, the *yajñas*, extending over many months if not years, were rituals which combined the function of the potlatch with various degrees of gift-exchange. Gifts established status among chiefs. The distribution of gifts by the *yajamāna* (the one who holds the sacrifice) to the priests established his status as well as that of the priests. The rituals were a source of legitimacy for the chief but they also prevented the investment of wealth into economically more productive channels.

The diversion of wealth into such channels did take place in the succeeding period, the middle of the first millennium BC, and in the adjoining area to the east, the central Ganges valley. The change of geographical location is referred to in the story of Videgha Māthava who, we are told, travelled east, but stopped and waited at the River

Gandaka until Agni, the god of fire, had purified the land across the river, after which he settled there. Being a low-lying, wetter area, pastoralism met with problems and gave way to a predominantly agricultural economy. The cultivation of wheat and rice was possible in Kośala (eastern Uttar Pradesh) where one of the early kingdoms arose. Further east, the marshlands of north Bihar were more conducive to rice.[15] Rice is essentially a single-crop cultivation, and even with the assistance of irrigation in the form of river channels and tanks, as mentioned in the sources, it was difficult to ensure a regular second crop. The need to obtain a larger surplus led to the extension of agriculture and the references to fields under rice run into hundreds of acres in the descriptions of wealthy landowners.[16] The larger acreages of cultivated land were either held by clans or by individual owners where clan holdings had ceased. This was regarded as private ownership with full rights of alienation. Irrigation was either the concern of the clan or was maintained by local landowners, a pattern which was to persist in most parts of northern India for many centuries. The state rarely provided irrigation facilities.

The extension of plough agriculture and the organisation of irrigation have often been regarded as sufficient requirements for the emergence of the state. That the emergence of the state was not an automatic or mechanical development from these changes is suggested by the co-existence in the central Ganges valley of two types of political system, where in the one case the state remained in limbo, while in the other it flourished. The contrasting picture is presented on the one hand in the *gana-sangha* systems often represented as republics, oligarchies or chiefdoms, and on the other, in the monarchies which increasingly became the norm for the state in early India.

The existence of chiefdoms was not restricted to the central Ganges valley. They are referred to in other parts of India well into the first millennium AD.[17] Those of the central Ganges valley have however been described more fully in early Buddhist sources. The chiefdoms were either those of a single clan such as that of the Śākyas, to which the Buddha belonged, or of a confederacy of clans such as the eight which went into the making of the famous Vrijji confederacy. The clans were uniformly of *kṣatriya* status but there was a sharp demarcation between the ruling clans (*rāja-kula*) who claimed ownership of the land, had the right to sit in the clan assembly and were accorded the highest social status, and the other half, as it were, which consisted of the hired labourers and the slaves who worked the land for the ruling clans and who were excluded from claiming social and political rights.[18] No mention is made in the chiefdoms of private property in land, or of the *grihapatis* as landowners. In case of conflict, as over the distribution of water for irrigation on one occasion, the ruling clans as a group entered the fray and fought it out.[19] There was, however, a fairly complex system of administration in which all the members of the ruling clans had equal status. Matters of importance were discussed in the assembly hall and voted upon, and problems of administration were given due weight by the assembly. The *gana-sangha* chiefships seem therefore to conform to the category of stratified societies prior to state formation, as defined by some theorists.

In the chiefdoms, the religious ritual was the worship of ancestral tumuli, the brahminical sacrificial ritual being alien. The status of the brahmin therefore even in the caste hierarchy was lower than that of the members of the *kṣatriya* clans who were the ruling families and the landowners.[20]

The *varṇa* system is treated as a theoretical notion with little relevance to actual social stratification. Social functioning was based on the *ñāti,* which has been translated as the minimum effective lineage and on the *jāti,* a larger group frequently defined by occupation but whose membership was conditional on being born into the group. A dual stratification divided *jātis* into high and low. The absence of an emphasis on ritual ranking led to these areas being categorised as impure and outside the social pale in brahminical sources.[21] That there was a powerful religious alternative to brahminism in the chiefdoms is evident from the loyalty of many of these clans to religious teachers who emerged from their midst, such as Gautama Buddha who was a Śākya, and Mahāvīra, associated with Janinism, who was of the Vrijji confederacy.

Whereas the chiefdoms remained, as it were, on the edge of state formation, the monarchies such as the kingdoms of Kośala and Magadha indicate the emergence of fully-fledged states. This transition appears to have followed from a number of other major changes. The more evident of these changes were the emergence of a professional, commercial group as well as of a peasant economy. Both developments broke the limitations of the prestation system of the western Ganges valley and led to a more liberated economic expression.

Urban centres were often in origin the residences of the ruling clans and, as such, each *janapada,* or territory, identified with a clan, had at least one large centre which was the political capital. This was true of the *janapadas* of north-western India as of those of the central Ganges valley. The Kuru capital of Hastināpura and the Pañcāla capital of Ahichhatra were equally important as political centres as the Śākya capital of Kapilavastu and the Vrijji centre at Vaiśāli. A significant change in urbanisation came about when some of these centres acquired commercial importance both as places of production and with incipient markets. The combination of political and commercial activity was what led them to be called the 'great cities', *mahānagara,* in Buddhist texts.[22]

The process can be traced through various stages. One of the by-products of kingship and the concentration of political power in the hands of one family was a change in clan relations. The heads of the households, the *grihapatis*, as private owners of land, and as the main supporters of the economy, had improved their status. With the extension of agriculture in the central Ganges valley, the *grihapati* became the symbol of wealth and the main taxpayer propping up the kingdom. Wealth was increasingly computed in measures of grain, and later in coined money.[23] The wealth released to the *grihapati* from both the extension of agriculture and the decline of a prestation economy could now be invested in trade. Trade developed out of more simple exchanges at the level of the village and of the market, the *nigama*. Itinerant smiths working on the new technology of iron doubtless encouraged itinerant trade. This may gradually have stabilised into regular trading circuits. The growth of settlements around the river system in the Ganges valley provided a natural means of communication by river. The locations of the 'great cities' associated with the early trade are at nodal points in relation to the river system, and are generally at the confluence of at least two ecological zones. Literary descriptions of cities exaggerated their size, sometimes up to fifty square kilometres, which is not corroborated by archaeology.[24] Nevertheless the urban levels at excavations are considerably larger in area than the pre-urban levels and the literary exaggeration symbolises the sense of a larger size. There is also a recognisable uniformity of some archaeological artefacts which characterise urban levels at sites in many parts of the Ganges valley. Associated with these levels is the discovery of punch-marked coins in particular which have been found in many thousands. These form the archaeological counterpart to references to coined money gradually becoming the basis of transactions in the cities. Not only did this extend the reach of trade, but it also brought with it the profession of the banker who financed trade. Usury is frowned upon in brahminical sources. The good brahmin is permitted to lend money on interest only in the direst of circumstances, and then too is required to perform an expiatory ritual to absolve himself of the accruing sin.[25] Buddhist ethics on the other hand recognise usury as a legitimate activity open to any member of society. The term used for the banker is *śreṣṭhin/seṭṭhi* meaning he who has the best, and the banker was a highly respected person in non-brahminical sources. Frequently, the wealthy *grihapati* moved into the banking profession and became the respected *śreṣṭhin*.[26] The existence of the heterodox religious sects, recognisably the Buddhists,

Jainas, and a large variety of non-conformist groups such as the Cārvākas and the Lokāyatas, helped to legitimise the *grihapatis'* investments in trade, rather than the burning up of wealth in ritual prestations at the sacrificial ceremonies. The brahminical sacrifices did not die out, since kings still sought legitimisation of their status through these rituals, but they became increasingly a formality. What is more important, the consumption of wealth at such gatherings was now marginal to the total wealth produced. Brahmin specialists in the rituals were rewarded with grants of fertile agricultural land and some of the wealthiest landowners in the new kingdoms were such brahmins, despite the injunctions in the legal texts against brahmins making a living from agriculture.[27]

The householding economy based on the private ownership of land which emerged from the gradual disintegration of clan ownership not only led to a diversion of wealth into trade and commerce, but also brought about changes in the agrarian economy. Where the heads of households took increasingly to trade, their supervision over agriculture was reduced. Thus fields tended to be cultivated not by their employees, but were leased to peasant cultivators who paid a share of the produce to the owner. These may well have been the erstwhile labourers, but their function and status had changed when they became tenants. In many cases the sizes of holdings were too large for the household to work them directly and, consequently, tenants had to be installed. In one case we are told that after renouncing a major part of his wealth, the head of the household still retained 500 ploughs, 100 acres of land and 40,000 cattle. Impoverished *grihapatis*, those who, because of drought and lack of a harvest were unable to retain any wealth and were reduced to the status of poor peasants, are also mentioned.

Peasant tenures were developed further through the settling of waste land by agriculturalists. This was done through the entrepreneurship of the state which then claimed ownership over such lands. In thus extending the agricultural economy the state obtained larger revenue.[28] Where the state owned the land a system of tenures was established with the cultivators paying a percentage of the share to the state. In such tenurial systems there was a direct relation between the state and the cultivator without the intervention of the landowning intermediary. In caste terminology the *śūdra* in the agrarian context gradually became the cultivator in the sense of a peasant. The *śūdra* as peasant and artisan and the *vaiśya* as the *grihapati* become the main bearers of the burden of tax, and taxation comes to be an important element in the theory of the state.

Changing theories of the state

In the period during which the state emerged there is a noticeable change in the explanation for the origin of kingship and government.[29] Whereas earlier, qualities of leadership were stressed and prowess in battle prized, later texts speak more frequently of other elements. In these theories the contractual aspect is added deriving from a condition in which society itself was supposed to have undergone a change. The earliest society is described as a Utopian remote past in which there were no kings, laws or social distinctions. But gradually virtue declined and this made it necessary for laws to be instituted and for authority to be vested in the king as the protector of society both from external threats and internal dissensions. The description of the decline of virtue varies in brahminical and Buddhist sources in accordance with the perspective of each on social change. Another important distinction is that the brahminical king is the nominee of the gods, but the Buddhist version speaks only of people electing one from among their midst and investing him with power.

In the fourth century BC the theory of the state is elaborated upon in the notion of the seven elements, later to be called the seven limbs, which constitute the state.[30] These are discussed in the *Arthaśāstra* of Kauṭalya, who lists them as the ruler, the ministers and administrators, the territory, the capital, the treasury where the revenue was brought, physical force and allies. These constituents existed in a somewhat nebulous form in the chiefdoms of the central Ganges valley and one may therefore describe the Vrijji confederacy as a state in the making. But they are more firmly and clearly recognisable in the monarchies of this area such as that of Kośala and Magadha. The texts which describe them regard the monarchical state as its only legitimate form.

The legitimisation of the monarchical state is also reflected in the conflated and interpolated versions of the two epics of early India. The *Mahābhārata* which has as its main location the Kuru territory of the western Ganges valley records the anguish of the chiefdoms slowly giving way to the coming of the state. The narrative depicts a society prior to the rise of the state, but the heavily conflated additions which take on the character of didactic interpolations are equally clearly a defence of the monarchical state. The *Rāmāyaṇa* has as its base the kingdom of Kośala in the central Ganges valley, and possibly the earliest version of the epic was restricted to this area. But with the extension of its geography in later redactions, the horizon was also extended. The conflict between the state and the non-state is much more clearly crystallised in the *Rāmāyaṇa* where Rāma the hero, a prince of the state of Kośala, battles against *Rāvaṇa* whose society of *Rākṣasas*, said to be demons, is strongly suggestive of a chiefdom.

The *Rāmāyaṇa* in particular has a chequered history. It was translated into various Indian languages and with each version some changes were introduced. It is significant that the rendering of the text into regional languages tends to coincide with the establishment of strong monarchical kingdoms on an extensive scale in the same areas. The translations therefore, apart from the religious message of propagating the cult of Vishnu, were also a subtle means of eulogising the monarchical state.

As a continuing process in Indian history, in areas beyond the Ganges valley, the pattern of change from lineage-based societies to state systems is a recurrent pattern. The process is not in every case entirely identical to the one described here, but broadly approximates to it. Where clan lands lay juxtaposed with monarchies, clan ownership was eroded by the conquest of the area or by the encroachment of the monarchical system through the clearing of waste land and the establishing of agricultural settlements. Ruling clans took on *kṣatriya* status and with the break-up of clan-held lands the lesser *kṣatriya* families claimed ownership over private holdings.[31] The ruling clans became the feudatories to the neighbouring monarchies, and if the control of the latter weakened the feudatories gradually acquired independent status. As local élites they emulated the lifestyle of the monarchies and included in this was patronage of courtly literature in Sanskrit, the building of temples, the granting of land to brahmins learned in the Veda and the encouraging of a new phase of Hinduism reflected in the Purāṇic texts. Those reduced to the condition of peasant tenants were given the rank of *śūdras* as also were those who worked as artisans and craftsmen. Trade in the early stages remained the occupation of the outsider though gradually the wealthier local families were inducted into this circuit as well.

The *varṇa* system in such areas soon became the model for social organisation with the introduction of caste society. Brahmins were imported since legitimisation through the sacrificial rituals was necessary for the new order. In return they were given substantial grants of land and other forms of patronage and often became the focal point of cultural assimilation. Legitimisation did not merely mean the centring of a monarchical state but also the provision of *kṣatriya* genealogies and lineage links for those who had succeeded in acquiring political power. The genealogical component of the historical tradition is therefore given priority in the historical chronicles written after the middle of the first millennium AD. The *vaiśya* even as a caste category tends to be less important in later centuries when occupations connected with trade are often relegated to *śūdra* status. With the acceleration in the formation of small states in the late first and second millennia AD, there is a mushroom growth of *śūdra jātis*, reflecting the assimilation of new clans on an extended scale, as well as the proliferation of occupational groups in newly opened areas.[32]

The ritual hierarchy of the *varṇa* system was maintained with the introduction of religious forms into newly established states and the attempt to absorb the existing religious cults and sects into what might be called the great tradition of Purāṇic Hinduism. The rituals sought to assimilate the local clan deity, to incorporate its territory as part of the new state and to convert its priests either into the brahmin caste or as special functionaries in temples built to the deity. This has been demonstrated for example in the history of the Jagannath cult at Puri which becomes such a focus in a late phase of the growth of the state in Orissa.[33] In such situations there was sometimes a convergence of caste and economic statuses. Even where this did not happen the *varṇa* system helped convey a sense of orderliness, uniform with other areas despite such economic transformations as the emergence of a peasant economy and commercial groups.

The transition from lineage to state was not the only pattern of change, nor was conquest the only avenue of state formation as has been asserted by many commentators on the pre-modern Indian past. Areas with a long history of state systems underwent intensive historical changes through time, the varying forms being integral to the nature and role of the state. The latter ranged from centralised unitary states to what have recently been described as segmentary states, not to mention various relatively decentralised systems in which varieties of peasant tenures and commercial interests constituted the variables. The relationship between metropolitan areas and peripheral areas was by no means unchanging or uniform. Nevertheless there is a tendency among theorists on the pre-modern state to insist that the Indian data supports a single system having prevailed throughout the sub-continent and valid virtually for all time.

Briefly summarised, the discussion of the state in pre-modern India assumes a static situation until the colonial period, the only change being from clan systems to the engulfing of society by the despotic state, a change believed to have occurred on an extensive scale in antiquity. With the absence of private property in land, ownership was vested either in the state or in the village community which was in any case subservient to the state. A despotic king extracted revenues from the village communities. These were described as otherwise auto-nomous and autarchic except that production being entirely agricul-tural was dependent on irrigation facilities controlled by the state through a hierarchy of officials who also collected the revenue. In such a situation the rare town was an administrative centre, there being a total absence of commerce. The only commodities produced were luxury goods for royal or courtly consumption.

This image of what was in essence regarded as oriental despotism was elaborated upon in Marx's 'Asiatic mode of production' and remains the most influential theoretical model for discussion of the traditional Indian political economy. Attempts have been made to show that the empirical data do not support such a model or that the model itself contradicts the very theory of a dialectical process, but nevertheless insistence on its applicability continues.

Recently, a more refined definition of the Asiatic mode of production has been suggested on the basis of data relating to the Inca state in Peru and its environs.[34] The pre-Inca situation was one in which land was owned communally by clans, was redistributed periodically between extended families, who worked it but did not own it, and labour was communal, with the villagers acting in co-operation. The Incas conquered these clans and declared that all land was the property of the state, some of it being declared crown land. The rest of the land was worked not by members of the clan, but by forced labour. The clans lost their rights over the land in terms of ownership but continued to have rights of possession and use, and production therefore remained communal, despite a changed mode of production. The Inca state maintained some of the earlier customs of providing food, drink and seed to the cultivators in an apparent attempt to suggest that the earlier system still prevailed. There was also an administrative organisation to control the clans. The state, in such a system, was the collective landlord and therefore the superior community. Kinship relations as ties in production were destroyed, as was the earlier social formation.

The application of such a model to the early Indian situation remains inappropriate. There is some ambiguity on the question of the ownership of land by the state other than in the clearly defined state lands. But there are frequent references to private ownership and to the alienation of land by its owners. Where the state system already existed, bringing new land under cultivation was in many instances carried out through the agency of the state either by land grants to individuals or by settling the area with agriculturalists. Mention is made in the *Arthaśāstra* of Kauṭalya of settlements of *śūdra* agriculturalists brought from overpopulated areas or induced to come from neighbouring kingdoms.[35] Elsewhere the same text makes special mention of state lands, and refers to these as being cultivated either by share-croppers or by hired labourers and slaves or even by those undergoing judicial punishment.[36] However, these settlements did not eliminate the independent owners of the land.

The question as to which type of agrarian structure predominated, privately owned or state-owned land, remains without a statistically proved answer. Possibly the short duration of large-scale states and the availability of new lands until recent centuries would suggest that the extension of agriculture through settlements by the state was not utilised to the point of its becoming the predominant system. In any case, the increasing incidence of land grants made by members of the élite to religious and secular beneficiaries from the first millennium AD onwards would have militated against the absolute control over land by the state. The continuation of independent clan systems juxtaposed with peasant economies until recent times would also suggest that state entrepreneurship in agriculture was not uniform throughout the various kingdoms.

The major form of peasant protest against oppressive taxes until the middle of the second millennium AD was not revolt but migration to new lands outside the jurisdiction of the state to which the peasant belonged. Kings are warned not to overtax the peasants, lest they migrate and thereby impoverish the kingdom. Migration would again point to access to fresh lands for settlement. Such protestors were doubtless welcome in neighbouring kingdoms for their settlement would result in additional revenue.

Theories of state formation relating to pre-modern India tend to either ignore or to underplay the importance of both the peasant economy and the rise of commercially based urban centres as factors in historical change. Lineage or clan systems were weakened by the strengthening of these two features in particular. Ritual status in so far as it was expressed in the *varṇa* or caste hierarchy acted as a continuing undercurrent of lineage systems, particularly in societies dominated by brahminical values, and where caste and economic status tended at times to converge. Such societies were often those in which the commercial economy was weak or else was controlled by the ritually high castes. The strength of the commercial economy is not recognised by modern commentators at other times perhaps because of the debate on the preconditions necessary for capitalism and the emphasis given to what was seen as the marginal role of the commercial economy in India.

State formation in early Indian history may be seen as a process of change from social formations broadly classified as lineage-based systems to those dominated by a peasant state system. But the nature of the state and the changes which it underwent through time do not conform easily to any of the existing models. Nor is the change from one social formation to another clear-cut, for there is much that survives from the earlier to the latter and many overlaps. Apart from the interpretational preconceptions of many theorists on pre-modern India, it is also these overlaps which have often helped to maintain the interplay between ritual and economic status, leading to the clouding over of the one by the other, and thus effectively hiding both the essential points of historical change and the complexities of Indian society in its early phases.

Notes

1   L. Krader, *The Asiatic Mode of Production*, Assen, 1975, traces the sources of the idea in various European writings from the seventeenth century onwards.

2   Such as the articles by Irfan Habib and S. Naqvi in *Science and Human Progress*, Bombay, 1974, and Romila Thapar, *The Past and Prejudice*, New Delhi, 1979.

3   H. Claessen and P. Skalnik, *The Early State*, The Hague, Mouton, 1978; M. Fried, *The Evolution of Political Science*, New York, 1967.

4   A more detailed discussion of state formation in the middle of the first millennium BC in northern India is available in Romila Thapar, *From Lineage to State*, Oxford University Press, 1982.

5   *Śatapatha Brāhmaṇa*, XII. 7.1.15.

6   Romila Thapar, 'The Study of Society in Ancient India' in *Ancient Indian Social History: Some Interpretations*, New Delhi, 1978.

7   R.S. Sharma, 'Class Formation and its Material Basis in the Upper Gangetic Basin', *The Indian Historical Review*, July 1975, vol. II, no. 1, pp. 1–14.

8   *Śatapatha Brāhmaṇa*, XII.7.1.12.

9   *Gautama Dharmasūtra*, X.47; *Āpastambha Dharmasūtra*, II.11.28.1.

10   H.W. Bailey, 'Iranian Arya and Daha', *Transactions of the Philological Society*, 1959, p. 71 ff. *Śudra* is sometimes linked to the Kṣudraka or Oxydrakoi tribe mentioned in accounts of Alexander's campaign in northern India. J.W. McCrindle, *The Invasion of India*, pp. 324–5, London, 1896; Plutarch, *Lives*, IX.

11   L. Dumont, *Homo Hierarchicus*, London, 1972.

12   Sharma, op. cit.

13   *Manu Dharmaśāstra*, X.12 ff.

14   Ibid., IV.205 ff.

15   O.H.K. Spate, *India and Pakistan*, p. 514 ff, London, 1964.

16   N. Wagle, *Society at the Time of the Buddha*, Bombay, 1966; R. Fick, *The Social Organization in North-east India in the Buddha's Time*, Calcutta, 1920.

17   V.S. Agrawala, *India as Known to Panini*, p. 426 ff, Varanasi, 1963.

18   H.N. Jha, *The Licchavis*, Varanasi, 1970.

19   *Kunāla Jātaka*.

20   Wagle, op. cit.

21   *Manu Dharmaśāstra*, II.23; X.45.

22   Fick, op. cit., p. 251 ff.

23   *Vinaya Piṭaka*, I, p. 240–1.

24   A. Ghosh, *The City in Early Historical India*, Simla, 1973.

25   *Baudhāyana Dharmasūtra*, I.5.10.23.

26 This is also attested to by the epigraphical evidence of donations to the Buddhist *sangha* from the second century BC onwards in western India and in the Andhra region.
27 *Baudhāyana Dharmasūtra*, I.5.10.28.
28 Kauṭalya *Arthaśāstra*, II.1; II.14; II.24.
29 R.S. Sharma, *Political Ideas and Institutions in Ancient India*, Delhi, 1968.
30 *Arthaśāstra*, VI.1.
31 Surajit Sinha, 'State Formation and Rajput Myth in Tribal Central India', *Man in India*, vol. 42, no. 1, January–March 1962, pp. 35–80.
32 R.S. Sharma, *Social Changes in Early Medieval India*, Delhi, 1969.
33 H. Kulke, 'Royal Temple Policy and Structure of Medieval Hindu Kingdoms' in A. Eschmann *et al., The Cult of Jagannath and the Regional Tradition of Orissa*, New Delhi, 1978.
34 M. Godelier, *Perspectives in Marxist Anthropology*, p. 186 ff, Cambridge, 1977.
35 *Arthaśāstra*, II.1.
36 Ibid., II. 24.

4 Strategic interactions and the formation of modern states: France and England

Aristide R. Zolberg

Introduction

Whether it is based on a Weberian or a Marxist approach, or on a more or less happy blend of several macro-sociological traditions, any theoretical analysis of the origins of the state in modern Europe, the dynamics of its subsequent development, its diversification and its dissemination, is sooner or later confronted with an epistemological dilemma arising from the very nature of its object. Such exercises are commonly founded on the comparative method — which assumes a universe whose units are mutually exclusive and independent of one another. The comparative analysis of the state is thus based on the image of a world made up of *societies*, regarded as largely self-sufficient human entities and therefore articulated by a mainly endogenous dynamic. However, anyone who takes that course is very soon made to realise that such a construction differs widely from historical fact. The path of history is strewn with cases which amount to a demonstration that in every age, societies are permeable to outside factors attributable not only to the repercussions of global processes set in train by interactions among the many societies that make up the universe in question, but also to the individual volition of one or another of those societies.[1]

Although it is true that this problem crops up in practically every branch of the social sciences, it raises special theoretical difficulties in relation to the subject under consideration, for in the European region, at the time when the state began to loom on the horizon, the relevant societies consisted of a limited number of relatively powerful protagonists whose interactions set off collective processes on a very large scale, and whose individual actions could determine the very existence of other units making up the whole. This is particularly true of what we shall call here politico-strategic action; that is to say, the set of pressures which are exerted directly or indirectly by political protagonists of a given aggregate in order to influence the organisation and individual behaviour of other protagonists in the aggregate or even the structure of the aggregate as a whole, and of which resort to armed force is merely the most obvious expression. If we consider that it is not simply a matter of the consequences, for a given state, of the actions undertaken by other protagonists in relation to itself, but also of the internal consequences of its own external enterprises, it would seem that any comparative macro-sociology of the state which ignores this factor is doomed to leave out of the explanatory schema a set of residual variables whose weight sometimes exceeds even that of the variance explained. Alternatively, the act of taking this factor into consideration tends to divert the analysis from the general towards the particular.

Does the revival taking place in this field indicate a return from historical macro-sociology to political history, rejected by many historians on the grounds that it deals with mere events? H.G. Koenigsberger, for example, seems to suggest as much in a recent analysis of the variation between European regimes at the beginning of the modern age, taking the theories of Otto Hintze and Norbert Elias as his starting-point.[2]

In the last analysis, while rejecting the illusory claims of a certain theoretical formalism, Koenigsberger seems to regard historical macro-sociology and historians' history as complementary approaches starting from two poles of a continuum rather than as mutually exclusive enterprises. If we accept the rules of the game, the task incumbent on political macro-sociology is precisely to push back as far as possible the point at which it enters the zone of history pure and simple. More particularly, in relation to the subject we are discussing, what matters is to determine whether the international politico-strategic aspect will necessarily stay beyond the reach of macro-sociology, as Koenigsberger assumes, or whether it can be subjected to this sort of treatment. Although history certainly has the upper hand in this field, that is not because theoretical reflection has failed but because it has rarely been undertaken. The reason for this might be that the appearance of the state as a two-faced political structure, as J.P. Nettl put it, one face looking inwards and the other outwards, brought about a parting of the intellectual ways that led to the split which is found today in history and in political sociology, into sub-disciplines which favour one face or the other.[3] Thus, while recent decades have witnessed, on the one hand, an abundance of theories concerning international relations and, on the other, a proliferation of comparative analyses dealing with the regime of the state, very little effort has been directed towards the interface. We find ourselves confronted, on the one hand, with the globalism of historians such as Fernand Braudel, William McNeill or again Geoffrey Barraclough, which has the merit of being comprehensive but is too eclectic to fit easily into the simplified presentation necessary to any theoretical exercise; and, on the other hand, with the theoretical globalism of sociology, which tends towards reductionism, either vaguely idealistic, as in the case of Talcott Parsons, or else strictly materialistic, as in that of Immanuel Wallerstein, whose enterprise is doomed to fail precisely because it regards the politico-strategic dimension of the international sphere as an epiphenomenon.[4] As for constructions based directly on the process of politico-strategic interaction — in other words, the theories propounded by specialists in international relations — they suffer in their turn from a fatal flaw: that of concerning themselves solely with this process, without considering the exchanges between it and the other processes that contribute to the overall structure or even, in most cases, the interface between states and the system of the states.[5]

Far from claiming to resolve these difficulties, I wish merely to point out that a global-type aggregate cannot be conceived exclusively as a 'world economy' or an 'international political system', but might be thought of as the result of exchanges between three distinct analytical structures: the economic, the politico-strategic, and the cultural, each of them in evidence both at the societal and the inter-societal levels.

The medieval origins of the state and the system of the states

The appearance of the state in the medieval West, considered in its morphological aspect as a type of organisation distinct from both the empire and the city, is inseparable from the more or less simultaneous emergence of several collectivities of that type in the region. The fact that this morphological unit materialised in multiple forms may be attributed not only to iteration — that is to say, to the fact that the cultural, social and economic factors which contributed to the process of political transformation we are considering crystallised more or less simultaneously in several parts of the region — but also to a relational dynamism peculiar to the political field itself. The dynamism in question sprang from the pluralism of the structures of authority which was the characteristic distinguishing Europe at the end of the invasions from other Euro-Asiatic civilisations, and which was itself a factor in what Perry Anderson has termed the 'detotalization of sovereignty'.[6] We shall try to show, first, how the interactions set in train by this pluralism, regarded here as the initial situation, gradually reduced it but did not eliminate it in favour of a single centre of political domination; and, second, how the crystallisation of these multiple centres produced effects which helped to give them a common morphological character. The precocious division of part of the region into a set of mechanisms for domination at a fairly high level of territorial aggregation helped to turn each of them into a state.

The chief factors which contributed to the pluralism of the structures of authority are well known. Resulting from the superimposition, in one and the same space, and of the protracted interactions, of structures inherited from the Roman Empire, Christianity and Germanic tribalism in a material and demographic environment that varies from region to region, these factors included, at the structural level, the differentiation of the respective spheres of spiritual and temporal authority, and at the territorial level, the fragmentation of feudal power that conflicted with its theoretical concentration at the level of kingdoms, although traces of that concentration remained. Lastly, Europe also contained an archipelago of urban islets grouped around trade routes and tending to develop a relatively autonomous power. The transformation we are considering should therefore be understood as two simultaneous processes: the emergence of territorial sovereignties out of entities aspiring to universal scope, and the aggregation of domination starting from widely scattered territorial power.

The differentiation of spiritual and temporal authority took shape at a fairly early stage with the emergence of the structures of the Empire and the Papacy, including not only separate legal institutions but also machinery enabling the Emperor and the Pope to extract from society as a whole the necessary resources for autonomous action. By means of such structures, the two areas of authority were transformed into two poles of power whose interactions constituted a field of tension that manifested itself in various forms including even armed conflict. According to Otto Hintze, the fissures opened by such clashes provided interstices within which other protagonists could grow, among them those who formed the nuclei of future states.[7] J. Strayer, taking up the same subject, lays particular stress on the unforeseen consequences of the Church's victory over the Empire towards the end of the eleventh century, when important economic and social changes took place. The Gregorian concept of the spiritual primacy of the Church unintentionally helped to crystallise the conception of

75

temporal authority. Europe maintained its religious unity, but henceforth the Church had to deal with each kingdom or principality separately. In this way, according to Strayer, the foundations of a multi-statal system were laid.[8]

The same process can be explained more generally by the logic of a bi-polar conflict. Given the danger represented by a strong and united Empire, the Church's interest lay in encouraging the development of multiple temporal power, for the rivalries engendered by such a system would enable her at any time to obtain the support necessary for bringing this or that unruly prince to heel. Such rivalry did not, however, have only one outcome. Where the confrontation was direct, as in Italy, coalitions formed around each of the antagonists, thus leading to the fragmentation of territorial power. On the western flank of the Empire, on the other hand, Rome's interest lay in helping to bolster the power of a prince capable of acting as a counterweight to the Empire itself. In fact we observe that throughout the thirteenth century the Church played an important role in the rise of the French monarchy, not only by bestowing on it the seal of legitimacy but also by giving it material aid, albeit indirectly, in allowing it to call upon the clergy for a financial contribution. What had been a custom was made official practice at the end of the conflict between France and the papacy that lasted from 1296 to 1311.[9]

By lending her support to kings, the Church was merely strengthening from the top a process of accumulation of power which had started from the bottom since the feudal parcellisation.

Norbert Elias has suggested that the process, which under the social and economic conditions arising in Western Europe towards the eleventh century led to the emergence of a limited number of powerful protagonists, might be compared to the model of a market in which the play of competition leads to the concentration of economic power in the hands of a few large units.[10]

Having territory as its main object, the process of accumulation developed on the basis of the 'rational' behaviour of the competitors present at the start: they did not set out to gain control over a particular domain but merely wished to control the lands adjacent to those they already possessed, so as to strengthen their security. A somewhat random selection thus operated among them and, in the resultant new pattern, interactions of the same kind among the survivors spread the struggle for hegemony to wider and wider regions. Competition itself played a part through two complementary mechanisms: the deployment of the apparatus of domination through the institutionalisation of new organisations. We should add that, over and above the advantages of territorial accumulation pure and simple, there was a qualitative transformation which might perhaps be compared to the economic concept of 'value added'. These units thus reached a critical mass at which they began gaining advantages over residual units. As Elias suggests, competition thereafter operated in a market that was no longer free: the only course left to the residual units was to attach themselves to one or other of the critical masses.

This process seems to have crystallised, towards the beginning of the thirteenth century, in a set of very varied patterns in each of the great European regions: a development which Elias does not attempt to explain, merely observing that the formation of hegemonies was highly probable but that the location of their centre and the line of their boundaries could not be predicted. We should remember that at this period, according to Yves Renouard, the 'lasting lineaments of modern Western Europe' were shaped by a series of decisive battles between 1212 and 1216.[11] While the Anglo-French frontier was being hammered out at Bouvines, the Christians were gaining control over the Iberian peninsula and the struggles between the kings of France and Aragon in the region of Toulouse were delineating a frontier between France and Iberia. Thereafter none of the big states waged any major war for nearly a century. It was a period of relative stabilisation at the international level and hence of coexistence between a number of relatively isolated politico-strategic areas during which the kingdoms entrenched themselves by absorbing their earlier conquests. In Iberia various aggregates were thus built up on the basis of three columns of the Christian advance; in France the royal domain, having been enlarged by the capture of the North-West, had become a critical mass that enabled the kings to launch a policy of annexation. Nevertheless, not only did Burgundy, Brittany, Guyenne and Flanders remain outside the scope of the central power, but the extension of the territory led to the formation of what Strayer calls a 'mosaic', that is to say an entity which remained similar to an empire, and whose management problems, exceeding the capacity of the centre, set off a new trend towards decentralisation; this was the period of the apanages. In contrast the English king's defeat on the Continent, together with Scottish resistance, reduced him to a political power which in territorial terms was much more modest, and in which his defeat forced him to bow to the barons. In the next century this double limitation facilitated the formation of a much more highly integrated whole than that of the French victor. The early development of the state in England, which made it easier for its kings to mobilise the resources needed for action abroad, made up for the advantages conferred on France by its size and wealth.

A more detailed analysis would probably convey more clearly the distinctive nature of this North Atlantic area, where the process of monopolising domination became organised at a fairly early stage around a bi-polar axis. In this area, as Elias points out, by the end of the thirteenth century 'of the five great warrior houses which retained some competitive power, two played a special role: the Capetians and their successors as Kings of France, and the Plantagenet Kings of England'.[12] The next two centuries were to be dominated by the duel between the two dynasties, with the monopoly of domination in the lands of the former Frankish Kingdom of the West as the prize. The internal political development of each of the antagonists was inextricably bound up with the progress of this duel, which had begun its see-saw in the decades that followed the Norman Conquest. In the long term, their interactions contributed to the break-up of the global political system and went to strengthen political integration within a smaller territory. The first stage in the transformation of the French and English kingdoms into states also made an essential contribution to the formation of a system of European states; the two processes thus determined each other reciprocally.

However, J. Strayer's interpretation of the genesis of state institutions in these two countries seems at first glance to challenge the hypothesis of the important role played in that genesis by their interactions. He lays great stress on the fact that the first central administrative institutions set up in the two countries, towards 1100, owed their existence to internal considerations; the high courts of justice and the treasuries, he notes, were permanently established long before the departments of foreign affairs and defence made their appearance.[13] He advances a hypothesis that is the reverse of ours: namely that state institutions went on developing throughout the thirteenth century, when there were few wars, whereas that development was checked in the next century, when war became almost continuous, because then the antagonists often relied upon improvisation rather than administrative innovation. More generally he considers that, in the Anglo-French area, the period 1300–1450 marks a hiatus between two fruitful periods of political development.

However, Strayer's objections lose much of their substance if we consider that the appearance of specialised administrations holds a privileged place in his conception of the state, at the expense of a broader — but also, it is true, more abstract — conception of a set of processes constituting a system of 'monopolistic' domination within a given territory. It is quite evident, for example, that the treasuries were multi-purpose institutions which from the very beginning mobilised the resources needed for royal action both at home and abroad. Strayer points out that in England, towards the end of the twelfth century, the emergencies caused by foreign wars were such that the vassals' contributions were insufficient to cover the king's needs and had to be transformed into a general tax. Furthermore, he seems to consider that the Anglo-French duel constituted an indispensable stage in the formation of the state in a broader sense, which comes close to our view of things. According to his thesis, the successes gained by the princes in the thirteenth century made the wars of the fourteenth century 'necessary and possible', for they served as the transition to the stage of sovereign states. But around 1300 it was not at all clear who was independent and who was not. What about Wales, Brittany or Flanders? It was impossible to draw definitive frontiers in a Europe which had known only interlocking spheres of influence and fluctuating boundaries. The wars, especially those for the conquest of peripheral regions by the state centres, thus helped to define the areas controlled by the two most advanced European states. Here Strayer agrees with the interpretation we put forward, on Elias's authority, earlier. What Strayer has to say about institutions between 1300 and 1450 in no way conflicts with our hypothesis. As already noted, he lays the emphasis on administrative improvisation. The establishment of war chests, for example, did not give rise to permanent administrative departments because, he maintains, the conduct of military operations and of diplomacy was to be left to professional administrators. The fact remains that such improvisations paved the way for an ever increasing mobilisation of resources on behalf of the political centre and that, furthermore, the 'reserved area' status assigned to external action suggests that, in the king's mind, the entire system was merely an instrument for such action.

When we turn our attention more specifically to the methods of mobilising resources on either side, we obtain a better insight into the internal processes which were set in motion by the Anglo-French duel, and which might be analysed in the terms employed by S. Finer in discussing the role of military organisation in building the state; he speaks of interlocking 'cycles', that is to say, of a series of exchanges prompted by mobilisation requirements between the various social structures and leading to a transformation of the whole.[14] As M. Howard shows,[15] because the vassalic obligation had proved obsolete long before, a wider obligation on the Italian model had been adopted (Statute of Westminster, 1285; *arrière-ban* (call-up of vassals and rear vassals) under Philip the Fair). Towards the beginning of the fourteenth century, it became clear that it was dangerous to arm the mass of subjects, whose military performance was in any case unsatisfactory, and also that the progress of the royal monopoly was creating underemployment in the traditional military class. The military labour market was thus favourable to the central power, provided only that it had the means of paying the warriors. Hence, during the Hundred Years War, the English armies in France served essentially under contract, as did the French armies from the second half of the fourteenth century onwards. The additional expense incurred by this system could only be covered by the revenue derived from trade, in the form either of dues payable directly to the king, or of loans granted by the merchants, or of contributions from representative bodies in the towns or other productive classes. Thus the parliaments, the estates and representative assemblies of the non-military and common sections of the population began to play an important part in the prince's capacity to make war.

This brings us to Hintze's hypothesis concerning the role played by conflicts resulting from the multiplicity of European sovereignties in the origins of the *Ständestaat* (that is to say, not only the state but also the estates), which helped to give the mode of domination that was becoming generalised its original form. As Hintze has it, in order to prosecute their wars the princes at first called upon those elements of the population whose possessions and local authority equipped them to make financial and military contributions. These elements were thus constituted in estates. As the needs of the sovereigns (who were also anxious to become independent of the notables) increased, the estates strove to have their privileges strengthened in exchange for their contributions. Hintze declares that, for the prince, the alternative to such concessions was often the outright loss of a region.[16] The French and English representative institutions (estates) developed more particularly during the long wars fought between the two countries in the fourteenth and fifteenth centuries when, according to B. Guénée, the royal governments continuously poured 'more than half their resources' into war and everything connected with it.[17]

Hintze uses this observation to rough out a more general model concerning the positive contribution of external conflicts to the development of representative institutions in Europe. But what, then, does he make of the absolutism that developed, as we shall see, out of the international conflicts of the sixteenth and seventeenth centuries, and which, he admits, constitutes a notorious exception to his generalisation? His answer is very disappointing: he merely explains to us that absolutism was only a transitional stage, based on the fact that in many places the estates had become an obstacle to the development of larger states, and that that stage was followed 'as soon as this development required by political necessity had been completed' by a rebirth of the representative principle. Let us instead restate the problem as follows: is it possible, on the one hand, to think of a given international pattern as a 'variable' possessing a particular value for each of the protagonists and, on the other hand, to specify the conditions under which this or that form adopted by that variable was able to contribute to the development of a certain constitutionalism, and the conditions which tended rather to atrophy it? Without elaborating this scheme further, let us note that it brings us back to what has been termed the 'interface'. Even when the exigencies of a given strategic pattern led the central power to look within the country for more efficient means of mobilising necessary resources, the effects produced were by no means determined exclusively by the external stimulus. It seems, for example, that at the period we are considering, a set of economic and social conditions dictated to the English state a strategy for mobilising resources based primarily on trade, whereas France, while developing the salt tax, lived mainly on direct taxes, and that this difference contributed to the differentiation of their representative institutions. The internal pattern did not dictate either solution, but made one more likely than the other at a critical time; however, once the choice was made, its repercussions led to the institutionalisation of certain mechanisms which thereafter reduced the range of future options. Furthermore, such internal transformations also moved the initial international pattern away from its original shape.

Thus, in the case of France, the Hundred Years War helped to free the monarchy from the limitations of the previous fiscal and military system[18] through the abandonment of the seigniorial call to arms and the creation of a paid army, in which artillery was the deciding factor. The royal talliage (*taille royale*) of 1439, to which the aristocracy consented for the purpose of raising such an army on condition that the aristocracy itself should be exempt from payment, and which was transformed into a levy on the military (*taille des gens d'armes*) during the next decade, was the first truly national tax.

As we know, the time came when the title to nobility was based on hereditary exemption from this tax. However, the coercive machinery at the disposal of the state centre was still limited; as Perry Anderson points out, Charles VII's orderly companies did not total more than 12 000 men — hardly a sufficient force to control a population of 15 million. Consequently the nobility, as sword-bearers, kept a large measure of autonomy at the local level. Thus, the new monarchy, which for the first time succeeded in gathering round it all the ducal provinces, did not yet constitute a centralised or integrated state. Contrary to what took place in England, where the monarchy's military requirements strengthened the role of Parliament, the consolidation of the States-General as a permanent national institution was blocked by the regional assemblies and, since the nobility was exempt from taxation, it had no interest in urging that they should be convened. This institutional blank contributed to the French monarchy's setbacks in the sixteenth century, but subsequently made it easier for absolutism to take hold. Since the situation was very often one of war, there can be no disregarding the technological factor and everything connected with it, including the military organisation proper. It is no exaggeration to say that the advent of artillery set off, on the basis of the 'economy–technology' cycle, a transformation whose repercussions still further accentuated the trend towards state monopoly and towards the formation of an international pattern which was to become a constituent factor in the transition to the modern era. The introduction of gunpowder in a civilisation which had already mastered the art of casting bells produced the cannon, which very quickly transformed armed combat. Howard does not hesitate to assert that the English were driven out of France, not by the mounted knights or by Joan of Arc, but by the gunners who were so early brought into the French armies; whereas the English, emboldened by the legendary success of their archers, resisted the innovation longer. Not only did the archers stand up poorly to the impact of even the rudest artillery, but, more important, the new weapon completely transformed siege technique, making the maintenance of strong points in a foreign land a very precarious undertaking.[19] In this way the new technology helped to complete the division of the North Atlantic region into two sovereign political entities separated by a sea. More generally, by giving the monarchies the decisive advantage, this new technology contributed to the process of institutionalising the monopoly of political domination at a given territorial level, a process which at the same time marked a big step towards the formation of a system of states. For it was not simply a matter of a few cannon, but of organising artillery trains whose effective use entailed very heavy investment, beyond the capacity of all save those entities that enjoyed the advantage of economies of scale; in other words, those which had attained critical mass. In France, for example, the cost of the royal artillery increased tenfold between 1375 and 1410, and by the end of the fifteenth century it fielded 149 pieces of ordnance served by hundreds of men and thousands of horses.

Formation of the inter-state system of modern Europe

Strategic interaction between states was an irreducible factor in the processes which wrought profound transformations in the European region from 1450 to 1750 and in its relations with the outside world. Having already had occasion to demonstrate the force of this argument in relation to Immanuel Wallerstein's economistic reductionism concerning the origins of the 'Western world-system', we shall confine ourselves here, first, to underlining the contribution of this factor to the formation of a true 'system' of states in Europe; second, to suggesting how political aggregate differentiated from 'civil society'; and lastly, considering the pattern formed by this system as a 'variable' in the sense defined earlier, to exploring how this variable might fit into the explanation of the differentiation that arose between European regimes.

It should be pointed out that the imagery based on the notion of the interface which we shall use in discussing this subject implies no taking of sides in the controversies between the main schools of historical or sociological thought. As it happens, this imagery does not seem far removed from that used by Perry Anderson in relation to the link between the internal and external processes which combined to lead Europe towards the formation which he calls 'absolutism', although we prefer to this term the less downright one of 'Renaissance states' suggested by H.R. Trevor-Roper.[20] In this connection, Anderson, taking his cue from Althusser's couplet on which he bases his general approach, says that, although the relations of production within each state certainly 'determined' the type of regime, once formed, the state also 'overdetermined' absolutism, for the state itself was shaped by external forces which can be thought of as a 'system of states'. Although Anderson attributes very great importance to this process, showing, for example, how Castilian absolutism 'overdetermined' the more general emergence of this formation through the dominant role played by Spain on the European scene, his discussion of the international factor remains rudimentary, and comes to an abrupt end with a favourable reference to the suggestions of the Soviet historian B.F. Porshnev.[21] In a historical analysis of political relations between Western and Eastern Europe at the time of the Thirty Years War, Porshnev refers to what he calls the scientific potential of the notion of a 'system' of states which, he says, has been used 'for quite some time by historians', among whom he mentions Lenin in particular. It is quite plain that the system is based on politico-strategic interaction.

Concluding his historical analysis, Porshnev advances the following schema:[22]

1. While 'all states without exception showed a tendency to external expansion as long as their internal social structure remained based on exploitation', as a rule 'this tendency was paralysed by similar tendencies in other states . . .'

2. 'In each period, one or other main centre of aggression arose against this background. This is precisely what transformed the sum of states into a system . . .' because 'such and such forces always united to deal with aggression and a second centre of the system was formed. The adjacent states and those which cast themselves in the role of *"tertius gaudens"* occupied the middle

ground; such and a such a counterweight was formed to stand up to them and so on.'

3. There are thus 'objective and general laws for any system of states whatsoever: that is to say, laws independent of individual wishes'.

4. Changes of pattern within a given system, or even passage from one system to another, are ultimately attributable to the 'no less objective and implacable laws of economic development' and to 'class contradictions' whose repercussions may modify the role of a state in the system and hence, the system itself.

It will thus be noted that, while Porshnev shares the views of Western historians and theorists as to the international dynamic itself (we are thinking here, in particular, of Ludwig Dehio, on whom we shall largely rely for the sixteenth and seventeenth centuries, and of Morton Kaplan), he has the merit of trying to forge a formal link between that dynamic and other social processes.[23] If we avoid giving too much attention to differences of terminology, and if we add a fifth point concerning the retroaction of the system of states towards the 'class contradictions' within some of them, as Theda Skocpol has done in her comparative analysis of the great revolutions, this scheme is a good approximation of the guiding thread of the analysis which follows.[24]

Let us briefly review the transformation that led to the emergence, towards the middle of the seventeenth century, of a particular type of inter-state system: that which has been described as the 'balance of power'. The processes of monopolisation had resulted in the appearance in the western part of the continent, during the second half of the fifteenth century, of two territorial aggregates inordinately larger than all the others: on the one hand France which, after recovering the English possessions in the South-West, had destroyed the Burgundian state and absorbed its possessions, except the Low Countries, and whose population was some 15 million; and on the other hand the Spanish aggregate which, in spite of France's efforts, had been formed in 1469 on the basis of the personal union of the crowns of Castile and Aragon (the latter being itself a complex amalgam) and whose subjects totalled 7 million. Having contrived to strengthen their state apparatus (in the Spanish aggregate this applied mainly to Castile) the two great powers lost no time in coming to grips with Italy, the former favourite battleground of Empire and Papacy, whose economic wealth and strategic weakness made it an attractive prize (the strategic weakness was due to the stabilisation of regional conflicts towards the mid-fifteenth century into an equilibrium among half a dozen small-scale political units).

After two decades of warfare (1494–1516) during which the Empire, strengthened by the acquisition of the Burgundian Low Countries, and England also entered the game, the two leading protagonists were more or less in balance. Partition of the Italian peninsula into two seemed the most likely outcome. However, the election of the King of Spain as Emperor in 1519 changed the situation completely: the emergence of such a superpower held out the possibility of reconstituting a universal empire embracing all Western Christendom. At this critical moment, the unexpected success of the overseas expeditions launched by the Crown of Castile gave the Habsburgs a tremendous additional advantage: not only did the extraordinary financial benefits gained by plundering the Amerindians play a role in the election of Charles I of Spain as Emperor, but the opportunities created by these ventures attracted into his camp Genoese and German entrepreneurs: in other words international capitalism, for which the Habsburg dominion, with the strategic capacity to make a success of its projects, formed the best conceivable field for investment. The activities of the Habsburgs in Europe and the West Indies sustained one another: having obtained, through their primacy and the support of a subjugated Pope, the virtual monopoly of colonisation in the New World, they then made use of the advantages this gave them to pursue their European ambitions; at the same time their European successes strengthened their position overseas, delaying by a full century the penetration of the periphery by other European states. Even Portugal and her possessions were annexed, after a time, to the gigantic aggregate that was in the making. This close connection between what was happening on the European scene and overseas likewise explains the reversal of the empire-building process in the next century, when the repercussions of the failure to achieve hegemony in Europe triggered the disintegration of the Spanish monopoly overseas, thereby helping to give the periphery a structure that reflected Europe's own evolution towards a multi-statal system. We shall see later how, in its turn, organisation of the periphery on these lines contributed to this trend.

If the universal European Empire failed to be achieved in the sixteenth century, causes are not to be found in the domain of socio-economic determinism. The failure of the project must be attributed primarily to French resistance. Moreover, that resistance itself can in no sense be explained by France's position in the 'world economy' in process of formation, because at the critical moment France happened to be at a disadvantage in relation to it. The causes, then, must be sought in strategic capacity *per se*: that is to say, the armed might which France could mobilise on the basis of the political organisation forged by the monarchy in the previous century. While the defeat at Pavia clearly shows that armed might was insufficient, the policy subsequently pursued by France bears out our hypothesis concerning the relative autonomy of the strategic factor. Threatened by the Habsburgs on three fronts and more or less bereft of European allies, France appealed for support to the historic enemy of Christian Europe. Towards 1525 Francis I initiated negotiations with Suleiman the Magnificent, and his envoys encouraged the Turkish advance leading up to the siege of Vienna four years later.[25] This broadening of the theatre of conflict wrought a profound change in the situation, since it was now the Empire that was threatened at its two extremities, and France could take advantage of the position she held in relation to its centre. Nor should we forget that France did not hesitate to support the German princes against the Emperor, in the same way as the Empire had done during the previous century in the struggle which pitted certain princes against the French monarchy.

The result of these interactions, of which we have retraced only the main trend here, was the restoration of a degree of balance about the mid-sixteenth century. But, as historians — among them F. Braudel — agree, the two antagonists had worn each other out with their conflicts.[26] Here the notion of 'feedback' which we added to Porshnev's schema proves its usefulness: the repercussions of the processes set in train by inter-state conflicts led on either side to crises on the plane of what the Marxists call 'class contradictions', a term which covers roughly what we mean by 'internal interstructural exchanges'. Thus France was rent by religious conflicts while the Spanish branch of the Habsburgs had to deal with the revolt of the Low Countries, which was both symptom and cause of the obstacles impeding the extension of Iberian absolutism beyond its original cradle, Castile.

Out between the fissures in the impasse once again there emerged on to the European chessboard two pieces that were to make a decisive contribution to the evolution of the international pattern. England, driven back to the British Isles and protected from undue outside interference during the first half of the sixteenth century by the struggle between the two great powers, differed from other states in that henceforth it had the choice between war and peace. The variable which the strategic pattern formed for England was such that her protection could be guaranteed by a fleet; but it turned out that the development of such an instrument could also give her a power in the inter-state system out of all proportion to what she could mobilise from a small population and strictly limited wealth. We shall return later to the significance of this variable in the political development of that country. On the plane of the international system, sea warfare was reducing to a few days, or even a few hours, crises which on land might spread over several decades.[27] Thus the defeat of Spain by England in

1588 marked a decisive turning-point in the evolution of the system by making the most likely issue to the European conflict — that is to say, the maintenance of a multi-statal system — a virtual certainty.[28] In the immediate result, this situation proved especially favourable to the emergence of the second piece on the chessboard: this time a completely new one, the United Provinces. As the recent work of G. Parker shows, the evolution of the Low Countries' revolt towards independence for part of the region can only be explained by the strategic constraints imposed on Spain throughout her eighty years of effort to put down the revolt, beginning with the naval defeat of 1588, or even perhaps with the Turkish pressure brought to bear in the Mediterranean during previous decades.[29] Here the chain of cause and effect ran both ways: the revolt helped towards the English victory, which in turn ensured support for the rebels; these events reduced Spain's freedom of action, which facilitated the settlement of the religious wars in France and soon enabled that country to stage its comeback on the international scene — a development that favoured England and the Dutch rebels; and so on.

Thus at the end of the sixteenth century Spain found herself faced with three European adversaries in addition to the Ottoman Empire, and was led to treat successively with each of them. This was the signal for the free-for-all overseas. The Iberian aggregate managed to defend the greater part of its New World empire, but England, the United Provinces and, after a time, France were able to gain a foothold in the West Indies (including Brazil) and in the north of Florida. The Dutch also infiltrated into Asia at Portugal's expense.[30] A large part of the outside world was thus transformed into a periphery exploited by Europe. However, the European merchants and colonists could make headway only where they enjoyed the military and naval support of their governments, not only against the indigenous inhabitants or non-European entrepreneurs already established in such and such an area, but also against their European competitors. Hence the formation of the new 'world economy' cannot be attributed solely to the inexorable drive of capitalism; the striking force which the state organisation of the Europeans enabled them to mobilise contributed to the success of their merchants, and hence to the rise of capitalism itself.

Conversely M. Howard suggests to us how the division of the periphery into areas controlled by each of the antagonists strengthened the trend towards the development of a state system in Europe itself. He maintained that, at a period when war, evolving *pari passu* with the more general transformations overtaking European societies, was increasing by the pressure of the mercenaries (*'pas d'argent, pas de Suisses'*), the means which the combatants could mobilise at home remained strictly limited. The bankers who had kept the princes going during the previous decades had been reduced to bankruptcy by the insolvency of their clients, who had not yet established tax systems with which to tap the wealth of their subjects regularly; the latter, moreover, had not yet accumulated wealth on the scale necessary to finance what were now long-drawn-out and indecisive campaigns. Thus the capacity to sustain warfare, and hence to maintain political power in Europe, became, in the course of the seventeenth century, more and more dependent on access to the wealth extracted from the world outside Europe or created by the trade which, in the last analysis, was derived from that wealth.[31]

Evocative though this hypothesis may be, it calls for some qualification, for it is obvious that the situation was not the same at all times and in all cases. Among the protagonists who played a leading political and military role during the first part of the seventeenth century, neither France nor Sweden, for instance, had the benefit of such support. This may even help to explain why, in these two cases, international constraints led the state to bring stronger pressure to bear on society at home, thus starting the 'cycles' which had the effect of institutionalising absolutism in the full sense of the term. The fact is that in Europe at this time there were virtually only two protagonists for whom the world outside Europe already presented a major source of wealth: these were the Spanish branch of the Habsburg (which also ruled Portugal up to 1640) and the United Provinces. However, although there can be no doubt that this financial resource increased in a general way the military might of each of them, and hence their position in the inter-state system, it had a very different impact on the internal pattern of each and thus contributed to the formation of distinctive political structures. On the Spanish side, the wealth extracted from the world outside Europe primarily served the Castilian monarchy, giving it a degree of autonomy in relation to Aragon and the southern Low Countries in carrying out its projects, and thus helped to bolster up an absolutism which in appearance was very powerful but in reality increasingly devoid of substance, and which, failing to promote any profound changes in society, soon ceased to develop.[32] In the United Provinces, on the other hand, that wealth chiefly served the merchants — or 'civil society' if that term is preferred — enabling them to prevent the constraints born of the century-old struggle for national independence (after Spain, France became the principal source of danger) from precipitating the cycles of transformation leading to the constitution of an absolutist-type state. Organising itself into an oligarchic confederation, this mercantile society turned war into a specialised activity which it entrusted to 'subcontractors' led by the House of Orange-Nassau, applying to it innovations of the same kind as those that brought about the country's spectacular economic growth in the seventeenth century: that is to say, chiefly a capital-intensive method of investment.[33]

In fact, it was then and there that the 'military revolution' took place, which was to continue throughout the seventeenth century in Sweden, France and the Electorate of Brandenburg. Howard points out in this connection that the armies of the United Provinces formed the great exception to the deplorable state of the mercenary armies of the period: they were exceptionally efficient, for the very simple reason that they were regularly supplied and paid. The merchants' earnings enabled their military agents not only to pick the most skilful mercenaries but to make sure of their services by paying them on a yearly basis. This professional system facilitated tactical innovations such as formations of musketeers with a far more effective fire-power, and the practice of entrenchment, an activity which was beneath the dignity of all other mercenaries but which vastly increased defensive capacity. More generally, the economic successes of the mercantile society enabled it to cover at the same time, without having to increase the pressure of taxation or of recruitment, the huge investments needed in building an unequalled line of fortifications and a fleet, which also came to be manned by professionals. Needless to say, this fleet did much to secure the position which the United Provinces had carved out for themselves on the periphery.

Although the Treaty of Westphalia, which ended the Thirty Years War, sanctioned the crystallisation of a 'European balance' and the legal recognition of the sovereignty of constituted states, that balance was maintained by the interplay of mechanisms of conflict arising mainly out of the bi-polar tension between Bourbons and Habsburgs. Thus, the second part of the seventeenth century (with which we shall conclude this outline of the inter-state system in order to return to the internal changes that accompanied its formation) was marked by the challenge to this balance represented by France's drive for a predominant position in relation to the Spanish branch of the Habsburgs; that is to say, not only Spain but also the Spanish Low Countries. At the same time, the various motives which had prompted European expansion overseas during the previous two centuries were being reduced to a search for the necessary means to strengthen the power of the states confronting one another in Europe. While the Dutch, after breaking forcibly into one or other trade networks, developed an economic system which enabled them to profit from any subsequent share-out of the spoils, the English and the French were striving to build up mutually exclusive trade systems which could only be maintained by force. The result was an escalation of the conflict to virtually world-wide proportions, after which naval warfare became increasingly the decisive factor.

In an initial phase, French designs led the maritime and Protestant powers — the Anglo-Scottish combination and the United Provinces — to set aside the differences born of their commercial rivalry and band together to prevent the elimination of their centuries-old enemy, whose already diminished power threatened them less than the power of the empire that was building. However, in a second phase, France was able to take advantage of this very rivalry to obtain British support in an enterprise whose aim was purely and simply to eliminate the United Provinces. The latter, however, emboldened by their defensive organisation, not only managed to resist invasion but were shortly able to take advantage, in their turn, of the internal tensions which racked Great Britain to reverse the situation and come to the aid of those in that country who opposed the political evolution directed at turning it into a satellite of France and transforming it into a Catholic monarchy of the absolutist type. The association of Great Britain and the United Provinces under the leadership of William of Orange who, 'prevented from ruling as a monarch in Holland, became a European statesman', formed the main pole of an alliance of all the states threatened by French hegemony, including the Papacy. The naval defeat of France at La Hogue (1692) ensured the survival of the new regime in Great Britain and confirmed the multi-statal orientation of the system, as the destruction of the Spanish Armada had done a century earlier. But France, far from renouncing her ambitions, soon regained the initiative, thus reviving a conflict which quickly assumed global proportions. In its wake Great Britain raised itself to the status of a world power, while elsewhere Russia took over from the Ottoman Empire and Sweden on the eastern and northern flanks of the European inter-state system. Great Britain's predominance enabled her to call the tune by imposing a policy of balance on the continental powers. Not wishing to replace French hegemony by that of the Austrian Empire, she had no interest in eliminating France and negotiated a separate peace with her in 1713; a year later the Empire was obliged to fall in with the new pattern.

As Howard further points out, while the greater capacity of the maritime powers to provide themselves, by exploiting the periphery, with the financial resources needed to sustain an immense strategic effort, was the deciding factor during the period 1689–1713, it was also at that time that an alternative method of obtaining such resources was developed on a hitherto unprecedented scale: namely the growing capacity of European governments to control, or at any rate tap, the community's wealth and to use it in setting up machinery — a bureaucracy, tax systems, armed forces — that enabled them to extend their control over the community still further. Even before 1700, the master plan had been laid down: that of a state machine capable of managing a full-time force and of maintaining it in time of peace as in time of war, a force composed of a coherent hierarchy of men imbued with a distinct sub-culture.[34] All the European states without exception were transformed by this; but let us consider how significant variations were able to take shape in the common melting-pot of these two centuries of interactions.

Interface dynamics in France and England

We have already alluded to the contributions of the international variable to the decline of the French monarchy in the second part of the sixteenth century and to the subsequent preservation of France's territorial integrity. Although the wars of religion ended with the reaffirmation of a royal state of which Paris became the true centre, there was nothing yet to suggest that during the next century France would become the very model of an absolutist state. It should be remembered, for example, that the Edict of Nantes sanctioned the existence of a veritable archipelago of autonomy within the state — a situation so uncommon that in 1625 Hugo Grotius dedicated his *De Jure* to Louis XIII in tribute to the most tolerant of monarchs — and that the peripheral regions, such as Brittany, still retained their own institutions. France's weakness made a pacific policy necessary and the maintenance of peace made administrative economies easier; Sully contrived to double the royal revenues without overweighting the state apparatus.

However, the demonstration that concerted action by the two Habsburg states would enable them to dominate the whole of Europe soon compelled France to intervene. From the very start of his military and diplomatic intervention in the Thirty Years War, Richelieu did his utmost to build up a rationalised administrative machine for royal intervention throughout the country, and he put an end to the consociational society by wiping out the Huguenot strongholds. Since France, despite the cardinal's efforts, had not yet succeeded in establishing herself in the overseas periphery, his foreign policy necessitated a sudden huge increase in the fiscal burden, which quadrupled in one decade from 1630 onwards.[35] France's intervention, at first mediatised by subsidies to Sweden (which, incidentally, with the addition of those Sweden obtained from Russia, were of considerable help to Gustavus Adolphus in building up a strong state), and by the employment of German mercenaries, ended with large French armies in the field.[36] The need to improvise such an army, rendered urgent by the death of Gustavus Adolphus, prompted the innovation that was decisive for the future development of the French political system: the creation of a civil bureaucracy to administer the army, a remarkable feat considering that at the time no formal bureaucracy existed to administer anything.[37] Military emergencies facilitated the imposition of the system of administrators in regions that were invaded or threatened; the royal troops were regularly deployed in the interior of the country to back up the demands of the central power; and the expansion of the administrative apparatus contributed, more generally, to the emergence of a new social formation, the *noblesse de robe* (magistrate nobility), which by common consent is generally credited with a crucial role in building up the French absolutist system.

As in the middle of the previous century, the repercussions of a long period of murderous and costly international conflicts heightened internal tensions and thus helped to precipitate a general crisis in European societies, which in France took the form of the Fronde. After this hiatus, evolution gathered speed with the accession of Louis XIV for whom, according to Perry Anderson, absolutism was not an end in itself but an instrument of military expansion. France, having as yet managed few moves on the overseas chessboard, logically turned her attention to the conquest of a European centre that appeared vulnerable in the small size of its territory and population and the limited degree of organisation of the state. After ten years of internal preparations, including the departmental reorganisation of ministries including those of the Navy, War and Foreign Affairs, and refinement of the system of administrators which made it possible to double the net revenue of the monarchy, came the invasion of Holland and what followed. During the reign of Louis XIV the strength of the royal army increased tenfold from 30 000 on his accession to 300 000 by 1713. Anderson, referring here to the works of Goubert and Mousnier, says that the growth of such a military machine meant both the final disarmament of the provincial nobility and the capacity to put down popular revolts quickly and effectively.[38] French culture was itself transformed: the 'culturisation of the warriors', to which Elias attached great importance as a mechanism of royal absolutism, was matched by what might be termed the 'bellicisation of society', which showed itself not only through the transformation of standards revealed by Michel Foucault but also through the invention of a new kind of town planning — that of fortified towns.[39] However, it is in the more humdrum field of public finance that the profound consequences of the systematic constraints imposed by the international variable were most apparent. The escalation of international conflicts at the end of the century resulted in a parallel increase in the expenditure of the French state, which between 1689 and 1714 totalled nearly 5 million livres (£300 million sterling): that is to say, very little less than the combined expenditure of the three principal members of the opposing coalition.[40] Not counting the service of the public debt already incurred as a result of the war, by the end of the reign the war was swallowing up between two-thirds and three-quarters of the public expenditure. Since nearly half the realm was exempt from taxation — a result of the institutionalisation of earlier choices concerning the nobility and clergy, which could not be disavowed without endangering the regime — the talliage weighed very heavily on the mass of the population, who were also liable for generalised military service — while covering only 30 per cent of expenditure. Despite the tendency to institutionalise specialised central bureaucracies, the constraints of the political system prevented the state from applying that technique in the crucial matter of revenue, in this respect falling short of the state centralism achieved in the United Kingdom. Since the device of tax farming responded poorly to the increased fiscal pressure, the total revenue obtained by the French state through indirect taxes probably diminished during the war; in view of the limitations on what it could extract from society by this means, the state resorted to borrowing, but, as its credit inexorably shrank, borrowing grew more and more expensive. Furthermore, having been ousted from the foreign money markets controlled by its enemies, it lent itself increasingly to venal transactions. When the war ended, the total debt came to more than the state could expect to collect from ordinary revenue sources in thirty years, and the debt charges alone ate up nearly the entire annual revenue. The problems created by this deadlock were never really solved; by the time the war was over, the most unwieldy state apparatus in the world was turning over only in order to stay in place.

It would also be possible to retrace step by step the influence of the constraints imposed by the role France was coming to play in the international pattern with regard to the final solution of the Protestant problem before, during and after the revocation of the Edict of Nantes (1685) and in the evolution of the links between the state centre and the territorial peripheries, of which the case of Brittany affords a good illustration. At the beginning of Louis XIV's reign this province still enjoyed a broad autonomy, arranged by its estates and trading freely with foreign countries, with England as its principal partner. On Colbert's initiative, Brest was created out of nothing as the great naval port of the Atlantic fleet. Since the province thus acquired outstanding strategic importance, the king could no longer afford not to keep it well in hand. Brittany rebelled during the war with Holland (1675) as the result of the introduction of new fiscal obligations (it was a question of stamped paper) without consultation with the estates. The movement developed into a more general uprising against the seigniorial regime and impressment, and was brutally crushed. This was the prelude to the ending of regional autonomy. After a difficult start, the royal administrators, established at Rennes in 1689, succeeded in imposing, without consulting the estates, the two new taxes created for the purposes of the war: the poll-tax and the tithe. In becoming for administrative purposes a province like the others, Brittany also began its economic decline. When Paris closed the kingdom to English cloth through prohibitive customs duties, England quickly turned away from her Breton suppliers, and the war at sea itself dealt the trade based on regional industry a blow from which it was never to recover. Once more, of the two kinds of France possible, the state gave priority to the continental one because of the pressures of the international system.[41] Though we do not propose here to consider war as the sole and unique source of causality, we nevertheless subscribe to Roland Mousnier's view,[42] which fits in with the one we ourselves have outlined on the basis of the notion of 'cycles', as suggested by Finer. War made necessary a level of taxation that went far beyond what the king's subjects considered lawful. This fiscal pressure helped to provoke revolts, thereby forcing the royal government to use its armed forces inside the country, but at the same time causing it to encourage economic development to increase the country's taxable wealth. Although war was not permanent from 1625 to 1789, the governments in power during periods of conflict nevertheless acquired habits which persisted when peace returned. They thus assumed a despotic and tyrannical aspect which led to criticism of the monarchy and of society. In conclusion, let us not forget that the ultimate crisis of the *ancien régime* clearly began as a result of the repercussions of a war whose cost was beyond the capacity of the system.

The sequence of processes contributing to the very different development of the English political system must be attributed not to England's insularity, considered as a geographical fact, but to the manner in which that insularity, at a given period, was woven into a particular inter-state pattern and thus became part of a variable with respect to the country's internal composition. It is noteworthy that historians such as L. Stone, C. Hill and P. Anderson, who in other respects hold very diverse views, all agree more or less about the initial cause of the country's originality. Although England, at the beginning of the modern age, was subjected to a centralising pressure just as powerful as that which prevailed among the continental states, that pressure did not lead to the establishment of a standing royal army. This omission in the monarchical apparatus subsequently imposed very strict limits on action by the monarchy, regardless of what the political aims of any particular sovereign were to be. And England's position in relation to the international pattern is clearly what made the persistence of that omission possible.

We must look beyond the early establishment of a parliamentary system to the international situation as a whole in Europe at the time of the Renaissance. During the first half of the sixteenth century, whereas Spain and France were engaged in a struggle the momentum of which drove them inexorably to turn themselves into war machines, England was not directly threatened and did not need either an army or even a navy to defend itself. However, because the Tudors shared ambitions similar to those of the other European monarchies, they intervened on the Continent in 1512–14, 1522–5 and again in 1543–6. Nevertheless, as they were only able to mobilise a very small force compared to that of the continentals, the campaigns of the Tudors cost them a good deal of money without bringing them any substantial successes. L. Stone explains very clearly the structural nature of the limits of their action. First, given the population factor, the only way in which the English Crown could develop a striking force was by engaging the services of foreign mercenaries, mostly Italians and Germans. Second, the Crown was highly dependent on the taxes allowed to it, since it had not been able to develop any direct resources of its own, like gold and silver in the case of the Spanish Crown, salt in the case of the French monarchy, or copper in that of the Swedish.[43] Hence, only by selling the greater part of the Church lands which it had recently seized was the English monarchy able to undertake the campaigns of 1543–6. But this decision represented a decisive turning-point for the monarchy, because of its unforeseen results. First, the Crown now retained, in the form of revenue independent of parliamentary vote, only what was necessary for its peacetime requirements, and second, the sale of 'national property' further precipitated the emergence of a new social class, the 'gentry', who henceforth would influence English society against any transformation of an absolutist type, making it less and less likely that the monarchy would at some future date ignore Parliament and go its own way.

Thus the monarchy had landed itself in an impasse. It could maintain itself on a small revenue so long as it did not raise an army, but if it did so it would be obliged to apply to Parliament, and Parliament would take advantage of the situation to oppose any attempt by the monarchy to establish absolute power. This did not apply when it came to building up a fleet. During the second half of the sixteenth century, this was found to be necessary not only for the country's defence but also to serve the ambition, shared by the monarchy and the English ruling classes alike, to carve a place for themselves in the overseas periphery then in the process of formation. By its very nature, a strategic instrument of this kind could not be used internally.

Given these facts, one can understand how the European crisis of the seventeenth century took the form, in England, of the collapse of the Stuart monarchy followed by a revolution. During the first decades of the century, in foreign affairs, the Stuarts did not stray to any great extent from the tradition established by their predecessors. The danger from Spain had been reduced by the peace of 1604; France was emerging from her civil wars weakened and cautious; the United Provinces formed a friendly Protestant power; Scotland, also Protestant, had been joined to the English Crown; and, from 1618 onwards, the spectacular rise of Sweden under Gustavas Adolphus ensured the maintenance on the Continent of a certain balance between Catholics and Protestants, so that in their conflicts the belligerants turned away from the British Isles. This pattern favoured a policy of retrenchment under the protection of a fleet — which also served the interests of the merchant adventurers and the investors who backed them up, including the Crown itself — and there was still no pretext whatever for the formation of a royal army. Without any such army, the state had no reason to build up the bureaucratic machinery for supplying the manpower and finance that an army needed, as we saw in the case of France.

Thus, when the Stuart monarchy tried to enter the stream of European politics, attempting to be as independent as possible from Parliament and to form England and Scotland into a unified whole, it turned out that it lacked the two keys to absolutist power: namely a standing army which it could use against its subjects, and a local bureaucracy paid by the central government and upon which it (the monarchy) could depend.[44] It is significant that the crisis arose as a result of a Scottish rebellion that occurred when the king and his archbishop attempted to impose the English form of religious organisation on the Scottish clergy, appearing at the same time to threaten the nobility whose rise to power had been based on the acquisitions of ecclesiastical property. We shall say nothing here about the period of the civil war which led to the rise of Cromwell's absolutism, particularly from the military standpoint. His coercive powers were based on a level of taxation five times higher than under the monarchy, but the system collapsed following the Protector's death, after London had refused to pay its taxes. Thus, a situation similar to the one which had contributed to the collapse of the monarchy in 1638–42 now brought about the opposite result, i.e. its restoration.

Shortly after the Restoration, the tension between the absolutist aims which the Stuarts still harboured and the aims of those sectors of society in favour of development towards a parliamentary form of government, manifested itself simultaneously in both internal and external policy, since the choices that were being made in each of these spheres were complementary. At the risk of oversimplifying, it is fair to say that in view of the monarchy's lack of means at the start, it could only succeed in strengthening its power by calling upon outside support. And this, for lack of any alternative, meant calling on France. This involved the pursuit by the monarchy of a foreign policy contrary to the economic interests of those who wanted parliamentary government, and of a religious policy that went against what had, for over a century, come to be one of the pillars of national identity. The balance of internal forces is not enough to explain the result of this conflict, for in spite of all the opposition to its plans inside the country, the monarchy, strongly supported by the greatest European power of the time, only narrowly missed being successful. Those who were opposed to this political trend were able to halt it by exploiting the opportunities presented by the international situation. Thus, the crystallisation of a decisive differentiation in the morphology of the European state — absolute monarchy, parliamentary monarchy — can be explained by the coming together of internal and external processes at the interface of the most crucial case.

Let us recall very briefly the sequence of events.[45] Whereas from 1668, England formed part of a triple alliance with Holland and Sweden against France, in 1670 the English king signed a secret agreement with France in which he undertook to declare himself a Catholic as soon as circumstances permitted, and in return he obtained the necessary funds to free him from parliamentary restrictions. In spite of the state's bankruptcy, Charles II started a war with the United Provinces in 1673 in alliance with France. Two days before the declaration of war, he issued an indulgence to the Catholics (as well as to the Protestant minorities), while Parliament reaffirmed the supremacy of the Anglican Church. As Parliament had been prorogued and remained suspended throughout nearly the whole of the period 1674–9, Charles II became more dependent than ever on his foreign patron. However, those who were opposed to the king's action placed every possible obstacle in his way. In an effort to turn foreign policy from its too exclusively French leanings, his own minister, Sir Thomas Osbourne, started negotiations for the marriage between Mary, the king's elder daughter, and Prince William, the ultra-Protestant head of the House of Orange and Stadtholder of the United Provinces. At the same time, a movement was launched to replace, in the order of succession to the throne, James, the Catholic, by his elder brother, the Duke of Monmouth, the king's illegitimate but Protestant son. Charles II, after proroguing Parliament yet again in 1679, excluded Monmouth from the succession and, in 1685, on his deathbed, declared himself a Catholic.

James II, having made the first step towards a reconciliation with Parliament on his accession, took advantage of threats of invasion (the Duke of Argyll in Scotland and Monmouth in England) to obtain parliamentary approval at last for the creation of a royal army whose numbers quickly rose to 30 000 men. The new king had the advantage, for the army's maintenance, of a considerable increase in customs duties as a result of the very protectionist policy on which all parties concerned were agreed, and he was therefore less dependent than his predecessor on French subsidies, which by this time accounted for only an eighth of the government's annual revenue. Matters were now very rapidly coming to a head. Bent on building up an organisation on which he could rely, James, contrary to the law, put Catholic officers into the army, a large part of which was concentrated near London, and tried in vain to obtain the repeal of the laws in question. When Parliament, scandalised by the revocation of the Edict of Nantes, attempted to wrest the army from the king's hands through a return to the militia, it was finally dissolved. The king now went straight for his aim. Having succeeded in obtaining office, he proceeded to appoint Catholics, one after the other, as Governor of Ireland, as Admiral of the Fleet, and even in such sacrosanct strongholds of Anglicanism as the Universities of Oxford and Cambridge. In 1688, in spite of the whittling down of French subsidies, James II felt sufficiently sure of his success to proclaim the complete emancipation of the religious minority to which he belonged, having the Anglican bishops who opposed this measure imprisoned in the Tower of London. At the same time, the birth of his son meant that his sister (a Protestant) was no longer in the direct line of succession to the throne and ensured continuity for his plans.

Although the courts helped to strengthen the opposition by proclaiming the bishops innocent, what turned the tide was the decision taken by the Earl of Danby, backed by the Bishop of London, to invite William of Orange to come over to England. Despite feelers for compromise put out by both sides, William finally landed at the head of 11 000 infantry and 4000 cavalry. While the nobility and gentry rallied slowly to the side of this imposing force, the king's supporters deserted him *en masse*. Receiving no help from Louis XIV, then engaged in a campaign in the Palatinate, and unable even to prevent William from sailing, James II was forced to disband his army that had not received its pay and to seek refuge himself in France. A group of peers, alarmed by the danger of a popular uprising in London, thereupon asked William to enter London with his army to keep order. As Koenigsberger points out, it was not just a coincidence that a Prince of Orange, the representative of a regime which stood out particularly from the current of absolutism, was the one who thus contributed to laying the foundations of a parliamentary monarchy in Great Britain.

Without going into details about the internal and external processes which combined to institutionalise the new regime, let us remind ourselves that although the need for an army was acknowledged now that the regime could only survive by actively opposing French hegemony, the first thing that Parliament did on being summoned in February 1689 was to impose the Act of Mutiny on the king. This allowed him to maintain an army for one year only, at the end of which his authority over the troops had to be renewed. That, in turn, could be done by seeking the approval of Parliament. This was followed by the Act of 1701 stipulating that no sovereign might engage in war for the defence of a foreign territory, or even leave the country without the consent of Parliament. This Act marked the first constitutional step towards parliamentary control over foreign policy.[46] With the danger of a French invasion removed by the victory of the reorganized British fleet off La Hogue in May 1692, Parliament proceeded to consolidate its ascendancy by a very strict limitation of the Crown's revenues, at the same time encouraging state centralisation by abandoning the system of farming out taxes and replacing it by the Treasury. It gave extra impetus to the strategic policy already established by cutting army expenditure below the level desired by the king, while increasing the navy's budget above what he desired. Thus, between 1688 and 1713, the number of naval units increased by 40 per cent and naval tonnage by 60 per cent.

Disagreements between France and Great Britain became accentuated during the struggle which opposed them for nearly a quarter of a century. How was it that Great Britain, in spite of all the drawbacks from which it suffered, and whose ordinary revenue at the end of the Stuart period was not one-fifth that of France, managed not only to carry on during the struggle but even, eventually, to triumph over a nation far richer than itself? Let us note, first, that in Great Britain state expenditure prior to the Revolution amounted to some £2 million sterling a year. This rose to £72 million during the following decade. The war, as in France, swallowed up most of this. But to deal with this huge burden, Great Britain organised itself differently from France. In the first place, with the establishment of the new regime, Parliament was able, in 1692, to bring in a property tax, from which the big landowners were in no way exempt. This tax, which alone brought in £2 million a year, was more fairly distributed and so weighed relatively less heavily on those at the bottom of the scale that did the talliage. In addition there were customs duties which, increasing fourfold between

1690 and 1704, accounted by the end of the war for nearly half the national revenue. While, as in France, the bulk of the revenue in Great Britain came from indirect taxes, the establishment of the Treasury ensured that a larger share went to the central government. Under this new system, the state was able to triple its ordinary revenue between 1689 and 1714. A fairer and more efficient taxation system inspired public confidence and helped to give the state a reliable image. The credit system, which got slowly under way in and around the year 1690, when government borrowing still accounted for only one-tenth of the expenditure, was subsequently regularised through the setting up of the Bank of England which, after the state's near-bankruptcy in 1696, provided for its short-term financing. This institution, which later replaced the Exchequer in the management of long-term loans, was merely one of the many innovations leading to the development of the London market as a centre for transactions in government bonds. Thus the interest rate, which stood at 10–14 per cent in the 1690s, had dropped ten years later to between 5 and 6 per cent. It is likely that the greater efficiency in mobilising resources through the taxation and credit systems was matched also by a greater military efficiency.

The results of the conflict were thus not all the same in the two cases. As Finer points out, the Whig nobility and their Bank of England associates, founders of the new regime, supported the war on land and sea by which they maintained themselves. So did the merchants, for it brought them good business; and the army could not be used by the monarchy to abolish the constitution, as the officers were mostly the younger sons of the Whig families that supported the Revolution. Meanwhile the Tories, jealously protecting the local power on which their status in the country was based, preferred to keep to the traditional form of war at sea; supporting and controlling the militia as they did, they were opposed to any attempt to create a military monopoly or a centralised bureaucracy. It will be observed, however, that in Great Britain, as in France, the international conflict brought about profound changes in the relationship between the centre and the peripheral regions. This was precisely the period at which the United Kingdom was formed, through the abolition of the Scottish Parliament, the setting up of a highly centralised and repressive administration in Ireland, and by the exclusion of the Catholic minority from full citizenship.

The contrasts between the two countries remain striking. In the case of France, the variable resulting from the international situation had helped to create an absolute monarchy which tended to play a role in this system that sharpened all internal tensions and was an obstacle to the development of the economy. In Great Britain, however (with the exception of Ireland, which nevertheless accounted for nearly half the population of the United Kingdom as a whole), this variable, after first rendering the absolutist solution less probable and then finally contributing to its elimination, offered the country the chance to choose a foreign policy which facilitated the rallying of the ruling classes to the new regime, and even the integration of the middle classes. As it grew stronger, so the British state became increasingly parliamentary. Because the interactions between France and England formed one of the principal poles around which the inter-state system was being reshaped, both countries were forced to commit themselves fully to the role this system imposed on them, and the differences in their internal organisation could only become more and more marked during the second 'Hundred Years War' that had already started.

Conclusion

Our purpose has been to show the need to include the international strategic factor as an explanatory variable in any comparative macro-sociology of the formation of the Western state and of its development and differentiation. We have also been concerned to demonstrate the possibility of subjecting this factor itself to a sociological type of treatment, which would enable it to be included in a more elaborate theoretical framework. Though we have concentrated on Great Britain and France for the purposes of example, what we have said could of course be extended to other cases, as we have suggested by referring to Spain, the United Provinces, Sweden and Prussia. We should add that a demonstration of this kind could equally well be made with regard to later periods, including our own.

The theory that emerges from this exploratory essay might be summarised as follows: during the period in question, the internal transformations that took place in each state in the process of formation helped to bring about the emergence of an inter-state system of which these states were the component parts. This system developed its own particular dynamism whose repercussions may be regarded as specific variables having feedback effects upon each unit of the whole. This cycle of exchanges occurred also in the reverse sense, with internal mutations leading to changes in the international pattern, thus modifying the variable formed by the international pattern in relation to its component units. If one were to continue in this way, one could conceive of a complete series of political structures and processes itself a part of a more comprehensive cultural and social system of which it would form an irreducible component. Even if it is unlikely that we shall come to conceive this complete series in any very clear way, it is useful to take it, on an ontological level, as the starting-point for our studies, so that they are more firmly grounded in historical fact.

As regards the contributions made by the international political and strategic factor to the development of states and regimes, is it a matter of 'overdetermination' in relation to a more basic factor acting both inside a country and at a global level (as claimed by those who consider the political structures of the modern world to be merely epiphenomena with respect to the formation of the capitalist system, extending on a 'world-economy' scale) or else as Hintze puts it, is it a matter of 'co-determination'? Let us say, rather, that we are confronted with two sets of constraints which come together at the interface and whose relations are themselves indeterminate. Although it is true that we have learned to visualise how the constraints brought about by relations of production and everything connected therewith, as well as those that can be attributed to already established internal political structures, combine to determine the subsequent development of a given political system, it is equally true that the constraints that we have identified intervene decisively at crucial moments of that development. As these constraints are of a systematic nature, it would be a mistake to relegate their manifestations to the purely *événementiel*, in other words, to assign them arbitrarily to the lowest level of a hierarchy of determinisms. Everything points to the fact, however, that the relative importance of each of these series of constraints varies from one period to another and one situation to another. How, why, and with what results? This is precisely what has to be established. It follows from this that we shall stand a much better chance of achieving our legitimate theoretical ambitions if we begin from the outset to work out our theories in relation to relatively precise parameters, in other words, by limiting both in time and in space the universe to which they are supposed to apply. In this way, history and sociology will be able to join together in the pursuit of a common task.

Notes

1   These remarks apply equally to sociology and political science. The chief works which spring to mind are: Barrington Moore, Jr., *The Social Origins of Dictatorship and Democracy*, Boston, Beacon Press, 1966; the introduction by Charles Tilly to the collective work he edited, *The Formation of National States in Western Europe*, Princeton, Princeton University Press, 1975; the contributions made to that work by Stein Rokkan and Samuel Finer, to which we shall return later; Raymond Grew (ed.), *Crisis of Political Development in Europe and North*

America, Princeton, Princeton University Press, 1979; Reinhard Bendix, *Kings or People: Power and the Mandate to Rule*, Berkeley, University of California Press, 1978; Bertrand Badie and Pierre Birnbaum, *The Sociology of the State*, Chicago, University of Chicago Press, 1983. It will be noted, however, that others besides ourselves have already raised the problem we are discussing. Among them we may mention Perry Anderson, *Lineages of the Absolutist State*, London, New Left Books, 1974; Theda Skocpol, *States and Social Revolution*, New York, Cambridge University Press, 1979; and above all Immanuel Wallerstein, *The Modern World-System*, New York, Academic Press, 1974. Indeed, a detailed criticism of this last work, A.R. Zolberg, 'Origins of the Modern World-System: A Missing Link', *World Politics*, vol. 33, no. 2, 1981, pp. 253–81, started us on the analysis of which this paper represents the second stage.

2   H.G. Koenigsberger, 'Monarchies and Parliaments or Dominium Politicum et Regale', *Theory and Society*, vol. V, March 1978, p. 214.

3   See J.P. Nettl, 'The State as a Conceptual Variable', *World Politics*, vol. 20, no. 4, 1968, pp. 559–92. From this analysis we arrived at the notion of the 'interface'.

4   Our reading of Fernand Braudel is based on the American edition of *The Mediterranean and the Mediterranean World in the Age of Philip II*, New York, Harper & Row, 1976; as regards historians, see also William McNeill, *The Rise of the West: A History of the Human Community*, New York, New American Library, 1963; and Geoffrey Barraclough, *An Introduction to Contemporary History*, Baltimore, Penguin, 1967. As to the sociologists, see Talcott Parsons, *Societies: Comparative and Evolutionary Perspectives*, Englewood Cliffs, NJ, Prentice-Hall, 1967; and Wallerstein, op. cit.

5   This is the flaw in the otherwise highly evocative model proposed by George Modelski, 'The Long Cycle of Global Politics and the Nation-State', *Comparative Studies in Society and History*, vol. 20, no. 2, April 1978, pp. 214–35. Further on, however, we shall refer to B.F. Porshnev's schema, which tries to make good this omission.

6   Anderson, op. cit., pp. 21, 405, 409, 412, 423–4. This conception, based on the works of Marx and Weber, whom Anderson regards in this connection as complementing rather than contradicting each other, comes close to that of McNeill, op. cit., who emphasises the 'heterogeneity' of the medieval West.

7   Otto Hintze, 'The Formation of the States and the Constitutional Development: A Study in History and Politics' in Felix Gilbert (ed.), *The Historical Essays of Otto Hintze*, New York, Oxford University Press, 1975, p. 167.

8   Joseph R. Strayer, *On the Medieval Origins of the Modern State*, Princeton, NJ, Princeton University Press, 1970.

9   Here we rely on the American edition of Robert Fawtier, *The Capetian Kings of France*, New York, St. Martin's Press, 1960, pp. 88–95.

10   Norbert Elias, *La Dynamique de l'Occident*, Paris, Calmann-Lévy, 1975, pp. 44–64.

11   Yves Renouard, '1212–1216: comment les traits durables de l'Europe occidentale moderne se sont définis au début du XIIe siècle', *Annales de l'Université de Paris*, Vol. XXVIII, January–March 1958, pp. 5–21.

12   Elias, op. cit., p. 63.

13   Strayer, op. cit., pp. 26–7.

14   Samuel E. Finer, 'State and Nation-building in Europe: The Role of the Military', in Tilly, op. cit., pp. 84–163. This approach resembles that outlined by Elias concerning the 'sociogenesis of the fiscal monopoly' (Elias, op. cit., pp. 153–83).

15   Unless otherwise stated, our discussion of military development throughout this essay is based on the seminal book by Michael Howard, *War in European History*, Oxford, Oxford University Press, 1976.

16   Hintze, op. cit., pp. 312, 340, 345 ff.

17   Bernard Guénée, *L'Occident aux XIVe et XVe siècles: les Etats*, Paris, Presses Universitaires de France, 1971, p. 205.

18   Anderson, op. cit., p. 86.

19   Howard, op. cit., p. 13.

20   See H.R. Trevor-Roper, 'The General Crisis of the Seventeenth Century, in Trevor-Roper, *The European Witch-Craze of the Sixteenth and Seventeenth Centuries*, New York, Harper & Row, 1969, pp. 46–89.

21   Anderson, op. cit., pp. 32–9, and particularly note 37, p. 37. As regards the attribution of 'overdetermination' to Spain, see ibid. p. 60.

22   B.F. Porshnev, 'Les rapports politiques de l'Europe occidentale et de l'Europe orientale à l'époque de la Guerre de Trente Ans', *Comité International des Sciences Historiques*, Uppsala, Almqvist & Wiksell, 1960, pp. 138, 161, 162n. 1.

23   Ludwig Dehio, *The Precarious Balance*, New York, A.A. Knopf, 1962. Unless otherwise stated, our discussion of the formation of the inter-state system at the beginning of the modern era will be based on this unjustly neglected classic (published in 1948 under the title *Gleichgewicht oder Hegemonie*). From the theoretical standpoint, see especially Morton Kaplan, *System and Process in International Politics*, New York, John Wiley, 1957, pp. 21–36.

24   Theda Skocpol, op. cit., pp. 22–4, and her discussion of individual cases.

25   G.R. Elton, *Reformation Europe, 1517–1559*, New York, Harper Torchbooks, 1963, p. 119. Dehio, after Ranke, sees in this the first sign of a counterweight being brought to bear by a maritime power on the periphery of Europe (Dehio, op. cit., p. 38). It will be noted that this analysis agrees entirely with Porshnev's schema. Was Lenin a disciple of Ranke?

26   Braudel, op. cit., vol. II, p. 945.

27   Dehio, op. cit., p. 55.

28   Garrett Mattingly, *The Armada*, Boston, Houghton Mifflin, 1959, p. 401.

29   Geoffrey Parker, *The Army of Flanders and the Spanish Road, 1567–1659*, London, Cambridge University Press, 1972; and, by the same author, *The Dutch Revolt*, Harmondsworth, Penguin Books, 1979.

30   In the opinion of J.H. Parry, for example, the activities of England and France in the New World resembled 'tactical counter-moves on the chessboard' (Parry, *The Establishment of the European Hegemony, 1415–1715*, New York, Harper Torchbooks, 1966). See also K.G. Davies, *The North Atlantic World in the Seventeenth Century*, Minneapolis, University of Minnesota Press, 1974, pp. 25–31, 35–45; and for the United Provinces, C.R. Boxer, *The Dutch Seaborne Empire 1600– 1800*, London, Hutchinson, 1965.

31   Howard, op. cit., p. 51.

32   Here we rely in the main on P. Anderson's interpretation, op. cit., pp. 71–84.

33   The connection between the political organisation and the economic rise of the United Provinces is underlined by Douglas C. North and Robert Paul Thomas, *The Rise of the Western World: A New Economic History*, Cambridge, University Press, 1973, pp. 132–45. These authors, however, minimise the contribution made by exploitation of the periphery to the development of Dutch capitalism.

34   Howard, op. cit., pp. 49, 54.

35   Anderson, op. cit., p. 98.

36   We cannot, unfortunately, linger over the case of Sweden which showed, as that of the Duchy of Brandenburg (Prussia) was to do still more spectacularly a little later on, that the international pattern could also take the form of a variable allowing a state to be built up almost exclusively on the basis of military organisation. These examples illustrate a process of state-building through 'value added' where certain social factors were present in a particular context. For the role of French and Russian subsidies in Gustavus Adolphus's enterprise, see Porshnev, op. cit., pp. 150–1.

37   Howard, op. cit., p. 64.

38   Anderson, op. cit., p. 62.

39   This 'curialisation' has been the subject of a detailed study: Norbert Elias, *La société de cour*, Paris, Calmann-Lévy, 1974. With regard to the term 'bellicisation', see Michel Foucault, *Surveiller et punir*, Paris, Gallimard, 1976. Our reference to the planning of fortified towns is the result of a visit in 1980 to the Musée des Plans-Reliefs in the attics of the Hôtel des Invalides, Paris.

40   All the facts quoted in the paragraph which follows have been taken from the well-stocked paper by P.G.M. Dickson and John Sperling, 'War Finance, 1689–1714, in J.S. Bromley (ed.), *The New Cambridge Modern History*, Vol. 6: *The Rise of Great Britain and Russia, 1688– 1725*, London, Cambridge University Press, 1970, pp. 284–315.

41   Here we are alluding, of course, to the very interesting interpretation given by Edward W. Fox, *History in Geographic Perspective, The Other France*, New York, W.W. Norton, 1971.

42   Roland Mousnier, *Les institutions de la France sous la monarchie absolue*, Vol. II: *Les organes de l'Etat et la Société*, Paris, Presses Universitaires de France, 1980, p. 7 ff. See also his general conclusion.

43   Lawrence Stone, 'The English Revolution' in Robert Forster and Jack

P. Greene (eds.), *Preconditions of Revolution in Early Modern Europe*, p. 68, Baltimore, Md, Johns Hopkins University Press, 1970.

44   Ibid., pp. 103–8. Christopher Hill, *The Century of Revolution, 1603–1714*, New York, W.W. Norton, 1961, pp. 13–14, may also be consulted.

45   Here we are following Christopher Hill, op. cit., pp. 193–311.

46   The following paragraph is based on David Ogg, 'The Emergence of Great Britain as a World Power' in Bromley (ed.), op. cit.

5 The triple heritage of the state in Africa

Ali A. Mazrui

The state was not a universal category in pre-colonial Africa. From a political point of view the African continent was a miracle of diversity — ranging from empires to stateless societies, from elaborate thrones to hunting bands, from complex civilisations to rustic village communities. In this essay we address ourselves especially to the emergence of the state in Africa, relating that phenomenon to the triple political and cultural heritage of the African continent — the indigenous, the Islamic and the Western.

Let us first explore some of the main attributes associated with the state. The first is the centralisation of authority. When Louis XIV said *'L'Etat, c'est moi'*, he was formulating this doctrine of centralism at its most extreme, when it actually focused on a single individual at the pinnacle of authority. In reality the centralism can be relative rather than absolute. After all, although the United States of America uses the term 'states' in the plural, the country as a whole is a nation-state within the tradition of the Treaty of Westphalia of 1648. The federal government of the country becomes both the focus and the mechanism of centralised authority.

Related to such centralisation is Max Weber's principle of 'the monopoly of the legitimate use of physical force'. Weber regarded this principle as virtually the definition of the state.

But from our point of view we may accept the twin principles of centralised authority and centralised power as the defining characteristics of the state. What should be borne in mind are additional

107

accompanying characteristics usually associated with the state but not necessarily of definitional import. One of these accompanying characteristics of the state concerns a fiscal system of some sort. This could be a case of collecting tribute from integral units of the state, or an evolving system of taxation still in the making. A relatively centralised system of revenue collection has come to be associated with institutions of this kind.

Also basic as an accompanying characteristic of the state in history has been a centrally supervised judicial system. The judicial system may in fact be internally pluralistic, accommodating different religious or customary courts, but the centralisation is partly a case of overall jurisdiction, with the state sometimes modifying customary law to conform with certain central principles. The state would in any case keep an eye on the system which selects those who interpret religious or customary law and those who implement it.

In Africa's experience state formation has been linked to the broader triple heritage of Africa's history and culture — a heritage which encompasses indigenous, Islamic and Western traditions. Some states in Africa were primarily products of purely indigenous forces; some were products of interaction between indigenous and Islamic elements; and others were outgrowths of a basic interaction between indigenous and Western ideas. There have been occasions when the heritage has indeed been a fusion of all three — indicating a historical meeting point involving Africa, Islam and the West. However, in this essay our approach will be particularly comparative, focusing more on at least two traditions at a time, rather than on pure models of the state. After all, Africa has indeed been a melting pot of political cultures, a laboratory of diverse experiments in political formations.

African polities and Islamic states

Africa's interaction with Islam antedates European colonisation of Africa by at least a millennium. In the seventh century Islam conquered Egypt and started the process of penetrating North Africa. Islam then spread down the Nile Valley as well as into North-West Africa. The politics of those societies responded to the impact of Islam, and some of those societies began to evolve institutions which reflected this basic interaction between Islam and indigenous responses.

Especially important in state-formation is the precise balance between trade and warfare, between economic aspects and military dimensions.

The history of Islam itself from the days of Muhammad is partly an equation involving exchange of goods and balance of arms. The Prophet Muhammad was himself a trader in his earlier years before he became a warrior in the name of Allah.

Islam has divided the world conceptually between *Dar el Harb*, the abode of war, and *Dar el Islam*, the abode of Islam. Within the world of Islam political co-operation and economic trade would be facilitated. Between the world of Islam and the world of war lines of difference and strategies of protection would be evolved.

Islam's penetration of the African continent continued this dialectic between the economic and the military. When Islam became an empire, Egypt for a while became the pivot of an international Muslim economic system. There was a time when the merchant class of Egypt became what has been described as a group so influential that it 'increasingly shaped the policies of the Muslim states, developed commercial law and custom, and gave the civilisation of Islam its strong emphasis on the bourgeois virtues of saving and sobriety, avoidance of waste or ostentation, and respect for scholarship'.[1]

Then the spread of Islam into West Africa accompanied another economic process. The trans-Saharan trade produced missionaries in the market places. The Muslim shopkeeper was at times the equivalent of the clergyman. Islam was spreading as an additional commodity accompanying the grand paradigm of trade.

Out of this began to emerge special kingdoms and emirates in West Africa, instances of new state-formation. There is a Hobbesian concept in Islamic statecraft — encouraging obedience to those who exercise authority, provided they do no violence to the principles that Muhammad advocated and God willed. This side of Islam is concerned with submissive fatalism.

But Islam is also a product of defensive fanaticism. While submissive fatalism might encourage acceptance and peaceful conformity, defensive fanaticism could generate rebellion.

Again it went all the way back to the life history of the Prophet Muhammad. Against the political establishment of Arabia in his own day, Muhammad decided that his duty was to resist or go into exile. Under pressure he decided to flee into exile. The Islamic calendar to the present day is a commemoration of exile — since it begins neither with the birth of Muhammad nor with his death, nor indeed with the moment when he felt that God had favoured him with the revelation. On the contrary, the Islamic calendar goes back to the hegira, the moment when Muhammad decided to flee from persecution and seek refuge in another city, Medina.

When Islam came to West Africa it certainly displayed the same dialectic between submissive fatalism and defensive resistance. Islam was mobilised to resist European imperialism. Indeed, a substantial portion of Western Africa's primary resistance to European colonisation was Muslim-inspired:

> Militant Islam presented the greatest challenge and mobilised the sternest resistance to the European occupation of Africa in the nineteenth century. Muslim polities, with their written languages, their heritage of state-making, and the cohesive force of a universal religion preaching the brotherhood of all believers, could generally organise resistance on a wider scale than political units whose extent was limited by the tide of common ancestry. Muslims also had a strong incentive to oppose the advance of Christian power.[2]

When European pressures were getting too strong for the leadership of the Sokoto caliphate in nineteenth-century Nigeria, the leadership thought of the hegira — 'obligatory flight from the infidels'. Sultan Attahiru Ahmadu led a hegira after the conquest of Sokoto, going eastwards. As a historian has put it: 'The British finally overtook him at Burmi and killed him. However, many of his followers continued to the Sudan where their descendants still live today under the chieftaincy of his grandson, Mohammadu Dan Mai Wurno.'[3]

In Sudan Muhammad Ahmed el-Mahdi revealed his own potentialities in the realm of defensive fanaticism. He was the precursor of Sudanese nationalism, rallying religion behind nationalistic causes, marrying piety to patriotism.

But Islam also had its other face — the face of submissive fatalism, a readiness to accept the inevitable. The same Islam which had fought so hard against European colonisation later seemed to be ready to accept the inevitable hegemony of the West. Again no one has put it better than the British Africanist, Michael Crowder: 'Islam, whose hatred of subjection to the infidel would have provided, as it did for a short while between 1889 and 1893 in the Western Sudan, a unifying theme for resistance against the French and British, also held the seeds of a fatalist acceptance of the inevitable.'[4]

Subsequently Islam profoundly influenced the colonial policy of at least one major imperial power, Great Britain. My own thesis is that the British policy of indirect rule was born out of a marriage of Islam, on one side, and the Anglo-Irish philosopher Edmund Burke, on the other. In a sense the legacy of Edmund Burke is what British political culture is all about. As a rule of political prudence Burke advised: 'Neither entirely nor at once depart from antiquity.' If a society does aspire to change direction, it will be a mistake to do it either totally or in one sudden move. Political prudence, according to Burke, requires political sensitivity to history. As he put it: 'People will not look forward to posterity who never look backward to their ancestors.'[5]

British political culture is a reflection in part of this broad political philosophy. The British are reluctant to turn their back on antiquity either entirely or at once. So they maintain ancient institutions and modernise them as they go along, and they are slower to modify traditional habits than many of their peers.

This same Burkean gradualism in British domestic political culture came to influence British colonial policy. Indirect rule was based on a Burkean principle of gradualism. Many colonial policy-makers felt convinced that you could not persuade Africans to look forward to posterity unless you respected their tendency to look backward to their ancestors.

But British indirect rule assumed a presence of defined institutions in African societies, rooted in the history of those societies. And yet many African societies were relatively decentralised without the state-like institutions of authority that the British would have preferred to use for purposes of government.

Where was indirect rule to find its paradigmatic formulation? Lord Lugard, the architect of Britain's policy of indirect rule, found those institutions in the emirates of Northern Nigeria. As Lord Hailey came to put it in his classic, *An African Survey:*

It was in Northern Nigeria that this procedure of using Native Authorities was given a systematic form by Lord Lugard during the years which followed the declaration of the Protectorate in 1900. The area which was brought under British protection was the scene of the most effectively organized system of indigenous rule to be found south of the Sahara. Most of the old-established Hausa Kingdoms had embraced the Islamic faith, and under its influence there had by the early sixteenth century developed a well-organized fiscal system, a definite code of land-tenure, a regular scheme of local rule through appointed District Heads, and a trained judiciary administering the tennets of the Muhammadan law.[6]

The Fulani, who gained the ascendancy in the greater part of the Hausa country, used and helped to develop further this organised system of administration. And then Lugard and the British came. In the words of another writer, Cyril Whittaker:

Like the Fulani conquerors, Lugard perceived that a solution for his problems presented itself in the form of the already effectively functioning system of government, which by then offered such obvious additional advantages as religious justification for authority, a formal code of law (the Islamic Shari'a), specialized judicial institutions, a more centrally controlled apparatus of administration, the custom of taxation, and above all, the people's habit of obeying state authority.[7]

From this appraisal of the Hausa-Fulani institutions the British then evolved an elaborate system of native authorities in Nigeria, utilising existing structures for indirect British control. Northern Nigeria especially afforded the British classical local instruments for indirect imperial rule. The old institutions of Hausa-Fulani states became part of the new institutions of the colonial state.

On the one hand, this appeared to be a healthy strategy of transition. African societies were not being disrupted precipitately, ignoring their habits and lifestyles. African societies were being ruled through institutions which they had come to understand across generations, but which were subject to gradual change.

On the other hand, indirect rule in Nigeria aggravated the problems of creating a modern nation-state after independence. The different groups in the country maintained their separate ethnic identities by being ruled in part through their own native institutions. Northern Nigeria became particularly distinctive in its fusion of Islam and Africanity. The missionaries were kept out of that part of Nigeria and missionary education — which had helped to Westernise the South fairly rapidly — was relatively inaccessible to large parts of Northern Nigeria. Different sections of the population perceived each other as strangers, sometimes as aliens, increasingly as rivals, and ominously as potential enemies. As it happens, the stage was being set for the events which ultimately led first to the military coup in Nigeria in January 1966, then to the slaughter of the Ibo in Northern Nigeria in the same year, and then ultimately to the outbreak of a civil war from 1967 to 1970. The preservation of pre-colonial state institutions, especially in Northern Nigeria, had made the consolidation of post-colonial national institutions more difficult. Clearly the British had been more respectful of African institutions through their policy of indirect rule than the French had been through their policy of assimilation. After all, the French policy of assimilation denied validity to indigenous structures and values, asserting a supremacy and uniqueness of French culture, and proclaiming a mission to Gallicise those over whom France exercised hegemony. The British policy of indirect rule, in contrast, allowed for cultural relativism among societies and was based on an assumption of cultural diversity in the universe. Hence British reluctance to tamper with local native institutions where they could be recognised by them, and British eagerness to use those institutions instead of inventing new ones. But there was a heavy political cost in places like Nigeria. Pre-colonial statehood militated against post-colonial statehood. The survival of the emirates of Northern Nigeria and the Kabakaship in Buganda, legacies of pre-colonial statehood, came to militate against the construction of one Nigeria or one Uganda after independence.

112

The sultanate of Zanzibar in East Africa presented distinctive problems of its own without altering the basic tension between the pre-colonial and post-colonial African state. From the days before European colonial rule Zanzibar had been a racially and ethnically plural society. By the end of the eighteenth century the ascendancy of the Arabs was already clear. It was consolidated by the rise of Seyyid Said bin Sultan. Sultan Barghash later provided the transitional rule from pre-European Arab ascendancy to the Arab oligarchy under European overlordship. Once again the British, having recognised monarchical institutions in Zanzibar reminiscent of their own in England, proceeded to give some kind of validity to those monarchical institutions and use them as a basis of indirect rule. In one sense the Arabs of Zanzibar were the equivalent of the Hausa-Fulani of Northern Nigeria. In both cases the maintenance of their particular political institutions from pre-colonial days augured ill for the transition to post-colonial nationhood. In the case of Zanzibar, the tensions between the privileged ethnic group and the others could not be mitigated by a shared rivalry of all of them against still other groups elsewhere. After all, the tensions between the Hausa-Fulani and others in Northern Nigeria were helped by the fact that all northerners had a sense of defensiveness against southerners. Zanzibar was too small a society to have those built-in safeguards of cross-cutting alignments. The result was the disastrous revolution of January 1964, barely a month after the British had departed. Those very Arab institutions of statehood which the British had so affectionately protected became the Achilles' heel of the new nation as it struggled to modern statehood after independence.

African polities and the westernised state

But why were pre-colonial state-formations so difficult to reconcile with the demands of post-colonial statehood? Why did indirect rule in Nigeria, by preserving greater recognition of traditional institutions of statecraft, make the business of building the modern Nigerian nation-state tougher? Why was respect for the Kabakaship in Buganda a disservice to the task of state-formation in Uganda?

Here it is worth bearing in mind another triple heritage — the heritage of the city-state, the empire-state and the nation-state. To some extent Zanzibar was a city-state, though it gradually established enough hegemony in parts of what is today coastal Kenya and coastal Tanzania to be on the verge of becoming a proper empire-state. In the case of Zanzibar the empire in the making was a dynastic empire, with an Arab sultanate at the top.

113

In the history of Europe the city-state antedated the empire-state. In African history it is more difficult to disentangle the origins of the city as against the empire. Some of the emirates in West Africa were at once city-states and part of a wider empire at the same time.

Subsequently the names of some of the greatest African empires were used after independence as names of the new nation-states. The empire-states of Ghana and Mali had bequeathed their historical names to modern states. We know less about ancient Zimbabwe than we do about ancient Ghana or ancient Mali, but Zimbabwe too may be a case of a former empire-state bequeathing its name to a modern nation-state. There is the alternative theory that Zimbabwe was an ancient city-state — but it had still contributed a name to a modern nation-state. No modern African country has as yet adopted the name of Songhay, but that is yet another ancient empire-state in search of a modern reincarnation.

The most durable of all Africa's empire-states turned out to be Ethiopia. Its last Emperor was Haile Selassie, an incarnation of pre-colonial statehood bound to confront sooner or later his moment of truth with post-colonial statehood.

There is a basic conflict within the demands of a dynastic ancient empire and the responsibilities of a modern nation-state. Ethiopia had had a severe famine which was under-publicised, seemingly because a famine of such magnitude was considered by the royal household as an embarrassment to the Empire.

When the Ethiopian Revolution began, in February 1974, it has been suggested that a major contributor to the revolution was precisely the famine and the long delay by the Imperial Order in responding to it. By that time, it appeared that the dynastic empire-state would no longer be permitted to masquerade as a modern nation-state. The soldiers of Ethiopia, for a while cheered by the students and peasants of Ethiopia, solved the dilemmas by abolishing the ancient imperial statehood and replacing it with a modern ideology dedicated in the long run to the principle of the 'withering away of the state' itself.

We might therefore conclude that one of the difficulties in the transition from a pre-colonial to a post-colonial state is precisely the normative and moral gap between the two. The values have fundamentally changed, the responsibilities redefined, the perspectives newly focused, the policies demanding reformulation.

An important disruptive factor was the evolution of the principle of equality. In Africa this principle was by far better realised among the so-called stateless societies than among either city-states or empire-states. Many indigenous societies along the Nile Valley, or societies like the Tiv of Nigeria and the Masai of Kenya and Tanzania, have relatively loose structures of control and substantial egalitarianism. In contrast, societies like those of Buganda, Northern Nigeria, Ashanti, and other dynastic empires of West Africa, were hierarchical and basically unequal.

The new nation-state provided a basic contradiction. On the one hand, it championed almost as much equality as the so-called 'primitive' and stateless societies which did not have kings or identifiable rulers. On the other hand, the new nation-state explicitly expected identifiable rulers, and asserted what Max Weber called the state's 'monopoly of the legitimate use of physical force'. The new post-colonial state was supposed to be as egalitarian as the Masai and the Tiv, and as centralised as the Baganda, the Asanti, and the Hausa-Fulani. The new nation-state was supposed to be morally as egalitarian as the stateless societies of Africa: but politically as structured as the nation-states of Europe.

This basic tension between moral equality from acephalous societies in Africa and political hierarchy from monarchical societies in Africa, has been one of the central divisive elements in the post-colonial experience. In places like Rwanda and Burundi this dialectic pitched hierarchical Tutsi against egalitarian Hutu; in Nigeria it pitched deferential Hausa against individualistic Ibo; in Uganda it pitched monarchical Baganda against neo-republican Nilotes.

Another area of tension between the pre-colonial African states and the post-colonial concerned attitude to territoriality. Most African societies have a high degree of land reverence. On the other hand, the principle of the modern nation-state includes a high sensitivity to territoriality. The mystique of land reverence in traditional Africa has had to seek a *modus vivendi* with the principle of territoriality of the modern state.

The mystique of land reverence in Africa is partly a compact between the living, the dead and the unborn. Where the ancestors are buried, there the soul of the clan resides, and there the prospects of the health of the next generation should be sought. Land was quite fundamental to both stateless African societies and to empires and city-states.

On the other hand, territory grew increasingly important in Europe, becoming almost sacrosanct in the legacy of the Treaty of Westphalia of 1648. Political communities under the new doctrine of the nation-state became increasingly definable in terms of boundaries, between one nation-state and another. Sovereignty was subject to territoriality; power was land-bound.

But while the pre-colonial African state indulged in this land worship in relation to both agriculture and the burial of ancestors, the post-colonial state indulged in the worship of territory in relation to power and sovereignty rather than cultivation and ancestry. The dichotomy between the land worship of old and territorial worship in post-colonial states has not yet been resolved. All we know is that the last legacy of the colonial order to be decolonised is likely to be the territorial boundary between one African country and another. That colonial boundary currently helps define one African political entity as against another. Each is jealous of its own inherited boundaries. Kenya defies Somalia; Ethiopia defies Somalia; Niger defies Nigeria; Morocco defies Mauritania; and most post-colonial African states defy any territorial changes. The ghosts of ancestors and land worship have been overshadowed by the imperative of sovereignty and territorial possessiveness.

Conclusion

We have attempted to demonstrate in this essay that there are two levels of a triple heritage of state-formation in the history of Africa from pre-colonial times to independence. At one level the triple heritage consists of the indigenous heritage, the Afro-Islamic heritage, and the Western heritage of state formation. The purely indigenous takes us to Buganda before the European impact, and then explores the implications and repercussions of British colonisation of that part of the world. The Afro-Islamic dramatises the impressive diversity of Nigeria, and illustrates the interaction between an Afro-Islamic heritage, on the one hand, and an indigenous heritage, on the other hand, in the South of the country, and the repercussions of the stimulation which European contact inaugurated. But the Afro-Christian component in the history of state-formation in Africa did not always include European stimulus. The striking exception to the intrusion of European Christianity is in fact Ethiopia, which has been Christian for a longer period than many parts of Europe, going back to the fourth century AD. The rise of the Ethiopian state was quite indistinguishable from the rise of Christianity in Ethiopia just as the nature of statehood in Nigeria, especially in the North, was often indistinguishable from the nature of Islam in Nigeria. But there was the subsequent impact of the system of Westphalia of 1648, consummated after the Thirty Years War in Europe, and clearly an aftermath of the conclusion of religious wars in Europe and the emergence of the nation-states in the global system.

We have also attempted to demonstrate another level of the triple heritage — the heritage involving the city-state, the empire-state and the new modern nation-state. Places like Kano and Zanzibar were partly settings for the city-state. But Songhay, Ghana, Mali, the

Hausa-Fulani empire, Ashanti, and possibly Zimbabwe, were manifestations of the second tradition of empire-states.

The third structure of statehood was the nation-state, very much a product of European history and very much a legacy of the Treaty of Westphalia of 1648.

This essay has attempted to point out a basic discontinuity between the pre-colonial African state and the post-colonial state. In the transition the British especially attempted to provide a *rite de passage*, a ceremony of transition from pre-colonial to post-colonial statehood. This ceremony of transition was the British policy of indirect rule, which attempted to use native institutions of government as instrumentalities for colonial control and as intermediate stages before full African incorporation into the global state system.

But in the ultimate analysis the transition from pre-colonial to post-colonial statehood was bedevilled by two crises — the crisis of normative egalitarianism and the crisis of territoriality. The crisis of normative egalitarianism arose because African city- and empire-states were, on the one hand, less egalitarian than African stateless societies, and, on the other hand, less egalitarian also than the evolving European nation-states. The kingdom of Buganda was less egalitarian than England; the religious Marabouts of Senegal were less egalitarian than at least the legacy of France after 1789. As for Dahomey (now the Republic of Benin), it was in some ways more sexist than Europe and in other ways decidedly less sexist. The rise of the Amazons, female soldiers in combat, indicated an impressive ambivalence about a sexist division of labour between male warriors and female domestics.

But it was not merely the normative and moral cleavage which distinguished pre-colonial statehood from post-colonial manifestations. It was also the nature of responsiveness to land. Pre-colonial statehood had a kind of mystical deference to land, an obsession with the aesthetics and religiosity of the soil. The grand compact between ancestors, the living, and the unborn, found an area of fulfilment in the religiosity of the land. The land was where crops were cultivated so that the living could continue to live, and the future infants could be sustained. But the land was also a graveyard, a place where the ancestors were indeed laid to rest, a place where the last incarnation found repose before a new incarnation received stimulus.

But the second major cleavage between the pre-colonial and the post-colonial is not land but morality. This is a conflict of values and principles, a tension between preferences. The pre-colonial state was basically inegalitarian, tracing its roots to hierarchy, privilege and power. Indeed the pre-colonial state sometimes began as a city-state and then expanded enough to become an empire-state.

One of the great ironies of the European era in Africa is that the era colonised the African imperial state and, by so doing, disimperialised it. Thus Buganda under British rule was indeed colonised, but after a while Buganda's capacity to imperialise the rest of Eastern Africa was blunted. British colonisation of African empires reduced the imperial capacities of those empires.

This was repeated elsewhere in the continent. British colonisation of the Hausa-Fulani helped to disimperialise the capacities of those groups to exert hegemony over others. British colonisation of Zanzibar helped to disimperialise Zanzibar's expanding hegemony over parts of Tanzania and Kenya.

After independence, in any case, some of the most acute tensions of African societies were tensions between legacies of egalitarianism and legacies of hierarchy. Legacies of egalitarianism had dual ancestry — the ancestry of the values of African stateless societies and the ancestry of the values of European liberalism and European socialism. The legacies of African hierarchy could be traced, on the one hand, to the impact of the city-states and the empire-states in pre-colonial Africa, and, on the other hand, to the legacy of the inequalities of European imperialism and European capitalism.

Perhaps the state system, whatever its origins, ought to give way to a more humane and more equitable global system. But while the state system persists, it is important to bear in mind that its African manifestation is indeed tripartite in two fundamental senses. It covers the basic interaction among indigenous cultures, Islam and Westernism. That basic interaction also includes the accompanying tripartite communication between the city-state, the empire-state, and the nation-state in the agonising tensions of Africa's political experience.

Notes

1　Basil Davidson, *The African Genius*, Boston, Little, Brown, 1969, pp. 211–12.
2　A.S. Kanya-Forstner, 'Mali-Tukulor' in Michael Crowder (ed.), *West African Resistance*, New York, Africana Publishing Corporation, 1971, p. 53.
3　Michael Crowder's introduction to Crowder (ed.), op. cit., p. 15.
4　Ibid.
5　E. Burke, *Reflections on the Revolution in France* (1790), *Works*, London, World Classics Edition, 1907, Volume IV, p. 109.
6　Lord Hailey, *An African Survey*, London, Oxford University Press, 1957, revised edn, p. 453–4.
7　C.S. Whittaker, Jr., *The Politics of Tradition: Continuity and Change in Northern Nigeria, 1947–1966*, Princeton, Princeton University Press, 1970, pp. 26–7.

6 Paradigms of modern state formation in the periphery

Ali Kazancigil

Globalisation of the modern state

The vast cultural, political and economic diversity of the Third World countries contrasts with their near universal aspiration to develop a modern state (Carroll, 1984, p. 364). The 'globalisation' of the modern state (Lefebvre, 1978, p. 25), which has gained momentum in the last few decades, is a dominant characteristic of our time.

The formation of this state can be situated geographically and historically: Western Europe between the sixteenth and twentieth centuries (Tilly, 1975). It has a specific cultural context: separation between the religious and secular spheres (Badie and Birnbaum, 1983). And it is intimately linked to the development of capitalism and the rise of the bourgeoisie (Poggi, 1978). The modern state has at its disposal a bureaucratic apparatus, established along the legal-rational pattern, with a precise division of tasks and functions, and a personnel which identifies with it, reproduces a specific ideology and carries out the tasks of administration, taxation, justice, police and defence. It exercises, over a precisely delimited territory, a control far greater than any other form of political domination known in history, such as the empires and the absolutist states. It intervenes very actively in the economic, cultural and ideological spheres of society, as well as in the private lives of its citizens.

Why, then, do non-European formations, which have not met a similar combination of historical factors, want to create the modern

119

state, rather than seek other state forms? Why are societies, in which the dominant ideology (for example Islamic fundamentalism) is opposed to the nation-state, not able to go beyond the stage of rejection, and fail to generate alternative political models?[1]

Most probably, this trend is linked to certain fundamental aspects of the transformation of Third World societies. Colonial heritage and the accession to power of Westernised élites are sometimes put forward to explain the extension of the modern state in the Third World. But such explanations, while not completely unfounded, appear to be rather limited to account for such a global phenomenon.

Third World societies, to promote their development, their modernity and their democratisation — the state being a crucial factor in such processes — must enjoy conditions of autonomy and display capacity for social innovation in order to find political solutions for their problems (Lapierre, 1977). This is exactly what Western Europe did: a product of specific economic, cultural and social processes, the modern Western state was gradually established as an innovation generated by the European societies in response to the crisis that struck them at the end of the Middle Ages (Tilly, 1975). In the past, other societies and cultures in Asia, in the Middle East, in Africa or in pre-Columbian America, also displayed social and political innovation. At present, however, the Third World countries are facing considerable difficulties in this respect.

How then can the question be formulated? Should the globalisation of the modern state be seen as the corollary of the Third World countries' cultural, economic and political inability to build the state forms which would suit them? Must answers be sought among cultural factors or such structural factors as the economic relations between industrialised and developing countries? Is today's world system incompatible with the coexistence of several types of state?

Global processes and fragmented paradigms

The analysis of the reproduction of the modern state at the global level involves a series of questions about the nature of the state, its relations with social classes, culture and economy, as well as its internal and external role. The imbrication of the cultural, social and economic processes of the state on the one hand, and, on the other, the world market and the inter-state system, which Lefebvre (1977) described as the '*mode de production étatique*', is still a long way from being clarified in all its dimensions, the more so because it forms a dynamic process.

The complexity of the question would call for a renunciation of 'disciplinary parochialism and paradigmatic parochialism' (Alker and Biersteker, 1984, p. 140). The title chosen for this essay, which juxtaposes the concept of the modern state with that of the periphery, aims precisely at drawing attention to this need for a paradigmatic decompartmentalisation in the study of state. The first concept is found mainly in historical and political sociology, which put the main emphasis on internal political and cultural processes (Badie, 1983). Here, the unit of analysis is the national society. The second concept is found in structural approaches, putting the accent above all on exogenous processes, such as the theory of *dependencia* (Cardoso and Faletto, 1978), that of centre–periphery (Amin, 1976), the world-system perspective (Wallerstein, 1974, 1979, 1980) or the long cycle theory (Modelski, 1978). Here the unit of analysis is the global system, the state being considered as a more or less autonomous component of this system.

However, the globalisation of the modern state calls for analyses which would go beyond such paradigmatic compartments. The endogenous approach is necessary for an explanation of the genesis of the state. But even in its structural/dialectical versions — for example the neo-Marxists — this approach does not provide an adequate analytical framework that can shed light on the globalisation of the modern state, on its extension in the periphery. This process is linked to relations between national societies and the global system, and it requires that economic, political and cultural dynamics be taken into account at the intra- and inter-state levels (Andrews, 1982, p. 136).

Compartmentalisation does not only concern internal and external processes, but also economic/political factors and empirical/dialectical approaches.

These paradigmatic fragmentations can be illustrated in a simplified form, in a diagram (Figure 6.1), in which approaches to the state are shown on three axes, at the extremities of which are the endogenous/exogenous, economic/political-cultural-strategic, and empirical/dialectical variables.

According to this diagram, the paradigmatic triads characterising approaches to the state are (with some authors' names to illustrate each case) as follows:

- exogenous/dialectical/economic: world-system perspective (Wallerstein, 1974, 1979);
- exogenous/dialectical/political-strategic: long cycle of world leadership theory (Modelski, 1978);
- endogenous/dialectical/economic-political: neo-Marxist approaches (Anderson, 1974);
- endogenous/dialectical/cultural-political: diffusionist approaches (Badie and Birnbaum, 1983);

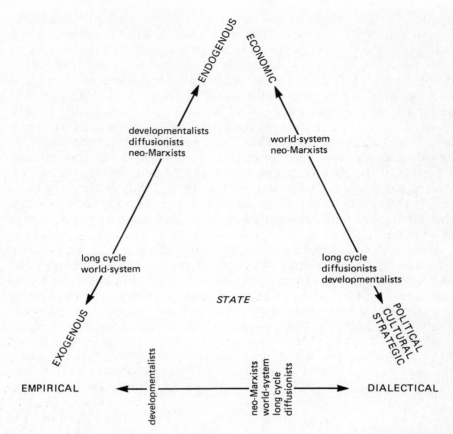

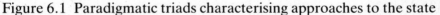

Figure 6.1 Paradigmatic triads characterising approaches to the state

● endogenous/empirical/cultural-political: developmentalist
approaches (Almond and Powell, 1966).

The analysis of globalisation processes of the modern state should
ideally be situated at the intersection of these paradigms, which would
benefit from communication and cross-fertilisation with each other.

Certain recent research has gone in this direction. The behavioural
and empirical social scientists do not trust the centre–periphery
paradigms, such as *dependencia*, or the world-system perspective,
which they consider to be teleological and unscientific, on the grounds
that they cannot be tested by empirical and quantitative methods
(Waltz, 1979). However, quantitative studies aimed at testing the
theories of dependence have demonstrated the latter's capacity to
explain many aspects of relations between industrialised and developing countries, and the negative consequences of a dependent position

on such areas as economic growth (Bornschier, 1981; Jackson *et al.*, 1979), democratisation (Bollen, 1983) or foreign policy (Moon, 1983) in the peripheral countries.

Conversely, more and more dialectical/structural theorists agree that their propositions would benefit from the scrutiny of empirical, quantitative methods (Alker and Biersteker, 1984; *Review*, 1985).

Another fragmentation with adverse effects on analyses of the state is the isolation of the economic from the political, and this too is gradually being overcome. Quantitative research (Venieris and Gupta, 1983) has confirmed the empirical validity of theoretical approaches which establish correlations between political institutions, economic growth and social change. Such crossing of the epistemological boundaries between endogenous and exogenous, economic and political, as well as empirical and dialectical approaches are very beneficial for analysing the globalisation of the modern state.

Two types of paradigm are examined below, particularly from the point of view of the heuristic advantages they offer for an explanation of the origin and evolution of the modern state in the periphery.[2]

Developmentalist and diffusionist approaches to the formation of the peripheral modern state

One of the major paradigms of social change and state formation falls into the endogenous/empirical/cultural-political category: developmentalism, the unit of analysis of which is the national society, and which places cultural factors, values and norms at the origin of social action. The term 'developmentalism' covers the various functionalist and evolutionist theories of modernisation. There is no need here to review the numerous criticisms that have been aimed at this non-linear view, which sees humanity evolving by predetermined steps (Rostow, 1971) towards a given type of society and political culture. The analytical categories used are pattern variables (Parsons and Shils, 1951), empathy (Lerner, 1964), or achievement orientation (McClelland, 1961). The proposed political culture is based on rationalisation, differentiation and secularisation. It contrasts essentially universal modernity with traditional local values, which are thought to be obstacles to modernisation (Almond and Verba, 1963; Pye and Verba, 1965). In this analysis, the political culture is the major variable which conditions the others. Internal and external economic processes are not taken into account. Social and political change is dealt with separately from questions such as capitalism, relations of domination or social classes, the consideration of which is dismissed as economism (Ashley, 1983).

These theories of modernisation base their intellectual legitimacy on a questionable interpretation of Max Weber, according to which the Weberian theory is built around the idea that at the source of social change are to be found exclusively cultural and ideological factors, particularly religion (Parsons, 1963). Such an interpretation comes from a strictly subjectivist and reductionistic view of Weber, which situates the analysis of structural elements of social change such as the state, the economy and the classes, at the level of interpersonal relations (Turner, 1981, pp. 234–56).

The idealist and culturalist interpretation of Weber has produced theories that shed little light on internal, and still less on external processes of the modern state formation in the periphery. If the modernisation process was the internal unfolding of a certain kind of culturally determined rationality and it was situated as the level of mentalities and interpersonal relations, then non-Western societies, which do not display such 'modernizing' patterns, could not possibly even start developing the modern state. This approach, which focuses on internal processes, paradoxically makes rather implausible the development from within of the modern state in non-Western societies. The culturalist interpretation is capable of explaining certain aspects of modernity in European societies, although this cannot be isolated from structural factors. But obviously its explanatory capacity is very low when it comes to the extension of the modern state in social formations of the Third World. This shortcoming must be attributed to developmentalist theories and not to Max Weber, whose analysis does not in fact exclude structural factors. However, as far as external dynamics are concerned, there is indeed an inherent weakness in the Weberian theory, which primarily focuses on endogenous processes. In conformity with his definition of the state as the holder of the monopoly of legitimate physical violence, Weber sees exogenous dynamics and inter-state relations through the military-strategic perspective of 'the fact of conquest'. The Weberian theory, which is essential for understanding the internal dynamics of the historical development of capitalism and the state, is better suited to explaining inter-state relations of the pre-capitalist world. It is less so as far as the contemporary world-system is concerned.

Within the internalist/culturalist framework, a solution more appropriate than developmentalism to the problem of explaining the globalisation of the modern state is offered by the theory of diffusion, inspired by anthropological studies of the cultural flows between 'transmitter' and 'receiver' societies. In this approach, the political and cultural are the independent variables which determine the nature of the state at the internal level. At the global level, cultural dynamics are accompanied by the political, economic and military hierarchies which countries establish within the international system. The state, which is essentially a politico-cultural construction, spreads from the centre towards the periphery of the system. The diffusionist model (Badie and Birnbaum, 1983, p. 97), which posits the extension of the modern state from the centre towards the periphery, also maintains that in view of its cultural characteristics, the periphery should generate types of political centres other than the modern state. Diffusion is explained either by voluntary adoption (mimetism) or by the use of brutal methods (colonialism and the use of force in general).

Thus of the two factors of diffusion, the first is subjective, stemming from the attitude of Westernised élites, and the second is objective, but limited to the fact of conquest. Diffusionism does not escape the difficulties of the culturalist approach when it comes to explaining the establishment of the modern state in the non-Western social formations. Such analytical difficulties arise mainly from the absence of articulation between the different variables, particularly between the cultural/political variables and the economic ones, which is crucial for the analysis of the modern state. The diffusionist approach maintains that the latter 'was a product neither of the rise of capitalism nor of the opening up of new trade routes, let alone of the growth of industry' (Badie and Birnbaum, 1983, p. 135). According to this view, the state is shaped by religious and cultural factors proper to the West, and essentially of the cultural principle of dissociation. Founded on the heritage of Roman law and the cultural vision of the Renaissance, it does not suit societies where an 'organic' religion prevails, such as Islam or Hinduism, which reject all separation between the temporal and the spiritual. Incapable of functioning on the principles of differentiation-autonomisation, the modern Western state succumbs, where it has been exported to the periphery, to the logic of authoritarianism.

The diffusionist analysis is relevant from many points of view, but it does not explain why the countries of the Third World, where the brutal imposition of foreign models through the use of force is nowadays the exception rather than the general rule and where the cultural and ideological influence of the centre is at least partly offset by an awareness of the drawbacks of mimetic behaviour, persist in their desire to construct modern states. The underlying difficulty of this approach comes from the primordial status given to the cultural determination of the modern state and the secondary importance accorded to economic factors and relations of dependence.

Because of the limited autonomy of peripheral societies resulting from such relations, the culturalist analysis, convincing in explaining certain aspects of the rise of the modern state in the autonomous European societies of previous centuries, is no longer so in accounting for the creation of the modern state in the periphery.

Structural approaches to the formation of the peripheral modern state

As the analysis founded on cultural determinism and the taking into account only of endogenous dynamics in the state processes cannot convincingly explain the fact that in the twentieth century virtually every national society is trying to build a modern state, explanations must be sought elsewhere, on the side of what might be called 'structural' theories.

The structural theories of the state have mostly developed within the Weberian and Marxian scholarship, but a Weberian approach delivered from the reductionism imposed by the functionalist interpretation, and a Marxian approach delivered from the evolutionist version which distorts it into a one-way 'historical highway' to be necessarily taken by every society (Gellner, 1984). If we refer to the typology described above (Figure 6.1), the ideal theory of the globalisation of the modern state would be one that could integrate the exogenous/endogenous variables with the economic/political-cultural-strategic ones, as well as the dialectical/empirical analysis. Obviously, such a theory does not exist. It would present insoluble epistemological and methodological problems. One could, however, try to identify the theories and approaches that would be best suited to our subject. Such is the case of dialectical approaches which, in so far as they are more inclusive, are preferable to others (despite certain analytical problems they entail, which is why it is worth testing them, as we saw above, through quantitative methods). Though essentially inspired by Marxism, they owe a good deal to Weber as well. They give first place sometimes to the economic, sometimes to the political, but at the same time they try to integrate both these factors, and are well equipped to analyse the connections between internal and external dynamics.

In the analysis of the globalisation of the modern state, another heuristic advantage of the structural theories lies in their integrating a particularly important dimension which Wolfram Eberhard (1965, p. 13) has conceptualised as the 'world time'. This concept refers to the fact that apparently or formally similar social processes can cover up realities or have consequences that are quite different, depending on the phases of world development in which they occur (Giddens, 1981, p. 167). It corresponds to a time lived at the world's dimensions (Braudel, 1979, p. 8) or again, to 'the world context of any given era' (Wallerstein, 1974, p. 6). This concept has a central place in the explanation of the inter-societal dynamics which are associated with the globalisation of the modern state. For the present era, it refers to the existence of a world-system which exerts considerable influence on state processes, on relations between the market, the social classes and the ideologies, as well as on the interactions between internal and external dynamics of societal change.

World time also has an epistemological implication: having been conceived earlier, when the world-system was a long way from its current magnitude and pervasiveness, the theories of Marx and Weber were internalist constructions mainly based on endogenous dynamics. However, in Marx the processes of production and exchange, and of the formation of classes and states, had inter-societal dimensions. Thus Marxism generated approaches which took world time into account. In particular, most of the present structural approaches to the modern state can be traced back to this origin.

With Weber, on the other hand, this aspect remains a weak point. The Weberian approach does not fundamentally take the world context into account. Weber's strength, from the point of view that interests us here, is to have developed concepts which shed light on the endogenous structural and cultural characteristics of non-European social formations.

One of Weber's main concerns was the emergence of organised capitalism, of which he studied the structural and cultural aspects. His theory of modernity relates the state to capitalism and its material foundations, such as the market, technology and the work-force. The modern state has a major role in the process, with its rational bureaucracy, its codified law, its principle of citizenship and the actions it takes to promote a homogenised market and stable systems of taxation, currency, credit, property and contract (Collins, 1980). It is into this context that the role of a particular ethic intervenes (such as the Protestant, the Hindu or the Islamic) as a cultural or psychological variable influencing rationality and modernity (Turner, 1974). According to Weber, the fact that Islamic, Hindu or other such societies could not embark on capitalist development is not the result of religion as an individual, subjective factor, but of certain structural, economic, political and social characteristics which have prevailed in these societies. One such characteristic is prebendalism (Weber, 1951), which has always been the mode of disintegration of oriental empires (and not feudalism, more favourable to the emergence of capitalism and the modern state). Patrimonialism is another, with its extreme form of the ruler's control over society, which Weber calls 'sultanism' (Weber, 1968, p. 1020). Structural factors of this kind, and not religion as such, explain the decline of the monetary economy, the precarious status of private property and the absence of secondary structures (such as autonomous cities and corporations) or a legal system based on formal rationality.

Marx's analysis of non-European pre-capitalist formations is rather marginal to his general theory of social change. The latter, based on class struggle and the contradictions between the forces of production and the social relations of production, which lead to the replacement of the old mode of production by a new one, was conceived against the background of industrial societies of the nineteenth century. To Marx, the social formation is characterised by the interactions between the infrastructure (relations of production) and the superstructure (the state, the law and culture). Though the former is more important than the latter, the autonomy of the state is not denied (Marx, 1959) and the two-way relations between the base and the superstructure are stressed.

To explain the non-European societies, Marx resorted to a model which differed from his general model of social change, by proposing, in the *Grundrisse* (1974), the concept of the Asiatic mode of production (AMP). However, apart from the fact that he did not have time to develop further this theory, his analysis was handicapped both by the limited knowledge available on non-European societies at the time of his writing, and by the influence which the concept of oriental despotism had on him. This concept, highly valued in classical political thinking, from Aristotle to Montesquieu via Machiavelli, corresponds more to a fantasy produced by imagination of the classical West than a serious study of oriental societies (Grosrichard, 1978). The validity of certain characteristics attributed by Marx to the AMP, such as the weak status of private property, is generally accepted today, but others have not been confirmed by contemporary anthropological and historical research. This applies particularly to such matters as societal stagnation, the complete isolation of village communities, the absence of social classes, the gap between the despotic state and the rest of society, chronic political instability in contrast to the lack of economic development, etc. The concept of AMP has often been criticised for its incoherence: the state is attributed a crucial role in it, but in the absence of social classes, the conditions for the emergence of the state do not exist (Hindess and Hirst, 1975).

Compared to the impasse into which AMP leads (Anderson, 1974, pp. 462-549), Weberian theories seem to be in a better position to explain the endogenous conditions that have prevented non-European societies from participating in the rise of capitalism and the modern state, in the initial stages of the process. However, once capitalism developed as a system in continuous expansion, progressively incorporating the whole of the inter-societal system, exogenous dynamics acquired exceptional importance, which they did not have in the proto-capitalist era. Here, Weberian theory is inferior to Marxian theory, which offers a conceptualisation better suited to exploring the connections between internal and external processes. The Weberian perspective does a better job of showing the links between political and cultural processes within non-European social formations, while the Marxian approach is indispensable for linking the endogenous and exogenous dynamics, and for taking world time into account. Thus, among the current theories of the modern state and the world system, those inspired by both Marx and Weber and which are trying to take into account the politico-cultural and economic processes, as well as the endogenous/exogenous dynamics, seem preferable from a heuristic point of view, and better placed to respond to the question of the globalisation of the modern state.

The paradigm which comes closest to fulfilling these criteria is the world-system perspective (Wallerstein, 1974, 1979). It is a Marxian/ Weberian approach, basically exogenous/dialectical. While giving priority to the external variables and to processes of production and exchange, it incorporates endogenous and exogenous political variables in its analysis — the states and the inter-state system — as well as cultural variables — nations and nationalism.

The world-system perspective broaches the issue of the extension of the modern state in the periphery, by taking into account the fundamental fact that 'capitalism for the first time in human history initiates the creation of an intersocietal system that is truly global in scope' (Giddens, 1981, p. 168).

Wallerstein's work gives on the whole more weight to non-economic factors than certain other global dialectical approaches, such as that of Samir Amin (1976), for example. It also differs from exogenous approaches based exclusively on political factors and wars, such as the theory of the long cycle of world leadership (Modelski, 1978; Thompson, 1983), which do not take into account the role of global economic processes in the establishment of hierarchical patterns within the world-system.

The world-system perspective is the most relevant theoretical construction, and covers the largest ground with regard to the globalisation of the modern state. Even so, however, the question of the formation of the modern state in the periphery calls for complementary approaches, particularly with regard to the subsequent transformations of the peripheral state and the particular forms it takes. In this respect, the endogenous and empirical approaches are particularly useful in analysing the peripheral state on the basis of its concrete practices and its economic, social, political and cultural policies. The neo-Marxian and Weberian analyses are likewise useful in studying the relations of the state with the social classes, civil society, the market, the nation, nationalism and strategic factors

(Anderson, 1974; Giddens, 1981; Skocpol, 1979).

The world-system perspective has been criticised for ignoring the strategic dimension in the hierarchisation of the states (Zolberg, 1981) and for relegating the political variable to a secondary position (Skocpol, 1977). Such criticisms are relevant, although it should be said that the world-system perspective does not altogether exclude endogenous, political, cultural and even strategic variables (Chase-Dunn and Sokolovsky, 1983; Hopkins, Wallerstein *et al.*, 1982). It integrates them as dependent variables. It is not the state that is the primordial entity, but the world-system, in the context of which relatively amorphous political entities have gradually been consolidated and transformed into modern states. At the base of the evolution of social formations, there is what Wallerstein calls the 'production processes', while the state is the most convenient institutional intermediary for subjecting the market to the control of this or that particular class. The political is the dependent variable, while the economic is the independent one. The system, which is essentially determined by capitalism, functions on the basis of an international division of labour and involves a multiplicity of political entities (states) and cultural ones (nations), organised hierarchically and situated at the centre, the semi-periphery[3] and the periphery (Wallerstein, 1979). At the centre of the system, the processes concerning capital, labour and commodity production mostly follow the logic of the market, while in the periphery, such processes are controlled more by the political and state logic.

Within the capitalist world-economy there is continuous interplay between the processes of capitalist production and geopolitical and national processes. Like Weber (Collins, 1980), Wallerstein stresses the importance of the political variable, of the state, in the development of capitalism. A dialectical relation exists between the type of state (empire or absolutist state), the mode of its disintegration (feudal or prebendal) and the rise of capitalism. The first modern states were formed in societies where the merchant and capitalist classes dominated, such as the Netherlands and England, not in empires, where patrimonial domination and the prebendal mode of disintegration constituted endogenous obstacles to the emergence of capitalism and the formation of the modern state. These endogenous obstacles were added to an exogenous factor, which was fundamental: the incorporation of the social formation within the capitalist world-economy and the subsequent dependence.

The two components of the modern world-system are the capitalist world-economy and the inter-state system. The existence of a global political structure, which is polycentric and multi-cultural, fits the processes of capitalist accumulation which characterise the world-economy. These processes call for an inegalitarian and hierarchical economic and political system, with relations of domination and dependence between the societies and states situated at the centre and in the periphery. The hierarchies between states are established, in the modern world-system, primarily through the international division of labour and the processes of production and exchange, and secondarily by wars and territorial expansion. All these processes form part of a single logic, in which the politico-strategic factors, and the surplus appropriation on the world market through the mechanisms of production and exchange, are in constant interaction (Chase-Dunn, 1981, p. 31).

The emergence of the capitalist world-economy in Western Europe coincided with the territorial and administrative consolidation of the nation-states. While there were 500 political entities in Europe in 1500, not more than twenty-five nation-states existed in 1900 (Tilly, 1975, p. 12). On the other hand, every attempt to create empires in Europe — from the Habsburgs in the sixteenth century to Napoleon in the nineteenth and Nazi Germany in the twentieth — failed. The colonial empires, which marked the nineteenth century, finally turned out to be an extremely costly way for the centre to exploit the periphery. The modern state is indeed the political form of the capitalist world-economy, while empires, which imply political control over the division of labour and the production and exchange processes, could not survive, still less be constituted, in the modern world-system. The extraction of surplus at the world level, for the purposes of capitalist accumulation, is achieved more efficiently and more cheaply by economic methods, rather than political and military ones (Wallerstein, 1974, 1979).

Modes of articulation of the peripheral state and the modern world-system

The continued expansion of the capitalist world-economy has thus been accompanied by the expansion of the inter-state system, through the globalisation of the modern state. Whereas in the past very different types of political domination, such as tribal states, absolutist states and empires, could co-exist, at present only the modern state is developing, in three categories of country: capitalist industrialised, social industrialised and developing. Thus the modern nation-state imposes itself as the sole form of political, military and territorial organisation (Giddens, 1981, p. 179).

In the periphery, the emergence of the modern state has often been achieved at the expense of the colonial possessions of the metropolitan states. Such transformations are consistent with the logic of the modern world-system, in which the transfer of economic surplus from the periphery to the centre is made essentially through the mechanisms of the international division of labour. Violence, conquests, wars, though far indeed from being eliminated, particularly on the regional scale, play a relatively secondary role in the global processes of capitalist accumulation and the hierarchisation of states.

Beyond such processes, which are mostly connected with the genealogy of the peripheral modern state, the further evolution of this state and the roles it is to play depend on the specific circumstances of its articulation with the capitalist world-economy and the inter-state system. Such circumstances are shaped by the particular endogenous, historical, political, cultural and economic factors of each country.

A fundamental aspect of this articulation is common to all peripheral states. While in the West the modern state was formed within autonomous social formations, situated at the centre of an expanding economic system, in Latin America, Asia, Africa, the Balkans and the Middle East its emergence took place mostly within social formations that had previously been incorporated at the periphery of the world-economy and rendered dependent. The modern state in the periphery bears the marks of its late emergence, within the context of world capitalism.

The circumstances of this link-up have varied: in some cases the modern state in the periphery emerged in a dependent, but not colonised, social formation. This was the case, for example, of the modern state in Turkey, which came out of the Ottoman Empire in the first three decades of the twentieth century. In the vast majority of cases, however, the peripheral modern state is post-colonial; it emerged from casting off the yoke of colonialism. In this regard the following distinction should be made. On the one hand, there are states which have freed themselves from pre-capitalist empires: the Latin American states, which emerged from the Spanish and Portuguese Empires of the nineteenth century, the Balkan States and the Arab states of Mashrek, which came out of the Ottoman Empire, the former in the nineteenth century, the latter in the twentieth. On the other hand, there is the majority of states of the Third World, in Africa, the Caribbean, Asia and the Pacific, which have gained independence by detaching themselves from colonial empires, dominated by the industrialised capitalist states. Such differences have had important consequences in political and cultural areas, and in ways in which these modern states have achieved their institutionalisation and constituted their bureaucratic apparatus (O'Donnell, 1980).

Another differentiating factor, which takes on more importance in the formation of the peripheral modern state, is whether accession to independence took place before or after the consolidation of the capitalist world-economy, with its global division of labour and its transnationalised processes of production, exchange and accumulation (Hopkins, Wallerstein *et al.*, 1982). The peripheral modern states created between the middle of the nineteenth century and the Second World War — for example the Latin American countries such as Argentina, Brazil, Chile, Uruguay and Mexico, or the Balkan countries such as Greece, Bulgaria, Romania, Yugoslavia and Turkey — were able to exercise a certain amount of autonomy, to achieve a national capitalist accumulation, form a local bourgeoisie and strengthen the nation-state. In the countries where the formation of the modern nation-state began after the Second World War, the consolidated capitalist world-economy has, as a general rule, made this type of evolution very difficult. Hence the enormous problems encountered by numerous African and Asian states, with a few exceptions.

A particular comment would be in order on the socialist states. The industrialised socialist states of Eastern Europe, the whole organisation of which is aimed at insulating them from the capitalist world-economy, are none the less surrounded and affected by this system (Wallerstein, 1974, p. 351; Chase-Dunn, 1982). As for the socialist states belonging to the Third World, they feel even more strongly the constraints of this system. It should be noted that the existence of such socialist states, and the role they play in the inter-state system, has been a significant factor in the processes that led to independence and the creation of modern states in the Third World.

A question related to the periodisation which concerns us here, that is the anteriority of the world capitalist system to the modern states in the periphery, is: why the social formations of Latin America, the Middle East, Asia and Africa could not embark upon the development of capitalism which is inseparable from the rise of the modern state? This question is particularly relevant for the social formations that were geographically close to Western Europe. In the initial stages of the process leading to the modern world-system (the sixteenth and seventeenth centuries), the impact of Europe on its neighbouring countries was less powerful than at later periods. To explain the non-emergence of capitalism in these countries, one can therefore only partially invoke the exogenous dynamics, which later (in the eighteenth and especially the nineteenth centuries) played such a crucial role in the incorporation of non-Western social formations into the periphery of the world-system. In the context of the proto-capitalist world, then, it was mainly the endogenous dynamics which determined the transformation of oriental social formations, and which made it impossible for them to participate at first in the movement towards capitalism and the modern state. They thus lost the chance of taking their place at the centre of the system, and were subsequently incorporated in its periphery. These endogenous processes have continued to be important in the subsequent phases of the protracted incorporation of the social formation in the capitalist world-economy, but they yielded primacy to exogenous factors. A case which illustrates these processes particularly well is that of the Ottoman Empire (Kazancigil, 1981, 1984), or that of the Iranian Empire (Turner, 1981, pp. 217–33).

Modern state, society and economy in the periphery

At the centre of the modern world-system, the state, capitalism and the nation developed simultaneously, autonomously and interactively. The state has played a crucial role in the rise of capitalism. Within the framework of these organic relations of state, nation and capitalism, which generated the modern state, a division of labour between the public and the private sphere developed (Giddens, 1981, p. 212). While in the pre-capitalist formations, the groups controlling the processes of production commanded the legitimate use of violence, in capitalism this monopoly is reserved to the state (the public sphere). As a counterpart, the management of the economy, the accumulation and valorisation of capital are left to the capitalist class (the private sphere). The basis of the private sphere consists of capital/wage-labour relations, the appropriation of surplus value taking place through economic means. The use of violent means is excluded from this process, unlike the extraction of surplus by politico-administrative means, which had been the dominant method in the world-empires.

In the capitalist economy, the worker is 'free' in the sense that his relations with the employer are based on a work contract, which he is free to cancel; but then he loses his means of subsistence. He does not participate in management or decision-making. In the economic realm (the private sphere, subject to private law), he only has at his disposal the possibility of selling his labour force. In the public sphere, on the other hand, the state recognises him extensive 'political' rights, as part of his citizenship, which include the right to strike, acquired through very long struggles. The state itself depends for its subsistence on the private sphere, to which it leaves the task of capitalist accumulation. In this whole edifice, there is a certain balance between capital and labour, the political and the economic, the private and the public. This balance, achieved over the centuries in the industrialised social formations, through bourgeois revolutions and labour struggles (and which does not exclude the exploitation of labour by capital, as well as the exploitation of the peripheral societies by the metropolitan societies at the world-system level) exists only very imperfectly, and often not at all, in the peripheral social formations. A crucial aspect of this edifice is the solidity of the capitalists' position, from which they exercise their control and hegemony by non-violent means. The managers of the state pursue policies which are on the whole in conformity with the interests of the capitalist class on which they depend. But they also have their own strategy of expanding their influence and power. Here, we encounter the phenomenon which is called, in different theoretical perspectives, the autonomy of the state (Poulantzas, 1978; Skocpol, 1979) or the corporatist state (Schmitter and Lehmbruch, 1979). The strategy of state managers involves the defence of the interests of the subordinate classes (workers and peasants), so as to ensure the stability of the political system. But they cannot go beyond certain limits without risking the loss of the indispensable confidence and support of those who control the capital. Thus the rationality of the capitalist state is built on a triple relationship between the managers of the state, the capitalist class and the subordinate classes (Block, 1978, p. 33).

In the peripheral societies, there have been two cases: either an autonomous political centre has been non-existent for a long time, having been destroyed by colonisation, or it has remained outside the processes that have led to the development of the state/nation/accumulation triad. As a general rule, the modern peripheral state was formed under conditions of dependence, in the absence of a local bourgeoisie, based on autonomous capitalist accumulation. The dependent social formations situated at the periphery of the capitalist world-economy have been gradually making the transition from a status order to a class society, while a still embryonic bourgeois class was not strong enough to bear on the state.

Because the impact of the capitalist world-economy renders autonomous accumulation so difficult, the peripheral capitalist class cannot strengthen its position, so as to offset the preponderance of the state bureaucracy and exercise class domination through economic and ideological hegemony. It is forced to rely on the state and its managers for the purposes of accumulation and revalorisation of capital. To perform specific tasks related to the production processes, the capitalist class in the periphery is thus obliged to resort to the mediation of groups which draw their strength from, and owe their status to the positions they hold within the state apparatus. In this situation, quite different from the one prevailing in the metropolitan states, the peripheral state plays an active part in the production processes, and above all takes care of the control of the working class by political and often violent means, so as to lower the cost of labour.

135

Such a utilisation of the state to maximise the advantages available on the market is not altogether absent in the capitalist states at the centre, but it is most characteristic of the peripheral states, where it corresponds to the incapacity of the private sphere to appropriate surplus value by economic means. Hence the weakness of the hegemony of the capitalist class and the intervention of the peripheral state in the production processes, through violent means. The subordinate classes, which have no say in the management of the private sphere, also suffer in the private sphere from the lack of solidly established political and union rights. The structural characteristics, which are fundamental to the capitalist nation-state, thus exist very partially in the periphery.

All this provides an explanation of the state violence and the military *coups d'état* which affect a large number of Third World countries. Confronted simultaneously with the triple task of creating a modern state, a nation and a national economy, under conditions of dependence, these countries do not manage to break the vicious circle of underdevelopment, violence and authoritarianism. By one calculation, there were 108 *coups d'état* in the countries of the Third World between 1960 and 1982, which shows how widespread is the phenomenon (Sivard, 1982).

Often incapable of bringing together the conditions needed for an autonomous accumulation and for creating a legal and ethical environment conducive to economic development, which Max Weber designated as one of the principal functions of the modern state, the peripheral social formations do not possess the structural foundations of democracy. However, it would be erroneous systematically to oppose democracy and economic accumulation and maintain that the latter must necessarily precede the former (Vergopoulos, 1983). For accumulation without democracy does not create satisfactory conditions for development, but conversely, without autonomous accumulation, no durable democracy can take hold.

The periphery is dominated by the capitalist mode of production and class relations, but all the structural elements needed by the state and society to function properly are not available. The exclusion of methods of violence from the solution of class contradictions and other issues concerning production processes, as well as the accumulation and the revalorisation of capital, the control of the working class and the modification of wage rates by the private sphere through economic means, which characterise the modern capitalist state are still a long way off.

The confusion of the economic and the political, of the public and the private spheres, which is particularly evident in the political control of the production processes and of labour conflicts, characterises the peripheral state. The worker and the peasant enjoy neither economic nor political rights. In the modern state these rights are not merely a deceptive appearance to mask the domination of the capitalist class (Giddens, 1981, p. 213). Given the prevailing market order, the 'free' and contractual nature of wage labour has made it possible for the working class to organise and defend itself. As for political rights, there is no need to insist on their importance for democracy and the defence of freedoms. Within the peripheral modern states these rights are flouted; often there is neither economic development nor political democracy.

What legitimacy for the peripheral modern state?

If that is so, the question of the legitimacy of the modern state in the periphery may be raised. Its globalisation is induced by the modern world-system. It enables the peripheral social formations to take their place within the world-economy and the inter-state system. But what are its functions in the societies of the Third World? Can it be a mediation and a basis for economic development and political democracy?

The answer must be sought in the two dialectically linked functions that the peripheral modern state performs: being, simultaneously, a relay in the process of surplus extraction and accumulation by the centre at the expense of the periphery, as well as a structure of sovereignty, liberation and autonomy for peripheral societies.

The chances of economic development and democracy in the peripheral formations depend above all on the capacity of the modern state to act more as a structure of sovereignty and autonomy than a relay in the capitalist world-economy, i.e. to overcome, to its own advantage, the dialectical contradiction that opposes these functions. This contradiction is tied to the inegalitarian nature of the capitalist world-economy and may well persist for as long as the latter operates.

The legitimacy of the peripheral modern state must thus be founded on two pillars: first, its capacity to maximise political sovereignty and the economic, political, strategic and cultural autonomy of the social formation, within the world-system. This should work in favour of democratisation and respect for human rights. Indeed, quantitative research, referred to above, shows the negative impact of dependence and of a peripheral position in the world-system upon economic development and political democracy (Bollen, 1983).

In this connection, it should be noted that the controversial concept of 'the rights of peoples' is not antinomic but consistent with 'human rights', since it has been coined as the normative expression of the autonomy of peripheral social formations, without which there would be no serious hope of progress in the Third World towards the establishment of democracy and respect for human rights.

Such progress would call for the recognition of certain endogenous factors, which would provide the second pillar of the legitimacy of the peripheral modern state. Such factors are linked to the characteristics of local societies, which precede and are often foreign to the formation of the modern state in the periphery. In the countries of the Third World they form a dense and lively social fabric of institutions, social movements, brotherhoods, networks of communitarian solidarity, modes of political action and behaviour, traditions of power and specific representations and symbols (CERI, 1984). They have religious or ethnic foundations, as the case may be. The peripheral state, completely absorbed in the task of constituting itself, building up the necessary apparatus and integrating segmented communities into a nation, has ignored or often seen them only as obstacles to be overcome. Because of this, popular movements and networks of institutions and solidarities, some of which could have been transformed and mobilised into societal resources for the formation of the modern state in the periphery, have functioned as counter-powers and centres of resistance against a state that excluded them.

The state in the periphery should take these societal forces into account in order to consolidate itself and create the conditions for economic development and democratisation. It is a difficult undertaking, for a number of such popular processes do not lend themselves to the transformations required by the construction of a modern state. Compared to the latter, they appear as alternative and parallel forms for aggregating social demands and exercising power. However, if the state in the Third World is to be more than a dysfunctional, externally dependent and domestically authoritarian copy of the modern Western state, political and social innovation is called for. And the road to innovation involves taking into account such popular political and cultural processes.

The deployment of such endogenous dynamics in the formation of the peripheral modern state, in itself a fairly problematical undertaking, is made even more difficult by the capitalist world-economy and the inter-state system, which limit the autonomy of Third World countries and set up formidable obstacles to their development. The transformation of the modern world-system into a new and less inegalitarian global configuration would certainly be a necessary — though insufficient — condition for the consolidation of states and the democratisation of societies in the Third World.

Notes

1   A distinction is to be made between concepts of the state, on the one hand, and of the political regime or constitutional form, on the other. We are concerned here only with the modern state, which is found in Third World countries with political regimes as different as traditional monarchy, the one-party system, parliamentarianism and presidentialism. Other categories of political regime can be conceived, such as the civil and the military, those dominated by the state bureaucracy and those in which non-bureaucratic political institutions (such as elections or elected assemblies) play a leading role. For precise data on which typologies of political regimes can be based, see, *inter alia*, Taylor and Jodice (1983).

2   This analysis is based on Kazancigil (1984).

3   In this essay we have put aside the somewhat questionable distinction between semi-periphery and periphery. The semi-peripheral states present characteristics which differentiate them from both those at the centre and those in the periphery, making them closer sometimes to the former and sometimes to the latter. Wallerstein includes in this category states which are very different, such as Norway, Australia, China, Eastern European countries, Saudi Arabia and Israel (Wallerstein, 1979, p. 100). Our working hypothesis is that the periphery includes all of the developing countries (those of the group of 77 plus some others, like Turkey) which already makes a very heterogeneous category.

References

Alker, H.R., Jr. and Biersteker, T.J. (1984). 'The Dialectics of World Order: Notes for a Future Archaeologist of International Savoir Faire', *International Studies Quarterly*, vol. 28, no. 2, pp. 121–42.

Almond, G.A. and Powell, G.B., Jr. (1966). *Comparative Politics: A Developmental Approach*. Boston, Little, Brown and Co.

Almond, G.A. and Verba, S. (1963). *The Civic Culture: Political Attitudes in Democracy in Five Nations*. Boston, Little, Brown and Co.

Amin, S. (1976). *Unequal Development*. Sussex, Harvester Press.

Anderson, P. (1974). *Lineages of the Absolutist State*. London, NLB.

Andrews, B. (1982). 'The Political Economy of World Capitalism: Theory and Practice', *International Organization*, vol. 36, no. 1, p. 135–63.

Ashley, R.K. (1983). 'Three Modes of Economism', *International Studies Quarterly*, vol. 27, no. 4, pp. 463–96.

Badie, B. (1983). *Culture et politique*. Paris, Economica.

Badie, B. and Birnbaum, P. (1983). *The Sociology of the State*. Chicago. University of Chicago Press.

Block, F. (1978). 'Marxist Theories of the State in the Capitalist World Economy' in B.H. Kaplan (ed.), *Social Change in the Capitalist World Economy*, Beverly Hills, Sage, pp. 27–37.

Bollen, K. (1983). 'World System Position, Dependency and Democracy: The Cross-national Evidence', *American Sociological Review*, vol. 48, no. 4, pp. 468–79.

Bornschier, V. (1981). 'Dependent Industrialization in the World-Economy: Some Comments and Results Concerning a Recent Debate', *Journal of Conflict Resolution*, vol. 28, pp. 157–64.

Braudel, F. (1979). *Civilisation matérielle, économie et capitalisme*, Vol. 3: *Le temps du monde*. Paris. Armand Colin.

Cardoso, F.E. and Faletto, E. (1978). *Dependency and Development in Latin America*. Berkeley, University of California Press.

Caroll, T.G. (1984). 'Secularization and States of Modernity', *World Politics*, vol. 36, no. 3, pp 362–82.

CERI (Centre d'étude des relations internationales, Fondation nationale des sciences politiques) (1984). 'Modes populaires d'action politique', *Bulletin de liaison*, no. 3, September.

Chase-Dunn, C. (1981). 'Interstate System and Capitalist World-Economy: One Logic or Two?' in W.L. Hollist and J.N. Rosenau (eds.), *World System Structure: Continuity and Change*, Beverly Hills, Sage, pp. 30–53.

Chase-Dunn, C. (ed.) (1982). *Socialist States in the World-System*. Beverly Hills, Sage.

Chase-Dunn, C. and Sokolovsky, J. (1983). 'Interstate Systems, World-Empires and the Capitalist World-Economy: A Response to Thompson', *International Studies Quarterly*, vol. 27, no. 3, pp. 357–67.

Collins, R. (1980). 'Weber's Last Theory of Capitalism: A Systematization', *American Sociological Review*, vol. 45, no. 6, pp. 925–42.

Eberhard, W. (1965). *Conquerors and Rulers: Social Forces in Medieval China*. Leiden, Brill.

Gellner, E. (1984). 'Along the Historical Highway', *The Times Literary Supplement*, 16 March.

Giddens, A. (1981). *A Contemporary Critique of Historical Materialism*. London, Macmillan.

Grosrichard, A. (1978). *Structure du Sérail*. Paris, Seuil.

Hindess, B. and Hirst, P.Q. (eds.) (1975). *Pre-capitalist Modes of Production*. London, Routledge and Kegan Paul.

Hopkins, T.K. and Wallerstein, I. *et al.* (1982). *World-Systems Analysis: Theory and Methodology*. Beverly Hills, Sage.

Jackson, S., Russett, B., Snidal, D., and Sylvan, D. (1979). 'An Assessment of Empirical Research on Dependencia', *Latin American Research Review*, vol. 14, pp. 7–28.

Kazancigil, A. (1981). 'The Ottoman-Turkish State and Kemalism' in A. Kazancigil and E. Ozbudun (eds.), *Atatürk: Founder of a Modern State*. London, Ch. Hurst, pp. 37–56.

Kazancigil, A. (1984). 'Théories de l'Etat et l'analyse de l'Etat moderne turc', *Peuples méditerranéens*, nos. 27–8, April–September, 63-81.

Lapierre, J.W. (1977). *Vivre sans Etat? Essai sur le pouvoir politique et l'innovation sociale*. Paris, Seuil.

Lefebvre, H. (1977). *De l'Etat*, Vol. 3: *Le mode de production étatique*. Paris, 10/18.

140

Lefebvre, H. (1978). *De l'Etat*, Vol. 4: *Les contradictions de l'Etat moderne*. Paris, 10/18.

Lerner, D. (1964). *The Passing of Traditional Society*. New York, Free Press.

Marx, K. (1959). 'The 18 Brumaire of Louis Bonaparte' in L. Feuer (ed.), *Basic Writings on Politics and Philosophy*, Garden City, N.Y., Doubleday.

Marx, K. (1974). *The Grundrisse: Foundations of the Critique of Political Economy* (transl. N. Martin). New York, Random House.

McClelland, D. (1961). *The Achieving Society*. Princeton, N.J, Van Nostrand.

Modelski, G. (1978). 'The Long Cycle of Global Politics and the Nation State', *Comparative Studies in Society and History*, vol. 20, no. 2, pp. 214–35.

Moon, B. (1983). 'The Foreign Policy of the Dependent State', *International Studies Quarterly*, vol. 27, no. 3, pp. 315–40.

O'Donnell, G. (1980). 'Comparative Historical Formations of the State Apparatus and Socio-economic Change in the Third World', *International Social Science Journal*, vol. 32, no. 4. pp. 717–29.

Parsons, T. and Shils, E.A. (eds.) (1951). *Towards a General Theory of Action*. Cambridge, Mass., Harvard University Press.

Parsons, T. (1963). 'Introduction' in Max Weber, *The Sociology of Religion*, Boston, Beacon Press.

Poggi, G. (1978). *The Development of the Modern State: A Sociological Introduction*. Stanford, Stanford University Press.

Poulantzas, N. (1978). *State, Power, Socialism*. London, New Left Books.

Pye, L. and Verba, S. (1965). *Political Culture and Political Development*. Princeton, NJ, Princeton University Press.

Review (1985). Special issue on 'Quantitative Studies of the World-System', vol. VIII, no. 4, Spring.

Rostow, W.W. (1971). *Politics and the Stages of Growth*. London, Cambridge University Press.

Schmitter, P. and Lehmbruch, G. (eds.) (1979). *Trends towards Corporatist Intermediation*. London, Sage.

Sivard, R.L. (1982). *World Military and Social Expenditures 1982*. Washington, D.C., World Priorities.

Skocpol, T. (1977). 'Wallerstein's World Capitalist System: A Theoretical and Historical Critique', *American Journal of Sociology*, vol. 82, no. 5, pp. 1075–90.

Skocpol, T. (1979). *States and Social Revolutions: A Comparative Analysis of France, Russia and China*. Cambridge, Mass., Cambridge University Press.

Taylor, C.L. and Jodice, D.A. (1983). *World Handbook of Political and Social Indicators: Third Edition*. New Haven, Yale University Press.

Thompson, W.R. (ed.) (1983). *World System Analysis: Competing Perspectives*. Beverly Hills, Sage.

Tilly, C. (ed.) (1975). *The Formation of National States in Western Europe*. Princeton, Princeton University Press.

Turner, B.S. (1974). *Weber and Islam: A Critical Study*. London, Routledge and Kegan Paul.

141

Turner, B.S. (1981). *For Weber: Essays on the Sociology of Faith*. London, Routledge and Kegan Paul.

Venieris, Y.P. and Gupta, D.K. (1983). 'Sociopolitical and Economic Dimensions of Development: A Cross-section Model', *Economic Development and Cultural Change*, vol. 31, pp. 727–56.

Vergopoulos, K. (1983). 'L'Etat dans le capitalisme périphérique', *Tiers-Monde*, vol. 24, no. 93, pp. 35–52.

Wallerstein, I. (1974). *The Modern World-System: Capitalist Agriculture and the Origins of the European World-Economy in the Sixteenth Century*. New York, Academic Press.

Wallerstein, I. (1979). *The Capitalist World-Economy*. Cambridge, Cambridge University Press and Paris, Editions de la maison des sciences de l'homme.

Wallerstein, I. (1980). *The Modern World-System II: Mercantilism and the Consolidation of the European World-Economy 1600–1750*. New York, Academic Press.

Waltz, K.N. (1979). *Theory of International Politics*. Reading, Mass., Addison-Wesley.

Weber, M. (1951). *The Religion of China* (transl. H.H. Gerth). New York, Free Press.

Weber, M. (1968). *Economy and Society* (ed. G. Roth and C. Wittich), Vol. 2. Berkeley, University of California Press.

Zolberg, A.R. (1981). 'The Origins of the Modern World-System: A Missing Link', *World Politics*, vol. 33, no. 2, pp. 253-81.

Part II
Structures and Functions

7 The states in the institutional vortex of the capitalist world-economy

Immanuel Wallerstein

Words can be the enemy of understanding and analysis. We seek to capture a moving reality in our terminology. We thereby tend to forget that the reality changes as we encapsulate it, and by virtue of that fact. And we are even more likely to forget that others freeze reality in different ways, using however the very same words to do it. And still we cannot speak without words; indeed we cannot think without words.

Where then do we find the *via media*, the working compromise, the operational expression of a dialectical methodology? It seems to me it is most likely to be found by conceiving of provisional long-term, large-scale wholes within which concepts have meanings. These wholes must have some claim to relative space-time autonomy and integrity. They must be long enough and large enough to enable us to escape the Scylla of conceptual nominalism, but short enough and small enough to enable us to escape the Charybdis of ahistorical, universalising abstraction. I would call such wholes 'historical systems' — a name which captures their two essential qualities. It is a whole which is integrated, that is, composed of interrelated parts, therefore in some sense systematic and with comprehensible patterns. It is a system which has a history, that is, it has a genesis, an historical development, a close (a destruction, a disintegration, a transformation, an *Aufhebung*).

I contrast this concept of 'historical system' with that of the more usual term of 'society' (or of 'social formation', which I believe is used more or less synonymously). Of course, one may use the term 'society' in the same sense I am using 'historical system', and then the issue is simply the choice of formal symbol. But in fact the standard use of 'society' is one which is applied indiscriminately to refer to modern states (and quasi-states), to ancient empires, to supposedly autonomous 'tribes', and to all manner of other *political* (or cultural-aspiring-to-be-political) structures. And this lumping together presumes what is to be demonstrated — that the political dimension is the one that unifies and delineates social action.

If boundaries drawn in every conceivable way — integrated production processes, exchange patterns, political jurisdiction, cultural coherence, ecology — were in fact always (or even usually) synonymous (or even highly overlapping), there would be little problem. But, as a matter of empirical fact, taking the last 10 000 years of human history, this is not all the case. We must therefore choose among alternate criteria of defining our arenas of social action, our units of analysis. One can debate this in terms of philosophical a priori statements, and if so my own bias is a materialist one. But one can also approach this heuristically: which criterion will account for the largest percentage of social action, in the sense that changing its parameters will most immediately and most profoundly affect the operation of other parts of the whole?

I believe one can argue the case for integrated production processes as constituting this heuristic criterion, and I shall use it to draw the boundaries which circumscribe a concrete 'historical system', by which I mean an empirical set of such production processes integrated according to some particular set of rules, the human agents of which interact in some 'organic' way, such that changes in the functions of any group or changes in the boundaries of the historical system must follow certain rules if the entity's survival is not to be threatened. This is what we mean by such other terms as a social economy, or a specific social division of labour. To suggest that a historical system is organic is not to suggest that it is a frictionless machine. Quite the contrary: historical systems are beset by contradictions, and contain within them the seeds of processes that eventually destroy the system. But this, too, is very consonant with the 'organic' metaphor.

This is a long preface to a coherent analysis of the role of states in the modern world. I think much of our collective discussion has been a prisoner of the word 'state', which we have used transhistorically to mean any political structure which had some authority network (a leading person or group or groups, with intermediate cadres enforcing the will of this leading entity). Not only do we assume that what we are designating as 'states' in the twentieth century are in the same universe of discourse as what we designate as 'states' in, say, the tenth century, but even more fantastically, we frequently attempt to draw lines of historical continuity between two such 'states' — of the same name, or found in the same general location in terms of longitude and latitude — said to be continuous because scholars can argue affinities of the languages that are spoken, or the cosmologies that are professed, or the genes that are pooled.

The capitalist world-economy constitutes one such historical system. It came into existence, in my view, in Europe in the sixteenth century. The capitalist world-economy is a system based on the drive to accumulate capital, the political conditioning of price levels (of capital, commodities and labour), and the steady polarisation of classes and regions (core/periphery) over time. This system has developed and expanded to englobe the whole earth in the subsequent centuries. It has today reached a point where, as a result of its contradictory developments, the system is a long crisis.[1]

The development of the capitalist world-economy has involved the creation of all the major institutions of the modern world: classes, ethnic/national groups, households — and the 'states'. All of these structures postdate, not antedate, capitalism; all are consequence, not cause. Furthermore, these various institutions, in fact, create each other. Classes, ethnic/national groups, and households are defined by the state, through the state, in relation to the state, and in turn create the state, shape the state, and transform the state. It is a structured maelstrom of constant movement, whose parameters are measurable through the repetitive regularities, while the detailed constellations are always unique.

What does it mean to say that a state comes into existence? Within a capitalist world-economy, the state is an institution whose existence is defined by its relation to other 'states'. Its boundaries are more or less clearly defined. Its degree of juridical sovereignty ranges from total to nil. Its real power to control the flows of capital, commodities, and labour across its frontiers is greater or less. The real ability of the central authorities to enforce decisions on groups operating within state frontiers is greater or less. The ability of the state authorities to impose their will in zones outside state frontiers is greater or less.

Various groups located inside, outside, and across any given state's frontiers are constantly seeking to increase, maintain, or decrease the 'power' of the state, in all the ways referred to above. These groups are seeking to change these power constellations because of some sense that such changes will improve the particular group's ability to profit, directly or indirectly, from the operations of the world market. The state is the most convenient institutional intermediary in the establishment of market constraints (quasi-monopolies, in the broadest sense of the term) in favour of particular groups.

147

The historical development of the capitalist world-economy is that, beginning with relatively amorphous entities, more and more 'states' operating within the inter-state system have been created. Their boundaries and the definitions of their formal rights have been defined with increasing clarity (culminating in the contemporary United Nations structure of international law). The modalities and limits of group pressures in state structures have also been increasingly defined (in the sense both of the legal limits placed on such pressures, and of the rational organisation by groups to transcend these limits). None the less, despite what might be called the 'honing' of this institutional network, it is probably safe to say that the relative power continuum of stronger and weaker states has remained relatively unchanged over 400-odd years. That is not to say that the same 'states' have remained 'strong' and 'weak'. Rather, there has been at all moments a power hierarchy of such states, but also at no moment has there been any one state whose hegemony was totally unchallenged (although relative hegemony has occurred for limited periods).

Various objections have been made to such a view of the modern state, its genesis and its mode of functioning. There are four criticisms which seem to be the most frequent and worthy of discussion.

First, it is argued that this view is too instrumental a view of the state, that it makes the states into a mere conscious instrument of acting groups with no life and integrity of their own, with no base of social support in and for themselves.

It seems to me this counter-argument is based on a confusion about social institutions in general. Once created, all social institutions, including the states, have lives of their own in the sense that many different groups will use them, support them, exploit them for various (and even contradictory) motives. Furthermore, institutions large and structured enough to have permanent staff thereby generate a group of persons — the bureaucracies of these institutions — who have a direct socio-economic stake in the persistence and flourishing of the institution as such, quite independent of the ideological premises on which the institution was created and the interests of the major social forces that sustain it.

None the less, the issue is not who has some say in the ongoing decisions of a state machinery but who has decisive or critical say, and what are the key issues that are fought about in terms of state policy. We believe that these key issues are: (a) the rules governing the social relations of production, which critically affect the allocation of surplus value; and (b) the rules governing the flow within and across frontiers of the factors of production — capital, commodities and labour — which critically affect the price structures of markets. If one changes the allocation of surplus value and the price structures of markets, one is changing the relative competitivity of particular producers, and therefore their profit levels.

It is the states that makes these rules, and it is primarily the states that intervene in the process of other (weaker) states when the latter attempt to make the rules as they prefer them.

The second objection to this mode of analysis is that it ignores the reality of traditional continuities, as ensconced in the operative consciousness of groups. Such consciousnesses do indeed exist and are very powerful, but are the consciousnesses themselves continuous? I think not, and believe the merest glance at the empirical reality will confirm that. The history of nationalisms, which are one of the salient forms of such consciousnesses, shows that everywhere that nationalist movements emerge, they create consciousness, they revive (even partially invent) languages, they coin names and emphasise customary practices that come to distinguish their group from other groups. They do this in the name of what is claimed to have always been there, but frequently (if not usually) they must stretch the interpretation of the historical evidence in ways that disinterested observers would consider partisan. This is true not only of the so-called 'new' nations of the twentieth century[2] but of the 'old' nations as well.[3]

It is also clear that the successive ideological statements about a given name — what it encompasses, what constitutes its 'tradition' — are discontinuous and different. Each successive version can be explained in terms of the politics of its time, but the fact that these versions vary so widely is itself a piece of evidence against taking the assertion of continuity as more than a claim of an interested group. It surely is shifting sand on which to base an analysis of the political functioning of states.

The third argument against this form of analysis is that it is said to ignore the underlying centrality of the class struggle, which is implicitly asserted to exist within some fixed entity called a society or a social formation, and which in turn accounts for the structure of the state.

If, however, classes is the term we use for groups deriving from positions in relation to the mode of production, then it is to the realities of the set of integrated production processes that we must look to determine who constitute our classes. The boundaries of these integrated production processes are in fact, of course, far wider than the individual states, and even subsets of production processes do not correlate very often with state boundaries. There is consequently no a priori reason to assume that classes are in some objective sense circumscribed by state boundaries.

Now, it may fairly be argued that class consciousnesses have tended historically to be national in form. This is so, for good reasons we shall discuss below. But the fact that this is so is no evidence that the analytic perception is correct. On the contrary, this fact of the national form of consciousness for trans-state classes becomes itself a major explicandum of the modern world.

Finally, it is said that this mode of analysis ignores the fact that the wealthiest states are not the strongest states, but tend indeed to be relatively weak. But this is to misperceive what constitutes the strength of state machineries. It is once again to take ideology for analytic reality.

Some state machineries preach the line of a strong state. They seek to limit opposition; they seek to impose decisions on internal groups; they are bellicose *vis-à-vis* external groups. But what is important is the success of the assertion of power, not its loudness. Oppositions only need to be suppressed where they seriously exist. States that encompass relatively more homogeneous strata (because of the unevenness of allocation of class forces in the world-economy) may achieve via consensus what others strive (and perhaps fail) to achieve via the iron hand. Entrepreneurs who are economically strong in the market do not need state assistance to create monopoly privileges, though they may need state aid to oppose the creation by others, in other states, of monopoly privileges which would hurt these market-strong entrepreneurs.

The states are thus, we are arguing, created institutions reflecting the needs of class forces operating in the world-economy. They are not however created in a void, but within the framework of an inter-state system. This inter-state system is, in fact, the framework within which the states are defined. It is the fact that the states of the capitalist world-economy exist within the framework of an inter-state system that is the *differentia specifica* of the modern state, distinguishing it from other bureaucratic polities. This inter-state system constitutes a set of constraints which limit the abilities of individual state machineries, even the strongest among them, to make decisions. The ideology of this system is sovereign equality, but the states are in fact neither sovereign nor equal. In particular, the states impose on each other — not only the strong on the weak, but the strong on the strong — limitations on their modes of political (and therefore military) behaviour, and even more strikingly limitations on their abilities to affect the law of value underlying capitalism. We are so used to observing all the things states do that constitute a defiance of other states that we do not stop to recognise how few these things are, rather than how many. We are so used to thinking of the inter-state system as verging on anarchy that we fail to appreciate how rule-ridden it is. Of course, the 'rules' are broken all the time, but we should look at the consequences — the mechanisms that come into play to force changes in the policies of the offending states. Again, we should look less at the obvious arena of political behaviour, and more at the less observed arena of economic behaviour. The story of states with communist parties in power in the twentieth-century inter-state system is striking evidence of the efficacities of such pressures.

The production processes of the capitalist world-economy are built on a central relationship or antinomy: that of capital and labour. The ongoing operations of the system have the effect of increasingly circumscribing individuals (or rather households), forcing them to participate in the work process in one capacity or the other, as contributors of surplus value or as receivers.

The states have played a central role in the polarisation of the population into those living off appropriated surplus, the bourgeoisie, and those whose surplus value is appropriated from them, the proletariat. For one thing, the states created the legal mechanisms which not merely permitted or even facilitated the appropriation of surplus value, but protected the results of the appropriation by enacting property rights. They created institutions which ensured the socialisation of children into the appropriate roles.

As the classes came into objective existence, in relation to each other, they sought to alter (or to maintain) the unequal bargaining power between them. To do this, they had to create appropriate institutions to affect state decisions, which largely turned out over time to be institutions created within the boundaries of the state, adding thereby to the world-wide definiteness of state structures.

This has led to deep ambivalences in their self-perception and consequently contradictory political behaviour. Both the bourgeoisie and the proletariat are classes formed in a world-economy, and when we speak of objective class position, it is necessarily classes of this world-economy to which we refer. As, however, the bourgeoisie was first to become class-conscious and the proletariat only later, both classes found disadvantages as well as advantages to defining themselves as world classes.

The bourgeoisie, in pursuit of its class interest, the maximisation of profit in order to accumulate capital, sought to engage in its economic activities as it saw fit without constraints on geographic location or political considerations. Thus, for example, in the sixteenth or seventeenth centuries, it was frequent for Dutch, English or French entrepreneurs to 'trade with the enemy' in wartime, even in armaments. And it was frequent for entrepreneurs to change place of domicile and citizenship in pursuit of optimising gain. The bourgeoisie then (as now) reflected this self-perception in tendencies towards a 'world' cultural style — in consumption, in language, etc. However, it was also true then, and now, that, however much the bourgeoisie chafed under limitations placed by particular state authorities for particular reasons at one or another moment, the bourgeoisies also needed to utilise state machineries to strengthen their position in the market *vis-à-vis* competitors and to protect them *vis-à-vis* the working classes. And this meant that the many fractions of the world bourgeoisie had an interest in defining themselves as 'national' bourgeoisies.

The same pattern held for the proletariat. On the one hand, as it became class-conscious, it recognised that a prime organisational objective has to be the unity of proletarians in their struggle. It is no accident that the *Communist Manifesto* proclaimed: 'Workers of the world, unite!' It was clear that precisely the fact that the bourgeoisie operated in the arena of a world-economy, and could (and would) transfer sites of production whenever it was to its advantage, meant that proletarian unity, if it were to be truly efficacious, could only be at the world level. And yet we know that world proletarian unity has never really been efficacious (most damatically in the failure of the Second International to maintain an anti-nationalist stance during the First World War). This is so for a very simple reason. The mechanisms most readily available to improve the relative conditions of segments of the working classes are the state machineries, and the political organisations of the proletariat has almost always taken the form of state-based organisations. Furthermore, this tendency has been reinforced, not weakened, by whatever successes these organisations have had in attaining partial or total state power.

We arrive thus at a curious anomaly: both the bourgeoisie and the proletariat express their consciousness at a level which does not reflect their objective economic role. Their interests are a function of the operations of a world-economy, and they seek to enhance their interests by affecting individual state machineries, which in fact have only limited power (albeit real power, none the less) to affect the operations of this world-economy.

It is this anomaly that constantly presses bourgeoisies and proletariats to define their interests in status-group terms. The most efficacious status group in the modern world is the nation, since the nation lays claim to the moral right to control a particular state structure. To the extent that a nation is not a state, we find the potential for a nationalist movement to arise and flourish. Of course, there is no essence that is a nation and that occasionally breeds a nationalist movement. Quite the contrary. It is a nationalist movement that creates an entity called a nation, or seeks to create it. Under the multiple circumstances in which nationalism is not available to serve class interests, status-group solidarities may crystallise around substitute poles: religion, race, language, or other particular cultural patterns.

Status-group solidarities remove the anomaly of national class organisation or consciousness from the forefront of visibility and hence relax the strains inherent in contradictory structures. But, of course, they may also obfuscate the class struggle. To the extent that particular ethnic consciousnesses therefore lead to consequences which key groups find intolerable, we see re-emergence of overt class organisations or, if this creates too much strain, of redefined status-group solidarities (drawing the boundaries differently). That particular segments of the world bourgeoisie or world proletariat might flit from, say, Pan-Turkic to Pan-Islamic to national to class-based movements over a period of decades reflects not the inconsistency of the struggle but the difficulties of navigating a course that can bridge the antinomy: objective classes of the world-economy/subjective classes of a state structure.

Finally the atoms of the classes (and of the status groups), the income-pooling households, are shaped and constantly reshaped not only by the objective economic pressures of the ongoing dynamic of the world-economy but they also are regularly and deliberately manipulated by the states that seek to determine (to alter) their boundaries in terms of the needs of the labour market, as well as to determine the flows and forms of income that may in fact be pooled. The households in turn may assert their own solidarities and priorities and resist the pressures, less effectively by passive means, more effectively, when possible, by creating the class and status-group solidarities we have just mentioned.

All these institutions together — the states, the classes, the ethnic/national/status groups, the households — form an institutional vortex which is both the product and the moral life of the capitalist world-economy. Far from being primordial and pre-existing essences, they are dependent and coterminous existences. Far from being segregated and separable, they are indissociably intertwined in complex and contradictory ways. Far from one determining the other, they are in a sense avatars of each other.

Notes

1   I have developed these theses at length in I. Wallerstein, *The Modern World-System*, New York, Academic Press, 1974, and I. Wallerstein, *The Capitalist World-Economy*, Cambridge, Cambridge University Press, 1979.

2   In 1956, Thomas Hodgkin wrote in a 'Letter' to Saburi Biobaku, *Odù*, no. 4, 1957, p. 42: 'I was struck by your statement that the use of the term "Yoruba" to refer to the whole range of peoples who would nowadays describe themselves as Yoruba (as contrasted with the Oyo

peoples simply) was due largely to the influence of the Anglican Mission at Abeokuta, and its work in evolving a standard "Yoruba" language, based on Oyo speech. This seems to me an extremely interesting example of the way in which Western influences have helped to stimulate a new kind of national sentiment. Everyone recognizes that the notion of "being a Nigerian" is a new kind of conception. But it would seem that the notion of "being a Yoruba" is not very much older. I take it from what you say that there is no evidence that those who owed allegiance to the kingdom of Oyo — or to the earlier State system based upon Ife? — used any common name to describe themselves, although it is possible that they may have done so?'

3   George Bernard Shaw has the nobleman in *Saint Joan* exclaim: 'A Frenchman! Where did you pick up that expression? Are these Burgundians and Bretons and Picards and Gascons beginning to call themselves Frenchmen, just as our fellows are beginning to call themselves Englishmen? They actually talk of France and England as their countries. Theirs, if you please! What is to become of me and you if that way of thinking comes into fashion?'

8 The functions of the modern state: in search of a theory

Philip Resnick

In the late 1960s, a British political scientist observed: 'The concept of state is not much in vogue in the social sciences right now'.[1] Less true for continental Europe where concepts such as *état* and *Staat* have roots going back over centuries than for the English-speaking world where the term 'state' has seldom enjoyed a good press, Nettl's point was none the less well taken. 1968 — the high point of student protests and challenges to established state systems east and west — was not a propitious time for theorists of the state. Two decades later, with state power more firmly in the saddle than ever before, with the economic and non-economic functions of the state experiencing continuous enlargement and refinement, writings on state power pour from the presses in English, French, German, Italian and a score of other languages.

Our purpose is to try to make sense of some of the ever growing literature on the state. As such, its focus will be primarily thematic and descriptive, leaving the much thornier question of developing an actual theory of the state — on the assumption such a quest is more than a twentieth-century version of the search for the Holy Grail — in abeyance. Much can be gained from critically scrutinising efforts that have been made in recent years. For in a sense the problem of the state is at the very heart of the twentieth century, of ideologies ranging from Marxism through Fascism,[2] of political systems in every corner of the globe.

To be sure, the problem of the state is the current expression of a

155

much older problem — the nature of political power. And there have been forms of power in earlier societies, so anthropologists tell us, in which the state as such does not seem to have existed.[3] This helps explain why classical writers were preoccupied with uncovering the *origins* of the state, whether through contract theories (Hobbes, Locke and Rousseau), conquest theories (Herbert Spencer) or class theories (Marx and Engels).

Another aspect of the definitional problem has been the difficulty of disentangling the concept of state from that of society. For in so far as power is dispersed through various levels of complex societies, boundary problems of the first order arise for any would-be theorist of the state. Hence the attempts of judicial writers going back to Bodin to ground the discussion of the state in terms of sovereignty, the attempt of sociological theorists like Weber to define the state in terms of 'a legitimate monopoly of force', and the attempt of twentieth-century Marxist theorists from Gramsci to Althusser to extend the concept of state to elements of the civil society.[4]

These persistent questions of genesis and definition are not our focus. For the most interesting question posed by the twentieth-century literature on the state has less to do with its abstractly conceived nature, than with its actual *functions* in different societies. It is here that debate is joined among Marxists and non-Marxists, economic historians, sociologists and political theorists. It is through this debate that we can perhaps come to formulate better the question of the nature of the state.

The economic function

What then are the principal functions of the modern state and to what extent have they taken on a special importance in the twentieth century?

Let us begin with the *economic*, which probably is the most important, and certainly the one which has attracted the greatest attention. Contrary to what writers like Poulantzas contend,[5] there is an important non-Marxist literature on this subject going back to the late nineteenth century when Adolph Wagner, the German conservative political economist, coined his famous law of increasing state expenditure relative to community output.[6] For Wagner, the development of capitalism brought with it certain new needs which could only be met by the state. For example, the national and international division of labour, more complicated commercial and legal regulations, entailed a more important role for the police, army, navy, foreign service and judiciary (*Rechts- und Machtfunktion*). As civilisation developed, there was also a tendency for the state to become responsible for the 'higher and finer needs' of society, even while accepting greater responsibility for its economically weaker members (*Kultur and Wohlfahrtsstaat*). Wagner's organicist sympathies, not unrelated, one suspects, to the strain of romantic anti-capitalism that pervaded German universities in the decades prior to World War I,[7] also made him sceptical of the ability of joint-stock companies to handle large amounts of capital effectively or to develop new technical processes, further reinforcing the trend towards increased state expenditure.

While Wagner's law has been subjected to criticism in the literature of public finance, it has helped spark some of the most important empirical research into twentieth-century state expenditure. More importantly still, its broad predictive tendency has overall been sustained — i.e. state expenditure as a percentage of Gross National Product has shown a secular tendency to increase in both relative and absolute terms in this century, though the curve has been neither as continuous nor the causes nearly as simple as Wagner might have believed.

The most important empirical studies which make reference to Wagner's law include those of Fabricant, Peacock and Wiseman, Andic and Veverka, Bird and André, Delorme and Terny.[8] The Fabricant study, for example, documents the increase in total American capital assets held by government from 7 per cent in 1900 to 20 per cent by 1949 and the parallel increase in the government labour force from 1 million to 7 million, stressing the increased importance of public welfare, health and public works, alongside defence, as the chief factors in state growth.

The Peacock and Wiseman study documents the growth in government expenditure in England as a percentage of GNP from 9 per cent in 1890 to 37 per cent by 1955, and tries to develop a more sophisticated explanation for leaps in patterns of state spending, linked to what it sees as the inspection, displacement and concentration effects of war. In a nutshell, it argues that situations like war provide a setting for leaps forward in state expenditure, making people more aware of injustices in social conditions, displacing public expenditures to new levels, and concentrating power at the centre where it can later be brought to bear more effectively on these problems.

Peacock and Wiseman's conceptualisation was in turn influenced by Titmuss's study of the levelling effects of war:

The aims and content of social policy, both in peace and war, are thus determined — at least to a substantial extent — by how far the cooperation of the masses is essential to the successful prosecution of war. If this cooperation is thought to be essential, then inequalities must be reduced and the pyramid of social stratification must be flattened.[9]

It was also indirectly influenced, though its authors do not sufficiently acknowledge it, by Pitrim Sorokin's apocalyptical view of the role of calamities in history.[10]

For Sorokin, the result of a major calamity such as war, famine, plague or revolution is to concentrate both the individual mind and the attention of society on that calamity to the exclusion of everything else. Old loyalties and social ties are loosened while

> a favorable ground [is laid] for the swift transformation of social institutions . . . the main uniform effects of calamities upon the political and social structure of society is an expansion of governmental regulation, regimentation and control of social relationships and a decrease in the regulation and management of social relationships by individuals and private groups.[11]

The *Zwangsökonomie* of World War I, the development of collectivistic economic policies in post-revolutionary Russia, the turn to a totalitarian economy among all belligerents in World War II are modern versions of a much more ancient phenomenon. From the war and famine economy of ancient Egypt to the increase in governmental functions in Republican and Imperial Rome, from the role of medieval communes and states in periods of plague or famine down to today, government intervention has been the direct result of calamity.

War and depression have certainly been major contributors to increased state expenditure in this century. Andic and Veverka's study on Germany, for example, underlines the importance of World War I and the economic crisis of the late 1920s to the growth of the public sector. 'It was the virtual breakdown of the economic system based on private initiative and national circulation which explains the continuation of the displacement after the end of hostilities.'[12] A study on France also shows a major leap upwards in state expenditures as a result of World War I and again in the 1930s.[13] And the same would probably hold good for Canada and the United States.

Yet important as all this is, do we yet have an adequate explanation for the economic functions of the state? How does one account for the continuing growth in state expenditures in Western countries through much of the post-World War II period, not a period of calamity, so that by the middle 1970s OECD data could show most Western societies with state expenditures ranging from 30–50 per cent of GNP?[14] Are there not perhaps other structural explanations that must be brought to the fore?

It is here that Marxist theory has attempted to fill the void. While Marx never completed his projected volume on the state, while Luxemburg and Lenin in their economic writings focused more on the international process of accumulation than on the domestic economic activities of the state, others paid greater attention to the latter.

On the Marxist-Leninist side, the Third International, influenced by Bukharin, developed the germs of a theory dubbed 'state monopoly capitalism', which essentially saw the capitalist state as acting at the behest of the giant monopolies, organising and integrating the process of capital accumulation on their behalf, and repressing the working class and traditional democratic liberties, as under fascism. Since World War II, this theory, with some modifications, has become the official doctrine of Soviet, the GDR, French and other communist parties in analysing contemporary capitalism. While some, such as the French, have shown greater sophistication than others,[15] the theory of state monopoly capitalism tends to what has been dubbed an instrumentalist theory of state action. The state is seen as acting pretty well in the interests of the large monopolies with only minor concessions here and there to other classes, and having little autonomy, hence French communist analysis in the early 1960s of de Gaulle and the Fifth Republic as 'the agents of monopoly capital'.[16]

A much more interesting formulation, I would agree, can be traced back to the writings of Rudolf Hilferding, the Austrian theoretician of finance capital and 'organised capitalism'. Already in his oft-cited but seldom read *Finance Capital* of 1909, he had underlined the interests of large-scale finance in a less competitive form of capitalism:

> What finance capital wants is not liberty but domination. It has no sympathy for the independence of the individual capitalist . . . It abhors the anarchy of competition and demands organization in order to be able to engage in the struggle for competition at an ever-higher level. To achieve this, it requires the state.[17]

In a 1915 article in the Austrian socialist newspaper *Der Kampf*, he perceived the movement sparked by the war, from an economy of individual entrepreneurs opposed to state control to a highly concentrated, bureaucratically organised economy, entailing much state intervention.[18] And to be sure, such ideas were being voiced by von Moellendorf and Rathenau, the economic tsars of wartime Germany.[19]

Some ten years after the war, Hilferding, in an address to the 1927

Kiel Congress of the German SPD, analysed what he considered to be a more permanent trend in twentieth-century capitalism:

> Finance capital has a tendency to temper the anarchy of production and bears the seeds of a transformation of an anarchist-capitalist into an organized capitalist economic order . . . The formidable strengthening of the state's power works in the same direction. Instead of the victory of socialism, we see the possibility of a society taking shape organized, to be sure, but along authoritarian (*herrschaftlich*) and non-democratic economic lines.[20]

To Hilferding, capitalism had by the mid-1920s become stabilised, the proletariat tamed, while the capitalist economy had gone from the road of competition to monopoly, with ever greater emphasis placed upon organisation and planning. While Hilferding was clearly wrong in emphasising the stability of the system, his analysis of organised capitalism did draw attention to the decisive role the state had come to play by the mid-1920s in the operation of European capitalist economies. A number of contemporary historians have drawn on his work and one can find in his term 'organized capitalism' the germs of what other writers today refer to as 'the drift to corporatism'.

The term 'organized capitalism', once shorn of its subordination to finance capitalism, has certain advantages over 'state monopoly capitalism'. It is a less ideologically charged term, and more importantly, does not ignore the relative autonomy of the state apparatus from monopoly capital. What is common to both terms, as a German historian suggests, are the following factors: the tendency to centralisation and concentration of production and capital, a fusion of financial and industrial capital, changes in productive forces sparked by the growth of new industries, the increased role of knowledge and science, the organisation of class conflict, the role of imperialism, and the increased linking of politics with economics.[21]

It also has certain advantages over the term 'corporatism', which experienced a certain vogue in Western Europe and North America from the mid-1970s on. Not only does the term 'corporatism' involve a rather dubious throw-back to the fascist economies of the interwar years, but it lacks precision. It has been used by some writers to describe 'Japan Inc.', by others to describe European social democracy at its zenith, by still others with reference to more peripheral capitalist economies from Southern Europe to Latin America, where military regimes have often prevailed.[22] We can save ourselves unnecessary anguish by recognising the more organised and statist quality of capitalism in our time, without having to dub the phenomenon corporatist.

160

At the heart of current Marxist and neo-Marxist discussion of the state, then, lies the attempt to relate its increased economic role to transformations in the nature of contemporary capitalism. Of course, non Marxist writers have recognized some of this as well (Shonfield, Galbraith, not to mention Keynes). But in explaining the state's new role, the Marxist school places emphasis on structural changes in the capitalist mode of production, on the ever greater need for organisation and centralisation of the process of capitalist accumulation.

Within the contemporary Marxist camp, there are major differences of emphasis. Some, a bit foolishly, try to read an economic theory of the state back into *Capital*.[23] Others explain increased state expenditures as a form of devalorisation of capital,[24] still others as a means of arresting the falling rate of profit.[25] Some would emphasise the role of military expenditures,[26] while others, more accurately in my view, stress the increased importance of social spending in most Western economies, which O'Connor rather narrowly terms the 'legitimation function'.[27] What contemporary Marxist theorists share is a view of the state as a sort of 'overall capitalist', not without contradictions, but it entails greater planning, state expenditure and organisation of the economy than in earlier periods of capitalism.

Overall, I would hold the Marxist emphasis on changes in the capitalist mode of production to be most useful in accounting for the state's increased *economic* function. Yet, as I shall shortly argue, when we examine the non-economic functions of the state, Marxism proves much less adequate. One of the ironies of the increased role of the state under 'organised capitalism' is that the much-vaunted distinction between base and superstructure formulated by Marx has broken down (on the assumption it was ever entirely accurate). The state becomes a good deal more than 'the executive committee of the whole of the executive class', coming to influence and shape human behaviour in ways more reminiscent of Sophocles than Marx:

Crafty inventions, subtle beyond believing, now onto evil bring them, now onto good. (Antigone)

The political function

From the economic, let us turn to a more traditional function associated with the state, namely *sovereignty*. Not surprisingly, jurists tend to pay it the greatest attention. For example, the influential early twentieth-century French jurist, Carré de Malberg, defined the state in the following terms: 'A human community, established on a territory of their own and possessing a higher power of command and

161

coercion.'[28] And a contemporary Hungarian jurist, reflecting the ideology of 'real socialism' if not the reality of certain practices, writes in his turn: 'Sovereignty is nothing else but independence of state power from all other powers both within and without the borders of the state . . . The socialist state is not subordinate to another state, to the power of either a capitalist or socialist state.'[29]

Sociological and political writers have not been far behind. Werner Sombart, in his classical study of capitalism, placed great emphasis on the external arena in explaining the state's increased power. Economic competition, military threats, imperialist rivalries had all strengthened the state system of Europe, and with it the importance of sovereignty.[30] For Charles Eisenmann, 'the international function' is one of the three main functions of a modern state,[31] while Bertrand de Jouvenal points to the development of a popular conception of sovereignty, from the eighteenth century on, authorising the extension of state power:

> As long as we represent sovereignty concretely in a single man, since we know that all men are fallible, we cannot admit an unlimited sovereignty. But, on the other hand, we cannot conceive of limits to the sovereignty which is that of all. It would be unfair to say that the idea of popular sovereignty dictates a very great governmental power, but it would be fair to say that it authorizes it.[32]

For many Marxist writers, sovereignty has been a less certain value. While the twentieth century world is clearly one of nations and states, which Marxism has pragmatically come to terms with, its original impulse was strongly internationalist. Moreover, its emphasis on the underlying class nature of institutions such as the state, its tendency to regard foreign and military policy, along with domestic policy, as the emanation of a ruling class in capitalist society, the absolutist origins of the very term 'sovereignty', have considerably reduced its attractions to Marxist writers, especially in the West. Not surprisingly, then, contemporary metropolitan Marxist treatments of the state, for example those of Miliband, O'Connor, Poulantzas, give little or no place to sovereignty in their discussion of state functions.

Elements of sovereignty have, however, been reintroduced into Marxism through Third World literature. The Marxist theory of imperialism emphasises the domination of certain powerful states over others within the international system and the impediment this constitutes to the sovereignty of smaller powers. Concepts of national liberation and self-determination are twentieth-century forms of sovereignty much influenced by Marxist thought. In a related way, distinctions between national and 'comprador' bourgeoisies or metro-politan and peripheral capitalism, so fashionable today, are attempts to come to grips with the implications of the international system for ostensibly sovereign states. The work of Samir Amin, André Gunder Frank and Immanuel Wallerstein comes rapidly to mind here, helping to elucidate the connection between sovereignty, at least in its economic aspects, and accumulation at the world level. Some of this had penetrated into Western Marxism, though arguably, not enough.

There is another aspect to the discussion of sovereignty — the claim of the state to represent some absolute or ultimate power against its own citizenry. Recent challenges to the modern state have stemmed from this, whether on the part of student radicals, militant workers, ecologists, 'autonomists', urban guerrillas and other practitioners of extra-parliamentary activity in the West, or on the part of workers and dissidents from party rule in the East. What the Pierre Elliott Trudeau of October 1970, the Helmut Schmidt of the autumn of 1977, the de Gaulle of 30 May 1968, or the party leaders of the Soviet Union, Poland and Czechoslovakia faced with dissidents have in common is a belief in the higher interests of the state they rule against some ostensibly small and disloyal group of citizens. The wholesale scuttling of civil liberties in various countries around the globe, the limits to dissent even in so-called liberal societies in times of trouble, the role of police, intelligence services and military establishments attest to the continuing importance of sovereignty as the doctrine of governors against governed and as the justification for the state's repression of threats internal, no less than external, to its authority. Marxism has usually recognised this where capitalist societies are concerned, but it is no less true of socialist regimes.

This comparative neglect of sovereignty by Western Marxists points to a more fundamental deficiency in Marxist thought. It is a failure to recognise that there may be a uniquely political dimension to social life (a perception, after all, that goes back at least to Aristotle), and that the origin of the political division of labour in society as between rulers and ruled is not in some mechanical or determinist sense coterminous with the economic division of labour. When Poulantzas tells us that '[t]he state is the strategic centre of organization of the dominant class in its relations with dominated classes. It is the place and centre for the exercise of power, but lacks any power in its own right',[33] he is echoing the reductionist tendency that creeps into some of Marx's own writings on the state[34] and that certainly dogs most twentieth-century Marxist writers. It underlines an inability to recognise the autonomy of the political — not merely some relative autonomy in which the economic instance always wins through in the end — but one which itself often determines the final outcome.

Is there a tendency for the state to be an instrument of domination over the citizenry, regardless of what institutional safeguards may or may not be built into a system? Is the state, as the examples of Hitler, Stalin, Idi Amim, Pinochet and countless others suggest, a demonic power in no ways explicable in purely economic or material terms? Should we not in Hobbesian-Freudian fashion speak of a *libido dominandi*, at least where rulers are concerned?[35]

For certain theorists, the answer is crystal clear. Carl Schmitt, for example, student of Max Weber and Nazi supporter in the 1930s, made the distinction between enemy and friend the very essence of politics.[36] A theory of the state could only be grounded in a view of human nature as corrupt, imperfect, trying to arrogate power onto itself and designating its rivals as the foe. Whatever classical liberalism, with its religion of progress, harmony and minimal state interference may have posited, the logic of history pointed to a powerful state grounded in domination. It was the state which came to define the economic system, rather than the other way round, reserving to itself the power to designate its enemies and crush them. Hence for Schmitt, the Bolsheviks, with their rediscovery of the enemy in the form of the bourgeoisie, were better students of politics than their liberal rivals.

Schmitt's French pupil, the sociologist Julien Freund, follows his master in speaking of an essence of politics: 'There is an essence of politics . . . there are no politics without a real or potential enemy.'[37] For Freund, politics is based on divisions external no less than internal, and on the affirmation of 'relations of command and submission' in society. Class struggle is but one aspect of struggles between city-states as in ancient Greece, between collectivities and groups aspiring to domination one against the other. Politics, accordingly, is to be seen as a fully autonomous activity, and the state as the expression of the friend–foe distinction and of an inherent desire for domination in human nature.

The Social Darwinian, not to say worse, undertones of such a political theory scarcely need underlining. Yet we would be foolish to discard it entirely in our analysis of the modern state. The attempt to locate a uniquely political form of activity merits consideration. We may not wish to limit this to the friend–enemy distinction — fortunately there is Rousseau to counterbalance Hobbes's view of human nature. But we will, however reluctantly, have to recognise that the exercise of domination seems to be an all too human activity in this century, that has in numerous instances led to the extermination of 'enemies of the state'.

A less chilling theory of domination is outlined by Michel Maffesoli. Not unlike Marcuse, he sees all aspects of daily life, from language to

164

sexuality, integrated into a system of value: 'The legitimation of domination . . . constitutes itself through work and its organization. Planning, efficacy, productivity become the modern gods.'[38] Marxism comes to resemble liberalism, ceasing to be a critique *of* political economy as opposed to a critique *within* political economy. The symbolic aspect of state domination recalls that of religion: 'A profane form of religion, politics reproduces the same schema of delegation and substitution.'[39] This analogy between state power and religion is, of course, not new. The Greeks had made it a central aspect of the polis.[40] Cicero, some centuries later, had exclaimed: 'Nowhere do men so approach the power of the Gods as in the founding of new states';[41] Rousseau had argued the case for a civil religion in his *Social Contract*, while Hegel in his deification of the state had not been far behind. In the twentieth century, the analogy between politics and religion has come to be applied to political parties (e.g. between Leninist parties and the organisation of the Catholic Church), to significant state occasions (e.g. coronations, assassinations)[42] and more generally as well: 'the concept of the state with the distinction it implies between power and those who govern is as socially indispensable as were, in their time, the *mana* of the chief, the superstition of warriors, and divine anointment.'[43]

Yet Marxist and neo-Marxist writers have great difficulty tackling the symbolic dimensions of power. The psychological dimensions of rule are ignored, along with the symbolism attached to state offices such as President or Prime Minister, or the quasi-religious authority exercised by successful political leaders. This does not mean that economic relations should be neglected or that we should take the symbolic level as constituting the essence of politics, any more than the friend–enemy distinction of Schmitt and Freund. But we should at least recognise that forms of political domination cannot be explained soley by economic domination.

After all, twentieth-century capitalism has known a variety of political regimes with Fascism through to liberal democracy, all presumably within the same mode of production. The same was true for pre-capitalist modes of production, e.g. ancient Greece. How then is one to account for the different *forms* of political power the same mode of production gives rise to? To be sure, the position a state occupies within the international system, the level of class struggle, the degree of development of the forces of production provide partial explanations. But are they sufficient to explain why Fascism came to power in Germany rather than England, why socialism in the Soviet Union engendered Stalinism rather than some twentieth-century variant of the Paris Commune? Is it not the political theory of Marxism that is sorely deficient?

A few contemporary Marxists have seen as much. For example, the Yugoslav philosopher, Rudi Supek, acknowledges the overwhelming power of party and state bureaucracy, not only in the sphere of production but in daily life. If under classical capitalism political power derived primarily from economics, under East European regimes, the contrary is true.[44] In the latter, ideological and political sanctions may play a more important role than economic, in the operation of the system, which in his discussion of bureaucracy in Eastern Europe, A. Hegedus seems to suggest.[45]

Henri Lefebvre, the French sociologist-philosopher, advances a more ambitious theoretical formulation in his four-volume treatise *De l'état*. He subjects classical Marxist conceptions of the state to critical scrutiny, discerning the emergency of a new mode of production dominated by the state: 'When each member of a civil society, each individual, group or class has the state as its partner, when the latter enters directly into each relationship, then begins the statist mode of production.'[46] Lefebvre's analysis goes on to underline structural similarities between state growth east and west and the predominant role the state *per se* has come to assume in the world political economy. To be sure he recognises other structural forces as having potentially equal power, e.g. the multinational corporation, but the gist of his interpretation is to challenge much of the current neo-Marxist literature that continues to read the state in terms of an ongoing capitalist mode of production.[47]

There are hints of a similar approach in Claus Offe, Jürgen Habermas and a number of other German writers, though few seem to have gone as far as Lefebvre. Offe, for example, argues that 'any attempt to explain the political organization of power through the categories of political economy becomes implausible'.[48] And Habermas credits the state with a legitimation function in late capitalism that transcends the purely economic: 'it is not possible to derive all the socio-economic-political problems of our community exclusively from the process of capital formation . . . The assumption that capitalism, through state policies, has merely been stabilized, but otherwise unaltered, is fundamentally untenable.'[49]

Fruitful as these openings may be, they leave unresolved a crucial question. If political domination is indeed as important as various writers, past and present, suggest, is it still meaningful to search for a theory within the confines of Marxism alone? Or is it not more honest to recognise that there are important areas of state activity in which Marxism proves just as inadequate, as does non-Marxist theory in other areas?

The function of legitimation

This question becomes all the more important when we turn to one final function which more than any other defines the limits of the modern state, legitimacy or legitimation. Ever since Max Weber's delineation of three types of legitimacy — the traditional, the bureaucratic-rational, and the charismatic — this term has enjoyed great popularity in the social sciences.[50] The term, however, is much older, having roots in Roman and medieval times, and coming into widespread use in the modern period.[51] Racine speaks of '*légitimes princes*' in *La Thébaïde*,[52] while the early nineteenth-century liberal, Benjamin Constant, rhapsodizes: 'There is something miraculous in the consciousness of legitimacy.'[53]

That legitimacy is more than mere legality has been recognised by a number of writers, pointing to such cases as the Weimar Republic as an example of legality without legitimacy, or de Gaulle's leadership of wartime French Resistance from London, as an example of legitimacy without legality.[54] Be this as it may, there is one element in definitions of legitimacy that bears particular attention: 'Whatever is founded on values and recognized as such by public opinion is legitimate.'[55] This recalls in a way the classical Leninist conditions for revolution, in which a ruling class having lost the will to rule, another class is aspiring to replace it.

Now there are enough cases in the contemporary world as in the past of regimes lacking popular support by any measurable index, yet able to endure. Force, just like tradition, can create its own legitimacy and for long periods dispense with any measure of popular support. Yet one of the permanent effects of the democratisation of European and world policies over the last century has been to make popular support, even if manipulated, an important aspect of political rule. All states, in the long run, like to consider their authority as grounded in popular support. It is when such support is put into question by elements of the military, the working class, the peasantry, student movements, or the bourgeoisie — in short, by important social forces — that one can speak of a crisis of legitimacy, of institutions, or in relations of production.[56]

Some Marxist theorists pay considerable attention to legitimacy/legitimation as a function of the modern state. O'Connor focuses on the large expansion in social expenditure by Western governments since World War II as evidence of attempts to win working-class support for the system.[57] Miliband also stresses ideological factors — the role of education, religion or the mass media — in explaining legitimation, while Habermas, traumatised, like other German writers, by the historical crisis of legitimacy of the 1930s, makes it central to his analysis.[58] Earlier, Gramsci and members of the Frankfurt School had placed much emphasis on ideological factors in shaping the organic interests of a hegemonial class or manipulating mass public opinion, as in the fascist state.[59]

Much of their analysis carries us a good deal further than any mechanical interpretation of the relationship between base and superstructure, economy and state, would allow. In particular, it counteracts the tendency in Marxist economic discussions of state action to reduce the latter to a mere agent of capital accumulation with little regard to cultural, ideological or institutional factors in state behaviour. But do they provide an altogether adequate theory of legitimacy in the modern state?

When de Gaulle, addressing the British Parliament in 1960 observed: '. . . in your success, for how much did the value of your institutions also count? At the worst moments, who among you questioned the legitimacy and the authority of the state?'[60] he put his finger on the role of political institutions and national traditions in assuring the legitimacy of the state. Was he altogether wrong? When the German Admiral Von Tirpitz argued that '[t]he German cannot afford to abandon that uprightness which was the palladium of his old civil service . . . it is only by proud, unselfish devotion to the State that [Germany] can counterbalance the deficiencies of its geographical position . . . its religious differences, its too young and too uncertain national sentiment',[61] was he not invoking a concept of legitimacy that marked Germany far more than Britain or the United States? Or for that matter is not the legitimacy of the centralised French state rooted in a national tradition from Louis XIV's *'L'Etat c'est moi'* to Georges Pompidou's *'C'est l'Etat qui doit commander'*[62] (It is the state which must command), from the Jacobins to the French communist party, that transcends right–left divisions? And nowadays, it remains to be seen whether Mitterrand's commitment to decentralisation will significantly or permanently modify this pattern.

Forms of legitimacy, then, would seem to be bound up with questions of national history, geographical situation, cultural values no less than with class relations or mode of production. Can Marxism do full justice to these phenomena without a Copernican revolution that turns much of the base–superstructure division upside down? Would the ensuing theory, by any traditional standards, still be Marxist? At the very least, some doubts are in order.

A Copernican revolution

What is required then is nothing less than a reformulation of the problem of the state. Classical Marxist theory has paid little attention to non-material factors in developing a theory. But if political economy, as Marx and Marxism would have it, is the matrix within which the modern state develops, the modern state is itself the matrix for economic and non-economic forms of power.

Whether this quite adds up to Lefebvre's statist mode of production is another matter. I fear that such a formulation mutes the very real differences that exist between the still predominantly market-based politics of the West and the more centralised, planned politics of the East. Such a formulation, moreover, pays insufficient attention to the specificities of different Western states and uses the concept of 'mode of production' as a *deus ex machina* to maintain some ongoing continuity with an earlier Marxist orthodoxy.

This is not my concern here. There is a serious crisis in Marxist theory, no less serious than the crisis of liberal theory, and there is nothing to be gained in minimising its extent. It is not a matter of looking for the appropriate quotation in *The Communist Manifesto, The 18th Brumaire* or *The Civil War in France*, of bringing Rosa Luxemburg to the rescue or of making Gramsci the patron saint of a democratised Western Marxism. The crisis is thorough-going, rooted in a chasm between theory and practice and in the inability of Marxist theory adequately to address crucial aspects of power.

Marx nowhere developed the political theory of a transitional society, let alone of a fully-fledged socialist one. Marx and Engels' formula of the withering away of the state, while fine as a Utopian fantasy, bears no relation to the reinforcement of power in this century in societies both capitalist and socialist, and seems an uncertain star by which to guide our fortunes into the indefinite future.

Can it not be that Marxism is simply not radical enough in its analysis of political power, too prone to believe that with the ending of bourgeois domination and market capitalism, the problem of political power is itself solved? Classical Marxism, by and large, failed to address the problem of limits to state power and in the process opened the door to the abuses that have characterised certain twentieth-century socialist societies. It is well and good to underline the bourgeois premises of classical liberal theory in its search for checks and balances on state power. Can Marxism, after all that had been committed in its name, seek for less?

What is the Marxist explanation of the disputes and wars between socialist states? Is the nationalism of one socialist state objectively more progressive and proletarian than that of the other? Does sovereignty really take a back seat to material relations of production in the modern world?

Are we better off when we turn to questions of personality and leadership? At least Plato could talk of 'philosopher kings', Hegel of 'world historical personalities', Weber of charisma. What is the Marxist explanation of the role of personality in history, of the revolutionary founders like Lenin or Mao? A Marxist theory of the state which is to go beyond ritual denunciations of capitalism must address this.

The same is true when one thinks of the question of bureaucracy. It is a fact that Weber's theory of bureaucracy has had a greater influence on twentieth-century social science than any Marxist alternative. This is not because Marxist analyses of bureaucratic tendencies or deformations in capitalism or in socialism are valueless. But the latter fail to sufficiently recognise the link between bureaucracy and the political domination that characterises the modern state.

To be radical in thinking about the state is to restore politics to a central position in our analysis. It is to recognise that different forms of sovereignty and styles of leadership, centralised versus decentralised types of politics, unified versus separated governmental structures, historical concepts of legitimacy and national traditions can decisively affect a society's development. These interact with material relations and modes of production, but the interaction is by no means unidirectional nor the consequences easy to predict. To echo the position advanced by Theda Skocpol:

In contrast to most [especially recent] Marxist theories, [ours] refuses to treat states as if they were mere analytic aspects of abstractly conceived modes of production, or even political aspects of concrete class relations and struggles. Rather it insists that states are actual organizations controlling (or attempting to control) territories and people.[63]

Political power through time and across national boundaries shows a Protean character, ever-changing and difficult to pin down. Brief reference to a number of major twentieth-century states may help to bear this out.

In France, state expenditure has grown from some 12 per cent of GNP in 1815–19 to some 29 per cent a century later (1920–4) to an even higher 37 per cent by 1965–9,[64] a pattern not without parallel in other capitalist states. The French state employed some 25 per cent of all salaried workers in 1974 — some 3 million directly, and more than another million in nationalised industries — a far cry from the less than half a million who worked for the state on the eve of World War I.[65]

What is most significant, however, in examining the French state, is a tradition of centralisation and state power going back to the pre-revolutionary period: 'The furbishing of the greatest Kingdom, the construction of a great state for long absorbed the energies of a whole people. Who needed an America? In France, the state was an America . . .'[66] Nor is the modern French state, with the tremendous power which, as study after study shows, the administration exercises,[67] to be reduced to a mere appendage of the bourgeoisie: 'The determinism of the [administrative] milieu is greater than ever. The administration cannot be simply confused with the dominant bourgeoisie. It constitutes a force for domination in its own right.'[68]

The issue here is not to determine the exact degree of power the *énarques* and other senior civil servants have, and how much greater this may be than that of their counterparts in somewhat more decentralised societies, such as the Federal Republic of Germany, the United States or Canada. What is important is that the French state, to no smaller extent, constitutes a force for domination in its own right and that its 'autonomy' *vis-à-vis* the economy has, if anything, increased with the reinforcement of executive power under the Fifth Republic.

That the French state is not immune from attack was shown by the events of May 1968. But its legitimacy is not so easily destroyed. Nor is the sovereignty function of the French state likely to disappear, despite the thirty-year experience of the Community. It is no accident that Marx and Engels' concept of the withering away of the state should have been penned with the example of the Paris Commune in mind. Nowhere in the capitalist world is the weight of the state so heavy. Indeed: 'France is the country of the state . . . We have offered the world this superb thing . . . an unfeeling Leviathan amongst unfeeling Leviathans.'[69] Nowhere has the dream of its imminent demise been more persistently, and probably hopelessly, kept alive.

Germany in this century provides, even more than France, a model of the autonomy of state power. We shall leave the discussion of the whys and wherefores of Germany's lateness in developing a unified state to the historians and theorists of world systems. Suffice it to say that the absence of such a state preys heavily on German national and philosophical consciousness from the French Revolution on, e.g. in Fichte or Hegel, and that the Bismarcks and Wilhelms found relatively little opposition from a politically supine bourgeoisie and an as yet untempered working class to a fairly authoritarian form of Reich. The economic role of the state was a great deal more directive, even in the pre-World War I period, than in other European countries.[70] This was further intensified during World War I, with the state coming to appropriate nearly 60 per cent of GNP, and to mobilise 'all the nation's resources, human and national'.[71]

The defeat of Germany in World War I ushered in a liberal democratic regime whose legitimacy was continually in question. The revolutionary left had been crushed in 1918–19, and any socialist transformation headed off. Instead, a system of organised capitalism, embracing the major industrialists and trade unions, carried on in the early post-war years,[72] while a weak parliamentary regime presided over an unreformed and unpurged state apparatus. The punitive clauses of the Treaty of Versailles weakened the German economy and undermined her sovereignty.

We shall not enter the debate concerning the relative importance of big business as opposed to other forces in the coming to power of Hitler. Only the ideological blinkers of the Third International, however, would allow anyone to characterise the Nazi state as a mere servant of monopoly capital or underestimate its autonomy and freedom of action.[73] From the Nuremberg Decrees to the invasion of the Soviet Union, there is every reason to believe that politics, not economics, was in command. Which is not to say that, where economic policy was concerned, there was not the closest possible interaction between big business and the state. But that is quite a different proposition from one which would see Hitler as a mere puppet of the big capitalists.

The post-World War II state in the Federal Republic ostensibly tried to reverse the statist current. The federal structure was one important element in decentralising and delegitimatising a too powerful state. Another lay in the neo-liberal policies pursued from 1948 onwards. Yet the state has hardly proved an economic dwarf. Fully 44.1 per cent of GNP passed through the state in 1958, a slight increase from the 42.2 per cent in 1938, after five years of Nazi regime.[74]

Nor in the political field has it been all that weak. Willy Brandt, the least authoritarian of Chancellors, stated his political credo in these terms some years ago: 'The democratic state cannot be organized without a strong structure. It must have a right to sovereignty and, in certain precise cases, use force to assure peace inside the country, defend justice and combat criminality.'[75]

The state in the Federal Republic has not hesitated in using an iron fist against internal dissenters, such as the *Berufsverbot* of 1972 or anti-terrorist legislation passed in early 1978, in the process renewing a tradition of legitimacy with vulnerable roots in pre-1945 times.

Let us turn to the United Kingdom, which Tom Nairn has characterised as 'the first state form of an industrialized nation'.[76] What is most striking about Britain — and by extension the United States and the white dominions — is a political tradition which rejects the strong state in its continental form, placing major emphasis on limited government well into the twentieth century. True, the British state played no small part in fostering colonial expansion from the time of Elizabeth I, through Clive's plundering of India, to the partition of Africa in the nineteenth century. Nor was its role in policing the lower classes — the Peterloo Massacre, anti-combination legislation — or in alleviating some of the worst features of capitalist exploitation, such as the Factory Acts, negligible, even in the nineteenth century. Yet ideologically it was a state which for long refused to know its name.

We may make light of this ideological tradition, but it continues to characterise the English-speaking world down to present day. It is not only the word 'state' which rings much less true in English than in French or German, but the very conceptualisation of unified govern- mental, bureaucratic and legislative power.[77] De Jouvenel has pointed to the distinction between the English 'the people are' and the French *'le peuple est'*, as underlining the pluralist and individualist assump- tions characterising the English-speaking conception of government.[78] One might also point to the role of voluntary organisations indepen- dent of state action,[79] to a tradition of juridical independence from the executive, to the autonomy of municipal government and even state enterprises (the nationalised industries, the BBC) from Whitehall, in contrasting British with say French or pre-1945 German practice.

To be sure, the move to increased economic and social intervention by the state has been part and parcel of British history in this century and has been accepted by leaders of all political parties. The experience of two World Wars and a depression, the need to mediate deep-rooted class inequalities, the decline in Britain's competitive position within international capitalism, all contributed to increasing the economic role of the state. Monetarist policies pursued since 1979, however, suggest that the earlier suspicion of the state in British political culture still has considerable popular appeal to this day.

The question of the degree of state autonomy from the economy or of the importance of non-economic factors to state domination is not resolved, moreover, by simply analysing the rate of state expenditure in twentieth-century Britain. A writer such as Miliband seeks to underline the common interests between state and capitalism, and, within certain limits, does this effectively. Those limits, however, are the ones pointed to earlier: the functions of sovereignty, of legitimacy, of political domination — which can be only partly explained through Marxist analysis. To what extent do questions of sovereignty, as in two World Wars, the debate over the European Community or the 1982 war over the Falklands/Malvinas, defy a purely materialist explana- tion? To what extent is legitimacy in Britain grounded in ideological values — monarchy, religion, parliamentarianism — which have over time become independent institutional factors in determining political

173

behaviour? Are those who hold political power coterminous with the economically dominant bourgeoisie, and if not,[80] may we not find a degree of autonomy to state action which cannot be explained by the larger interests of the capitalist class? And what of the role of political leadership? Would Churchill have been as quick to disengage Britain from India as the Labour Party was? Would Macmillan have acted in the same way as Eden over Suez? Would Heath have pursued the same economic policies as Thatcher? Whatever the logic of the capitalist system, political leaders somehow develop wings of their own.

The United States, even more than Britain, denies the concept of the modern state. The roots of this attitude go far back in time, to the agrarian underpinnings of the American republic. The American governmental structure, carefully divided between federal and state governments, further subdivided into separate executive, legislative and judicial compartments, was meant to stay small and serviceable compared to the more powerful, absolutist states of much of Europe.

The imperatives and contradictions of capitalist development from the very beginning, coupled with the emergence of the United States as a global power of the first order in this century, were none the less to make the state, especially the federal part thereof, a much more important economic force. Still, certain important differences from twentieth-century European experience can be singled out.

The most important one is the relatively smaller importance of social security spending as compared to overall state spending, coupled with a generally lower level of overall state expenditure as a percentage of GNP in the United States compared to Western Europe. OECD figures, for example, show this percentage for the United States in the 1970s to be in the range of 30–35 per cent, as compared to 40–50 per cent in Western Europe.[81] At the same time, defence spending for much of the post-World War II period accounted for over 40 per cent of overall federal expenditure and close to 10 per cent of GNP,[82] a figure far larger than in any other major capitalist country. This vast military expenditure was of course linked to the United States' dominant political and economic position within the so-called 'free world' after 1945. War spending proved attractive to important sections of American big business otherwise hostile to state expenditure, and enjoyed a legitimacy in American public opinion, unchallenged until the period of the Vietnam War.

The second distinguishing feature of the American situation has been the continuing importance of an anti-state ideology. Even as public employment soared to some 14 million by 1974,[83] as the international role of American corporations and the American state loomed ever larger, the myths of laissez-faire and limited government continued to enjoy widespread support.[84] The United States is the capitalist country with the least public enterprise, with one of the least developed social security systems, with no socialist or social democratic party of any importance. Despite movement towards an enhanced executive power during the cold war years, the so-called imperial presidency, its state structure lacks the unity and coherence of older nation-states such as Britain and France. Institutional factors such as federalism and the separation of powers provide part of the explanation. Even more important, one suspects, are America's geographical position, her extensive resources, the lack of a feudal tradition, her place within a larger world system, all of which allowed a process of capital accumulation with relatively little support from the state. What remains unresolved, however, are larger questions concerning political domination and the nature of legitimacy in the American system. A crisis of legitimacy such as the United States experienced during the late 1960s or the Watergate period went far beyond issues of social expenditures which O'Connor stresses in his discussion of legitimation. The roots of legitimacy are moral and political, no less than economic, the challenge to the Moloch character of the modern state in the United States in the late 1960s rooted in questions of political domination and the external uses of sovereign power. To be sure, such questions were not unrelated to the nature of American capitalism or imperialism. But it is far from clear whether they are subsumed under the latter or whether in a socialist United States questions of state power, political domination, citizen participation or sovereignty would be any less acute.

If we needed to be convinced, let us turn to one final example of a twentieth-century state, the Soviet Union. Without getting into a long digression on the nature of the Soviet state, one thing is clear: it is not a Western-style capitalist state with the institutional structures or clusters of private economic power characteristic of France, the Federal Republic of Germany, the United Kingdom, the United States or Japan. What exactly it is, has of course been subject to much dispute.

For Soviet and Eastern European orthodoxy, the Soviet system is based on socialist relations of production; class exploitation has been abolished, and the state reflects the economic, cultural and social interests of the people. While some theorists continue to talk of the council system as 'the classical political form of dictatorship of the proletariat'[85] and others of forms of direct democracy that contrast with the fake pluralism of the capitalist system,[86] all acknowledge the leading role of the party: 'Under our historical conditions, it is impossible to conceive a political system which would provide for the development of new political centres, of political centres whose centre of gravity lies outside the party.'[87] The withering away of the state is retained as an ultimate objective under socialism, but this is impossible until 'the respective internal conditions — the building of the communist society — and the consolidation of socialism in the international arena' prevail.[88]

In practice, the history of the Soviet Union since 1917 and, more particularly, what the French historian, Jean Elleinstein, modestly calls *'le phénomène stalinien'*,[89] poses problems for state power that go far beyond the confines of Marxist-Leninist theses. Not only has the state not withered in the Soviet Union, but its power over civil society has known few restraints. The question is not to assess how much of Russia's earlier history — absolutism, centralisation — contributed to the type of regime that emerged by the 1930s, how much economic conditions or Bolshevik ideology played a part. What matters is simply to recognise that the state apparatus can be the source of an extraordinary degree of control in its own right. It is the economic base and civil society which lack autonomy. Or in Gramsci's telling phrase about the pre-revolutionary period: 'In Russia the State was everything, civil society was primordial and gelatinous.'[90]

Conclusion

Where then does our discussion of the modern state lead us? I stated at the beginning that I would not be so daring as to attempt to formulate an actual theory of the modern state. A number of strands can, however, be brought together.

(a) The state, as the modern form of political power, is here to stay into the indefinite future, regardless of what certain anthropologists[91] or Marx and Engels may have thought. The real question then becomes what limits can be placed on its repressive qualities, and how much power can in fact be devolved back to its citizens. That debate has really scarcely begun.

(b) The economic functions of the state have grown by leaps and bounds, confirming the predictions of old-world conservatives like Adolph Wagner, and imparting a new character to Western economic systems, even where large-scale private ownership over the means of production has been maintained. An unpdated Marxist economic theory of capital accumulation and concentration can account for a good part of this trend, coupled with an analysis of international capitalist relations and uneven development. In Hilferding's apt term, the twentieth century has seen the emergence of 'organized capitalism', at an increasingly global level.

(c) Concerning non-economic functions of the state such as sovereignty, legitimacy, domination, Marxism proves much less adequate. Indeed, some features of the modern state are better discussed by non-Marxist theorists, from Weber on legitimacy to Schmitt on the friend–enemy distinction, from Maffesoli on the logic of domination to various liberal writers on the autonomy of the state.

(d) There is no single type of capitalist state, as the different experiences of France, the Federal Republic of Germany, Great Britain and the United States show, and the argument could as well be extended to other countries. National history, international position, cultural factors of various kinds play a role which makes difficult all-embracing theorisation about the modern state. By the same token, socialist states also come in different guises — the Soviet Union, China and Yugoslavia, to name but three — and the political form socialism might take in the West would conceivably differ even more. The relationship between political domination and forms of economic relations is thus highly complicated; we need new typologies of possible political regimes, in the manner of Aristotle's classical delineation in the *Politics*, relating them to both capitalist and socialist modes of production.

(e) The state must not be elevated into a fetish towering over society, nor should it be reduced to a mere expression of the relationship of social forces at any point in time.[92]

A product of human history, it must be studied historically and, in that endeavour, philosophy, political theory and historical imagination have no less a contribution to make than political economy.

Notes

1   J.P. Nettl, 'The State as a Conceptual Variable', *World Politics*, vol. 20, no. 4, 1968, p. 559.

2   Here I must take issue with Professor Macpherson, who in 'Do We Need a Theory of the State?', *European Journal of Sociology*, vol. 18, 1977, pp. 223–44, asserts that only Marxism and social democracy need such a theory. On the contrary, conservative, liberal and fascist theorists have shown no less of an interest in this question as some of the references in my paper will suggest.

3   See, for example, the article on 'Stateless Society', *Encyclopedia of the Social Sciences*, Vol. 15, pp. 157–68, with its extensive bibliographical references. See also Pierre Clastres, *La Société contre l'Etat*, Paris, 1974

and the intelligent critique thereof in Jean-William Lapierre, *Vivre sans Etat?*, Paris, 1977.

4   Cf. Gramsci's discussion of the role of religion or the national press in 'State and Civil Society' in *Selections from the Prison Notebooks*, London, 1971, and Althusser's concept of state ideological apparati in his article 'Idéologie et appareils idéologiques d'Etat', *Positions*, Paris, 1976.

5   N. Poulantzas, *L'Etat, le pouvoir, le socialisme*, Paris, 1978, p. 180, maintains that the knowledge concerning the current economic functions and certain aspects of monopoly capitalism is to be attributed exclusively to Marxist theory.

6   The most extensive discussion of Wagner's law is contained in Herbert Timm, 'Das Gesetz der Wachsenden Staatsausgaben', *Finanzarchiv*, Tübingen, Vol. 21, 1961, pp. 201–47. The biographical article on Wagner in the *Staatslexikon*, Freiburg, 1963, Vol. VIII is also of interest in sketching his relationship to the so-called Socialists of the Chair (*Kathedersozialisten*). A.T. Peacock and J. Wiseman, *The Growth of Public Expenditures in the United Kingdom*, Princeton, 1961, pp. 18–24 provides a useful summary.

7   For a brilliant discussion of this intellectual climate, see Michael Loewy, *Pour une sociologie des intellectuels révolutionnaires*, Paris, 1976, Chapter I.

8   Solomon Fabricant, *The Trend of Government Activity in the United States*, New York, 1952, Peacock and Wiseman, op. cit.; Suphan Andic and Jindrich Veverka, 'The Growth of Government Expenditure in Germany', *Finanzarchiv*, vol. 23, 1964, pp. 169–277; R.M. Bird, *The Growth of Government-Spending in Canada*, Canadian Tax Foundation, 1970; C. André, R. Delorme and G. Terny, 'Les dépenses publiques françaises depuis un siècle', *Economie et Statistique*, March 1973, pp. 3–14.

9   Richard M. Titmuss, *Essays on 'the Welfare State'*, London, 1958, p. 86.

10   Pitrim A. Sorokin, *Man and Society in Calamity*, New York, 1942.

11   Ibid., pp. 120, 122.

12   Andic and Veverka, op. cit., p. 193 and Table 1, p. 183.

13   André, Delorme and Terny, op. cit., Graph 1, Table 3.

14   Cf. OECD, *National Accounts Statistics*, Paris, 1976.

15   Paul Boccara *et al., Le capitalisme monopoliste d'Etat*, 2 vols, Paris, Editions sociales, 1976.

16   Cf. H. Claude, *La concentration capitaliste. Pouvoir économique et pouvoir gaulliste*, Paris, Editions sociales, 1965.

17   Rudolf Hilferding, *Le capital financier*, Paris, 1970, p. 451.

18   Cf. the introductory article in H.A. Winkler (ed.), *Organisierter Kapitalismus*, Göttingen, 1974.

19   Cf. Jürgen Kocka, *Klassengesellschaft im Krieg 1914–18*, Göttingen, 1973; Charles S. Maier, *Recasting Bourgeois Europe*, Princeton, 1975.

20   Cited in Winkler, op. cit., p. 9.

21   Jürgen Kocka, 'Organisierter Kapitalismus oder Staatsmonopolistischer Kapitalismus?' in Winkler, op. cit., p. 25.

22　To cite but some of the literature on corporatism: J.T. Winkler, 'Corporatism', *Archives Européennes de Sociologie*, vol. 17, no. 1, 1976; Philippe Schmitter and Gerhard Lehmbruch (eds.), *Trends Towards Corporatist Intermediation*, London, Sage Publications, 1979; J.M. Malloy (ed.), *Authoritarianism and Corporatism in Latin America*, Pittsburgh and London, 1977; Leo Panitch, 'Recent Theorizations of Corporatism: Reflections on a Growth Industry', *British Journal of Sociology*, vol. 31, no. 2, June 1980.

23　John Holloway and Sol Picciotto, 'Capital, Crisis & the State', *Capital and Class*, 1977, no. 2, pp. 76–101; Joachim Hirsch, *Staatsapparat und Reproduktion des Kapitals*, Frankfurt, 1974.

24　Louis Fontvielle, 'Evolution et croissance de l'état français', *Economies et sociétés*, vol. 10, nos. 9–12, 1976.

25　E. Altvater, *Rahmenbedingungen und Schranken staatlichen Handelns. Zehn Thesen*, Frankfurt, 1976.

26　P. Baran and P. Sweezy, *Monopoly Capital*, New York, 1966; Michael Kidron, *Western Capitalism since the War*, London, 1968.

27　James O'Connor, *The Fiscal Crisis of the State*, New York, 1973.

28　R. Carré de Malberg, *Contribution à la théorie générale de l'Etat*, Paris, 1920, reprinted 1962, p. 7.

29　Gyoergy Antalffy, *Basic Problems of State and Society*, Budapest, 1974, pp. 116, 120.

30　Werner Sombart, *Das Wirtschaftsleben im Zeitalter des Hochkapitalismus*, Munich and Leipzig, 1928, Chap. VI.

31　Charles Eisenmann, 'Les Fonctions de l'Etat' in *Encyclopédie Française*, Vol. 10, *L'Etat*, 1964, p. 311.

32　Bertrand de Jouvenel, *Les Débuts de l'Etat moderne*, Paris, 1976, pp. 156–7.

33　Poulantzas, op. cit., p. 162.

34　Cf. the interesting contrast between Marx's inadequate theorising of political events in France during 1848–50 and the far superior *ad hoc* political analysis by Marx of the same events that Martin E. Spencer draws in his article 'Marx on the State: The Events in France between 1848–1850', *Theory and Society*, vol. 17, nos. 1 and 2, January–March 1979, pp. 167–98.

35　The term *libido dominandi* derives from St Augustine's *De Civitate Dei*. Henri Lefebvre makes use of the concept in his treatise *De l'Etat*, especially Vol. 1, *L'Etat dans le monde moderne* and Vol. 3, *Le mode de production étatique*, Paris, 1976–7.

36　Carl Schmitt, *La Notion de politique*, Paris, 1972, contains a translation of his most important essay of the early 1930s as well as a much later piece on the theory of the partisan.

37　Julien Freund, *L'Essence du politique*, Paris, 1965, p. 1.

38　Michel Maffesoli, *Logique de la domination*, Paris, 1976, pp. 158–9.

39　Ibid., p. 188.

40　Victor Ehrenberg, *The Greek State*, London, 1969, pp. 74–7.

41　Cicero, *De republica*, I 7, cited in Helmut Kuhn, 'Der Staat als Herrschaftsform', *Zeitschrift für Politik*, 1967, Vol. 14, p. 229.

42   S. Verba, 'The Kennedy Assassination and the Nature of Political Commitment' in B.S. Greenberg and E.B. Parker (eds.), *The Kennedy Assassination and the American Public*, Palo Alto, 1965; Edward Shils and Michael Young, 'The Meaning of the Coronation', *Sociological Review*, vol. 1, 1953.

43   Georges Burdeau, *Traité de science politique*, Vol. 11, *L'Etat*, Paris, 1967.

44   Rudi Supek, 'La "Main visible" et la dégradation de l'individu' in Alain Touraine *et al.*, *Au-delà de la crise*, Paris, 1976.

45   Andras Hegedus, *Socialism and Bureaucracy*, London, 1976.

46   Lefebvre, *De l'Etat*, Vol. 4, *Le mode de production étatique*, Paris, 1977, p. 248.

47   Lefebvre's analysis was heavily influenced here by the French translation of Kari Levitt, *Silent Surrender*. Cf. Vol. 2 of *De l'Etat: Les contradictions de l'Etat moderne*, pp. 190–3.

48   Claus Offe, 'Political Authority and Class Structures' in Paul Connerton, (ed.), *Critical Sociology*, London, 1976, pp. 393, 395–6.

49   Jürgen Habermas, *Legitimationsprobleme im Spätkapitalismus*, Frankfurt, 1973, pp. 105, 128, 130.

50   Max Weber, *Economy and Society*, Vol. 3, New York, 1968, p. 954.

51   Raymond Polin, 'Analyse philosophique de l'idée de légitimité' in Polin, *L'Idée de légitimité*, Annales de philosophie politique, Paris, 1967.

52   Racine, *Théatre complet, Thébaïde*, Paris, Garnier, 1960, 21.

53   Cited in Polin, op. cit., p. 23.

54   Cf. the articles by Noberto Bobbio and Sergio Cotta in Polin, op. cit.

55   Polin, op. cit., p. 23.

56   Cf. Habermas' discussion of economic, rationality, legitimation and motivation crises in *Legitimation Crisis*, Boston, 1975.

57   O'Connor, op. cit., Chapters 1, 4 and 5.

58   Ralph Miliband, *The State in Capitalist Society*, 1969, Chapters 7–8; Habermas, op. cit.

59   Gramsci, op. cit.; Phil Slater, *Origin and Significance of the Frankfurt School*, London, 1977.

60   Michel Droit (ed.), *Homme du destin*, Vol. 3, *Le Retour*, p. 365.

61   Cited in Peter Wiles, 'War and Economic Systems', *Science et conscience de la société, mélanges en l'honneur de Raymond Aron*, Paris, 1971, Vol. 2, p. 286.

62   Cited in Alain Peyrefitte, *Le Mal français*, Paris, 1976, p. 96.

63   Theda Skocpol, *States and Social Revolutions*, Cambridge, 1979, p. 31.

64   Fontvielle, op. cit., p. 1705.

65   André Piettre, *Les grands problèmes de l'économie contemporaine*, Paris, 1976, Vol. 1, p. 16.

66   Pierre Chaunu, 'L'Etat' in Fernand Braudel and Ernest Labrousse (series editors), *Histoire économique et sociale de la France*, Vol. 1, *1450–1660*, p. 223.

67   For example Ezra Suleiman, *Les Hauts fonctionnaires et la politique*, Paris, 1976; J. Siwek-Pouydesseau, 'French Ministerial Staffs' in Mattei

Dogan (ed.), *The Mandarins of Western Europe*, New York, Wiley, 1975; Pierre Birnbaum, *Les Sommets de l'Etat*, Paris, 1977.

68   *Pour nationaliser l'Etat*, Réflexions d'un groupe d'études, Paris, 1968, p. 31.

69   Henri Lefebvre, *Le Temps des Méprises*, Paris, 1975, p. 229.

70   W.O. Henderson, *The Rise of German Industrial Power 1834–1914*, Berkeley, University of California, London, 1976; W.F. Bruck, *Social and Economic History of Germany from Wilhelm II to Hitler, 1888–1938*, London, 1940.

71   Peter-Christian Witt, 'Finanzpolitik und Sozialer Wandel' in H.V. Wehler (ed.), *Sozialgeschichte Heute*, Göttingen, 1974, pp. 565–74; Walter Rathenau, 'German Organization at the Beginning of the War' in J.M. Clark, W.H. Hamilton and H.G. Moulton, *Readings in the Economics of War*, New York, 1918.

72   Maier, op. cit.

73   Among the better analyses of the Nazi state, one may cite Franz Neumann, *Behemoth*, Octagon, 1963 and A. Schweitzer, *Big Business in the Third Reich*, Indiana University Press, 1964.

74   Andic and Veverka, op. cit., p. 183. To be fair, however, social security spending would have accounted for a much larger share of total state expenditure in 1958 than 1938.

75   Willy Brandt, Bruno Kreisky and Olof Palme, *La sociale démocratie et l'avenir*, Paris, 1976, pp. 27–8.

76   Tom Nairn, 'The Twilight of the British State', *New Left Review*, nos. 101–2, 1977, p. 6.

77   Nettl, op. cit., p. 570.

78   De Jouvenel, op. cit., p. 69.

79   Nairn, op. cit., p. 16. 'State power was appropriated by a self-regulating elite group which established powerful conventions of autonomy: that is of forms of self-organization and voluntary action independent of state action.'

80   As is suggested in the essay of Christopher Hewitt in Philip Stanworth and Anthony Giddens (eds.), *Elites and Power in British Society*, Cambridge, 1974.

81   OECD, *National Accounts 1961–1972*, Paris, 1974; OECD, *Expenditure Trends in OECD Countries, 1960–1980*, Paris, 1972.

82   *Statistical Abstracts of the United States*, various years, cited in Piettre, op. cit., Annexe 7, p. 53.

83   *United States Monthly Labor Review*, May 1975, p. 80.

84   David Vogel, 'Why Businessmen Distrust their State: The Political Consciousness of American Corporate Executives', *British Journal of Political Science*, vol. 8, January 1978, pp. 45, 78.

85   Gyoergy Antalffy, *Basic Problems of State and Society*, p. 157.

86   J.A. Tikhominov, *Pouvoir et administration dans la société socialiste*, Paris, CNRS, 1973, p. 62.

87   Antalffy, op. cit., p. 186.

88   Ibid., p. 100.

89   Jean Elleinstein, *Histoire de phénomène stalinien*, Paris, 1975.

90   Gramsci, *Selections from the Prison Notebooks*, p. 238.
91   According to Prince Clastre, *La Société contre l'Etat*, Paris, Seuil, 1974, p. 12, it is not obvious that coercion and subordination do constitute everywhere and always the essence of political power. Though Clastre's account focuses on primitive societies, is it too much to suggest the prescriptive qualities he reads, much like Rousseau, into his anthropology?
92   Alain Touraine, *Production de la société*, Paris, Seuil, 1973, p. 259.

9 Pluralism, violence and the modern state

M.G. Smith

Modes of incorporation and plural societies

Most member states of the United Nations are multinational societies, and all or most of these are plural societies. Very few member states of the United Nations incorporate ethnically homogeneous populations or nations (Broom, 1960). In other words, we labour under misplaced identifications of society with nation, and nation with state.

Briefly, and in the broadest sense, by 'plural society' I refer to a society whose members are divided into categories or groups on the basis of such factors as language, race, ethnicity, community of provenance or descent, religion, distinctive social institutions, or culture. In some cases a single variable, such as race, provides the socially institutionalised basis for such divisions. In other cases, two or more variables together define the major lines of cleavage or division. The term 'pluralism' applies wherever societies are culturally or socially divided by variables of any kind, number and institutional significance. Such divisions and units are most manifest in the society's public domain (Smith, 1960, 1965, 1969a, 1969b, 1984).

The public domain of a society consists in all those institutions which regulate and coordinate its collective interests and affairs. The authoritative regulation of its relations with external units is always a critical responsibility of the central political institutions. The public domain of centralised polities corresponds broadly with the sphere of state regulation, and implicitly assumes the state.

The state is that set of structures which claims and exercises supreme regulative rights and functions over the society of which it is the central coordinative unit. For such a polity to win recognition as a state by scholars and by men of practical affairs alike, it is sufficient that its central political institutions enjoy the autonomy and authority required to regulate legitimately all the various interests, affairs and units which are entrusted by tradition or by the prevailing constitution to its control. We may therefore recognise colonial states, dynastic states, tribal states, tributary states, feudal states, city-states, and theocracies of various kinds, as equally interesting and valid varieties of the state.

Plural societies having been identified by deep internal divisions into social segments or sections that are, or are felt to be, inherently different by virtue of culture, race, ethnicity, language, religion, or by some complex combination of these variables, I shall distinguish two structural types, the *hierarchic* and *segmental*, while recognising a third, more variable category, the *mixed* or *complex*, in which hierarchic and segmental organisations are variously combined. In *hierarchic pluralities*, one section of the population which is culturally and/or racially distinct dominates and rules the rest. If the dominated population contains two or more plural divisions they may be ranked as superior and inferior, or equally as co-ordinates, despite their reciprocal closure. Alternatively, the major divisions of an inclusive plural society may hold or claim co-ordinate political and legal status, as in the ill-fated Nigerian Federation of 1959–66. In such a case, the plural society has a *segmental* structure, since its major components are social segments that hold or claim co-ordinate status and autonomy within it. While normally but not always regional, such segments are usually internally autonomous, self-regulating units.

In *hierarchic pluralities* the dominant cultural section, whether a demographic minority or not, monopolises or seeks to monopolise the societal public domain — that is, all those institutions and structures through which the state, whether directly or indirectly, regulates the society's public affairs. Accordingly, dominant and subordinate sections of such societies are *differentially incorporated*. By contrast, in segmentally structured pluralities, to avoid domination by others, the constituent segments assert and retain sufficient internal autonomy to regulate their own segmental affairs so that the societal public domain in which they all participate is structurally and substantively *consociational*. Either it will be explicitly federal or confederal in form, or implicitly and informally so, given some conventional or negotiated bases of coalition or power-sharing (Lijphart, 1977). Incorporation of individuals within such consociational polities is therefore indirect, and presupposes their prior membership in one or other of these

184

segments. Thus, just as status parities or complementarities are essential for consociational pluralities based on the *equivalent* or *segmental* mode of incorporation, so inequalities of status at collective and individual levels are basic to the structure of hierarchic pluralities grounded on differential incorporation (Smith, 1969b).

Various writers, remarking the hierarchic ordering of ethnic and racial blocs in many colonial societies, have treated these as simple instances of class organisation or social stratification, and argued that such concepts as social and cultural pluralism are redundant and confusing. There are several major difficulties with this view. Firstly, many plural societies consist of co-ordinate rather than ranked segments, and these may share or differ in their economic base, as for instance Cyprus, Yugoslavia, Czechoslovakia, Malaysia, Belgium, Nigeria and Belize (formerly British Honduras). In other cases, such as colonial and post-colonial Surinam, South Africa, Indonesia, and Zimbabwe, the plural divisions are incorporated and differentiated by complex combinations of hierarchic and segmental alignments, with similar and different economic bases. Clearly, such compartmentalised social structures differ notably in form, content and cultural implication from the familiar patterns of social stratification or class organisation. Yet if this is conceded for such segmentally structured and complex polyglot pluralities, precisely the same point holds, and for precisely the same reasons, in such hierarchic colonial societies as Kenya, Uganda, Jamaica, Guyana and Grenada.

Given the central significance of modes of incorporation for the establishment and structures of plural societies, it is clearly important to investigate the *de facto* realities as well as the *de jure* forms of these orders. For example, in the United States, while the ethnic divisions of whites lack *de jure* status in the common public domain, locally they often enjoy *de facto* validity. Conversely, while the *de jure* position of American negroes is that of formal equality with American whites, even today they are *de facto* incorporated as inferiors in the common public domain. We must therefore always attend to the convergence or divergence of *de facto* and *de jure* realities in studying human societies, plural or otherwise. As Max Weber observed: 'It is always the actual state of affairs which is decisive for sociological purposes' (Weber, 1947, p. 137).

We need then to recognise at least six distinct types of society: the homogeneous, weakly differentiated type; the heterogeneous, differentiated society that bears a common culture; the heterogeneous society which contains several cultural traditions and exhibits cultural pluralism without corresponding social pluralism; and plural societies of three types, namely the segmental, hierarchic, and mixed or complex.

185

Since many societies belonging to all of these different categories are not incorporated as states, clearly state and society differ fundamentally in their nature, bases, contents, relations and essential processes as well as their structures and history. While states of differing kind may incorporate societies of identical type, societies of differing type may have identical forms of state.

Criteria for a typology of states

Despite their many important common characteristics, contemporary states are a very mixed bag indeed. However, they all share pre-emptive claims to particular bounded parts of the earth's surface over which they assert their 'sovereignty', and exercise administrative, legislative and judicial authority. Though some monarchies still survive, most contemporary states normally allocate their supreme political offices on various non-hereditary bases and rely for their administration on relatively impersonal bureaucracies staffed on contract by career officials who co-ordinate the activities of elaborate hierarchies of ministries, departments, sub-departments, regions and parastatal bodies to ensure routine discharge of the usual state functions, however these are defined in a given unit. State bureaucracies generally operate with minimal publicity concerning their procedures, criteria and personnel. On behalf of their peoples, states monopolise the conduct of external relations with one another and with international bodies. Within their territories they monopolise the claim to legitimacy in the use of force for offence or defence, for police action and the like. Accordingly most contemporary states have relatively elaborate and expensive military establishments as well as police, prisons and security forces to ensure internal law and order as well as defence of their interests and boundaries. In addition each has a hierarchy of courts to administer its law.

Such expensive bureaucratic and defence establishments require an equally elaborate budgetary process and administration; and states are heavily preoccupied with the levying of taxes, collection of revenues, projections and regulation of expenditures, savings and investment in weaponry, public utilities, education and research, or in projects that promise substantial economic returns.

While all states nowadays undertake responsibility for construction and maintenance of public roadways, some do likewise for railroads, water supplies, light and power, radio, telephones, television and even newspapers, while others do not. Posts, ports, airports and water supplies are generally established and administered directly by states themselves or through some parastatal organisation such as a port authority set up to run an operation as far as possible on commercial lines with or without seeking profit.

Contemporary states also try to regulate market activities and relations within their borders, and may embargo external transactions. They seek credit as necessary from one another, and from international or commercial agencies. They regulate and often sponsor building and construction of differing kinds, research activities, town planning, education, training, health, housing and many similar spheres of action for their peoples.

While some states seek to control and manage the total economy of their countries, others prefer to share such controls with private interests in mixed economies; and yet others try not to engage in productive or commercial activities, directly or via subsidiaries. Such differences of scope correlate with ideological and organisational differences between Marxist states, capitalist states, and such socialist states as Sweden or Norway that operate mixed economies. They clearly involve corresponding differences in the organisations of their respective public domains.

All modern states elaborate some ideological justifications for their existence and activities, whether these are collectivist, individualist, theocratic, developmental or other. All contemporary states, including Marxist states, such as the Soviet Union and Poland, incorporate stratified populations that exhibit significant differences of wealth, prospects and social status. All contemporary states administer their interests and populations through hierarchies of units ordered in several levels from small local units up to the most inclusive central directorates. Requisite degrees of co-ordination and central control of the activities and relations of units at these differing levels pose important problems for all contemporary states.

While noting these common features, we should not underestimate the differences and varieties of modern states. Though most are secular, some are theocratic; and if, following Max Weber (1963, pp. 100f, 135), we regard certain current secular ideologies as religions, the theocratic category would be correspondingly extended. While some theocracies are revolutionary, others are not; but of course not all revolutionary states are theocratic, even in this extended sense; and some revolutionary states are not regarded as such by others of like persuasion. While, as noted above, some states are socialist and identified with mixed economies, others are Marxist and identified with totally managed and centrally directed economies, and yet others are ideologically capitalist and committed to self-regulating market economies. There are also many ex-colonial states, some of which proclaim their socialist identity, but differ variously from the preceding and from one another in the political regulation of their local economies.

Employing criteria of wealth and development, some states incorporate industrial societies with developed economies, whether centrally or market regulated. Others preside over economies classified as 'developing' by the World Bank, International Monetary Fund, United Nations, etc., though realistically most of these weaker economies are now collapsing. Yet others are identified simply as backward or underdeveloped economies, whatever their organisations, socialist, Marxist or neither. In short, most states are poor, some are rich, and some of middling poverty or wealth.

There are also several units that correspond to the ideal of 'nation-state', that is, where the state incorporates people of a single ethnic stock and cultural tradition, such as Denmark, Sweden or Portugal. However, most contemporary states, as mentioned earlier, are polyethnic; and most of these incorporate plural societies. Implicitly for Europeans, the conceptual opposite of the 'nation-state' was an empire, itself the goal and projection of most major European states during and after the sixteenth century.

While some modern states are continental in extent, or virtually so, for instance the United States, Canada, India, China, the Soviet Union, Brazil and Australia, others, especially those of Western Europe, such as France, Spain, Poland, Italy, are of moderate dimensions, and many of recent emergence are indeed minuscule, for example, Mauritius, Grenada, Barbados, Seychelles and the like. Evidently, size alone is no good guide to the relative homogeneity of state populations. Continental and minuscule units are equally likely to be plural societies; while those units of moderate size, the first crop of nation-states to emerge from feudalism in Western Europe and carve out foreign empires, began by forcibly incorporating such weaker groups at home as the Basques, Bretons, Catalans, Welsh, Scots, Irish, Flemings, Frisians and the like.

If we classify states by the basis and nature of their governments, then, as of 1982, besides 'bourgeois democracies', we have to distinguish the proletarian dictatorships of Marxist states; autocratic military governments, as in Benin and Chile; patrimonial autocracies as in Saudi Arabia, Morocco and Abu Dhabi; revolutionary and other theocracies as in Iran, and so on. Within the broad category of democratic states, moreover, we need to distinguish one-party from multi-party states. Some one-party states, i.e. 'People's Democracies', are self-proclaimed proletarian dictatorships that practice 'democratic centralism', following Lenin and/or Mao. Others lack such prestigious credentials but operate one-party organisations none the less, for example Mexico or Tanzania. Yet other dictatorships, both military and civilian, tolerate no political parties. Among multi-party states it is useful also to distinguish those with only two prominent parties from others with more. At issue here is the relative stability or instability of states as that relates to the conditions under which governmental power is typically transferred between their competing units; but the nature and status of these units are also of interest, whether these are legally registered parties, other civilian groupings, or cliques within some military or secret service, the 'party', etc. It is surely important to distinguish power seizures effected from within by monarchs and other rulers, by army units or by some inner party or other group that illustrates the general pattern of palace coups, from those transfers that proceed by free and open public elections, and others which follow effective outbursts of collective violence, as recently in Iran, Bolivia and Poland.

While well aware of these and other differentiae, it seems sufficient and appropriate for us to classify contemporary and recent states on two axes, by certain gross differences of status and structure. On the first axis we may group these units in four categories, as metropolitan, colonial, emergent or post-colonial, and other, this fourth residual category being reserved for all states which are patently neither metropolitan, emergent — i.e. recently independent — nor colonial, as for example Australia, Peru or Romania. On the second axis it is best to distinguish states by structure as unitary, consociational, ambiguous, and other (see Table 9.1).

In this classification all members of a unitary state are subject to a single central administration, as for example, Britain, Cuba, Israel, Poland, Sri Lanka and Vietnam. The central administration may be elected on a plurality basis or by proportional representation, or it may acquire and hold office under other rules and conditions, free or unfree. In the unitary state, the supreme directorate exercises power and responsibility for the regulation of public affairs, and for relations with other states and foreign bodies.

Consociations as conceived here differ from unitary states by their systematic dispersal of decisive power over policy formation and/or execution among a plurality of units, parties or other agencies within the common state. Thus, besides federations and confederations such as the United States, Switzerland, Canada and Australia, consociations include states with such divergent arrangements of power sharing as Lebanon during 1943–73, Malaysia 1955–69, Cyprus 1960–3 and Nigeria 1959–66 (Lijphart, 1977). Notably consociational regimes generate or facilitate pressures between their constituents to uphold or to modify the current patterns and conditions of power sharing.

On this axis, the residual category labelled 'other' caters for such apparent anomalies as the European Economic Community, which may later prove to be an emerging metropolitan super-state of

189

consociational type; Ulster during 1921–72 whose status *vis-à-vis* Britain was highly ambiguous; or Zimbabwe-Rhodesia during the years of its unsure transition from illegal '*Herrenvolk* democracy' based on white racism towards an independent populist democracy based on black military achievements and majority votes. Thus units classified as 'other' may or may not be fully independent states, but all are transitional.

Finally, it is useful to distinguish states of Marxist base and type such as Yugoslavia, Cuba, China, the Soviet Union, the German Democratic Republic and Poland, from others that lack such pronounced collectivist foundations and orientations. These collectivist states differ significantly in their scopes as well as their organisation from the rest of the species. They represent a quite distinct variety, however diverse internally.

It is obvious that, as a class, contemporary metropolitan states differ in power, status, wealth and many other important attributes from the colonial states that some of them created and controlled until very recently. It is equally obvious that, following their decolonisation, the ex-colonial states differ significantly in status, initiatives and other important features from the colonies that gave them birth, and from the metropolitan states on which they were so often modelled. There is also, as usual, value in the residual category labelled 'other' to include such units as Australia, Peru and China, which, though not metropolitan, are clearly neither colonial nor recently emergent. It is obvious that unitary and consociational structures are likely to be found among metropolitan, emergent and other states, thus demonstrating the independence of the two classifications and their underlying criteria.

State–society relations

For heuristic purposes I shall conclude this discussion by using the criteria and categories set out above to classify a sufficiently large set of recent and contemporary states to enable us to assess their appropriateness and utility. This is done in Table 9.1, which requires some introductory remarks.

The symbols used to indicate the societal typology are: (S) for segmental pluralities; (H) for hierarchic pluralities; (M) for mixed or complex pluralities; and (O) for non-plural societies of any kind. In thus classifying this set of societies I have paid special attention to their ethnic, regional, and religious composition, and to the alignments of their major population blocs, and have tried to avoid placements based on minor and exceptional phenomena. To illustrate: since

190

indigenous Indians and Inuits (Eskimos) in Canada today represent less than 5 per cent of that country's population, I give priority in summarising the Canadian society to relations between its component French, British, other European, and non-European ethnic groups. Likewise, since some 94 per cent of its population are Han Chinese, China is classified as culturally and ethnically homogeneous, even though its Zhuang, Uygur, Hui, Yi, Tibetan, Miao, Manchu, Mongol, Korean, Bui and other minorities together exceed 50 million, which is far larger than the population of most contemporary 'nation-states'.

Clearly I cannot expect general agreement on the societal classification in Table 9.1 since it involves subjective judgement and inference in the absence of specific data. Neither can I expect everyone to agree entirely with the classification of states, either as consociational, unitary or other, on the one hand, or as metropolitan, colonial, emergent or other on the other. The intent of the classification is thus illustrative and exploratory rather than definitive. It makes no claim either for clinical exactness or for sample representativeness. Indeed I doubt if any truly representative sample of recent and/or contemporary states is possible. Certainly the set of units reviewed in Table 9.1 does not provide any adequate basis for statistical generalisations about other contemporary states or societies, or about the varieties and distinctive properties characteristic of either of these units; but neither are all statistically sound generalisations useful or illuminating, nor are all useful or illuminating generalisations statistically sound. On the other hand, comparative analysis of the units in this classified set does illustrate the considerable value and suggestiveness of the leads that flow from our preceding reflections on the various types of state and society and their relations, as those varieties centre on differences of *de jure* and/or *de facto* corporate constitutions.

Most of the units in Table 9.1 are included either because I wished to test and demonstrate the applicability of the criteria and categories of the classification to problematical cases, or because, however wrongly, I felt I had some knowledge of the social and political history and organisation of the units concerned. An attempt was made in selecting countries to strike some balance between the various continents, religious, political, and historical traditions, and levels of economic development. None the less several entries in the Table cannot be defended on these or other grounds since some states appear twice and in different boxes, such as Nigeria before and after 1959; Egypt separately and during its brief honeymoon with Syria; Jamaica, Grenada and Trinidad separately, and as unnamed members of the defunct West Indies Federation; Malaysia and the Malay Federation; and Zimbabwe/Rhodesia, formerly a member of the Central African Federation. In each case such double entries reflect

Table 9.1
Classification of states and societies

	Consociational		Unitary		Other

Metropolitan	Canada (S)
	Switzerland (S)
	FR Germany
	  (O)
	Yugoslavia (S)
		Belgium (S)*
		Holland (S)
		U.S.A. (M)*
			France (O)
			Poland (O)*
			German DR
			  (O)*
			USSR (M)
				Norway (O)
				United
				  Kingdom (S)*
					EEC (S)

Colonial	[Malay Federation 1948–65 (S)]
	[Central African Federation
	  1953–64 (M)]
	[West Indies Federation
	  1957–64] (M)
	Surinam 1949–73 (S)*
			Uganda (M)*
			Jamaica –1962 (H)*
			Grenada –1974 (H)*
			Gold Coast (Ghana) – 1957 (S)
			Nigeria (1951–9) (S)
			French West
			Africa (M)		

Emergent	Malaysia (S)* Nigeria 1960– (S)* Cyprus 1960–4 (S)* Pakistan 1946–71 (S)* [Federation of Egypt and Syria 1958–61 (S)] [Mali Federation 1959–60 (S)] India (S)*		*Cuba* (O)* *Vietnam* (M)* Mauritius (M)* Sri Lanka (M)* Israel (M)* Indonesia (M)*	Trinidad (S)* Guyana (S)* Egypt (O)* Algeria (S)* Iran (M)* Iraq (H)*	Rhodesia 1954–78 (M)*
Other	Australia (O)		*China* (O)* Peru (H)* South Africa (M)* Brazil (O)* Mexico (H)	Chile (O)* Bolivia (H)*	

Key:		
	S – segmental plural society	[ ] – defunct federation
	H – hierarchic plural society	* – prone to violence (see text)
	M – mixed segmental/hierarchic plural society	*Italicised* are states of Marxist
	O – not a plural society	persuasion
	? – unclassified	

Across column (Mexico) – anomalies; states that are consociational in form but unitary in
practice.

significant changes of status and/or structure experienced by these
units. Together they show how the typology may be used to capture
and analyse changes of status, scope or structure in modern states.

To distinguish states of Marxist persuasion in Table 9.1, I have
italicised their names. Several defunct units of federal or quasi-federal
type are included, partly to illustrate retrospective uses of the present
scheme, and partly as relevant memorials of the closing decades of
European imperialism, but also to commemorate and illustrate the

futility of Utopianism in politics, as, for example, the two Islamic Federations. Given the significance our classification ascribes to differences between consociational and unitary states, it is also important to distinguish those states which, while formally consociational operate in practice as unitary structures, for example, the Soviet Union, India, and Mexico, by placing them directly across the line that divides the two categories. Such placements indicate the basic discrepancies between *de facto* realities and *de jure* formalities in these ambiguous regimes.

Being concerned to explore relations between pluralism and the structures of contemporary or modern states, I have restricted this selection to states that have flourished since the end of World War II, not all of which survive in 1982. Dates attached to a particular unit indicate the periods to which the classification refers. Asterisks are used to indicate states which have periodically experienced outbursts of internal collective violence since 1945 and seem likely to do so in the near future. Such internal upheavals are theoretically related to conditions of social composition and structure on the one hand, and to conditions of state organisation on the other. Since such incidents reflect and affect the relations and access of all members to the state structures and facilities, it seems useful to try to indicate, however crudely, the differing incidence and risks of collective violence within these states since World War II in order provisionally to test our political and societal typologies and to illustrate their application and implications.

Of 52 units in Table 9.1, 6 are defunct, 5 of these being unsuccessful attempts at federation, 3 of which were initiated by the British government in the process of its decolonisation, while 2 were constructed by the inexperienced leaderships of Islamic states shortly after achieving independence. The sixth defunct unit, French West Africa, though represented loosely as a federal group, was a colonial expression of the French passion for bureaucratic centralisation. Six other units, namely, Surinam, Uganda, Jamaica, Grenada, Gold Coast (Ghana) and Nigeria are cited in their colonial phases which have since passed. Thus only 40 of the 52 units in this Table figure there in their current status and form, all entries in the colonial row having since moved on or out of history together with the 2 well-meaning but misconceived Islamic federations announced in the 1950s. If we include the 6 surviving ex-colonial states, 46 of the 52 units in this selective list are currently afloat. Of these, Cyprus, Malaysia and Pakistan have recently experienced secessions or fission, while the Soviet Union, India, Mexico and Brazil, though formally constituted as federations, operate effectively as unitary states, and are placed accordingly in the Table so as to indicate their ambiguity. A fifth member of this ambiguous class, the now defunct French West Africa, though formally federal, operated in fact as a highly centralised unitary state. Excluding its defunct and duplicate entries, several of the 40 states remaining in Table 9.1 are national units only by fiction, force or faith.

Table 9.2
Distribution of states in Table 9.1

	Consociations	Consociational in Form, Unitary in Practice	Unitary States	Others	Total
Metropolitan	7	1	5	1	14
Colonial	4	1	5	–	10
Emergent	6	1	12	1	20
Other	1	2	5	–	8
Total	18	5	27	2	52

Table 9.3
Distribution of segmental pluralities in Table 9.1

	Consociations	Consociational in Form, Unitary in Practice	Unitary States	Others	Total
Metropolitan	5	–	1	1	7
Colonial	2	–	2	–	4
Emergent	6	1	3	–	10
Other	–	–	–	–	–
Total	13	1	6	1	21

Table 9.4
Distribution of hierarchic pluralities in Table 9.1

	Consociations	Consociational in Form, Unitary in Practice	Unitary States	Others	Total
Metropolitan	–	–	–	–	–
Colonial	–	–	2	–	2
Emergent	–	–	1	–	1
Other	–	1	2	–	3
Total	–	1	5	–	6

194

Table 9.5
Distribution of pluralities of mixed structure in Table 9.1

	Consociations	Consociational in Form, Unitary in Practice	Unitary States	Others	Total
Metropolitan	1	1	–	–	2
Colonial	2	1	1	–	4
Emergent	–	–	6	1	7
Other	–	–	1	–	1
Total	3	2	8	1	14

Table 9.6
Distribution of non-plural societies in Table 9.1

	Consociations	Consociational in Form, Unitary in Practice	Unitary States	Others	Total
Metropolitan	1	–	4	–	5
Colonial	–	–	–	–	–
Emergent	–	–	2	–	2
Other	1	1	2	–	4
Total	2	1	8	–	11

Although the units listed in Table 9.1 are selected to illustrate and explore various points, it is none the less useful to review briefly the details of their distributions as set out in Tables 9.2 to 9.6. As regards the distribution of states in this set of 52, 27 are unitary in form and practice; 5 are consociational in form but unitary in practice; 2 are included to illustrate anomalies; and 18 are consociations in practice, if not so by their constitutions.

Of the 52 states listed in Table 9.1, 21 incorporated segmental pluralities (Table 9.3), 6 incorporated hierarchic pluralities (Table 9.4), and 14 were based on plural societies of mixed constitution (Table 9.5). Thus 41 of these 52 states incorporated plural societies, a fact that should indicate the urgent need for adequate study of the political implications and aspects of pluralism in contemporary states.

Of the 21 segmental pluralities, 13 are or were explicitly incorporated as consociational states, 6 as unitary states, while India, though consociational in form, is unitary in practice, and the EEC is anomalous. Of 18 consociational states in the set, only 2, the Federal Republic of Germany and Australia, do not incorporate plural societies, while 2 others, the defunct Central African and West Indian

195

Federations, each combined hierarchic and segmental structures. Thus of 18 consociational states in Table 9.1, 13 incorporated segmental pluralities, 3 coordinated mixed pluralities, and only 2 were not plural societies.

Of these 18 consociations, the 5 hurriedly misconceived federations have disappeared with little regret. Three other consociational units, namely, Cyprus, Malaysia and Pakistan, have experienced secessions; a fourth, Canada, has recently faced a similar threat which is by no means over; and a fifth, Nigeria, has had to fight a bitter civil war against secession. All 5 units incorporate segmental pluralities. Altogether this record does not inspire great confidence in the capacities of consociational state structures to ensure order and stability in segmental pluralities. However, of 27 unitary states in the list, 6 incorporate segmental pluralities though 1 of these — colonial Nigeria before 1952 — should be excluded to avoid duplication. Of the remaining 5, Guyana and Mauritius have recently had to cope with internal violence that reflects their plural composition. Excluding the defunct Islamic federations and duplicate references to Malaysia and Nigeria, of the 15 remaining segmental pluralities in Table 9.1, 9 have experienced internal violence recently and risk its resumption in the near future.

Violence in plural societies

Of 14 units listed in Table 9.1 as states incorporating pluralities of mixed or complex structure, 3, namely French West Africa, and the Central African and West Indian Federations, were highly artificial groupings of colonial states and have ceased to exist. To assess, however tentatively, the incidence of internal violence in plural societies of mixed structure, I shall therefore exclude these three non-entities, thus leaving 11 cases of this type in our set, namely, the United States, Vietnam, the Soviet Union, Uganda, Indonesia, Iran, Israel, Sri Lanka, Mauritius, Zimbabwe/Rhodesia (1954–78) and South Africa. Excluding the Soviet Union, all of these societies have suffered internal violence during the past two decades; and some now continue to do so. All, with the possible exception of the United States and the Soviet Union can be expected to experience recurrent violence in the immediate future. Thus, on these data, societies of mixed or more complex plural structure seem to be even more at risk of internal collective violence than segmental pluralities.

Of 6 hierarchic pluralities in Table 9.1, namely, Jamaica, Grenada, Iraq, Peru, Bolivia and Mexico, 5 have experienced upheavals and violence of varying duration and intensity during the recent past, and seem more likely than otherwise to repeat the experience in some form in the near future. Thus if these unrepresentative instances and subjectively asserted classifications are accepted, it seems that pluralities of mixed and hierarchic structures are at least as prone to internal collective violence as segmental pluralities. Of the latter, however, on our data those incorporated as unitary states seem a little less at risk of internal violence than others organised as consociations.

Of the states listed in Table 9.1, 11 incorporate non-plural societies. Of these 11 non-plural societies, 5 are metropolitan, 2 emergent and 4, namely, Australia, Brazil, China and Chile, are bracketed as 'other', being neither metropolitan, colonial nor emergent on the criteria employed to distinguish these categories. Of these 11 states, 2, though clearly not plural, are organised consociationally, namely, Australia and the Federal Republic of Germany. Excluding Brazil, the remainder are all constituted as unitary states, 5 being of Marxist persuasion, namely, Poland, Cuba, China, Vietnam and the German Democratic Republic, while 4 others, Norway, France, the Federal Republic of Germany and the United Kingdom, operate mixed economies, and yet others, such as Brazil or Chile, are committed to capitalism and market-regulating economies. Clearly the modern state, whether unitary or consociational, is equally capable of promoting, organising and regulating economies of either kind in plural and in non-plural societies. Notably, although Cuba and China are pre-industrial societies, while the German Democratic Republic and Poland are not, both pairs rely equally on Marxist ideology and models of political organisation to regulate their economies.

Of these 11 'non-plural' societies, at least 2 non-Marxist units with recent histories of internal violence, namely, Chile and Brazil, are likely to experience its recurrence in the near future. A third, Poland, has experienced over the past two years profound industrial and social upheavals with some bloodshed. How we place the United Kingdom in this scheme turns firstly on our views about Northern Ireland, which is now clearly a segmental plural society, though formerly hierarchic. That unit, which still occupies an anomalous political status, has for years suffered internal violence. Secondly, racial conflicts have occurred recently in England and are likely to recur in the near future. To date, such outbreaks have been sporadic and sharply localised, thus indicating the need for more precise criteria to discriminate degrees, kinds and contexts of collective violence. Of the non-plural states in this set, Cuba, China, the German Democratic Republic, Poland, Brazil and Chile in recent times have experienced upheavals of the sort that Marxists theorise, together with others they do not, as in China and Poland. In contrast, conflicts already reported or expected in pluralities of segmental, hierarchic or more complex structure seem either to be exclusively or predominantly ethnic and racial, religious,

197

or otherwise non-economic in genesis, focus and character. If so, then only in non-plural societies, on our evidence, is it likely that class conflicts may give rise to collective violence of the kind that Marxist theory expects.

Of the Marxist states in Table 9.1, the Soviet Union and Vietnam incorporate mixed pluralities, Yugoslavia incorporates a segmental plurality, while, on our criteria, the German Democratic Republic, China and Cuba incorporate non-plural societies. Yugoslavia deviates from other Marxist states in at least two ways. First, the Yugoslav state is set up and operated as a genuine consociation, despite its Marxist commitment to democratic centralism under a Communist Party. Second, in recognition of its polyethnic basis, Yugoslav ideology and practice alike stress heavily the responsibilities of self-management by groups of all kinds and at all levels as a basic principle of Yugoslav socialism.

Altogether, the distribution in Table 9.1 suggests that under capitalism and socialism alike, contexts of cultural heterogeneity without pluralism are more favourable for class mobilisation and coordinated collective pursuit of economic interests on a rational basis by revolutionary or other means than contexts of ethnic, racial, cultural and social pluralism, even when polyethnic populations are incorporated in unitary states, as in Mauritius, Uganda, Peru, Sri Lanka or Iraq.

Of the 21 segmental pluralities in our list, 13 were incorporated as consociations, 6 as unitary states. Evidently the unitary model may be employed to co-ordinate segmental pluralities effectively. Hierarchic pluralities are the least numerous societal type in our set; and in their pure form they fit most readily within a unitary state structure. No example of the consociational incorporation of a hierarchic plurality occurs in this set, including Mexico, which neatly illustrates the rule by its conversion of a formally consociational regime into a unitary one in practice. Complex pluralities which combine differential and segmental incorporation are also more commonly coordinated as unitary states than as consociations.

The only extant example of a complex plurality ordered as a consociation in our list, the United States, is presently involved in extensive processes of structural change intended officially to eliminate its *de facto* differential incorporation of non-white citizens, and may therefore at some future point change its societal type. Interestingly, the other superpower, the Soviet Union, also incorporates a complex plurality of continental scale, but as befits a Marxist regime, despite its elaborately consociational constitution, regulates its population by proletarian dictatorship. On this evidence it seems that the unitary state structure is generally preferred by the dominant sections of complex and hierarchic pluralities for obvious reasons.

Of the 20 emergent nations in this set, only 2, Cuba and Egypt, are not plural societies of one kind or another. The great majority of the new states that have emerged from the colonial and semi-colonial rule formerly imposed by Europeans owe their plural structures and characteristics to that common though diverse formative experience. As the distributions set out in Tables 9.2 to 9.6 illustrate, alternative state structures, consociational and unitary, *de facto* as well as *de jure*, are to be found in societies of all differing kinds, except that no hierarchic pluralities in this set are ordered by consociational regimes.

To explore the possible connections of internal violence and societal type in states of differing structure, it is first necessary to eliminate from consideration all those improbable and short-lived units listed in Table 9.1, namely, the Malay Federation, the Central African and West Indies Federations, French West Africa and the two Islamic Federations of Egypt and Syria on the one hand, Senegal and the Soudanese Republic (the Mali Federation) on the other. With these excisions our set consists of 46 states (see Tables 9.7 and 9.8).

Table 9.7
Distribution of Internal Violence and Order in Extant States of Differing Status and Type

	Consociations	Consociational in Form, Unitary in Practice	Unitary States	Others	Total
Metropolitan	3/4*	0/1	3/2	0/1	6/8 = 14
Colonial	1/0	–	3/2	–	4/2 = 6
Emergent	4/0	1/0	12/0	1/0	18/0 = 18
Other	0/1	1/1	5/0	–	6/2 = 8
Total	8/5 = 13	2/2 = 4	23/4 = 27	1/1 = 2	34/12 = 46

* The first figure in each column is the number of units that have had internal violence between 1945 and 1981, the second the number that have not.

Of these 46 states, by my standards 34 have suffered internal collective violence since World War II, while 12 (Canada, Switzerland, the Federal Republic of Germany, the Netherlands, France, Norway, Australia, the Soviet Union, Mexico, the EEC, and the Gold Coast and Nigeria before decolonisation) have not. Of the 13 consociations, 8 have experienced internal violence. Of 4 formally consociational but *de facto* unitary regimes, 2 have done likewise. Of the two anomalies, while the EEC has enjoyed peace and order, Zimbabwe/Rhodesia was

Table 9.8
**Distribution of Internal Violence and Order in Societies and States
of Differing Type**

	Consociations	Consociational in Form, Unitary in Practice	Unitary States	Others	Total
Segmentary pluralities	7/3*	1/0	4/2	0/1	12/6 = 18
Hierarchic pluralities	–	0/1	5/0	–	5/1 = 6
Mixed pluralities	1/0	0/1	8/0	1/0	10/1 = 11
Non-plural societies	0/2	1/0	6/2	–	7/4 = 11
Total	8/5 = 13	2/2 = 4	23/4 = 27	1/1 = 2	34/12 = 46

* The first figure in each column is the number of units with internal violence
since 1945, the second the number without internal violence since 1945.

the arena of prolonged conflict. Of 27 unitary states in this set, 23 have
suffered but survived internal violence during the post-war years,
although often with abrupt changes of government and sometimes of
the regime itself.

Of these 46 states, 18 are segmentary pluralities, 10 of these being
organised consociationally and 6 as unitary states. Another 6 are
hierarchic pluralities, all operating *de facto* as unitary states though
one, Mexico, is formally a federation. Eleven are mixed or complex
pluralities; and of these only 1, the United States, is a genuine
consociation. Of the 11 non-plural societies in this set, 8 are incorporated *de jure* as unitary states while another, Brazil, operates thus in
practice though formally a consociation.

Of the 35 pluralities in this set, 8 have experienced no significant
internal violence since World War II, while 27 have experienced such
violence. Of our 6 hierarchical pluralities, only Mexico has escaped
substantial internal violence since World War II. Of 11 mixed or
complex pluralities in this list, only the Soviet Union, as far as I know,
has maintained internal order without public outbursts since World
War II. All other mixed pluralities have witnessed severe, sometimes
prolonged or periodic strife. Of the 18 segmental pluralities, 11 have
experienced internal violence since 1945.

Of the 11 non-plural societies in our set, the Federal Republic of
Germany, Australia, France and Norway have all been peaceful over

this period. Of the remaining 7, 4 have become Marxist states since World War II, namely, Cuba, China, Poland and the German Democratic Republic, the first 2 by independent revolutionary struggles and programmes, and the others as outcomes of Soviet liberation from Nazi forces during the closing phases of World War II. In Brazil, Chile and Egypt, internal violence has differing bases. In Brazil and Chile counter-revolutionary and pro-capitalist forces, including the army, have played prominent roles in overthrowing populist regimes and eradicating their leadership and active elements. While the cases of Brazil, Chile, Cuba, China, Poland and the German Democratic Republic all illustrate the processes of class struggle for economic and political control that Marx expected in capitalist societies, in several instances these struggles also occur in Marxist states. However, these are the only 6 instances of such economically motivated collective violence in the 34 cases under discussion. They all occur in societies which lack plural divisions. By contrast, in Canada, Belgium, the United Kingdom, South Africa, Israel, Peru and Bolivia, despite their capitalist economies, the primary lines of cleavage which have generated or threatened public violence are cultural, ethnic and/or racial. It seems then that while class-based violence in pursuit of rational economic and political objectives can be expected in some non-plural societies, pluralities, whether segmental, hierarchic or complex, tend to generate collective violence of a different kind, as functions of tensions between their plural rather than their class components.

Of these diverse pluralities, on our evidence, despite its explosive potential, the segmental variety, whether organised consociationally or as a unitary state, seems least violence-prone. The hierarchic plurality, formally or *de facto* organised as a unitary state, has a higher incidence and risk of violence. This is also the case with pluralities of mixed structure, since they are also fundamentally based on differential incorporation. Of 17 societies in the list that share this structural feature, namely, the six hierarchic and 11 mixed pluralities, only 2 have escaped significant internal violence since World War II, namely, the Soviet Union and Mexico, both perhaps because of the overwhelming concentration of resources, power and organisational capacity in their dominant sections, which are also demographically by far the largest in both societies.

Viewed from a different perspective, of the 46 societies under present view, those organised within consociations seem to have the best chance of avoiding violence, despite the friction which consociational arrangements often generate, perhaps because such arrangements may be tailored to fit or adjust to changing *de facto* segmental alignments and interests fairly well. Unitary states, despite their remarkable resilience and stamina as power structures, seem on the evidence of this 'sample' to provide fertile fields for collective violence, of class-based as well as plural kinds.

Conclusion

Although segmental pluralities are conducive to consociational regimes and forms of state, and those structures probably provide the most favourable and appropriate frameworks for such societies, they cannot guarantee internal order or successful nation-building, depluralisation, national integration or political development. Similarly, although pluralities of hierarchic or mixed structure are most appropriately incorporated as unitary states, such frameworks are often employed by their dominant sections to frustrate policies and programmes that might undermine their collective positions of privilege and power. In effect, in plural societies, the unitary state commonly serves as an effective structure for repression of trends towards depluralisation and national integration, whether these are hierarchic, segmental or complex at base. Such policies are equally compatible with industrialisation and governmental promotion of economic development, as South Africa, Guyana, Israel and Iran illustrate (Blumer, 1965). So long as the dominant sections of such pluralities enjoy favourable external relations with powerful metropolitan states and monopolise effectively the means of violence at home, their regimes remain beyond local challenge, as illustrated by Israel and South Africa. However, once either or both of these requisites ceases to hold, the regime is at risk, and with it the unity and future of the society it regulates.

Though primarily heuristic, given the arbitrary collection of states on which they are based, these 'conclusions' are sufficiently significant and interesting to indicate the value of our approach to such problems of state and society, and to warrant further work along these lines.

References

Blumer, Herbert (1965). 'Industrialisation and Race Relations' in Guy Hunter (ed.), *Industrialisation and Race Relations*, London, Oxford University Press.
Broom, Leonard (1960). 'Discussion' in Vera Rubin (ed.), 'Social and Cultural Pluralism in the Caribbean', *Annals of the New York Academy of Sciences*, vol. 83, art. 5, p. 889.
Lijphart, Arend (1977). *Democracy in Plural Societies: A Comparative Exploration*. New Haven, Yale University Press.

Smith, M.G. (1960). 'Social and Cultural Pluralism in the Caribbean' in Rubin, op. cit., pp. 763–77.

Smith, M.G. (1965). *The Plural Society in the British West Indies*. Berkeley and Los Angeles, University of California Press.

Smith, M.G. (1969a). 'Institutional and Political Conditions of Pluralism' in Leo Kuper and M.G. Smith (eds.), *Pluralism in Africa*. Berkeley and Los Angeles, University of California Press, pp. 27–65.

Smith, M.G. (1969b). 'Some Developments in the Analytic Framework of Pluralism' in Kuper and Smith, op. cit., pp. 415–58.

Smith, M.G. (1984). 'The Nature and Variety of Plural Units' in David Maybury-Lewis (ed.), *The Prospects for Plural Societies*. Washington, DC, American Ethnological Society, pp. 146–86.

Weber, Max (1947). *The Theory of Social & Economical Organization*, translated by Talcott Parsons and A.M. Henderson. Edinburgh, William Hodge & Co.

Weber, Max (1963). *The Sociology of Religion*, translated by Ephraim Fischoff. Boston, Beacon Press.

10 Neo-Marxist, pluralist, corporatist, statist theories and the welfare state

Göran Therborn

By the mid-1980s, it would seem from many accounts that one of the major participants in the 'great controversies about the state', over the past two decades, neo-Marxism, is fatally wounded, or even dead. According to Claus Offe (1983, p. 58), himself in the textbook literature still often referred to as a Marxist, 'as a consequence above all of the impact of French theorists such as Foucault, Touraine and Gorz . . . remnants of Marxist orthodoxy hardly have social scientific respectability any more'. (A reply to Offe is included in Therborn, 1986.)

In his broad overview of state theories, Pierre Birnbaum disposes of the 'four great schools' of Marxist political theory and finds a tendency in the latter towards dissolution into conceptions centring on what he calls the 'differentiation of the state'. This tendency was noticeable in Nicos Poulantzas's later works, and now, according to Birnbaum (1985, p. 670), we have arrived at

> a moment where certain Marxist theoreticians themselves come almost to conceive the state in a Weberian perspective, where the action of the State is exercised to the benefit of the personnel who controls it, considering that the power of the former increases to the extent that the power of the latter grows.

Michael Mann (1984, p. 185f) embarks on an attempt at grounding the autonomy of the state in its territoriality, after briefly dismissing

Marxist, along with liberal and functionalist, theories of the state as 'reductionist'.

On the Marxist side, there have been serious losses, evasions, and concessions. The greatest neo-Marxist political theoretician, Nicos Poulantzas, died in 1979. Confrontations with new challenges to liberal pluralism, such as corporatism and its two main variants, developed by Philippe Schmitter and Gerhard Lehmbruch (Schmitter and Lehmbruch, 1979; Lehmbruch and Schmitter, 1982), and statism as presented by Theda Skocpol (1979), have been evasive and are often simply avoided by Marxists.

Bob Jessop (1982) ends a penetrating book-length discussion of Marxist state theories with a chapter attempting to lead us 'Towards a Theoretical Account of the State', without even mentioning the corporatist and statist challenges. Ralph Miliband has tried to face up to the statist critique, but in a remarkably weak and conceding way. Arguing for viewing the relationship between the state and the dominant class as one of 'partnership', and reducing the state simply to 'certain people who are in charge of the executive power of the state — presidents, prime ministers, their cabinets, and their top civilian and military advisers' (Miliband, 1983, p. 60). If the state is no more than the government élite, there would seem to be no need for any state theory. Martin Carnoy, in another presentation of Marxism, wider-ranging than Jessop's does critically discuss other contemporary state theories. But he ends his book with a deep bow to the non-class-movement theories, which have so much impressed Offe, among others, asking: 'Is it possible that the class State degenerates through its own delegitimation to be replaced by other loci of political and economic power?' (Carnoy, 1984, p. 261).

The irony is that while many former protagonists and adherents of the various 'schools' of neo-Marxism are now proclaiming a post-Marxist, beyond-class stance (Laclau and Mouffe, 1985), a new, vigorous self-confident class theory of politics and the state is being launched, impeccably dressed in the best clothes of modern empirical social science, while making no secret of its inspiring commitment to the working-class movement. The most elaborate argument so far of this counter-tendency is probably Walter Korpi (1983). Other examples include Gösta Esping-Andersen's (1985b) comparative study of Scandinavia, and Esping-Andersen and Korpi's ongoing comparative welfare-state research project, a part of which has been published (Esping-Andersen and Korpi, 1984). Without, obviously, being competent to judge my own dress, qualities or significance, I might perhaps be allowed to add to this list some works of my own (Therborn, 1983a, 1984a,b, 1985a,b, 1986).

This renaissance of Marxist political analysis in the 1980s will appear unexpected, at least in two respects. First, its main empirical focus is the welfare state, a topic by and large absent not only in classical Marxism — for obvious historical reasons — but also in the first wave of neo-Marxist political theory, inaugurated by Poulantzas (1968) and Miliband (1969). Second, its geographical centre is Scandinavia — where it is paralleled by other major works of a similar orientation, such as that of Ulf Himmelstrand *et al.* (1981) — distinguished earlier as a nursery of Marxist thought.

A historical materialist, or if preferred, a social historian, may find some reasons for this development, beyond individual idiosyncrasies. Class politics is in the open, occupying centre stage in Scandinavian politics. The party spectrum is divided between parties claiming to represent the working class and constitute the labour movement and those designating themselves as 'bourgeois' parties. The labour movement is relatively strong, and the working class relatively homogeneous. National and religious issues play a smaller part in Scandinavia than in most other countries. The Scandinavian welfare states are very much developed and play a central part in the self-identification of Scandinavian society. Hinting at the basis for the endeavours of contemporary Scandinavian sociological Marxism, of course, tells us nothing about its explanatory range. Those questions will be taken up below.

There is, then, still a contingent of scholars arguing, that states are a function of classes, rather than the other way round. Let us now try to locate their arguments in the broader context of controversies about the state, beginning with their relationship to the first generation of neo-Marxism.

Neo-Marxism I and II

If we cut through the dense vegetation of jargon, fully on a par with sociologese, and dispense with the code-words of the sentinels and latterday guardians of the schools, the first generation of neo-Marxist political theory offered three major theses.

Firstly, political power even in democratic capitalist societies was not in the hands of the people, of the electorate, with its competing parties and interest groups. Instead, power and politics were dominated by a capitalist class, exerting its power through a number of mechanisms and in a number of ways. Miliband's work was primarily preoccupied with this question, although all brands of neo-Marxism I agreed on the conclusion, albeit along variegated routes of argumentation.

Secondly, Western democratic states were capitalist/bourgeois

206

states in a structural sense. Their organisation, internal mode of functioning and relationship to society were shaped primarily if not exclusively, by the social class relations of the capitalist societies they were governing. Poulantzas pioneered this conception, whereupon other variants followed, particularly in the Federal Republic of Germany.

Thirdly, not only the capitalist class but also the above-mentioned structural features of bourgeois states posed certain fundamental constraints on what even governments with the best intentions could actually achieve, constraints surmountable only by revolution or by quasi-revolutionary popular mobilisation. Here again, Poulantzas was the forerunner, although the structural limitations of governmental reformism above all preoccupied neo-Marxists in the Federal Republic, trying to cope with an initially ambitious reformist government.

This first neo-Marxist thrust left several important, lasting achievements, not yet reversed in mainstream political science and political sociology. It brought into focus the stark inequalities of power even in liberal democracies and the enduring reality of class even in booming capitalism, both phenomena soft-pedalled and often denied outright by liberal theory. Furthermore, it brought back the state, as an institutional/organisational ensemble, wider than 'the government' and more differentiated from society than 'the political system', to the centre stage of theory and investigation. It also highlighted the problem of the relationship between the state and the capitalist economy, then still largely neglected by political science, in spite of the massively increasing involvement of Western states in the running of their economies.

By any assessment, this was no small achievement. On the other hand, the limitations are also obvious, at least with the wisdom of hindsight. Three of them stand out: one empirical, one theoretical, and one political.

State theorising was little associated with or followed up by empirical research. Most empirical research from a ruling-class perspective was done by those least theoretically ambitious or elaborate, such as William Domhoff (1967, 1978, 1979) and Maurice Zeitlin and his students (Zeitlin, 1980). An attempt at empirical operationalisation of the class character of state structures and of ruling-class rule (Therborn, 1978) fell largely between scholastic approaches to both Marxism and non-Marxism. The outstanding Marxist empirical work on the state produced in this period (Anderson, 1974) did not deal with capitalist states at all, but with late feudal absolutist states.

The theoretical shortcoming of the first generation of neo-Marxist works concerned, above everything else, the very core of the state, the

207

relationship between state and class as actors. Poulantzas (1968, chapter IV.1) laid out the terrain of the ensuing controversies, and also sowed the seeds of enduring confusion. He put the relation in terms of the 'relative autonomy' of the former *vis-à-vis* the latter. Over preceding Marxist analyses, this was a clear advance, a recognition of a problematical and variable complexity. But this formulation begged the critical questions, which were soon to arise; how relative is state autonomy and how autonomous is a relatively autonomous state? (cf. Block, 1977, p. 9). The statist option was to assert the autonomy *tout court* of states and 'state managers', while recognising the state's 'intrinsically dual anchorage in class-divided socioeconomic structures and an international system of states (Skocpol, 1979, p. 32).

Behind 'the relative autonomy' or the 'anchored autonomy' and a number of other more or less contorted formulations, such as for example Block's (1977) 'behind the backs' non-rule of the ruling class or Therborn's (1978, p. 138) ruling class rule 'in the absence of a conscious inter-personal relation', lies a fact not explicitly recognised and theorised. That is, that states and classes are different animals.

States, like all formal organisations, are *decision-making* bodies; classes are not. Classes act — through the parallel or more or less complexly co-ordinated actions of class members — but classes *qua* classes do not decide. The latter incapacity is also a rationale for the specificity of class analysis. For if classes were reducible to the organisations claiming to represent them, we could more handily replace the former with organisational analysis.

Thus, rather than state managers competing with or being in partnership with a dominant class, we are faced, on the one hand, with a contextualised set of decision-makers and, on the other, with, first, a class-structured supply of social and organisational skills, second, a set of constraints on state action posed by class relations and class action, and, third, different demands upon the state pushed by class action, the effectiveness of which is dependent on class constellations of force.

Politically, neo-Marxism I was hung up on the problematic of a transition from capitalism to socialism, and its theorisation and analyses of contemporaneity focused on what was specifically capitalist, as opposed to socialist, or on what was characteristic of the current epoch or stage of capitalism in distinction to preceding ones. Neo-Marxism I shared this concentration on trying to grasp the basic features of modern times, as opposed to previous or post-modern ones, with classical sociological theory, often a chosen rival — with the latter's polarisations between *Gemeinschaft* and *Gesellschaft*, mechanical and organic solidarity, the traditional and the rational, etc. In both cases the result was a lack of interest in, and attention to, variation between epochs and the reasons for the latter. To many protagonists and adherents of the first neo-Marxism, this transitional problematic had an almost eschatological immediacy to it, which, as time went on, and capitalism remained while the Chinese Cultural Revolution ended, not infrequently led to intellectual crisis and breakdown.

This is not the place to give an extensive account of neo-Marxism II, mainly because the state has hitherto been rather out of focus in it. Instead, while the 'post-Marxists' have turned to 'new social movements' as topics of discourse and objects of hope and while state analysis has been increasingly impregnated with corporatism and statism, neo-Marxism II has concentrated, even more than the first wave, on class. Some examples are Korpi (1978, 1983), Roemer (1982), and Wright (1985). As far as the state is concerned, the major efforts have been orientated towards analysing welfare states.

Briefly, however, we may summarise some characteristic features of neo-Marxism II. In theorising, the idiom of classical social theory has largely been replaced by a more formalised language, sometimes with recourse to analytical philosophy (Cohen, 1978) or mathematical economics and game theory (Roemer, 1982), more generally by a language of hypothesised variation. Explanation, rather than interpretation has become the central task. While including a lively theoretical debate, on a very high level of abstraction, neo-Marxism II, in contrast to its immediate predecessor, is resolutely empirical and intimately links theorisation and empirical research. The political problematic of transition from capitalism to socialism still looms large (Korpi, 1978), but it has lost all traces of eschatology, and in the works of Swedish social democrats such as Himmelstrand and, particularly, Korpi, it takes on an assertively reformist and gradualist character. But increasingly, neo-Marxism II is interested in and concerned with variations within capitalism, between advanced capitalist societies and states.

State theory and the welfare state

General theories of states and politics have already been developed with the welfare state in mind. On the contrary, welfare-state research has been much more concerned with the relevance of politics than the nature of politics and political theory. Even the specialised welfare state researchers of neo-Marxism II, such as Esping-Andersen and Korpi, have had little interest in state and political theory *per se*.

In other words, the terrain for a proper confrontation between state theory and welfare-state realities will have to be laid out. From state theory, at least three explanatory hypotheses may be drawn with regard to the welfare state:

1 *Patterns of development*: Under what circumstances should we expect major welfare-state institutions to be installed, to grow rapidly, to stagnate, and to be cut back or abolished? Under what conditions should larger or smaller welfare states be expected to develop?
2 *Structural forms*: What are the circumstances which contribute to shaping various kinds of welfare state?
3 *Socio-economic implications*: How do welfare states influence social relations and relations of distribution?

There are some basic problems which have to be solved, before a proper testing of theories may be arranged, but this is beyond the scope of this paper. Since none of the major contending state theories of pluralism, neo-Marxism, corporatism and statism have as yet been explicitly formulated in these terms, further developments or extrapolations from existing modes of thought are necessary. The road already travelled by the theories in this respect is also uneven, the longest distance having been covered by pluralism and neo-Marxism II. Only rudimentary classifications of types of welfare state, such as Richard Titmuss's distinction (1974:30-1) between 'marginal' and 'institutional' types, have yet become established, although some more elaborate attempts do exist (Alber, 1982, p. 47; Esping-Andersen, 1985b, pp. 468ff; Mishra, 1977, pp. 90ff, 122ff; Rimlinger, 1971; Therborn, 1984a, pp. 18ff). What is to be explained with regard to welfare-state forms, and to some extent also, to effects upon social relations, has still to be specified.

Pluralism

Taken broadly and generally, a pluralist perspective entails that politics and political situations in liberal democracies are the result of competitive elections between parties and competitive pressures from a plurality of interest groups, all operating within a given constitutional framework.

The causal political forces, which may well be considered to be more or less influenced and constrained by economic and demographic parameters, will here be the constitutional structure, the cycles of elections and of electoral outcomes, and the basically *ad hoc* output of interest group mobilisations and rivalries.

Concerning patterns of development, certain propositions follow from pluralist theory. Welfare systems of social security should start earlier in countries with wide or universal suffrage than in countries having a more restricted franchise. Once full liberal democracy is established, welfare systems can be expected to grow gradually with economic growth — including general social rights and a certain guaranteed minimum security for everybody, after which the outcome of pluralist politics becomes logically indeterminate. Public social expenditure could either grow with further economic growth or decline with rising prosperity, making social security largely superfluous, or stay somewhere in between. The ageing of the population should in any case be expected to push social expenditure upwards.

Along this mainly economically and demographically determined trend, two cyclical patterns of expansion and holdback should be expected. One expresses an electoral cycle, with expenditure rising just prior to elections. Another governmental cycle, manifesting the governmental outcome of the previous election, is one in which governments striving primarily for the support of lower-income voters spend more and extend social rights, and governments appealing more to a better-off electorate do less so. Countries with a more complex and divided constitutional structure should exhibit more inertia in the face of changes and governmental oscillations than countries with unified and centralised forms of government. International variations in size of the welfare state should, at similar levels of wealth and similar age composition of the population, tend to become less significant over time.

About the determinants of different forms of welfare state, it seems to be very difficult to derive any propositions from pluralist theory, except that, with the development of liberal democracy there will be a substitution of social rights for personally humiliating forms of social support for those in dire need. The pluralist perspective would also suggest that ethnic and religious cleavages might have some special effects upon the organisation of the welfare state.

With regard to the socio-economic implications of the welfare state, again little appears to follow from pluralism. The welfare state should contribute to the establishment and consolidation of equal citizenship rights. Economically, it will tend to have a destabilising impact by adding a pattern of political (electoral) business cycles, to the cycles of the market itself. For an overview, the reader is referred to the very comprehensive works of review and testing by Jens Alber (1979, 1982, 1983) and Manfred Schmidt (1982).

A few things are noteworthy, however. Researchers in, or related to, the pluralist tradition have concentrated on quantitative patterns of development. Varying amounts of support for pluralist hypotheses have been found in this respect, but three major weaknesses of pluralist theory in accounting for patterns of development have

211

become clear. While political pluralism proper is indeterminate in its forecasting of long-term development, welfare states have tended to grow for about a century. Second, there is no international trend of convergence (Alber, 1982, p. 200). In 1981, the relationship between the largest social public spender (as a proportion of GDP, exclusive of education) (Belgium) and the smallest (Japan) was 2.4:1 (calculated from OECD, 1985, p. 79ff). Third, growth patterns tend to be temporally uneven, whereas pluralist politics would expect them to be continuous — before and after a possible breaking-point — with cyclical oscillations. The rapid growth of real benefits in 1960–75 (OECD, 1985, p. 30) and the uneven long-term social insurance growth in Western Europe (Alber 1982, pp. 28, 60, 152) are but two examples.

The apparently inherent weakness of pluralist theory with regard to the structural forms and the socio-economic implications of welfare states must be viewed as a serious deficiency. A final word of qualification is called for, however. The quality of the actually existing practice of research is not synonymous with the theoretical perspective which is behind it. Arguably, the best available work on comparative welfare-state arrangements and policies, in a broad sense, is largely written from a pluralist perspective, although with some ingredients borrowed from neo-Marxism II, in the second edition (Heidenheimer *et al.*, 1975, 1983).

Corporatism

From a corporatist viewpoint the key forces are monopolistic, central-ised and converted interest organisations bargaining with the state and with each other.

Though launched as a critique of and an alternative to pluralism, corporatism is less wide-ranging and elaborate than pluralism. Hitherto it has also been much less applied to welfare-state and social policy research. Both features make it more difficult to spell out what it may mean and imply in our context. Corporatism suggests that, as regards the patterns of development, welfare should be expected to follow not so much from citizens' demands or politicians' appeals to voters, as from negotiated and calculated trade-offs between the state and powerful interest organisations, where relations between the state and its population meet these limits. Schmitter (1984) has argued, for instance, that warfare is the origin of welfare, as a compensation for sacrifice and conscription. Welfare states may be expected to grow, when interest organisations benefiting from such growth are powerful and when governments have to demand from the population sacrifices which have to be traded off. Since social institutions can be tailored to the interests of a large variety of interest organisations, patterns of growth and international variations of welfare-state size appear theoretically largely indeterminate. Given another corporatist proposition, concerning the socio-economic effects of welfare states, a tendency towards an increasing divergence between more corporatist and less corporatist (and still pluralist) states should be expected. Welfare states strengthen interest organisations and their corporatisation, which then press for further welfare-state enlargement. In times of economic crisis, welfare states in strongly corporatist countries should be more resistant to cuts than less corporatist ones.

The forms of the welfare state should be expected to reflect deals between the state and interest organisations. Two more concrete hypotheses appear to follow from this. The more corporatist the polity of a country, the more corporatist is its welfare state. And, the more corporatist a country, the larger the gap between provisions for the organised and the unorganised.

Socially, the welfare state has meant a transfer of power and influence to interest organisations of workers, employers, and professionals. Therefore, we should expect that the larger the welfare state the bigger the power and influence of such organisations. As a corollary, we should expect the political equality of citizens in large welfare states to be lower than in less developed welfare states. Because of the strong link between corporatism and welfare states, we should expect that in the larger welfare state there would be more economic stability, less inflation and less unemployment.

There is a particular problem in advancing a considered opinion on the potential contribution of corporatist theory to an understanding of welfare states. What a fully corporatist animal looks like and what separates it from others in the zoo of political sociologists has not been firmly established. The corporatist community itself has not established an accepted ranking of countries in terms of corporatism (for a brief overview of conflicting rankings and criteria, see Therborn, 1985c, chapter III.3). Three countries which stand either at the top or very high on virtually every corporatist hit parade — Austria, Norway and Sweden — appear in Korpi's eyes (1983, p. 40) as countries exhibiting the largest working-class power resources.

One short way out of this entanglement will be to focus on the *social closure* thesis which is (explicitly or implicitly) particular to corporatist theory. In welfare-state terms, this would mean that in strongly corporatist countries there should be more marginalisation of unorganised or weakly organised groups, like one-parent families, the marginally employed and the unemployed, than in the less corporatist countries. Furthermore, in the strongly corporatist countries more poverty, in relative terms, should be expected and fewer of the unemployed would receive unemployment benefits (see Table 10.1). On the other hand, if what corporatists call strong corporatism involves stronger working-class power, we would expect the relationships to be inversed, class solidarity being broader than organisational interests.

Table 10.1
Beneficiaries of unemployed benefits as a percentage of the unemployed

Canada, 1982	87
Denmark, 1982	81
Finland, 1982	77
France, June 1983	52
FRG, June 1983	65
Italy, 1980	38
Japan, 1979	55
Norway	67
Sweden 1983	79
UK, 1980	43
USA, Nov. 1982	39

Sources: Calculations from OECD, *High Unemployment. A Challenge to Income Support Policies*, Paris, 1984; OECD, *Labour Force Statistics 1962–1982*, Paris, 1984; *Arbejsløshedens omkostninger i Norden*, Stockholm, NU 1983:15, 1984; *Arbetsmarknaden 1970–1983*, Stockholm, SCB, 1984.

From Table 10.1 it can be seen that, with the outstanding exception of Canada, which can hardly rank very high on any corporatist scale, leaving the unemployed out in the cold is above all a feature of countries scoring low, or at least not high, on corporatism, such as Italy, USA, UK and France.

While the decimal place gives a quite misleading impression of precision to a material of very fragile comparability, the evidence of Table 10.2 certainly gives no support to a corporatist hypothesis of social exclusion or marginalisation. It also shows that the large Swedish welfare state is not particularly effective in alleviating relative poverty. In contrast to the pluralist USA, however, the Swedish system is quite generous and effective. In Sweden, about 10 per cent of the pre-transfer gap in household income below the poverty line remains after transfers; in the USA the same figure is about a third (Gustafsson, 1984; p. 196; cf. the calculations by Lee Rainwater and Martin Rein reported in Heidenheimer *et al.*, 1983, p. 228).

On the welfare-state issue, where the corporatist argument can be clearly separated from the class-power hypothesis, corporatism fails to deliver. Although the evidence is by no means conclusive in this respect, there seems to be more promise in class-power theory.

With regard to patterns of welfare-state development, corporatist

214

Table 10.2
Relative poverty in Western Europe. Percentage of households having a disposable income below 50% of average disposable income per consumption unit

Belgium, 1976	6.6
Denmark, 1977	13.0*
France, 1975	14.8
FRG, 1973	6.6
Ireland, 1973	23.1
Italy, 1978	21.8
Luxemburg, 1978	14.6
Netherlands, 1979	4.8
Sweden, 1979	7.0–7.3
UK, 1975	6.3

* The Danish figure looks surprisingly high, and seems to be less firmly grounded than the others. See, on this point, R. Walker, 'Resources, Welfare Expenditure and Poverty in European Countries' in R. Walker *et al.* (eds.), *Responses to Poverty: Lessons from Europe*, London, Heinemann, 1984, p. 71n.

Sources: Commission of the European Communities, *Final Report from the Commission to the Council on the First Programme of Pilot Schemes and Studies to Combat Poverty*, Brussels, 1981, here quoted from Gustafsson (1984, p. 102); Gustafsson (1984, pp. 169, 187).

theory has not yet been much applied. As compared to pluralism, its thesis of divergence fits the reality better, and there is a tendency for corporatist countries to be high social spenders. But the picture is complex. Uniquely low-spending Japan is hardly a pluralist country in the sense of corporatist theory, and the unanimously top-ranking corporatist Austria and Norway are actually lower social spenders than France and Italy (OECD, 1985, p. 21).

Welfare-state organisation does not quite correspond to overall corporatist classifications. In the Nordic countries, welfare-state institutions are run by state administrators and elected politicians, apart from unemployment insurance, which in Denmark, Finland and Sweden are run by the trade unions. Tripartite welfare institutions do not exist, and the bipartite ones which exist are relatively marginal, and owe nothing to the state, and are the result of collective bargaining. In France, on the other hand, corporatist forms of welfare-state organisation tend to be the rule.

The hypothetical socio-political effects of corporatist welfare states remain to be investigated and demonstrated. As far as economic stabilisation is concerned, I have shown that corporatism has at most only dubious relevance to an explanation of the currently diverging rates of unemployment (Therborn 1985c, esp. chapter III.3).

Corporatism has made a major contribution to state theory by bringing into focus the political and social importance of the rise of a limited number of large and resourceful interest organisations and their complex relations and imbrications with the state. This phenomenon was neglected by neo-Marxism as well as pluralism. Its increasing importance in the 1970s explains much of the rapid success of corporatist theory. But the question now being raised is whether these interest organisations should be seen as *sui generis* or whether they are better grasped as rooted in class relations and class dynamics (cf. Korpi, 1983, pp. 7–14). Corporatism has as yet contributed little to an understanding of the welfare state and appears to hold little future promise in this area.

But there is another meaning to corporatism which may hold more potential. Corporatism is a peculiar, one might say dialectical, concept, with contradictory meanings. In social science parlance, it refers to concertation, compromise and collaboration among large interest organisations and between them and the state. In everyday French and Italian political language, on the other hand, corporatism rather refers to attitudes of *toujours plus*, to strivings for differentials and special privileges by small groups or particular segments of a class, without consideration of broader class or national interests. Corporatism in the latter sense is the opposite of class orientation and is an expression of class division and class weakness. That kind of corporatism has an interest group dynamic of its own and also has effects of social closure and marginalisation on those outside. Perhaps the concept of corporatism can make a successful second career as the opposite of its first meaning.

Statism

According to statism, or as it prefers to call itself, the 'state-centred approach' (Skocpol, 1982), the key actors are state managers, political rulers and administrators, 'maneuvering to extract resources and build administrative and coercive organisations' at 'the points of intersection between international conditions and pressures, on the one hand, and class-structured economies and politically organised interests, on the other' (Skocpol, 1979, p. 32). Another important independent variable is the state structure, defined first of all as administrative capacity. Statism has developed mainly through comparative or synthesising historiography (Skocpol, 1979; Skocpol and Ikenberry, 1983; Weir and Skocpol, 1983; Heclo, 1974), who may or may not agree with the programmatic statements of Skocpol, but whose work has been held forth as exemplary by the latter (Skocpol, 1982)). In a way it is more an approach than a theory, albeit with a sharp polemical edge against other theories. To formulate it theoretically then is both difficult and risky.

Welfare states develop, in this perspective, primarily through key interventions of state managers and experts, operating under and manoeuvring through various pressures and constraints, not excluding open political and social conflicts. The more resourceful and unified the state apparatus, the sooner and the more rapidly the welfare state should grow. Whether this may be extrapolated into hypotheses about long-term developments and contemporary international variations in the size of the state is unclear.

The form of welfare states should be expected largely to reflect inherited state structures, both as administrative parameters and as learning experiences. An explanation of modifications and extensions of these should be sought first of all in the actions of particular state managers, the outcome of which is theoretically indeterminate. From the theses of another leading statist theorist, Pierre Birnbaum (1985, p. 665), we should expect welfare institutions in countries where the state is strongly differentiated from civil society, such as in France, to be more strictly governmental than in countries with a weak differentiation of the state, such as the United Kingdom.

By deliberate choice, statist theory says little about civil society, which, of course, does not preclude writers drawing inspiration from it to make important contributions to, for instance, the study of social change. But from the theory or approach itself, it appears impossible to derive many socio-economic implications from welfare states. Birnbaum (1985, p. 670), however, considers the social power of state executives to be greater in large welfare states than in smaller ones.

The statist approach has made at least two very important contributions. First, a focus on the crucial effects of the inter-state system on domestic politics. This is something which again and again crops up in the political analyses of Marx, Engels and Lenin, and something which was also in the foreground of some neo-Marxist empirical studies (Anderson, 1974; Therborn, 1977), but which was, on the whole, seriously neglected by neo-Marxist political theory. Second, a historiographic approach to the actual processes and conditions of making and carrying out state policies, coupled with a bold confrontation with major issues of theory and explanation. Usually, political scientists and political sociologists, and often political historians as well, have left out one or the other.

Its significance for analysing welfare states, and states in general, however, seems circumscribed by some important limitations. One is simply its abdication, so far, from systematic theorising, which leaves us with no guidance on many burning questions. Another is the inherent danger of state- and even person-centred myopia.

It is certainly true that pre-existing state structures have heavily influenced the shaping of twentieth-century welfare states. The enduring legacy of nineteenth-century health-care systems (Abel-Smith, 1972) is one of the best examples of this. The importance of how labour exchanges had been traditionally organised for the adoption of modern labour-market policies was emphasised by the OECD Reviews of Manpower and Social Policies in the 1960s and 1970s. But even if concrete proposals are formulated and concrete decisions are made by a few key agents, their formulations and decisions are shaped not only by administrative structures and capacity, but also by vast social forces. With regard to the latter, there is in statist writings on the welfare state a strong tendency to omit, neglect or otherwise avoid them. For example, the reader of Hugh Heclo's careful book on Swedish and British social policy learns little of the social background to the fact that in 1913 Sweden was the first country to adopt a universal social insurance scheme (old-age pensions). This innovation stems from late nineteenth-century Swedish class relations. The Second Chamber majoritarian Yeoman Party amended a motion on investigating workers' insurance to include 'with them [the workers] comparable small farmers and artisans'. The Workers' Insurance Committee, of which the Yeoman Party leader was a member, included in its 1888 Report that on the basis of a class analysis it had made only 5.75 per cent of the Swedish population could not be counted as 'workers and with them comparable persons'. Later in the decision-making process, the Social Democrats, learning from their Austrian comrades' unhappy awareness of the socio-politically divisive effects of sectional insurance schemes, added a new force to that of early Swedish populism (Therborn, 1983; cf. Heclo, 1974, pp. 180–95).

The reader of Skocpol and Ikenberry (1983) is told nothing of the social mobilisations against social insurance in the United States in the 1910s, an agitation which is hardly understandable from their account of the basic incompatibility between the social insurance proposals and the American form of 'state-building' of that period. Similarly, Weir and Skocpol (1983) fail to recognise, as does Heclo (1974, pp. 100–1), the social context in Sweden in the early 1930s. Deficit spending was never a taboo in the labour movement, and so in that respect Keynesianism was hardly an innovation and was not an issue at that time. The 1933 Social Democratic budget was quite benevolently received by the leading participants of the Employers' Confederation, among others, in the budget debate at the Economic Club. Nor was this a new Swedish budget practice. The crucial economic issue was the wage level at public relief works. Should they be below the lowest market wage for unskilled labourers or not? In other words, it was a class issue, pushed first of all by the trade unions. The principle of public relief works had been a universally accepted and established practice since 1914. Weir and Skocpol contend, that 'Sweden's central-ized state with its tradition of administratively grounded policymaking was crucial to the eventual emergence [in the 1930s] of social Keynesian strategies for managing the national economy'. While it was clearly easier in a Swedish than an American type of state, the authors' arguments are sometimes unconvincing. That Keynesian-type economics emerged among Stockholm economists was hardly the effect of a state tradition of investigating commissions, and Keynesian economics was neither the political issue in the historical situation of 1932–3, nor very important to Sweden's relatively rapid economic recovery. (For a contrasting historical account, see Therborn, 1985a.)

Neo-Marxism II: Esping-Andersen and Korpi

The main factor in this view (mainly Korpi, 1983, Esping-Andersen and Korpi, 1984, and Esping-Andersen, 1985b), is the power resources of classes, and primarily those of wage-earners. The latter are principally made up of 'mobilisation', expressed in the rate of unionisation, first of all, and of the 'control', manifested in the amount and the duration of labour party government incumbency. Though its rootedness in class relations and their dynamics is always underlined, the key actor is, for all practical purposes, the labour party govern-ment.

With regard to patterns of welfare-state development, in the sense used here, the authors under review have said relatively little. What is clear is that with internationally differing distributions of working-class power resources, we should expect increasingly divergent paths of development. In countries with strong working classes, a vigorous growth of the welfare state is to be expected, accelerating with the duration of government control. What might be expected from countries with other allocations of power resources seems theoretically indeterminate, although it seems reasonable to assume that develop-ments would be later, slower, and less forceful. Countries with high mobilisation and stable control should be found at the top. Structural form, rather than size is, here, the most important and interesting aspect of welfare states. The latter are explicitly broadly defined, wider than social insurance, including social services, taxation systems, housing, labour-market policies. Where there are powerful working classes unified, universalistic, publicly organised social security should be expected, with high income-replacement ratios and little means-testing, large public consumption, and full employment. In countries with a weak working class more or less the opposite is to be expected. Without yet being theoretically developed and argued properly, the latter cases have been divided by Esping-Andersen (1985b, p. 474ff) into 'conservative' and 'liberal' welfare states. The former comprise continental Western Europe, and are characterised by attaching rights and duties to occupation and status. The latter are made up by the Anglo-Saxon nations and have social policies and arrangements tailored to primordial market relations.

Socio-economic implications are also held to be central to welfare-state analysis. The welfare state constitutes a tendentious overcoming of capitalist market inequalities, with their political as well as economic divisions and insecurities. Strong working classes should lead to more socially unifying and egalitarian welfare states.

This approach has had a great significance in bringing class analysis back into mainstream social research at a time when neo-Marxism I was faltering. Korpi's first major work (1978) effectively disproved the working-class integration or dissolution theses, at least as general propositions about capitalist development. The class theory's major contribution to welfare-state research has been its directing the spotlight to the forms and social and economic implications of the welfare state. The contribution mentioned is also an important one to general state theory. Although, this is the political theory most explicitly and directly developed with the welfare state in view, its major weakness is its theoretical underdevelopment. More brutally, one may say that it goes into the world with Swedish social democracy as a yardstick.

Empirically, the authors themselves (Esping-Andersen and Korpi, 1984, p. 203) conclude about Austrian and German social democracy, that 'their capacity to "social-democratize" their respective societies has differed considerably more than would be expected in terms of relative degrees of union strength and centralization, working-class political mobilization, and parliamentary power'. Their singling out 'the fact that in Austria and Germany, working-class parties were politically and socially ghettoized to a degree never experienced in Scandinavia' as an 'especially important' explanation for the former, either underlines a basic deficiency of their theory or indicates an empirical error, or both. If the *ad hoc* explanation points in the direction of formative history, then that is something which has to be theorised in terms of class formation, given the class political framework of the authors. (For an attempt in that direction, which perhaps bent the stick too far in a historically determinist direction, see Therborn *et al.*, 1978.) If it refers to more contemporary conditions, it is simply wrong, as far as German social democracy is concerned. Since Bad Godesberg the SPD proudly claims to have transformed itself from a 'class party' into a 'people's party', something which the Swedish SAP has never done, and the former has now in fact a socially more heterogeneous electoral support than the latter (Webber, 1983,

p. 36). The logic of the authors at this particular point is also difficult to follow. Why should (formerly) ghettoised working-class parties in power pursue less working-class policies than a non-ghettoised one, or than might be expected from their power resources?

On the subject of full employment, the theory of the authors is clearly deficient. The bourgeois governments of Japan and Switzerland have proved themselves much more committed to and successful in maintaining it in the current crisis, than the social democratic governments of Britain, France, and the Federal Republic of Germany (cf. Therborn, 1985c).

The final outcome of the authors' large-scale and resource-rich comparative welfare-state project still awaits to be seen, so a hasty judgement should be avoided. But it seems clear that if class theory is to prove itself capable of providing a fruitful theoretical framework for explanations and analyses of the welfare state, it will have to move far beyond Korpi's mobilisation-cum-control variables.

Some further neo-Marxist perspectives

Welfare states display a modern universality, which state theorists have to confront. Generally speaking, universal phenomena are fruitfully approached by some kind of functionalist reasoning. Marxist writers on the welfare state have often made use of functionalist arguments (Lenhardt and Offe, 1977; Ginsburg, 1979; Gough, 1979), but they all suffer from one basic deficiency. They start from capitalism, then turn to the functions of the welfare state in relation to it. But capitalism is no longer a universal type of modern society. Whatever one would like to call the societies directly or indirectly springing from the October Revolution of 1917, they could by no scholarly means be designated as capitalist. Welfare states, on the other hand, can be found in all of them as well.

It is with problems and deficiencies of the *market* that a theory about the development of welfare states should begin. (I am here indebted to Gunnar Persson of the University of Copenhagen, who is working on such a theory. Cf. also Arrow, 1963.) Human reproduction, the social importance of which has belatedly been highlighted by feminism, has never been predominantly run along market lines. A major part of it has been done in family or quasi-familial relations, by mothers, daughters, sisters, wives or by paid maids. A certain part has been played by fathers, sons, brothers, and male family servants too. Non-market enterprises such as churches were often important in education, health care, and as a last resort, income support. Guilds and later friendly societies and *mutualités* were also significant, and there were early pre-modern state arrangements, not only the notorious poorhouses but also public hospitals and pensions, often first catering to soldiers and veterans.

The rise of capitalism and its social concomitants eroded, marginalised or destroyed many of these institutions, but the market never came to replace them. Instead, the modern welfare state began, providing universal public education, public or publicly decreed or regulated income-maintenance programmes, and to varying extents public housing, public hospitals, and care for children and the elderly. Another line of development was state licensing and regulation of the professions of education and medicine, a seemingly paradoxical revival of pre-capitalist guilds simultaneous with the smashing of the latter by the market and free enterprise in other areas. Successful large enterprises also shouldered tasks of human reproduction for their labour force and their families, running insurance schemes, providing housing, medical facilities, and schools. What is referred to here is the deficiency of markets, not of the private sector. There may be private, non-market-determined provisions, by families, professions, and even business enterprises, while public enterprises may well operate as market actors.

A theory of the rise of the welfare state will have to be founded in an economic theory explaining the dysfunctionality of markets in ensuring human reproduction. In Marxist terms, the explanation may be expressed as a fundamental contradiction between the forces of human reproduction and market (simple commodity as well as capitalist) relations of production. But it is doubtful whether Marxian economics could be of much further help here.

A basic weakness of functionalist explanations, however, is that they tell us nothing about how and in what form solutions to a functional problem are found. Here a historical, causal theory is called for, although it should never be forgotten that Clio hardly ever gets firmly caught by any of her theoretical pursuers.

For grasping the early developments of the modern welfare state, with the establishment of universal educational and extensive hospital systems, the statist problematic of 'state-building' appears fruitful, at least if it is combined with a keen eye for the class and other social relations within which nineteenth-century state-building took place. Later institutions of social security and other social services, however, intervened more directly in the class relations shaped by industrial capitalism and should be better approached from a perspective of class politics, while keeping in mind the always complex and intricate relationships between class action and state decisions.

If the welfare state is a solution to an inherent deficiency of the market, class perspectives on the welfare state can hardly be strictly derived from the economic rationality used in what Adam Przeworski has called 'game theory Marxism'. Nor will it do to define the working-class perspective as (virtually) equal to the programme and practice of post-World War II Swedish social democracy, as Korpi has done.

Some sort of more general empirical historical anchorage, reinforced by a theoretical logic, seems to be required. The solution I have opted for in this situation (Therborn, 1983a) is as follows. The programmes and resolutions of, and the national party reports to, the First, Second, and Third Internationals and the programmes of the major parties of the Second International, primarily the German and the Austrian ones, have been systematically studied with regard to what they say about the workers' contemporary situation, immediate demands to improve it, and about governmental policies on 'the workers' question'. This should give us the perspective of organised labour before it was shaped by national constraints in conjunctures involving parliamentary responsibility and delimited governmental margins of manoeuvring. To check whether such early programmatic statements on immediate, short-term issues were in tune with the demands and strivings of workers, nineteenth-century labour and social policy historiography, in particular with regard to Britain, Germany, France, and Austria, has been culled. On this basis, a working-class perspective on the welfare state has been extracted, in the form of a limited set of core principles. To cautious and scrupulous empiricists, such an undertaking will perhaps appear dubious. But that something more than nineteenth-century organisational reporting and resolution-making was tapped, is indicated by the fact that a recent report on the welfare state by the OECD Trade Union Advisory Committee has been found to express the same principles. (Therborn, 1984a, pp. 28–30).

The working-class perspective contained the following elements:

1   As a guiding principle, an assertion of workers' rights to a livelihood and to a decent human life, rights above (and against) principles of insurance and charity and arguments about the requirements of capital accumulation, competitiveness and incentives.

2   A priority of tasks, setting *Arbeiterschutz* (workers' protection) above everything else: safety at work, leisure, union rights. A second top priority is the right to work, employment under non-punitive conditions.

3   The instalment of public social insurance and public income-maintenance programmes was not an early working-class demand. At issue was the *administrative control* of income-maintenance schemes and social services. This first concerned employer-run schemes and was later, when they appeared,

directed at state-organised ones. Working-class self-management of such schemes was a persistent demand, with bipartite or tripartite forms as a second best.

4   A wide coverage and uniform organisation of social regulations and institutions was a demand from very early on. This, of course, is a rational class point of view, maximising autonomy from particular employers and the unity of the class and its potential allies. Generally schemes, however, covering the whole population, can only be a second best alternative, being erosive of class unity and difficult to combine with a specifically working-class say in administration. Demands for such 'social citizenship' can be found in neither the early nor the classical pre-1914 labour movement.

5   A redistributive mode of social finance was also a running theme, through progressive taxation or through employers' contributions.

It has been found (Therborn, 1983a, 1984c pp. 15ff) that the welfare state which has developed in Sweden largely corresponds to this working-class perspective, in the sort of issues involved as well as in the actual outcomes. This is in agreement with Esping-Andersen and Korpi, though the reasoning sometimes differs. For instance, to them (Esping-Andersen and Korpi, 1984, p. 202), in a rare criticism of Swedish social democracy, Sweden's unemployment insurance is a 'second-rate programme'. From a working-class point of view, however, it is first class: it is run by the trade unions themselves, is mainly financed by progressive taxation, and has an effective coverage wider than most state schemes. The working-class perspective identified above was also found, by and large, to reappear in the (mostly defeated) labour point of view in the post-World War II welfare-state settlements in Austria, Belgium, France, the Federal Republic of Germany, the Netherlands and the United Kingdom (Berben, Roebroek and Therborn, 1985).

But for a class theory of the welfare state, a single class perspective is not sufficient. On this point, all varieties of class theory are still very underdeveloped. Therefore, what is suggested here is no more than a very first and provisional attempt.

A capitalist or bourgeois perspective may be constructed on the basis of the same historiographic reading referred to above and with a check of modern stances by looking at the welfare-state report of the Business and Industry Advisory Committee to the OECD (OECD, 1981):

1   The guiding principle is that welfare arrangements should be adapted to the requirements of capital accumulation, business competitiveness, and incentives to seek work on the labour market.
2   The priority task is to secure an adequately skilled, able, and loyal work-force.
3   Administrative control should be in the hands of the employers themselves or in specialised private enterprise or associations, in order to ensure efficiency and to avoid abuse. Bipartite or tripartite arrangements constitute a second best. Exclusive union or state control should be resisted.
4   Coverage and organisational form should not be universal and uniform, but tailored to particular market conditions and preferences of groups and individuals and should involve elements of competition.
5   Finance should be based on insurance principles, as far as possible on contributions from potential beneficiaries.

In the complex social formations in which welfare states have emerged there are also important social forces other than capitalists and workers. At least we have to take into account the landed aristocracy (a major force in most countries before World War I), the professional middle class, the farmers, the petite bourgeoisie, and the salaried middle strata. None of these has an unambiguous position in the capital– labour dynamic of capitalist societies, and a clear general class perspective on this dynamic can hardly be expected. A few hypotheses may, nevertheless be ventured.

Noblesse oblige is an old aristocratic maxim, and to the extent that the aristocracy was associated with running the state, certain paternalist welfare-state interventions to ameliorate the lot of capitalists' workers could be expected from the aristocracy, in particular if and when the latter posed a threat to social order and political rule. The forms of such interventions largely reflect traditional institutions and social relations, public or private. Agricultural workers could not be expected to be included in aristocratic benevolence.

The professional middle classes seem to have a general tendency to embrace general social causes, perhaps in part because their professional practice often pertains to society and social conditions at large. They should be expected to take an active interest in 'the social question'. We should expect them to be active proponents of extended education, better hygiene, and charity.

In these social categories, broad ideologies tend to be particularly important, given their social position hinted at above. In welfare-state history, two such professional middle-class ideologies appear to have been important. One is protestant liberalism, from which a double concern with asserting and maintaining market principles and with alleviating poverty tended to follow. The other is catholic and calvinist organicism, borne above all by the clergy and by church-associated intellectuals. From this corner, institutional arrangements of class harmonisation, drawn from precapitalist estate society, were promoted, as well as the principle of the secondary position of the state in relation to the church and other non-state institutions. A further particular concern of this variant of the professional middle class was protection and support of the family. The practical position and the relative social strength of the medical professional have had special effects on the forms of health care and insurance.

The welfare-state perspectives of the farmers and the petite bourgeoisie have probably varied most internationally. A main reason for this seems to be their general social location in relation to the working class. Where they have been rather close to the latter, as in Scandinavia and some of the North American prairie states, they have sided with the workers in demanding extended social security and social services, when the issue has come up. Since they usually have low cash incomes, they have later tended to part company with the labour movement over earnings-related benefits. Where the petite bourgeoisie and the farmers have been generally distanced from the class of industrial workers, they have tended to guard their independence by opposing welfare-state initiatives both for themselves and for all others, if necessary demanding separate schemes.

To the extent that the salaried middle strata have their social security arranged by or with their employer, private or public, they should be expected to play a rather passive role in general welfare issues. Their general attitude should be expected to be governed by the same topological conditions as those relevant to the farmers and the petite bourgeoisie, with the difference that middle strata strongly differentiated from manual workers should be more concerned with ensuring security for themselves, either directly with their employer or in separate public schemes. The distance of civil servants and public employees in general from workers is largely determined by the character of the state. It should be largest in countries with strong absolutist state traditions, such as Austria, France, the Federal Republic of Germany, and Italy, and we should expect this to be reflected in separate and particularly generous welfare provisions for civil servants and public employees.

Let us finally summarise the foregoing in a few hypotheses about the patterns of development, structural forms and socio-economic implications of the welfare state.

Welfare-state development cannot adequately be captured by the formula Jens Alber chose as the title for his monumental work: 'From the Poorhouse to the Welfare State'. Besides the poorhouse, there were also the family, the church, the friendly society, and the big enterprise. The welfare state has developed because markets are inadequate to ensure human reproduction, and because alternative non-market institutions for various reasons and to a varying extent have been found wanting. Over time, the latter have on the whole become relatively weaker. This holds, by and large, also for the domestic units of multinational corporations in relation to their home state—which is one reason why welfare states have continued to grow. The origin of developments of educational and hospital systems had better be seen as part of a class-contextualised process of modern state-building. Early social policy initiatives should be expected to come mainly from ruling aristocracies and from professional middle classes, spurred into action by actual or perceived threats from the working class to the existing order, or by initiatives abroad with a background of this kind. The universal development of welfare states has not been based on consensus or non-political, but conflicts have tended to centre more on form than size. The timing of welfare reforms is largely contingent and dependent on the interest and skills of state decision-makers. But we should expect periods of working class threat to the existing social and political order to speed up and simplify the normal procedures of policy-making. We should expect the welfare state in countries, or in periods, with a politically strong capitalist class to be relatively small, and in countries and periods with a strong working class to become relatively large. For the rest, variations in size remain theoretically indeterminate. Whether convergence or divergence between welfare states takes place depends on whether one or the other occurs with regard to social constellations of forces.

Welfare states should be expected to vary widely in structural form, and these forms should be expected to manifest the relative strength and interrelationship of the classes and their perspectives on welfare. International examples may provide important sources of inspiration for anticipatory moves, but their adopted forms should correspond much more to the social and power relations of the country of importation than to that of origin. We should also expect that the outcome of a welfare battle at time t_1 should shape not only the arena but also the line-up of social forces at time t_2 , primarily in the sense of an adaptation to previous defeat.

This hypothesis is connected with the important social effects of welfare states. A given form of the welfare state tends to strengthen the victorious forces which produced it. This is also a major reason for the cumulative and change-resistant character of welfare-state forms once they are in place. Welfare states have very important effects on the conditions of human reproduction, and above all on the position of women. In so far as public social services are extended, the growth of the welfare state should increase the independence of women. One part of the effects of the welfare state is the transformation of the state itself, a process which can also be analysed in social-class terms.

The place and meaning of the welfare state in the history of the state is another central problem of state theory which has largely been neglected. I have tried to deal with it to some extent elsewhere (Therborn, 1983b; 1984a, pp. 31–6; 1984b).

Also underdeveloped is the large and fascinating question of the welfare state in the history of gender relations. Variations of sexism and gender perspectives among major social forces are in principle amenable to an analysis similar to the one indicated here with regard to class perspectives on welfare. It awaits the arrival of a new kind of feminism. Meanwhile, neo-Marxism II claims to hold a certain promise in state theory and welfare-state analysis. It should make a proposal of marriage to an empirically gounded feminist theory of the state.

References

Abel-Smith, B. (1972) 'The History of Medical Care' in E.W. Martin (ed.), *Comparative Development in Social Welfare*. London, George Allen & Unwin.

Alber, J. (1979) 'Die Entwicklung sozialer Sicherungssysteme im Licht empirischer Analysen' in H. Zacher (ed.), *Bedingungen für die Entstehung und Entwicklung von Sozialversicherung*. Berlin, Duncker & Humblot.

Alber, J. (1982) *Vom Armenhaus zum Wohlfahrtstaat*. Frankfurt, Campus.

Alber, J. (1983) 'Einige Grundlagen und Begleiterscheinungen der Entwicklung der Sozialausgaben in Westeuropa, 1949–1977', *Zeitsschrift für Soziologie*, no. 12, pp. 93–118.

Anderson, P. (1974) *Lineages of the Absolutist State*. London, New Left Books.

Arrow, K. (1963) 'Uncertainty and the Welfare Economics of Medical Care', *American Economic Review*, vol. 53, pp 941–73.

Berben, T., Roebroek, J., and Therborn, G. (1985) 'Postwar settlements op het terrein van de sociale zekerheid', *Res Publica* (Revue de Science Politique), December.

Birnbaum, P. (1985) 'L'Action de l'état', in *Traité de science politique*, vol. 3, Paris.

Block, F. (1977) 'The Ruling Class Does Not Rule: Notes on the Marxist Theory of the State', *Socialist Revolution*, no. 1, pp. 6–28.

Carnoy, M. (1984) *The State and Political Theory*. Princeton, Princeton University Press.

Cohen, G. (1978) *Karl Marx's Theory of History: A Defence*. Oxford, Oxford University Press.

Domhoff, W. (1967) *Who Rules America*? Englewood Cliffs, NJ, Prentice-Hall.

Domhoff, W. (1978) *Who Really Rules*? Santa Monica, Calif., Goodyear.

Domhoff, W. (1979) *The Powers That Be*. New York, Random House.

Esping-Andersen, G. (1985a) *Politics Against Markets*. Princeton, Princeton University Press.

Esping-Andersen, G. (1985b) 'Politische Macht und wohlfahrtsstaatliche Regulation' in F. Naschold (ed.), *Arbeit und Politik. Gesellschaftliche Regulierung der Arbeit und der sozialen Sicherung*. Frankfurt, Campus.

Esping-Andersen, G., and Korpi, W. (1984) 'Social Policy and Class Politics in Post-war Capitalism: Scandinavia, Austria and Germany, in J. Goldthorpe (ed.), *Order and Conflict in Contemporary Capitalism*. Oxford, Clarendon Press.

Ginsburg, N. (1979) *Class, Capital and Social Policy*. London, Macmillan.

Gough, I. (1979) *The Politics Economy of the Welfare State*. London, Macmillan.

Gustafsson, B. (1984) *En bok om fattingdom*. Lund, Studentlitteratur.

Heclo, H. (1974) *Modern Social Politics in Britain and Sweden*. New Haven and London, Yale University Press.

Heidenheimer, A. *et al*. (1975) *Comparative Public Policy*. New York, St Martin's Press.

Heidenheimer, A. (1983) *Comparative Public Policy*, 2nd edn. New York, St Martin's Press.

Himmelstrand, U. *et al*. (1981) *Beyond Welfare Capitalism*. London, Heinemann.

Jessop, B. (1982) *The Capitalist State*. Oxford, Martin Robertson.

Korpi, W. (1978) *The Working Class in Welfare Capitalism*. London, Routledge & Kegan Paul.

Korpi, W. (1983) *The Democratic Class Struggle*. London, Routledge & Kegan Paul.

Laclau, E., and Mouffe, Ch. (1985) *Hegemony and Socialist Strategy*. London, Verso.

Lehmbruch, G., and Schutter, Ph. (eds.) (1982) *Patterns of Corporatist Policy-making*, London and Beverly Hills, Sage.

Lenhardt, G. and Offe, C. (1977) 'Staatstheorie und Sozialpolitik' in Ch. v. Ferber and F.-X. Kaufmann (eds.), *Soziologie und Sozialpolitik*. Opladen, Westdeutscher Verlag, Sonderheft 19 v. Kölner Zeitschrift für Soziologie.

Mann, M. (1984) 'The Autonomous Power of the State: Its Origins, Mechanisms and Results', *Archives Européennes de Sociologie*, vol. 25, pp. 185–213.

Miliband, R. (1969) *The State in Capitalist Society*, London, Weidenfeld & Nicolson.

Miliband, R. (1983) 'State Power and Class Interests', *New Left Review*, no. 138.

Mishra, R. (1977) *Society and Social Policy*. London, Macmillan.

OECD (1981) *The Welfare State in Crisis*. Paris, OECD.

OECD (1985) *Social Expenditure 1960–1990*. Paris, OECD.

Offe, C. (1983) 'Arbeit als soziologische Schlüsselkategorie', *Krise der Arbeitsgesellschaft?* Verhandlungen des 21. Deutschen Soziologentagen. Frankfurt, Campus.

Poulantzas, N. (1968) *Pouvoir politique et classes sociales*. Paris, Maspero.

Przeworski, A. (1977) 'Proletarians into a Class', *Politics and Society*, vol. 7, pp. 343–401.

Przeworski, A. (1980) 'Material Interests, Class Compromise and the Transition to Socialism', *Politics and Society*, vol. 10, pp. 125–53.

Przeworski, A., and Wallerstein, M. (1982) 'The Structure of Class Conflict in Democratic Capitalist Societies', *American Political Science Review*, vol. 76, pp. 215–38.

Rimlinger, G. (1971) *Welfare Policy and Industrialization in Europe, America and Russia*. New York, Wiley.

Roemer, J. (1982) *A General Theory of Exploitation and Class*. Cambridge, Mass., Harvard University Press.

Schmidt, M. (1982) *Wohlfahrtsstaatliche Politik unter bürgerlichen und sozialdemokratischen Regierungen*. Frankfurt, Campus.

Schmitter, Ph. (1984) Speech on 'Democracy and the Welfare State' at the European Center for Work and Society Conference on the Future of the Welfare State, Maastricht 19–21 December.

Schmitter, Ph. and Lehmbruch, G. (eds.) (1979) *Trends Towards Corporatist Intermediation*. London and Beverly Hills, Sage.

Skocpol, Th. (1979) *States and Social Revolutions*. Cambridge, Cambridge University Press.

Skocpol, Th. (1982) 'Bringing the State Back In', paper presented at a States and Social Structures conference in Mt Kisco, N.Y., 25–27 February.

Skocpol, Th. and Ikenberry, J. (1983) 'The Political Formation of the American Welfare State', *Comparative Social Research*, vol. 6, pp. 87–148.

Therborn, G. (1977) 'The Rule of Capital and the Rise of Democracy', *New Left Review*, no. 103, pp. 3–41.

Therborn, G. (1978) *What Does the Ruling Class Do When It Rules?* London, New Left Books.

Therborn, G. (1983a) 'The Working Class and the Welfare State. A Historical-Analytical Overview and a Little Swedish Monograph', paper presented at the Fifth Nordic Congress for Research on the History of the Labour Movement, 23–27 August.

Therborn, G. (1983b) 'When, How and Why Does a State Become a Welfare State?', paper presented at the ECPR Joint Workshops in Freiburg 20–25 March.

Therborn, G. (1984a) 'Classes and States, Welfare State Developments 1881–1981', *Studies in Political Economy*, vol. 13, pp. 7–41.

Therborn, G. (1984b) 'The Welfare State in State and in Class History', paper presented at a conference on The Labour Movement and the Welfare

State, at the Sociological Institute of Copenhagen, 21–22 March.

Therborn, G. (1984c) 'The Prospects of Labour and the Transformation of Advanced Capitalism', *New Left Review*, no. 145, pp. 5–38.

Therborn, G. (1985a) 'The Coming of Swedish Social Democracy', *'Annali' della Fondazione Giangiacomo Feltrinelli 1983/84*, Milan, Feltrinelli.

Therborn, G. (1985b) 'Beyond the (Relative) Autonomy of the State', paper presented at the Karl Marx Colloquium of the Vrije Universiteit in Brussels, 24–26 November 1983.

Therborn, G. (1985c) *Why Some People Are More Unemployed Than Others.* London, Verso.

Therborn, G. (1986) 'Class Analysis: A History and a Defence' in U. Himmelstrand (ed.), *Sociology. The Aftermath of Crisis.*

Therborn, G. *et al.* (1978) 'Sweden Before and After Social Democracy: A First Overview', *Acta Sociologica*, XXI, Supplement: pp. 37–58.

Titmuss, R. (1974) *Social Policy.* London, George Allen & Unwin.

Webber, D. (1983) 'Combating or Acquiescing in Unemployment? Economic Crisis Management in Sweden and West Germany, *West European Politics*, vol. 6, no. 1.

Weir, M., and Skocpol, Th. (1983) 'State Structures and Social Keynesianism: Responses to the Great Depression in Sweden and the United States', *International Journal of Comparative Sociology*, Special Issue, December.

Wright, E.O. (1985) *Classes.* London, Verso.

Zeitlin, M. (ed.) (1980) *Classes, Class Conflict and the State.* Cambridge, Mass, Winthrop.

11 States, ideologies and collective action in Western Europe

Pierre Birnbaum

Historical sociology has gradually brought to light the many processes which give rise to specific types of states. Rejecting all determinist or evolutionist explanations, it affirms the originality of the various mechanisms of political modernisation.[1] Political systems, then, do not follow one another in an inevitable sequence, as was maintained both by traditional political philosophy and by the reductionist theories, which derive the nature of politics from the successive stages of economic development, often on the basis of structuro-functionalist models of organicist origin, or of structural changes which, they claim, necessarily affect economic systems throughout history.

One of the least challengeable gains of contemporary political sociology lies precisely in the recognition of striking originality in the political formula which, at the end of the Middle Ages, took hold in certain European societies whose centres came up against resistance from obdurate feudal strongholds on the periphery. The birth of the state — particularly necessary in the case of France — is therefore perceived as a result of a process of differentiation which fostered the formation of an autonomised public area and of structures peculiar to it which attest to a gradual institutionalisation. Tied to a particular history in a specific socio-cultural and religious context, the state was above all the result of a tremendous differentiation of social structures. Its advent overturned once and for all the organisation of the social system, which henceforth took its structure from the state. The state thus emerged as an institutionalised politico-administrative machine, served by officials who identified themselves with their functions, and cut off from civil society, over which it tried to exercise total guardianship, supervising that society through its administrative authorities and private law, dominating it through its police, stimulating it through intervention in the economy, and ultimately mastering it by winning over the people and bringing them to accept its own values.[2]

Other societies, such as England, were not faced with crises of that kind. From the end of the Middle Ages onwards, save in exceptional times, the centralisation which affected all political systems was not matched there by a differentiation of politico-administrative structures. Civil society largely succeeded in regulating itself, the various social categories more or less managed to make their voices heard at the centre, and Parliament made it possible to install efficient machinery of representation. Thus England did not experience the building of a state on the lines of that taking shape in France and, to a lesser extent, for example, in Prussia. A legitimate centralisation prevented the emergence of a differentiated politico-administrative machine claiming the right to be separate from civil society, the better to rule it. In the United Kingdom to this day, a relatively permeable social aggregate, or Establishment, and not a true state, organises the workings of a civil society from which it does not differentiate itself.[2] Once brought to term, these two diametrically opposed processes of political centralisation each gave rise to a transformation of the entire social system which was destined to remain quasi-permanent. From then onwards, social groups developed different strategies, political parties organised themselves in their own way, according to the specific goals they pursued in one or other system, the intellectuals themselves instituted strategies and enjoyed an influence closely bound up with the mode of centralisation, and the ideologies arising on this side and that diverged totally, for they took root in contrasting realities. Political sociology must therefore take seriously the particularity of modes of political centralisation and the many kinds of states it brings forth. From this standpoint the state is seen as an independent variable around which the entire social system in all its aspects reorganises itself.

We would like first of all to show here how the ideologies that arise and manage to spread are in perfect correlation with the type of state in whose presence they develop; we shall then go on to consider their influence on the workers' movement, its structure, its values, the organisation it adopts and the strategy it employs both in relation to the state and in the course of the collective bargaining through which it strives to obtain advantages for all its members.

The sociology of knowledge establishes various kinds of links between ideologies and social settings. It endeavours to reveal a correlative or causal relationship between knowledge, in the general sense of the term, and the social system. Whether its inspiration is Marxist (from Marx to Lukács), Weberian (including the relationism of Mannheim) or functionalist or ethnomethodological, the sociology of knowledge interprets ideologies, world views or, indeed, values according as they are produced by a social class, a group or, again, an aggregate of interacting individuals. It never takes into account the specificity of politics, though this may revolutionise the conditions in which knowledge is produced. Marx, for example, saw the social classes as the only begetters of the ideologies which expressed their interests. In his view the representations, thought and intellectual commerce of men appeared here again as a direct emanation from their material behaviour.[3] Similarly, according to the model that predominates in the works of Marx and Engels, the state is the state of the most powerful class, that which is economically dominant and which, by means of the state, becomes the politically dominant class as well.[4] Marx never attempted, instead of linking forms of knowledge to social classes, to link them to the different types of states, although he did occasionally acknowledge their existence when, for example, he contrasted the French or Prussian state with the British or Swiss state.[5]

By placing the emphasis, as he occasionally did, on the specificity of states, Marx could have snapped the connection he ceaselessly forged between ideologies and social classes, and conceived of correlations between ideologies and types of states. Since he did not try, he was led to consider intellectuals solely in terms of their membership of a class and never according to their relationship with states. Hence, according to Marx, intellectuals could be regarded only as the political and literary representatives of the social classes whose interests they expressed. Having stated the problem in these terms, therefore, Marx ignored the ties which, in some cases, bound intellectuals to certain particularly institutionalised types of states — such as France or Prussia — with the result that the theories they developed and the ideologies that sprang up in such a setting were a function of the state and not of the social class. It may then be postulated that other theories and ideologies would come into being in the presence of a minimal state such as Great Britain. Although social relations in these countries were identical in nature, the difference in the type of state called into being contrasting world views and determined the particular roles played by the intellectuals in each case.

Within the Marxist tradition, the question of intellectuals and the role of ideologies were given particular attention by Gramsci. In his view 'they correspond to the function of "hegemony" which the dominant group exercises over the whole of society and to the function of "direct domination" or command which is expressed in the state and the "legal" government'.[6] Going even further than Marx, Gramsci considered that intellectuals were the agents of the dominant class, and that they enabled it to exercise its hegemony both over society and over the state. Once again, the specific intellectual/state relationship was effaced. Yet in contrasting the states of the East with those of the West, Gramsci emphasised that in the East 'the state is everything', whereas in the West the state was the 'moat' of the fortress of civil society which, unlike the 'primitive and gelatinous' society of the East, was seen as a 'sturdy structure'. On the basis of this distinction, Gramsci could have shed light on the different roles played by intellectuals not only in relation to social classes but also according to the different types of state. Unfortunately he did not take that course. Perry Anderson sums up Gramsci's thought in the following model:[7]

East	*West*
State	Civil society
Coercion	Consent
Domination	Hegemony
Movement	Position

He takes the view that, according to Gramsci, 'the preponderance of civil society over the state in the West may be paralleled with the predominance of "hegemony" over "coercion"'.[8] This model has the merit of outlining a comparative and differentiated sociological approach to intellectuals and ideologies. However, it remains inadequate. The fact is that, in his interpretation of Gramsci, Perry Anderson maintains his own East–West antithesis, which does not enable him to account for the substantial differences that separate Western societies themselves from one another.[9] In the same way, he sees them as having been equally aristocratic societies in the seventeenth century but ignores the phenomenon of institutionalisation of the state in France and relegates to the background the factors that make the French absolute monarchy, where the state became autonomous and differentiated itself from the nobility, distinct from the English aristocratic system where, in contrast, the state remained minimal and non-differentiated.

Marx, Gramsci and Perry Anderson aside, therefore, it is essential to recognise the diversity of the modes of political centralisation which operated in the West if we are then to attempt to study the emergence of ideologies according to the type of state they encounter, if it is true that in the West domination is not only exercised through civil society but sometimes, on the contrary, transmitted essentially by the state.[10] Here we would like to employ a sociology of knowledge which depends not on social economic settings but *inter alia* on social political settings, and then to see how relationships develop between ideologies and types of states, taking as a first example Western Europe at the end of the nineteenth century. In so doing we aim to challenge both the developmentalist and evolutionist view, which ties the advent of a particular kind of ideology, such as communism, closely to a particular moment in industrialisation,[11] and those models which deny the diversity of historical political processes and claim that identical sets of state ideological apparatus perform, to the profit of the bourgeoisie, similar activities in all Western countries.[12]

The French model

As we have seen, highly institutionalised, differentiated and auto-nomised states — of which France is the ideal example — can be distinguished from those that have undergone a process of political centralisation leading to a minimal state. On the basis of this distinc-tion, which makes politics the independent variable, we must take into consideration those relationships that exist, in each case, between the state and the dominant class (see Table 11.1); in some cases a fusion may be observed and in others a differentiation. But beyond this first political variable — state or non-state — which raises the question of fusion with the ruling class, we must also take into account another political variable, independent of the first because it is of entirely different origin: that of the political market through which, at different rates, democracy is attained. In order to account for the emergence of

Table 11.1
Relationships between state and ruling class

France	Germany	United Kingdom
E+	E+	E−
F−	F+	F+*
I+	I+	I−
M+	M−	M+

Note: E+ or E−   Differentiated or non-differentiated state (centre).
       F+ or F−   Fusion or absence of fusion of state with ruling class.
       I+ or I−   Industrialisation from above or industrialisation from below.
      M+ or M−   Open political market or closed political market.
* In the case of the United Kingdom, as we shall see, given the fact that there is no truly differentiated state, the problem of its possible fusion with the ruling class does not arise. The political area is occupied by an Establishment. In this case, therefore, the F+ represents a social fusion without real differentiation of political roles.

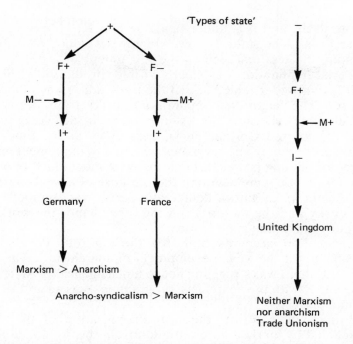

'Types of state'

Figure 11.1   Ideologies and social political settings in Europe at the
end of the nineteenth century

ideologies, therefore (and here we shall deal only with the ideologies which structure the collective action of the working class), it is essential to use both these political variables in order to analyse the results of their many combinations (see Figure 11.1).

Among the highly institutionalised states, the German state was unable to differentiate itself from the aristocracy. In this case, the result was a fusion of state with dominant class which, as Barrington Moore observed, was responsible for the revolution 'from above'[13] and favourable to change and to rapid industrialisation pursued with the active participation of the state.[14] In such a context it is easy to understand the rapid development of a Marxist social democracy that expressed the direct antagonism between the working class and a dominant class in close osmosis with the state. The rise of Marxism corresponded to the formation of a sturdy working class born of the rapid industrialisation and dominated by an alliance of the aristocracy and the bourgeoisie. Lassalle's version, in contrast, points to the weight carried by the state in the organisation of the dominant classes.[15] German social democracy was organised in the very image of the state it hoped to conquer; it was as centralised and disciplined as the state itself, and it is understandable that R. Hilferding spoke of 'Bismarckism'. The state, however highly developed or institutionalised, none the less emerged as the instrument of a dominant class. Thus social domination was clearly visible through political domination. It is thus understandable that the trade union was subordinate to the party. The factor that separated Kautsky from Bernstein, and which ultimately became the essential issue in the great theoretical debate that stirred German social democracy at the time, was the question of the state. The revisionists wanted to implement an indirect strategy for gaining power through the economy (which in our model represents an adequate action in the presense of a weak state) and to transform the party into a democratic party, trade unionist version. For Kautsky and the majority, on the other hand, the working-class party must make 'the state its own'.[16]

This situation accounts both for the vigorous development of Marxism and for the weak development of anarchism.[17] The workers' movement, then, was struggling not so much against the state *per se* — in accordance with the anarchists' programme — as against the state of the dominant class.

In France, in contrast, the institutionalisation of the state was accompanied by marked differentiation from the dominant class. The absolute state, or the bureaucratised state, presented itself as a machine for dominating civil society and not as the instrument of the dominant class. Domination was thus experienced first in its political dimension, which perhaps explains the initial upsurge of anarchist theories and the subsequent spread of anarcho-syndicalism.

In the second half of the nineteenth century anarchism spread in France, parallel with the great strengthening of the state.[18] The vast influence exerted by Proudhon over the workers' movement up to the beginning of the twentieth century testifies to the weight carried by anarchism. According to Proudhon, the state was far from being a mere tool of the dominant class; it was a differentiated machine that had to be fought as such. In his analysis of Napoleon III's *coup d'état*, he emphasised the specificity of the resultant state.[19] Confronted with the French state — whose originality, incidentally, he failed to perceive — Proudhon developed analyses identical with those advanced, from opposite ideological horizons, by both de Tocqueville and Marx. In Proudhon's view, 'centralisation being by nature expansive and intrusive, the purview of the state constantly grows at the expense of corporative, communal and social initiative'.[20] Marx, analysing the Second Empire in his turn, took up Proudhon's analyses only to refute them systematically; in his opinion the state hems in, controls, regulates, oversees civil society and holds it in tutelage; he saw it as a 'frightful parasitical body that enveloped the body of French society as though with a membrane, blocking all its pores'.[21] Faced with the French state, Marx abandoned his traditional analysis in terms of social class to acknowledge, like Proudhon, the specificity of the political domination exercised in this context. He also agreed with de Tocqueville, who emphasised that 'under the old regime, as in our time, not one city, town, village or tiny hamlet in France, not one hospital, factory, convent or school could dispose independently of its own property. Then as now the administration thus kept all Frenchmen in its tutelage'.[22] The fact that liberal thought, Marxist theory and anarchist analysis, despite their incompatibility, agreed in recognising the particularity of the French state reveals the profound influence exerted on ideologies by socio-political settings.

As Pierre Ansart rightly observes,[23] a structural homology can be perceived between the practice of mutualism among the workers, which flourished in France in Proudhon's day, and its theoretical creation, which also developed, in the image of the workers' friendly societies, by rejecting the state in favour of independent economic action. This being so it must also be recognised that the activity of the movement was perhaps determined primarily by the type of state to which it was opposed. A slower rate of industrialisation and the maintenance of an economic structure in which, as a result, small producers and craftsmen acted only as an intervening variable admittedly favoured the acceptance of anarchist theories, but were nevertheless overdetermined by the specificity of the state. We should also mention, with Yves Lequin, that anarchism was equally successful at the time in infiltrating the large-scale industrial sector.[24]

In these circumstances it is not surprising that, unlike what occurred in Germany, anarchism long held the upper hand over Marxism. As Édouard Droz observes: 'Through his own work and that of his followers, Proudhon did most to create the Confédération Générale du Travail [General Confederation of Labour].'[25] Similarly Jacques Julliard and Annie Kriegel both draw attention to the strong influence exerted by Proudhon, through Pelloutier, over revolutionary syndicalism.[26] The organisation of labour exchanges and the acceptance of the idea of the general strike[27] illustrate the working class's attempts at self-organisation. Pelloutier considered that it was in the workers' interest 'to unite, and to look upon the trade union and the co-operative society, not as an employment bureau and a compulsory savings bank, but as schools of revolution, production and self-government'.[28] It is striking to find in Pelloutier's writings the British concept of self-government; in both cases it expresses rejection of the state. However, whereas in the United Kingdom the limited character of the state was highly unfavourable to the development of anarchism or anarcho-syndicalism, in France the strength of the state was accountable for their rise.

In opposition to the development of a socialist party which would set out to conquer the state, and in opposition to Marxism and its Guesdist expression, Pelloutier, developing the labour exchanges, subscribed to the view which speaks of 'mutualism, co-operation, credit and association, and declares that the proletariat possesses in itself the instrument of its emancipation'.[29]

In these various forms — individualist and terrorist, mutualist, collectivist and syndicalist[30] — anarchism consequently developed on a tremendous scale in France, corresponding to the power enjoyed by the state in that country. From this standpoint, the antithesis between French anarchism and the Marxism which developed in Germany was attributable — in the opinion of both Bakunin and Kropotkin — less to a difference between the 'Latin mind' and the 'German mind' than to the type of state built up in each of those two countries and to its greater or lesser differentiation from the dominant class. It is thus understandable that at that time the attitude of the strikers reflected, in Michelle Perrot's view, 'a belief in the primacy and omnipotence of political factors'.[31]

It is true that at the Marseilles Congress in 1879 Guesdism triumphed over the corporatist and mutualist movement.[32] Nevertheless anarcho-syndicalism long maintained its control over the workers' movement, and the Amiens Charter of 1905 still reflected its influence.[33] In addition, 'Guesdism, which claimed kinship with Marx, in fact retained at the outset a strong anarchist or Blanquist influence'.[34] Whatever their differences in approach, these three movements sought to define themselves in relation to the state by fighting it or by organising themselves outside it and against it. Guesdism, the French version of Marxism, concentrated on action against the state: 'Let us say and repeat to the proletariat', declared Guesde, 'that unless the working-class party seizes the state there can be no transformation of society and no emancipation of labour'.[35] The French socialist movement gradually rejected co-operative organisations, friendly societies and anarchist trends, and the exclusion of anarchism became final in London in 1906 with the temporary backing of Jaurès, who cannot after all be regarded as a statist.[36] However, the French section of the Workers' International (Section Française de l'Internationale Ouvrière or SFIO) which was formed in 1905, while rejecting revolutionary syndicalism, long retained traces of Proudhonian influence[37] and was infinitely less structured than German social democracy.

The birth of the Communist Party at Tours in 1920 was to accelerate the organisation of the French workers' movement on state-like lines. As Annie Kriegel aptly observes: 'Each party constitutes itself as the negative of the state which, within its territorial sphere, it sets out to destroy — on the model of the German Social Democratic Party, whose design as the negative of the Prussian state so captured the attention of Lenin. . . . The French Communist Party rediscovered what gives the French political system its coherence and unity — the concept of absolutism.'[38] There could be no clearer demonstration of the weight carried by the 'state' variable in the organisation of the social system, of political parties, and of the ideologies sponsored by different social or political movements. Like anarchism, which found particularly favourable soil in France, Marxism, as it developed later, at a time when industrialisation was further advanced, adhered in its turn to state determinism. The successor to anarchism, the answer to the formidable French state, the Communist Party, which planned to take over the state and not to destroy it, constituted itself in its image: 'The Communist Party functions like a state because it is modelled on the state'.[39]

The British model

If we turn now to the British model of a political centralisation which took place without any true differentiation of state structures, we find that the installation of the machinery of representation — whatever the real difficulties of making it work, especially in relation to the working class — made possible some degrees of self-government for civil society as a whole. Although Great Britain was ruled by a dominant class — an Establishment which absorbed new arrivals from the middle classes — the working class did not embrace Marxism as it did in Germany, which had likewise experienced fusion of the ruling class with the state and fairly rapid industrialisation. The British working class did not go to war with the dominant class but negotiated, often violently, with the employers to improve its living conditions and its standing in society as a whole. It almost invariably rejected any recourse to the state and any growth of the state, preferring to strengthen itself, the better to assert its rights. Just as it did not embrace Marxism, the working class did not accept the anarchist or anarcho-syndicalist model which had been such a success in state-structured France. The works of Godwin and William Morris notwithstanding, anarchism never became acclimatised in Great Britain for the state itself remained weak. The state was not the main issue to be opposed or utilised.

As G.D.G. Cole observes, anarchism managed to entrench itself firmly only in countries ruled by a strongly dominant state, such as France, Italy or Spain; it had no *raison d'être* in Great Britain.[40]

Literary anarchism apart, such anarchist groups as arose in Great Britain were most often led by foreigners — at the end of the nineteenth century, Kropotkin; at the turn of the century, Jewish workers from Russia, Germany or Poland — all of them from countries where domination was maintained, often brutally, through state institutions or the use of force by a powerful empire. But anarchism remained negligible: 'Where state tyranny is little felt, for lack of experience of centralization and bureaucracy, it is much more difficult for revolt to start spontaneously, or for slogans like "neither God nor master" to find an echo.'[41]

Lastly, as George Woodcock notes, anarchism remained virtually non-existent in the Netherlands, the United Kingdom and the United States. All these are countries where the state is only slightly differentiated. The first type of state may be explained by the model of consociational democracy, in which respect for schisms is accompanied by an accommodation between élites to avoid building up the state; the other states are social systems in which civil society manages more or less to regulate itself, likewise avoiding differentiation of state structures.[42] The only form of anarchism which came to light in those societies was a peaceful one influenced by Tolstoy and remained within civil society.[43]

Anarchism remained an anarchism of civil society which was not directed against the state, and its theorists were more often poets or writers than movement organisers.[44]

According to David Apter, the new anarchism making its appearance in the English-speaking countries is a reaction against the system of roles in civil society and not the expression of a struggle against a state. The young people's counter-culture attacks the social identity of the protagonists; violence is directed against oneself and not against political authority.[45]

In the United States, as in the United Kingdom or again in the Netherlands, the type of anarchism which finds expression today may thus be seen as evidence of the absence of a truly institutionalised state. Here once again, in a negative sense, politics appear as the independent variable that determines the kind of ideology emerging.[46]

Thus Great Britain, unlike Germany or France, never really welcomed either Marxism or anarchism. As Henry Pelling observes, British trade unionism from the nineteenth century onwards was infinitely stronger than that of other European countries; highly self-organised and aware of its strength, 'the British movement was neither very Marxist nor clearly oriented towards party politics'.[47] Preferring economic action to political struggle, the leaders of the British workers movement even refused to take part in the Second International which met in London in 1896. The 1880s witnessed attempts to organise several Marxist movements, such as the Social Democratic Federation around Hynd, which sought to subordinate trade-union action to political action, and to assign a vital role to the state. These movements, extremely hostile to trade unionism, remained outside the popular culture of the British workers who, for their part, opted most often for a purely economic struggle.[48]

In the face of economic difficulties and employers' reactions, however, the trade unions themselves, as we know, gradually entered the political arena in order to defend their own rights. It should be remembered that this process led to the formation in 1900 of the Labour Representation Committee, which was broadly dominated by the trade unions; the representatives of the socialist movement were in the minority. In 1906 this committee became the Labour Party, which was to set itself the task of giving expression, on the political scene, to the workers' demands for improvements in wages and working conditions. Even though this parliamentary socialism triggered reactions of rejection, and gave birth to a revolutionary socialism that was sometimes Marxist in inspiration and to a direct-action trade unionism closely resembling French anarcho-syndicalism, it took lasting hold as the mode of representation of the British working class.

In contrast to the situation which prevailed in Germany, where the workers' movement confronted a state undifferentiated from the dominant class, the British working class, save in unusual times, has on the whole ignored Marxism. It has refused to subordinate the trade union to the party. Integrated into the political system and able to be 'heard' by representatives whom it controls, it has scorned French-style anarcho-syndicalism and its struggle against the state, and has never known separation and rivalry between union and party.[49] Through the payment of compulsory dues by unionised workers to the Labour Party, the practice of almost inevitable unionisation and the predominant position of the unions in the party, the working class has subjugated the political apparatus and communicated to it its own pragmatist and reformist ethos, the expression of its full participation in civil society. Hence the Labour Party does not betray the working class (Miliband), but speaks for it.[50] Marxism, anti-statism, and an economic pragmatism allergic to ideology — such are the three ideological responses in close correlation with the type of state which emerges, in the majority of cases, in each of the systems studied. Let us add that, whereas in France 'revolutionary syndicalism equals trade-unionism plus direct action',[51] conversely it may be contended that in the United Kingdom trade unionism equals revolutionary-inspired syndicalism, in so far as it seeks to cause civil society to evolve, minus direct action. Up to the First World War French syndicalism had its similarities to trade unionism; but while the British trade unions were subsequently to succeed in taking control of the Labour Party, in France they were to yield pride of place to the parties for a long time to come. The logic of the state or centre thus weighs heavily on the union–party relationship and on the ideologies through which it is expressed.

We may briefly note that this purely political logic also determines the methods of settling labour disputes. Trade unions in the United Kingdom and the United States always prefer to reach agreement directly with the employers in a contractual setting because, 'in contrast to French Jacobinism, Anglo-Saxon liberalism leads to a curbing of the state's power to intervene, even at the cost of a trade-union monopoly'.[52] In France, on the other hand, collective agreements do not exist, and recourse to the state and the courts is often the result. This Jacobin tradition is reflected in the very conception of the right to form and join trade unions, which the Waldeck–Rousseau Act raised to the status of a public freedom on the same footing as freedom of opinion; the state was thus to act as an arbitrator, with most disputes being settled in court.

In Great Britain, on the other hand, the situation was practically the reverse. Since the 1870s the law has developed negatively, intervening only rarely in collective relations in order that the state should not be called upon to rule in disputes. As a result, such disputes came to be treated mainly as matters of equity. Hence the 'voluntarism' characteristic of industrial relations in Great Britain, where free collective bargaining was for a long time the corollary of the absence of legislation.[53] A product of the 'weakness' of the state and the self-regulation of British civil society, this voluntarism, as we know, was gradually worn away, from the 1960s onwards, by the Industrial Relations Act (1971), the incomes policy and the social contract; whereas in France, in contrast, the state was trying during the same period to encourage collective bargaining[54] — a transformation which is perhaps indicative of the diminishing role of a state in France today as it turns towards liberalism. The differences between the two models nevertheless remain striking and continue to depend on the nature and role of the state. A further indication of the extent of these differences is the almost total absence of political strikes in Great Britain up to the 1960s, whereas in countries like France lacking a route of access to the state, the working class uses the strike as an alternative means of exerting collective pressure. The strike served in this case as an extra-parliamentary channel for political participation by the working class.[55] In contrast, with voluntarism in decline, the British labour movement managed to integrate itself into the machinery of the state in order to limit its action.

Rather than find itself regulated from above, the trade-union hierarchy preferred to legislate for itself. Hence the participation of the unions in the political centre, the rise of corporatism and the often violent reactions it provoked at the base.[56] From the difference in the impact of Marxism and anarchism in France and Great Britain respectively at the end of the nineteenth century to the contrasts which persist today in the matter of industrial relations, and, for example, the more or less effective application of corporatism, it is clear that, as time goes on, the 'state' variable continues to have its specific effect.[57]

As we have tried to show, the state emerges as the true independent variable, industrialisation being only an intervening variable in countries which are all capitalist in structure. The relationship between these variables explains why Great Britain and Germany, two countries where industrialisation was fairly rapid, produced profoundly different ideologies because their states were radically dissimilar. The same relationship accounts for the conflicting ideologies which flourished in France and Germany respectively — countries whose state structures were comparable. However, while Marxism spread in Germany, where the state was tied to the dominant class, anarcho-syndicalism developed in France, where domination mainly took a political form. The fact remains that, once industrialisation was widespread in France, anarcho-syndicalism gave way to variants of Marxist-inspired socialism.

This potency of the state seems to us an essential factor. In conclusion we may point out that it even influences the manner in which an ideology takes shape. Just as Proudhon, de Tocqueville and Marx agreed in recognising the distinctive character of the French state, so today Robert Dahl, Wright Mills, David Easton and James O'Connor, despite their conflicting theoretical approaches, accord little importance to the state itself in their analyses of American society. Again, within the contemporary Marxist movement, James O'Connor in the United States and Ralph Miliband in the United Kingdom concentrate mainly on the contradictions of capitalism or the homogeneity of the ruling class, thus ignoring the problems of the state, whereas Nicos Poulantzas and Claus Offe in France and the Federal Republic of Germany, in spite of their differences, agree in recognising its essential character as a constituted public area. This means that even the theoretical models thrown up within a single school of thought, e.g. Marxism, should not be interpreted solely in terms of their internal logic and that the controversy they arouse is not confined to the cognitive level but perhaps depends more upon the type of state in whose presence they have been constructed.[58]

Notes

1   See for example J. Peter Nettl, 'The State as a Conceptual Variable', *World Politics*, July 1968; Samuel Finer, 'State Building, State Boundaries and Border Control', *Social Science Information*, vol. 13, no. 4, p. 5; Charles Tilly (ed.), *The Formation of National States in Western Europe*, Princeton, NJ, Princeton University Press, 1975.

2   For a typology that offers a means of distinguishing states from centres, see B. Badie and P. Birnbaum, *The Sociology of the State*, Chicago, University of Chicago Press, 1983.

3   K. Marx, *The German Ideology*, London, Lawrence & Wishart, 1964.

4   F. Engels, *The Origin of the Family, Private Property and the State*, Moscow, Progress Publishers, 1977.

5   See Badie and Birnbaum, op. cit., chapter 1.

6   A. Gramsci, *Deuvres choisies*, Paris, Editions Sociales, 1959, pp. 266–8.

7   P. Anderson, *Sur Gramsci*, Paris, F. Maspéro, 1978. Adam Przeworski criticises Anderson's interpretation of Gramsci's work by showing that, in Gramsci's view, states in the West use both force and consensus depending upon the relations between social classes. At the same time he ignores, as do Gramsci and Anderson, the specificity of states in the West and its consequences for the mode of government: 'Material Bases of Consent: Economics and Politics in a Hegemonic System', *Political Power and Social Theory*, vol. 1, 1980, pp. 58–60.

8   Anderson, op. cit., p. 43.

9   P. Anderson, *Lineages of the Absolutist State*, London, New Left Books, 1974.

10 Stein Rokkan, for his part, draws his conceptual map of Europe according to the various modes of nation-building, and not according to the different types of state which have taken shape there. For example, he attributed the genesis of communism to the schism produced long ago by reaction to the Reformation. In Protestant countries, the resultant osmosis between political and religious élites favoured consensus, and rendered subsequent upsurges of communism impossible; in Catholic countries, the antagonism between those élites favoured dissension and later the appearance of communism. This explanation is primarily culturalist and ignores differences in state-building, for example between France and England, which appear in the same column in the conceptual map of Europe. See S.M. Lipset and S. Rokkan, 'Cleavage Structure, Party Systems and Voter Alignments: An Introduction' in *Party System and Voter Alignments*, New York, Free Press, 1967; and S. Rokkan, 'Cities, States and Nations' in S. Eisenstadt and S. Rokkan (eds.), *Building States and Nations*, Vol. 1, London, Sage, 1973.

11 See, for example, Seymour M. Lipset, *Political Man: The Social Bases of Politics*, Garden City, N.Y., Doubleday, 1960, chapter 2.

12 Louis Althusser, 'Idéologie et appareils idéologiques d'Etat, *La Pensée*, June 1970.

13 Barrington Moore, Jr., *Social Origins of Dictatorship and Democracy:*

Lord and Peasant in the Making of a Modern World, Boston, Beacon Press, 1958.

14 Alexander Gerschenkron, *Economic Backwardness in Historical Perspective*, Cambridge, Mass., Harvard University Press, 1962.

15 See G. Roth, *The Social Democrats in Imperial Germany*, 1963, pp. 10–11. Ottawa, Bedminster Press. According to Lassalle, 'it is the state's function to perfect the development of freedom, the development of humankind in freedom': F. Lassalle, *Discours et pamphlets*, Paris, Giard & Brière, 1903, p. 188.

16 A. Bergounioux and B. Manin, *La social-démocratie ou le compromis*, Paris, Presses Universitaires de France, 1979, p. 65. See also D.A. Chalmer, *The Social Democrat Party of Germany*, New Haven, Conn., Yale University Press, 1964.

17 George Woodcock, *Anarchism*, London, Pelican, 1963, pp. 404–9. A.R. Carlson, *Anarchism in Germany*, Methuen, 1972.

18 On the differences between the anarchists and Marx over the attitude to be adopted towards the state and the possibilities of transforming it, see Paul Thomas, *Karl Marx and the Anarchists*, London, Routledge & Kegan Paul, 1980, p. 344ff.

19 P.J. Proudhon, *La Révolution sociale démontrée par le coup d'Etat du 2 décembre* [1852], Paris, Marcel Rivière.

20 P.J. Proudhon, *Capacité politique des classes ouvrières*, Paris, Marcel Rivière, p. 287.

21 K. Marx, 'The Eighteenth Brumaire of Louis Bonaparte' in L. Feuer (ed.), *Basic Writings on Politics and Philosophy*, Garden City, NY, Doubleday, 1959.

22 A. de Tocqueville, *L'Ancien régime et la révolution*, Paris, 1953, p. 122.

23 Pierre Ansart, *Naissance de l'anarchisme*, Paris, Presses Universitaires de France, 1970, p. 131ff.

24 Yves Lequin, *Les Ouvriers de la région lyonnaise (1848–1914)*, Vol. 2, Lyon, Presses Universitaires de Lyon, 1977, p. 282.

25 Edouard Droz, *P.J. Proudhon*, Paris, Librairie des Pays Libres, 1909, p. 34.

26 Annie Kriegel, *Le Pain et les roses*, Paris, Union Générale d'Edition, 10/18, 1973, pp. 95–6. Jacques Julliard also likens Pelloutier to Proudhon, while pointing out the difference between their views on socialism and the idea of war. J. Julliard, *Fernand Pelloutier et les origines du syndicalisme d'action directe*, Paris, Le Seuil, 1971, pp. 209–10.

27 See F. Ridley, 'Revolutionary Syndicalism in France: The General Strike as Theory and Myth', *International Review of History and Political Science*, vol. 3, no. 2, 1966.

28 Quoted in Julliard, op. cit., p. 341.

29 Fernand Pelloutier, *Histoire des Bourses du Travail*, Publications Gramma, 1971, p. 99.

30 Jean Maîtron analyses all these currents in *Le Mouvement anarchiste en France*, 2 vols, Paris, F. Maspéro, 1975.

31 Michelle Perrot, *Les Ouvriers en grève, France 1871–1890*, Vol. 2, Paris, Mouton, 1974, p. 703.

32 Michelle Perrot, 'Le congrès de la scission', *Le Monde*, 9 December 1979.

33 See Henri Dubief, *Le Syndicalisme révolutionnaire*, Paris, A. Colin, 1979.

34 Michelle Perrot, 'Les Socialistes français et les problèmes du pouvoir (1871–1914)' in Michelle Perrot and Annie Krigel, *Le Socialisme français et le pouvoir*, Paris, E.D.I., 1966, p. 19.

35 Quoted in Dubief, op. cit., p. 12. See also Claude Willard, *Les Guesdistes*, Paris, Editions Sociales, 1965, part 2, chapter 11.

36 Madeleine Rébérioux shows how Jaurès later drew nearer to syndicalism, in *Jean Jaurès. La classe ouvrière. Textes prèsentés part M. Rébérioux*, Paris, Maspéro, 1976, pp. 14–15; see also, by the same author, 'Les Tendances hostiles à l'Etat dans la S.F.I.O. (1905–1914)', *Le Mouvement social*, October–December 1968; and 'Jean Jaurès et le marxisme', *Histoire du marxisme européen*, Vol. 1, Paris, 10/18, 1977, p. 233.

37 Madeleine Rébérioux, 'Le Socialisme français de 1871 à 1914' in J. Droz (ed.), *Histoire générale du socialisme*, Vol. 2, 1974, p. 196.

38 Annie Kriegel, *Communismes ou miroir français*, Paris, Gallimard, 1974, p. 149.

39 Christine Buci-Glucksmann, 'Pour un eurocommunisme de gauche' in Olivier Duhamel and Henri Weaver (eds.), *Changer le P.C.?*, Paris, Presses Universitaires de France, 1972, p. 133.

40 G.D.H. Cole, *Socialist Thought, Marxism and Anarchism, 1850–90*, Vol. 2, London, Macmillan, 1961, pp 336–7.

41 François Bédarida, 'Sur l'anarchisme en Angleterre', in *Mélanges d'Histoire sociale offerts à Jean Maitron*, Paris, Editions Ouvrières, 1976, p. 23.

42 Badie and Birnbaum, op. cit., part 3.

43 Woodcock, op. cit., p. 18.

44 April Carter, *The Political Theory of Anarchism*, London, Routledge & Kegan Paul, 1971, pp. 10–11.

45 David Apter, 'The Old Anarchism and the New—Some Comments' in D. Apter and J. Joll (eds.), *Anarchism Today*, London, Macmillan, 1971, pp. 8–10.

46 See David Stafford, 'Anarchists in Britain Today', and Rudolf de Jong, 'Provos and Kabouters', in Apter and Joll, op. cit.

47 Henry Pelling, *A History of British Trade Unionism*, 3rd edn, New York, St Martin's Press, 1977.

48 See F. Bédarida, 'Le Socialisme en Grande-Bretagne de 1875 à 1914 in J. Droz, op. cit., Vol. 2, p. 356 ff.

49 On party/union relations in various leading cases, see Jacques Julliard, 'Les Syndicats et la politique' in P. Birnbaum and J.M. Vincent (eds.), *Critiques des pratiques politiques*, Paris, Galilée, 1978. See also Alessandro Pizzorno, 'Les syndicats et l'action politique', *Sociologie du travail*, April–June 1971.

50 H.M. Drucker, *Doctrine and Ethos in the Labour Party*, London, Allen & Unwin, 1979, chapter 1. See also L. Panitch, Introduction to *Social*

Democracy and Industrial Militancy, London, Cambridge University Press, 1976. T. Nairn is one of the few authors to establish a relationship between the nature of the Labour Party and the relative weakness of the British state; 'The Nature of the Labour Party', *New Left Review*, nos. 27 and 28, 1964. In 'The Decline of the British State', *New Left Review*, no. 101, 1977, p. 23, he rapidly extends his study of the relationship between the 'backward' state and the working class, placing emphasis also on the separation between the intellectuals and the working class.

51 Jacques Julliard, 'Théorie syndicaliste révolutionnaire et pratique gréviste', *Le Mouvement social*, October–December 1968, p. 60.

52 Gérard Adam and Jean-Daniel Reynaud, *Conflits du travail et changement social*, Paris, Presses Universitaires de France, 1978, pp. 59–61. See also the comparative article by Colin Crouch, 'The Changing Role of the State in Industrial Relations in Western Europe' in C. Crouch and A. Pizzorno (eds.), *The Resurgence of Class Conflict in Western Europe since 1968*, Vol. 2, 1978, chapter 8.

53 A. Flanders and M.A. Clegg, *The System of Industrial Relations in Great Britain*, Oxford, Blackwell, 1954.

54 G. Lyon-Caen, 'Critique de la négociation collective', *Droit social*, September–October 1979. We may perhaps adduce as further evidence the rediscovery of the role of the conciliation boards (*conseils des prud'hommes*) which obviate recourse to the state and testify to its withdrawal from employer–employee relations. See Pierre Can, *Sociologie des conseils de prud'hommes*, Paris, E.P.H.E., 1979.

55 Walter Korpi and Michael Shalev, 'Strikes, Industrial Relations and Class Conflict in Capitalist Societies', *British Journal of Sociology*, June 1979, p. 181.

56 Colin Crouch, *Class Conflict and the Industrial Relations Crisis*, London, Heinemann, 1977.

57 Very briefly, for lack of space, let us observe in conclusion that in Italy the state has not succeeded in institutionalising itself and differentiating itself completely according to the French model. It continues to be infiltrated by civil society. In place of the state/civil society relationship, therefore, we find a power structure composed of multiple élites and not, as in the United Kingdom, a ruling class. This situation, accompanied by late industrialisation accomplished in reality neither on the initiative of the state nor on that of a ruling class, long lent strength to the community structures in resisting the development of social and political movements, whether Marxist or anarcho-syndicalist in inspiration. Although such movements took an increasingly organised shape towards the end of the nineteenth century, it should nevertheless be said that, in the setting of these community relations and of 'clientelism', the main feature was individual or small-group anarchism. See, for example, Richard Hostetter, *The Italian Socialist Movement*, Princeton, Princeton University Press, 1958, chapter 13, G. Woodcock, op. cit., chapter 11; Sidney Tarrow, *Peasant Communism in Southern Italy*, New Haven, Yale University Press, 1967, chaps. 3–4.

58 See Pierre Birnbaum, *La Logique de l'Etat*, Paris, Fayard, 1982.

12 'State', legitimacy and protest in Islamic culture

Bertrand Badie

Comparative analysis is faced with a formidable dilemma: in developing general and transcultural concepts like 'protest' or 'demand', which it relates to a universal process of modernisation,[1] it denies itself the possibility of understanding the specific types of claims generated within different cultural settings. It tends automatically to assimilate such particularities to phenomena of underdevelopment. But if it goes the other way, beginning with categories proper to each cultural system concerned, it limits the comparison to the construction of formal typologies or the juxtaposition of concrete forms, denying itself the possibility of finding a social logic of modern protests. However, provided that the pitfalls of developmentalism are avoided, the notion of protest is worth retaining as a hypothesis: the questioning of various types of communitarian solidarity, social mobilisation, the construction of a centre and competitive strategies between élites enjoying distinct legitimacies, maintain in different cultures, behaviour patterns of rejection and protest which share common characteristics.

Beyond the latter, one of the most clearly differentiated aspects of protest is the manner in which it is legitimised in various cultures, i.e. the formulation and the pattern of signification to which the social actors appeal to establish the validity of their protest activities and incorporate them in the political system. The contrast between Islamic and Western Christian models is striking from this point of view.[2] The latter conceives of the political domain as having its own autonomous legitimacy, which is distinct from religious formulae, being essentially a human matter, and it encourages evaluation, discussion and challenge. The former, on the other hand, denies the very possibility of any legitimacy other than religious, and makes it doubly difficult to protest against an order which is supposed to remain unitarian. The evolution of the Western model since the beginning of the Christian Middle Ages towards a culture of representation and delegation provided a legitimate foundation for protest and gradually ensured its institutionalisation, with the establishment of specialised channels, so that one could say that little by little an internal 'demand culture' was formed within the political space of Western Christian societies. The low compatibility of Islamic culture with the idea of delegation, on the other hand, has hindered efforts aimed at legitimising protest in the Muslim world and contributed more than anything else to maintaining it outside the institutionalised political space.

The process of modernisation aggravates the implications of this contrast. Resting as it does on the social division of labour and the specialisation of tasks, it also involves individualisation and the horizontal structuring of society, as well as the banalisation of demand, which thus becomes one of the fundamental elements of the social and political processes. The socio-economic changes which currently affect Islamic societies lead to the voluntaristic development of new strategies of protest and stimulate the emergence of rival doctrinal models which claim to legitimise them. The cultural identity of the Muslim world often makes this process contradictory, leading to practices which remain religion-oriented and are structured outside the institutionalised political space. Such practices contribute to the increasing complexity of Islam's status, which claims simultaneously to be a culture, a religion and an ideology.[3] Particularly they tend to confer on the political space a certain identity which separates it from the rationality of the State.[4]

Islamic culture and protest

The elaboration of this protest strategy is first characterised by the crisis of legitimacy which continually affects the Islamic political system and hinders the formation of a political space displaying authority.[5] This crisis is only partially resolved by the elaboration of formulae of substitution which limit the opportunities for protest.

The legitimisation of political power has appeared as a recurrent quest in the history of Islamic societies since the death of the Prophet, with civil wars and struggles for succession[6] sustained by a monist conception of authority as essentially divine, indivisible and which cannot be delegated. God being the sole sovereign, the prince who

251

claims an essentially political quality, and pretends to create a political obligation distinct from that of the believer, runs the risk of illegitimacy.[7] Political action is the duty of the man of faith when it contributes to the consolidation of the community of believers, but loses its legitimacy as soon as it ceases to have this function, as Jelal-ed-Din Rùmi, one of the great figures of classical sufism puts it: 'Princely rank (*miri*), vizirat (*vaziri*), royalty (*shahi*), what seductive terms these are, but behind them lurk death, torment and the loss of our days'.[8] This rejection of politics is similar to some of the arguments one finds in the Christian culture of Rome, in which politics is viewed as a degrading and inferior activity.[9] The two formulae are different, however: inferior though it is to religion in the Christian Roman tradition, the political has its own legitimacy, which makes rivalry between political projects or ideologies acceptable. But within the context of Islam, the political is part of the religious realm, in which case is appears as indisputable, and as protest when this link disappears.

Thus the political supports a system which will only be legitimised if it draws its strength from the law of God, and divests itself of every human attribute. It is in such circumstances that every human construction of political power has been seen from the outset as 'irregular', as an approach involving the danger of lending to the function of protest the legitimacy which the political power itself was lacking. The strategy of princes seeking to establish their own power has thus been to welcome foreign forms of legitimisation of political power, first from Persia and Byzantium, then from the Asiatic invasions, in an effort to reconcile them with classical Islamic culture, and to provide principles replacing a faltering legitimacy. History shows that this undertaking was based essentially on four lines of argument.

First, if the political power cannot put on the mantle of legitimacy, it can impose itself as a necessity. Sedition (*fitna*), being the main obstacle to the construction of the *ummah* (the community of believers), a human power is at any rate preferable to the anarchy which can result from recurrent protests. For lack of any hierarchy of legitimacies (which can only be unique), a hierarchy of *illegitimacies* clearly emerges, which necessarily condemns the protest more severely than power. Ghazali stresses this in the following way: 'Should we stop obeying the law? Should we revoke the *qāḍīs*, should we abandon all authority without values, should we stop getting married and proclaim that the acts of people in high places are null and void in every way? And are we to let people live in sin? Or should we continue, recognising that what is inanimate really exists, and that all the acts of the administration are valid, in view of the circumstances and necessities of the moment?'[10] Seditious protest is not all that is condemned here: 'exit' behaviour is denounced with equal vigour.

To this was added the argument that the power of the prince should be accepted, for all power — just like all empirical phenomena — could only be understood as a sign of God. The Islamic culture, like reformed Christianity, thus tends to see the tyrant as the incarnation of an evil, but an evil willed by God. Relations of power, if they are human and necessary, and not of a divine order and legitimate, cannot be seen as in the Christian mode, of a secondary cause abandoned by God, but as bound to his will. Thus they are to be accepted, just as usurpation or a palace revolution is to be accepted. This conception is altogether different from the one which would call for popular insurrection, and which one finds underlying political theories which have been produced since the birth of the great empires. An example is the *morjite* doctrine which helped to protect the Ummayad Empire from a movement of essentially religious popular protest.[11]

The monist understanding of authority held in the Islamic culture rejects the idea of princely political sovereignty as much as a national political sovereignty. Political obligation, being derived from obedience to a divine truth, can in no case emanate from the expression of national sovereignty, the very idea of which can only with difficulty be introduced into the constitutional theory of Muslim countries. The lack of the principle of national sovereignty protects the established political power, limiting the meaning and scope of protest. It also confines legitimate political relations to the religious realm, denying to individuals responsibility for political control, leaving that either to the *ummah* or the *fuqahā* (depositories of jurisprudence), or the *ulamā* (the doctors of Law), as the case may be. It was precisely on this basis that the caliph was able to attempt the establishment of a substitution formula for the legitimacy he had lost, by presenting himself, in conformity with Al Mawardi's theory, as 'the Prophet's replacement'. In this way he claimed not a divine authority but that of a lieutenant of God, holding a *bay'a* (a contract of allegiance) with the community of believers.[12] This is a false authority if one observes to the letter the coherence of a cultural model which rejects all delegation of authority, but it was an authority of substitution, which the caliph was able gradually to impose precisely in order to contain the risk of protest that was hanging over the political order.

The final element, which completes this orientation, is the failure of every attempt to produce a theory of the right to resistance. As we know, this right is central in the Western culture of the state based on the rule of law, and is none the less compatible with a culture which holds any command contrary to the Shari'a to be illegitimate. B. Lewis shows how the *faqīh*, who is an employee of the caliph, was never able to establish procedures of sanction against the prince, and how the different categories designating practices of resistance (*thawra, kharaja, qama, naza, baqua, ikhtilàl, inqilàb*) have never been established as categories of law.[13]

Certain Muslim political systems have succeeded in providing themselves with formulae of legitimacy derived partly from other sources, either from the nature of the social structure, as in Morocco, where the monarch is accepted equally as a conciliator of the tribes,[14] or from remnants of pre-Islamic cultures, as in Iran, where the Sassanid model of government has often prevailed against the rigours of shiism in matters of legitimacy, and where the king has often laid claim to an absolute or even divine right.[15]

Thus one cannot deny the power and complexity of doctrinal and institutional constructions aiming to contain different forms of protest and protect a political power in search of legitimacy for itself. But equally undeniable is the 'infrastructure' nature of these constructions which in all their ramifications fall a long way short of constituting a system of meanings which unifies the whole body of actors in societies of the Muslim world. Every extension beyond the idea of a heteronomous, illegitimate, but necessary polity provokes debates, and the motions this generates lead to doctrinal theories which are not shared commonly in all their implications. It is thus partly in reaction to the latter that discourses of protest have been elaborated, striving in turn to establish their own legitimacy.

Discourses of protest are characteristically pluralistic because of this, each founded on certain elements of Islamic culture and developed in support of actions taken by groups with divergent strategies.

One type of protest stems from a critique of the human dimension of political power, and is expressed by a refusal of the politics, or even by 'exit'. This approach is associated with the history of the brotherhood phenomenon, particularly Sufism, which first appeared in the ninth century as a communitarian reaction to the legalism of the *ulamā* and to the organisation of an imperial and centralised system. It reinforces a traditional mode of protest which is found throughout the ages, justifying resistance or boycott by referring to the religious claim and the degrading nature of politics. It may take the form of refusing to pay the tax or to frequent the market towns, or of splitting loyalties to construct counter-communities.[16] This attitude of 'exit', modelled exactly on the Prophet's hegira, finds great vitality in Muslim Africa, where C. Coulon notes the role of Senegalese brotherhoods in resisting the central political power and defending the peripheral communities.[17] This first form of protest can in no case be limited to the pre-modern period, as the example of Senegal reminds us. Other examples show how it can carry a demand for protection of identity in the face of political ideas or organisations viewed as foreign to the cultural patterns of a community. It is found in situations of drastic or erratic social mobilisation[18] and is expressed by a reactivation of religious behaviour which is misinterpreted as a form of depoliticisation. It is very often expressed as a possible mode of resistance to secularisation that has been imposed 'from above', as shown by the example of the 'religious resistance' of the Turkish villagers.[19] It may be seen in the prolific construction of mosques, particularly in the new districts of towns bearing the brunt of the rural exodus, as in Syria where, after 1967, more mosques were built in three years than during the preceding thirty years.[20]

This first discourse is extended with another one, still built on the view that power corrupts, but expressed this time in a ritual of rebellion directed not against the political role but against its incumbent. This was a familiar phenomenon in the pre-modern period, especially in the form of peasant rebellions against holders of authority, or even, more recently, against ministers or bureaucracies, but it is not sustained by any global plan of political protest, except perhaps the restoration of an order which has been corrupted by the person in charge of it. This arraigning of 'the bad prince' or the 'bad minister' seems like a form that is both legitimate and able to mobilise an expression of demands to a political system which is deprived of channels for socio-economic representation by the logic of neopatrimonialism.

A third type of protest discourse extends the accusation of corruption to politics itself, no longer stopping at the incumbent of the roles, holding it to be necessary to resist the deterioration which threatens all political power, adopting an entropic and pessimistic view of what the earthly polity must come to. The theme of corrupt and tyrannical power is particularly structured in the beliefs of shiite Islam, which were forged essentially to protest the construction of the Umayyad Empire. It is expressed particularly clearly in the 'paradigm of Karbala', which presents the martyrdom of Imam Hosein and his companions in their resistance to the oppression and injustice (*zulm*) of the caliph power.[21] Unlike the previous model, this form of protest is equipped with revolutionary relevance, being aimed at the political order itself.

Thus it comes close to a Messianic type of discourse, which constitutes a fourth variant of protest, basing its denunciation of the established political power on a religious obligation (the jihàd or holy war) or a religious tradition (the *mahdi*, the saviour and restorer of the polity in conformity with the divine will). At the same time this claim involves a powerful popular mobilisation, no longer only negatively but also towards the construction of a new political order. Reference to the jihad structures the argument of the Muslim Brothers in particular.[22] It rests on an inversion of the generally accepted postulate that *fitna*, frequently denounced in Islam, is a result of popular protest. Here the basic idea is that political power which no longer conforms to Islam gives rise to *fitna*, and should therefore be fought by any means available, including the jihad, which exists to liberate all people and those in the *dar al-Islam* first of all. Not only is protest then legitimate but it cannot stop at hegira or rebellion, and must go on to the reconstruction of the City of the Prophet, including, through tyrannicide, the elaboration of the new *fiqh* (jurisprudence)[23] and the constitution of a new polity based on total submission to God. The argument of necessity is thus reconsidered to favour a view of legitimacy which derives from fidelity to a perpetual revolution directed against human domination and positive laws. At this level, protest becomes an obligation for the believer, reinforced by the necessity of a political counter-plan which claims a legitimacy that excludes all others.

The coexistence of these formulae for protest thus constitutes another mark of Islamic culture. The absence within it of political legitimacy in the strict sense contributes to the tendency for such formulae to seek religious legitimacy. Such a phenomenon is doubly consequential. First it strikes fiercely at the political power in office, because in this way protest establishes its own legitimacy, which will impose itself against the established power. Second, it tends to place the protest *beyond* the reach of the institutionalised political system. This gives it an externality and a universality which can lead at any moment to a global condemnation of the political system. It seems that in these tensions and asymmetries one has a complex of factors which decisively influence Islamic cultural identity.

Modern strategies of protest

The modern function of protest was first organised in the Arab world towards the end of the nineteenth century, through the influence of foreign models, particularly where attempts were made to import the essential elements of the Western theory and practice of protest. The influence of the nationalist argument, then of social democracy and finally of Marxism, is very clear: it is found today as much as Ba'athism as in Nasserism, and is crystallised at first in their nationalistic and Pan-Arab themes. Both these currents then proceed to minimise Islam, describing it merely as a 'moment' in the history of Arab nationalism in the first case, or as a 'component' of national Arab identity in the second.[24] Basically they both articulate a triple protest, which is modulated, but not fundamentally changed, according to whether they are in power or not. Thus we see a new *mode of management* of protest emerging, directing against the division of the Arab peoples, against the established socio-economic order and power structure, and against the imperialism and bipolarisation of the international system which place the Arab world in a dominated and marginal position.

From this point of view, it is not so much Nasser — who was more pragmatic than doctrinaire — as Nasserism that should be studied as a diffuse mode of protest. The major themes of the programme it offered from 1954 onwards (against imperialism, feudalism and capitalism; for social justice, a powerful army and a democratic system) appealed to the new élites and social groups such as the military and the bureaucrats, who were calling for redistribution. But at the same time it appealed to groups who were the victims of economic modernisation, such as peasants affected by population increases and technological change, small shopkeepers weakened by competition, and communities in danger of being dispossessed, like the *ulamā* in particular.[25]

In this context Nasserism offered a triple strategic choice in the articulation of protest. First, it was a chance to express an inter-class, or at least inter-category, protest, with some demands involving a critique of modernisation, others an acceleration of it. Then, by maintaining this mode of protest one could make of it an instrument not only of mobilisation but of government. Hence the increasing importance of the nationalist and anti-imperialist themes, which made it possible to manage discontent by directing it towards the outside. Finally, it made the nation the central value of mobilisation, urging its construction as the demand that was capable of including the whole range of protests. The major difficulty with this stems from the fact that the national theme, which is essentially imported from the West, does not fit in very well with the cultural configuration of Islam which, rather than the secular idea of the nation, favours the more all-embracing one of the community of believers.

Nasserism and Ba'athism are the archetypes of this approach, which was dominant at the end of the 1950s and the beginning of the 1960s, when the challenge of modernisation seemed to be the necessary emphasis for the political élites, either imitating the Western model as a whole or selecting certain elements from it so as to arrive at an 'Arab' model of modernity. The first formula, which was used particularly in the traditional monarchies, had necessarily only a very slight effect on the protest movements, which found themselves reduced to a strategy of depoliticisation as an alternative, or to one of supporting or making use of the monarch's legitimacy. This was the case of Abd al Aziz ibn Saoud, for example, with his imposition of the first elements of a modernisation policy in Saudi Arabia.[26] The second formula, in addition to its Nasserian and Ba'athist variants, is found in Mossadeghism and Bourguibism. Their failure to satisfy and channel a whole set of contradictory processes is seen first of all in the more and more massive use they had to make of charismatic legitimacy, as a substitute for a nationalist legitimacy which never really managed to assert itself. But this failure was due above all to their inability — flagrant in Ba'athism, less so in Nasserism — to define themselves in relation to religion, which was thus able to assert itself all the more swiftly as a substitute formula for legitimising different forms of protest.

The decline of Nasser's charisma after the defeat of 1967 led, notably in February and November of 1968, to the outbreak of riots in Cairo, Alexandria, in the University of Ayn Shams, where the protest of the students and the workers were fused into religious terms.[27] Likewise, in February 1960, Bourguiba's attempt to base the non-observance of Ramadan on the nationalist argument of promoting Tunisian economic development set off a popular protest movement which forced the Tunisian President to back down.[28] Perhaps even more significant was the periodical failure of the Syrian Ba'ath in its efforts to establish this secular and nationalist legitimacy, and the rise of a religious dispute which resulted from it. This helps to explain the events of spring 1967, when the army newspaper called for 'a new Arab man', described in secular terms. At street level there was a violent reaction which led to the arrest of the author of this incriminating article.[29] We find a similar scenario in 1973 with the draft constitution, which recognised the Shari'a only as a source, among others, of legislation: Hafez el Assad had to face a new outbreak of rioting and accept a new compromise.[30]

Attempts to build secular structures and legitimacy for protest thus seem to be doomed to a triple failure: not managing to articulate different demands and forms of dispute in a cultural context which can command solidarity; not managing to mobilise demands behind a legitimising project; and finally reacting to this by developing protests on religious grounds which strive in their turn to monopolise the whole complex of dissident attitudes. This re-emergence of the religious as a dominant support for protest can thus be understood in two ways: as a new formula for legitimacy and mobilisation or as a larger arena of protest, in which pro-modernist demands are able to coexist with a critique or even a rejection of modernity.

The religious articulation of protest practices derives at first from the strategy of the religious élites themselves in their struggle to reinforce their power and influence, and above all to protect themselves against the risks of dispossession. The advantage of such a strategy is that, being essentially directed against the political power and its claim to autonomy, it is in a position to make multiple alliances and take up the most diversified interests and challenges. Fighting for their own interests and convictions against every attempt to install absolute monarchic power, the religious élites, first in the Ottoman Empire and then in Persia, could thus ally themselves with the constitutionalist forces. This explains the role of the *ulamā* side by side with the Young Ottomans in disputing the omipotence of the Sultan and his pretensions to law-making and to institutionalising a model of government that was closer to the Mongolian, Persian or Byzantine concept of authority than that of Islam.[31] It also explains the role of the Iranian clergy in the Persian constitutionalist movement at the beginning of the century, in sanctioning a growing opposition to the *qàjàr* dynasty which, since the second half of the nineteenth century, had sought to monopolise political functions to its own advantage by creating a secular education, reducing the scope of religious jurisdiction, abolishing the immunity of sanctuaries and claiming control of the revenues of the *awqàf* (religious foundations).[32] In these conditions the constitutionalist strategy made it possible for the Iranian clergy to participate in the limitation of monarchic power and play an active role in it by imposing the institutionalisation of religious supervision, to ensure that laws and procedures conformed to the Shari'a. This same anti-monarchic and anti-absolutist line is found in the support given by the *ulamā* to the free officers at the time of the Egyptian revolution.[33]

This expression of an essentially political dispute is further supported and amplified by the authoritarian reactions of most of the political systems, which fear that social mobilisation will involve a wave of demands for political participation whose destabilising effects threaten not to be containable by their all too fragile formulae of legitimacy. This authoritarian response then tends to produce the Islamic themes of the equality of believers, the duty of consultation or the culpability of the élite in confiscating the political power.

This strategy of protecting the religious élites from the risk of being dispossessed of their privileges can also take on anti-modernist dimensions. This is partly because modernisation is associated in the minds of some of these élites with the beginnings of irreversible secularisation,[34] or a socio-economic restructuring process at the expense of the clergy's interests, especially where they themselves are highly structured, as was the case in Iran at the time of the agrarian reform.[35] It is also because the religious élites are led to define themselves against a secular political power which systematically seeks to base its legitimacy on the fulfilment of a modernising function, as was the case in Kemalist Turkey or, from the reign of the Reza Shah onwards, in Persia.[36]

But above all this anti-modern orientation is reinforced by the proliferation of extremely varied protests stimulated by rapid social change, which the secular organisations have been unable to control. The demand for protection against the risks of social regression affect not only the religious élite but the artisans and shopkeepers as well.[37] At the same time, the rapid increase of social mobilisation, and particularly of urbanisation, disrupts community allegiances, and this is still quite inadequately compensated for by the timid construction of a citizens' allegiance, which is too constricted by the repressive character of most political regimes, with the artificiality of their mobilisation structures and the weakness of their literacy levels. The result of this is the appearance in the towns of political alienation patterns, expressed mainly in demands for the reconstruction of community solidarities which religion can help to form or even partially satisfy in itself, through the mosques,[38] or through the brotherhoods or, where there is a real religious bureaucracy, like in Iran, through a veritable wide networking and coverage carried out by the clergy. This communitarian reaction is particularly marked in the countries with strong social mobilisation like Iran, Syria or Egypt.

Alongside such protests directed against modernity, there are also those which go on within it. First, there are the protests arising from the frustrations modernity causes, particularly among young unemployed graduates or the members of proliferating bureaucracies who belong, in Senegal for example, to brotherhood organisations or religious reform movements.[39] Likewise, the new middle classes are frustrated by a sense of exclusion from political power or the wealth flowing from modernisation, and seek through traditional religious culture — which is made more available to them by the spread of education — ways of asserting themselves in the face of extreme Westernisation, using an initiative similar to that of the 'Sanscritisation' movement in India, referred to above.[40] Finally, we find the same religious vehicle in the expression, typically modern this time, of demands addressed to the centre for subsidies or other forms of redistribution of income, as seen in the pro-Khomeni character of the riots of January 1977 in Egypt, in reaction to the rise in prices.[41] It was also seen in Iran during the demonstrations of discontent over the economic difficulties of 1955 and 1956, which very quickly turned into riots against the Baha'is; and again in the demonstrations of the autumn and winter of 1977, which began with protest over the housing policy and a call for redistribution.[42]

These processes as a whole lead to the formation of a religious legitimisation of socio-economic protest, seen mainly in the promotion of the Islamic theme of social justice and community sharing; if the idea itself of private property is not challenged, it is none the less amended by the necessity of taking into account the needs of everyone and of considering production as something that should be for the good of the whole community.[43] This social theory, completed by the practice of community leadership and protesting against the established political authority, incontestably nurtures strategies of hegira and jihad of the kind we have described, which seem most compatible with the accomplishment of this type of vindication. These strategies place the most structured Islamic organisations in an advantageous position, whether they are the clergy in Iran, the marabout brotherhoods in Senegal, the *nurju* and *süleymanju* brotherhoods in Turkey, or movements within the constituency of the Muslim Brothers in Egypt, Syria or the Maghreb, and even in the countries of the Arab peninsula.[44] One should be careful not to overestimate their similarity, however: dissimilar beliefs on the acceptability of modernity exist among them, with some, like the *nurju*, for example, open to it in principle. One also finds different organisational forms among them, with varying degrees of secrecy and integration. Finally, one can also distinguish several types of tactics among them, ranging from the desire to Islamise society before taking power — thus capitalising on the advantages of taking over the protest movements — to terrorist approaches, aimed directly at the political centre.

The formation of this community counter-culture thus gives rise to new forms of protest directly concerned with protecting the identity of Islam. Thus one sees hostile opposition to the development of a new family code or the adoption of a new status for women.[45] But above all they involve the structuring of all forms of nationalist dispute religiously. This phenomenon appeared fairly early in the process, but has never ceased to gain ground. One sees it already in November 1945, with the demonstrations in Egypt during the commemoration of the Balfour Declaration, which turned into riots against the Jewish communities and the Catholic, Armenian and Coptic churches. It appears again in January 1952 in the anti-British demonstrations at Suez, which led to the burning of Coptic churches;[46] and again at the time of the demonstrations which followed the defeat of 1967 and the announcement of Nasser's resignation;[47] and yet again in the 'rumours' that were spread in October 1973 accusing a Coptic officer of being responsible for the Israeli army's crossing of the Canal.[48] All these events indicate a redirection of nationalist vindication and mobilisation towards a religious theme which both sustains and legitimises them.

This religious take-over has the effect of helping to make the protest all-embracing and part of what is often a Messianic or millenarian attack on political structures. This trend is somewhat reminiscent of protest patterns which took shape in the West at the time of the construction of the industrial society. M. Agulhon, in his study of the formation of these practices in nineteenth century Provence, observes the same communitarian origin in the protests of labourers and craftsmen and the role of Christianity in sustaining communitarianism.[49] We find here as in other places the relevance and effectiveness of the community forms of mobilisation.[50] The essential difference lies in the slow mutation of worker protest activities in the West which, partly through their imitation of a revolutionary bourgeoisie, gradually expressed themselves in an associative and secular way, built first on various categories of interest, then on class interests, finally to be crystallised in a culture of demand.[51] It was on this renewed basis that the politicisation of these movements was built up.

The practice of protest in Islamic societies seems to diverge from this model on several essential points. Defining itself again and again in relation to a breakdown in legitimacy of public power, it is liable in any moment of crisis to take up a position of a priori denunciation of the political order, which tends even to precede any statement of what is being vindicated. Furthermore, expressing itself on the basis of durable community and religious legitimacy, it can only with difficulty blend with the Western mode of focused claims which are institutionalised and by their very nature particular, so as to be included in an inclusive position, to which the critique of modernity is particularly well suited.[52]

These reference points help to explain the recent successes of fundamentalist movements preaching return to a strict application of the principles of Islam to solve problems facing modern society. However, the dominant role of the fundamentalist approach should not eclipse two sources of uncertainty. Having managed up to now to take charge of demands both hostile and favourable to modernisation, the Islamic organisations of today seem more and more confronted with a choice which is liable to bring schism or a split between the 'modernist' and 'anti-modernist' organisations. This trend produces a new rivalry which helps to anchor fundamentalism more deeply to the rejection of modernity while at the same time inciting an Arab 'reformist' protest.[53] In addition to this split, the accession, whether direct or not, of some of these movements to power, with the concomitant obligation of 'managing' modernity, is likely to undermine their credibility and put them in a position similar to that experienced earlier on by secular movements.

Notes

1 See on this, S. Eisenstadt, *Modernization, Protest and Change*, Englewood Cliffs, NJ, Prentice Hall, 1966.

2 We do not intend to suggest that there exists only one Islamic culture or a single Western Christian one. It just seems necessary, in a comparative approach, to isolate a few major characteristics which show the contrast between these two types of culture and whose importance makes it justifiable to use them in this way. On the use of the concept of culture in political analysis, see B. Badie, *Culture et politique*, Paris, Economica, 1983.

3 M.C. Hudson, 'Islam and Political Development' in J.L. Esposito (ed.) *Islam and Development*, Syracuse, NY, Syracuse University Press, 1980, p. 23.

4 Our hypothesis is based on a restrictive construction of the state, cf. B. Badie and P. Birnbaum, *The Sociology of the State*, Chicago, University of Chicago Press, 1983.

5 M.C. Hudson, *Arab Politics: The Search for Legitimacy*, New Haven, Yale University Press, 1977, chap. 4.

6 P.J. Vatikiotis (ed.), *Revolution in the Middle East*, London, Allen & Unwin, 1972, p. 9.

7 B.N. Borthwick, *Comparative Politics of the Middle East*, Englewood Cliffs, NJ, Prentice Hall, 1980, p. 64.

8 Quoted in G.E. von Grunebaum, *L'Identité culturelle de l'Islam*, Paris, Gallimard, 1973, p. 28.

9 On these questions, see Badie, op. cit., pp. 106–7.

10 Quoted in G.E. von Grunebaum, *L'Islam médiéval*, Paris, Payot, 1962, p. 185.

11 Cf. E. Kedourie, *Islam in the Modern World*, London, Mansell, 1980, p. 36.

12 Cf. M.C. Hudson, 'Islam and Political Development', p. 4, and G.E. von Grunebaum, *L'Islam médiéval*, p. 173.

13 R. Lewis, 'Islamic Concepts of Revolution', in Vatikiotis (ed.), op cit., p. 30ff.

14 E. Gellner, 'Patterns of Tribal Rebellion in Morocco' in Vatikiotis, op. cit., p. 126ff.

15 R. Savory, 'Sovereignty in the Shi's State' in M. Curtis (ed.), *Religion and Politics in the Middle East*, Boulder, Westview Press, 1981, p. 134ff.

16 M. Halpern, *The Politics of Social Change in the Middle East and North Africa*, Princeton, Princeton University Press, 1963, p. 93.

17 C. Coulon, *Les Musulmans et le pouvoir en Afrique noire*, Paris, Karthala, 1983, Part I.

18 This does not correspond to the hypothesis, which is much too linear, of D. Lerner, *The Passing of Traditional Society*, Glencoe, Free Press, 1958.

19 Cf. P. Magnarella, *Tradition and Change in a Turkish Town*, New York, Wiley, 1974.

20 Halpern, op. cit., p. 92ff.
21 Cf. M. Fischer, *Iran from Religious Dispute to Revolution*, Cambridge, Mass., Harvard University Press, 1980, pp. 7–9.
22 O. Carré, 'Le Combat pour Dieu et l'état islamique chez Sayyid Qotb, l'inspirateur du radicalisme islamique actuel', *Revue française de science politique*, August 1983, p. 687ff.
23 Ibid., pp. 692, 696.
24 Cf. R.I. Dekmejian, 'The Anatomy of Islamic Revival: Legitimacy Crisis, Ethnic Conflict and the Search for Islamic Alternatives' in Curtis (ed.), op. cit., p. 34ff.
25 L. Binder, *The Ideological Revolution in the Middle East*, New York, Wiley, 1964, pp. 213–14.
26 J.P. Piscatori, 'The Roles of Islam in Saudi Arabia's Political Development' in Esposito, op. cit., p. 131.
27 Borthwick, op. cit., p. 173.
28 B. Lewis, 'The Return of Islam' in Curtis, op. cit., p. 24.
29 Ibid.
30 S. Humphreys, 'Islam and Political Values in Saudi Arabia, Egypt and Syria' in Curtis, op. cit., p. 293.
31 S. Mardin, *The Genesis of Young Ottoman Thought*, Princeton, Princeton University Press, p. 102.
32 Cf. M.R. Djalili, *Religion et révolution*, Paris, Economica, 1981, p. 45.
33 Binder, op. cit., p. 214.
34 Humphreys, op. cit.
35 On this question see A.K.S. Lambton, *The Persian Land Reform*, Oxford, Oxford University Press, 1969.
36 Cf. for example, A. Kazancigil and E. Ozbudun (eds.), *Atatürk: Founder of a Modern State*, London, C. Hurst and Co., 1981.
37 Humphreys, op. cit., p. 290.
38 B. Lewis, 'The Return of Islam', p. 27.
39 Coulon, op. cit., p. 70ff.
40 Halpern, op. cit., pp. 138–9.
41 Dekmejian, op. cit., p. 37.
42 Fischer, op. cit., p. 191ff.
43 J.T. Cummings, H.T. Askari and A. Mustafa, 'Islam and Modern Economic Change' in Esposito, op. cit., p. 36.
44 Cf. B. Badie, C. Coulon, B. Cubertafond, P. Dumont and R. Santucci, *Contestations en Islam*, Paris, CHEAM publications, 1984.
45 Humphreys, op. cit., p. 302.
46 B. Lewis, 'The Return of Islam', op. cit., p. 19.
47 Borthwick, op. cit., p. 137.
48 B. Lewis, op. cit., p. 26.
49 M. Agulhon, *La République au village*, Paris, Plon, 1970, p. 149ff.
50 A. Oberschall, *Social Conflict and Social Movements*, Englewood Cliffs, NJ, Prentice Hall, 1973.
51 Cf. Agulhon, op. cit., p. 206ff.
52 This corresponds to 'type D' of Oberschall's typology, in Oberschall, op. cit., pp. 119, 122.

53 Cf. above, the example of Turkey, also that of Senegal (Coulon, op. cit., chap. 4) or that of Iran today.

13 The forms of the socialist state

V.E. Chirkin

Introduction

The term 'form of state' has three meanings: it is a sociological notion, a category of the science of the state, and an institution under constitutional law. There is no commonly accepted definition of the'form of the state' in the writings of Western political scientists. More often than not, the form of the state is identified with the form of government, which is one of its elements, and in some cases with the political regime and sometimes even with the political system as a whole.

The 'form of state' has been the subject of discussion in the legal literature of the socialist countries for a long time.[1] This discussion has centred recently on a clarification of the nature and components of the form of the state. Originally, most scholars supported a two-element approach, which distinguished the form of government — a method of organising the highest bodies of the state — and the forms of the state structure — a national-territorial and administrative-territorial organisation of the state. This approach is still used in some textbooks.[2]

Since 1955, most authors have begun to include a third element, which is the political regime, usually understood as the methods of exercising state power, and sometimes as a 'style of government'.[3] A fourth component, suggested in 1970, was called 'political dynamics' (the 'aggressive' or 'peaceful' nature of a state was cited as an example of such dynamics). On the other hand, some authors began to reduce the number of components. Some equated the form of the state with the political regime[4] and others with the form of government.[5]

New ideas emerged in the late 1960s, and in particular that of 'the state regime'. The supporters of this notion distinguish it from the political regime, maintaining that the latter develops not only as a result of the activities of the state bodies but also of those of other political institutions, thus going beyond the form of the state.[6] The state regime reflects the general characteristics of the methods of exercising state power in regulating political relations between the society, the state, the collectivity and the individual. It is considered as the third element in analysing the form of state (especially for teaching purposes).

In the 1970s a system approach was introduced. In addition to the components approach, this provided a clearer description of the form of the state. According to its proponents, the concept of the form of the state cannot be broken down into one or more selected elements without further considerations. It is equally important to bear in mind the interconnections between such elements and between the components and the whole (the form of the state); between the state form and its elements, on the one hand, and the social environment in which they exist and operate, on the other. In this case, importance is attached both to direct connections such as the methods of administration and to such feedback as popular support for various government policies.[7] Systems analysis indicates that the notion of the form of the state reflects a new quality, which cannot be reduced to its components and which is inherent neither in any single element nor in their mechanical combination. This means that, although the element analysis is useful, it cannot fully describe the characteristics of the form of the state.

The notion of the form of the state used in many social science disciplines and in specialised areas of political science (the theory of the state and law, the state law, etc.) is becoming one of the most important scientific categories, which is used in the analysing of the 'external' structure and the organisation of all types of state. However, the main element of the state is its social substance, and not its form. As Lenin observed, 'bourgeois states are most varied in form, but their essence is the same: all these states, whatever their form, in the final analysis are inevitably the dictatorship of the bourgeoisie'.[8]

The correct use of the concept of the form of the state implies taking into account its class essence, its social substance, which can vary at different stages of development, such as the capitalist state in the period of 'free' industrial capitalism and the bourgeois imperialist state or the socialist state of the dictatorship of the proletariat and the socialist state of all the people. Without such a consideration the

267

various classifications of the forms of the state would not only be superficial (for example, putting the socialist republics which have a president under the category of the presidential regimes), but also basically wrong, since it would amount to using the same form to designate states which in fact are different in their social substance and, consequently, possess different forms, even if they appear to be similar.

Finally, the form of the state is not only a notion or a scientific category, but also an institution of the state law. It constitutes a system of legal interconnections, through internally co-ordinated rules of the state law, regulating the organisation of the state, the methods of exercising the state power, the linkages between the state bodies and the population. These rules, as part of the state law, may be studied through an analysis of their concrete forms in such states as the Soviet Union, Cuba, the United Kingdom, the United States, India, Tanzania, Fiji, etc.

However, the analysis of the form of the state should go beyond the constitutional and legal standards. The state is not only a legal institution, but also a concrete establishment. This is why Marxist-Leninist studies look at the form of the state in both its legal and its social substance, which together — and indeed they are inseparable – form the basis of state law. In analysing the development of the forms of the socialist state, the form is seen dependent on the changing social substance of the state and the integral structure of the state law. This structure expresses the unity of the method of organising the state power and the principal methods of exercising it in the sphere of political relations, the territorial organisation, and the principal forms of linkages between the state bodies and the population.

The correlation between essence, content and form

More often than not, Western constitutional experts and political scientists fail to differentiate and to establish the necessary links between the essence of the state (a historical phenomenon linked with various socio-economic systems, such as slave, feudal, capitalist, and communist systems, socialism being the early phase of the latter), its content or substance (the concrete variety of the state power within each), and its form. For example, F. Giese singles out monarchy, aristocracy and democracy, as constitutional types of the state, and describes the forms of government as absolutism, constitutionalism and parliamentarianism.[9] H. Nawiasky singles out the liberal, democratic-egalitarian, socialist and nationalist types of state.[10] M. Imboden identifies four types: monistic, dualistic, trinitary and quadrative.[11] In their analysis of the form of government, P. Odegard, R. Carr, M. Bernstein and D. Morrison distinguish monarchy, democracy, the one-party and multi-party states, the welfare state, liberalism, totalitarianism, etc.[12]

In Marxist political science the classification of the forms of the state is based first and foremost on the essence and the nature of the state power and not on external features of the state, since it is the content which determines the form. This is also reflected in the terminology, which refers, in the case of eighteenth-century France, not simply to the monarchy, but to the 'absolute centralized feudal monarchy', or in the case of contemporary India, to the 'bourgeois-democratic federal state' and concerning present-day Poland, Cuba or Vietnam, the 'people's democratic state form of the dictatorship of the proletariat'.

The same approach is used in analysing the evolution of the forms of the socialist state. The major changes in the form are rooted in the changing social essence of the state and its substance or content, that is, the concrete nature of state power.

However, the essence and the substance as a whole do not always exert an identical influence on the form. The essence of the socialist state, reflecting its most important, stable quality, determines the basic features of the form. For example, the soviets, which have different names in different countries (soviets or Councils of Workers', Peasants' and Red Armymen's deputies before 1936, Soviets of Working People's Deputies before 1977, and, since then, the Soviets of People's Deputies in the USSR, People's Councils in the Democratic Republic of Vietnam, National Committees in Czechoslovakia, Assemblies of Deputies in the German Democratic Republic, etc.), are the basis of any form of socialist state. As to the differences in the substance of the socialist state (e.g. the dictatorship of the proletariat, or the government of all the people), they determine the peculiar features of these bodies and their varieties (e.g. the withholding of electoral rights from the exploiters under the dictatorship of the proletariat in the elections to the soviets in the USSR before 1936). As for the specific national conditions of various socialist states, they have determined the individual features of the representative bodies (e.g. the bicameral structure of the Federal Assembly in the Czechoslovak SSR which corresponds to the multinational nature of the state, the system of four deputy chairmen of executive administrative bodies, at certain levels of local representative assemblies, in the German Democratic Republic, in accordance with the number of political parties, etc.)

The republican form of government is determined by the very essence of the socialist state which rules out the monarchy. However, the specific features of a republic depend on the substance of the state

269

power (e.g. the Soviet and people's democratic republics) as well as on the concrete historical conditions prevailing in different countries (cf. the republican form of government in Romania, where the President exerts a major influence and Hungary, which has no President).

The essence of the socialist state makes it imperative to apply Leninist principles in solving the problem of nationalities and forming the basis of the state structure (a federalism, autonomy or unitarism). The specific national features of a state determine the concrete forms of the state structure (six socialist republics within Federal Yogoslavia, two in Czechoslovakia, 38 different autonomous units in the Soviet Union, the Kazakh Bayan-Ulegey Oïmak (region) in unitarian Mongolia, etc.). Consequently, the essence is important for the form of state, but it determines it only in its principal, most fundamental outlines. The essence shapes only the principal framework of the state. The form of the state as a whole, however, is determined by its substance, which is greater than the essence, although the latter is part of the substance and constitutes its basis. This is why the evolution of the form of the socialist state (while its type remains the same) is above all linked to its changing substance.

The social nature of power is the main component of the substance of the state. In the Soviet Union, the development of the dictatorship of the proletariat into the socialist government of all the people was completed in the late 1950s. As a result, the form of the Soviet Republic in the USSR changed. It ceased to be the form of a proletarian state and became a state of the entire people. Similar processes are now taking place in a number of other socialist countries (Bulgaria, the German Democratic Republic, etc.), although they have not yet been completed.

Significantly, the substance of the state is not limited to the concrete social nature of power. Relations among nationalities are also of considerable importance. A change in these relations may lead to a change in the form of state, although its class nature may remain the same (e.g. in 1969 Czechoslovakia changed its unitarian structure to become a federal state).

The notion of the substance of the socialist state may also include a number of other social aspects, such as, for example, the political-economic relations among the various regions in a country. A change in these relations may lead to a basic reorganisation in the administrative territorial units. Bulgaria, for example, set up two-tier administrative territorial units (communities and districts) in 1959, when industrial management was being restructured. The new structures replaced the old three-tier system. Mongolia introduced a new administrative territorial division when the process of forming cattle breeders' co-operatives was completed, as did Cuba after the introduction of socialist relations of production.

Finally, the change in the form of the state may be influenced by various practical needs such as the necessity to reorganise the structure of the state machinery (e.g. the abolition of the presidency in Poland in 1952 and its replacement with a collective body and the introduction of the office of President in the People's Democratic Republic of Korea in 1972).

The forms of the socialist state of the dictatorship of the proletariat

The socialist state comes into being either as a result of a peaceful victory of the socialist revolution (e.g. the Hungarian Soviet Republic in 1919), the development of a democratic revolution into a socialist one (in a number of East European countries in 1944–8, and in North Vietnam in 1945–54, or as a result of armed uprisings (in Russia in 1917, and Bulgaria in 1944). In all cases this victory signifies that the state power has been taken away from the exploiters and handed over to the people led by the working class. Therefore, the socialist state emerges and exists for a more or less considerable period of time as a state of the dictatorship of the proletariat until the exploiting classes are removed from the scene in the course of socialist changes.

Historical experience makes it possible to single out several forms of the dictatorship of the proletariat: (1) the 1871 Paris Commune as an incomplete state form of the dictatorship of the proletariat; (2) the Soviet Socialist Republic (1917–1950s) which took a variety of forms (the independent Soviet Socialist Republic, preceding the USSR set up in 1922); the unitarian Soviet Socialist Republics, members of the Soviet Union, such as Ukraine, Byelorussia, etc.; the autonomous Soviet Socialist Federal Republic (the Transcaucasian Soviet Federal Socialist Republic in 1922–36, and the USSR); (3) the people's democratic socialist republic in a number of East European countries, in several Asian countries and in Cuba.

Each kind has its own specific features. Its forms change in the course of development to reflect the main tendency: the gradual evolution towards the government of all the people and, accordingly, the further advancement and expansion of socialist democracy. On the whole, the state form of the dictatorship of the proletariat is an interim form of transitory socialist government. It corresponds to the period of transition from capitalism to socialism with the antagonistic relations inherent in this period and has a clear-cut class nature.

The state of the dictatorship of the proletariat continues to exist for some time, even after the transition period is over, until a developed socialist society has been constructed. At this stage, the vanishing traits of this form of the proletarian state intertwine with the emergent ones of the government of the whole people. The latter become predominant in the long run. In the Soviet Union, the turning point in this process came in 1936 when a new constitution was adopted. However, for various reasons the Soviet Union still remained a dictatorship of the proletariat until the end of the 1950s.

The form of the socialist state of all the people

Under the dictatorship of the proletariat, the state power which belongs to the working people is used to bring about socio-economic changes, leading to a transformation of the structure of society. In the Soviet Union, in 1928, eleven years after the Socialist Revolution, the socialist forms in the economy accounted for 44 per cent of the national income, 82.4 per cent in gross industrial output and 3.3 per cent in gross farm output. The figures for 1937 were 99.1, 99.8 and 98.5 per cent respectively.[13] In the course of further development a strong integrated national economy was built up to combine the achievements of the scientific and technological revolution with those of the socialist system. At present, it takes Soviet industry two-and-a-half days to produce as much as Tsarist Russia turned out in the whole year of 1913. As compared with the mid-1930s when socialist relations in production became prevalent in both town and countryside, the gross social product today has increased nearly 20 times while real incomes have increased more than fivefold as compared to 1936.[14]

Radical economic transformations have led to a major reshaping of the class structure. In 1913, factory and office workers made up 17 per cent of the country's population; family farmers and individual handicraftsmen accounted for 66.7 per cent, landowners, the petty and upper urban bourgeoisie, traders and capitalist farmers for 16.3 per cent. In 1928, the percentages were 17.6, 74.9 and 4.6 respectively. Besides that, a new though small social group emerged, made up of the co-operative farmers and handicraftsmen. In 1937, this social category already accounted for 57.9 per cent, factory and office workers for 36.2 per cent and family farmers and individual handicraftsmen for 5.9 per cent. There were no more bourgeoisie or capitalist farmers.[15] Consequently, the exploiting classes had been removed from the scene and a new class of socialist co-operative farmers emerged. The ideological and political unity of Soviet society became firmly established.

As regards the question of the nationalities, all the peoples inhabiting the country had been given legal equality immediately after the

1917 Revolution. They also became equal in actual fact. The formerly backward peripheral provinces of the Tsarist empire turned into the flourishing republics of the united multinational socialist federal state.

A new social and international community, the Soviet people, came into being in the USSR as a result of all those changes. As a result, there were substantial modifications in the political system: 'Essentially they consist in the growing of the state of the dictatorship of the proletariat into a socialist state of all the people.'[16] These changes were reflected in the new Soviet constitution, adopted in 1977.

The form of the state of all the people, while possessing the common features of the socialist state and preserving the typological continuity, nevertheless differs from the state of the dictatorship of the proletariat.

Changes in the form of the Soviet socialist state, deriving from its altered social nature, are reflected, first of all, in the different procedures employed in establishing the top government bodies, their structure and activities. The 1936 constitution abolished the system of Congresses of Soviets. Deputies to the soviets were elected for a fixed term of office (first for four and two years, and later for five and two-and-a-half years). Earlier restrictions on the electoral rights of the exploiting classes were abolished and equal representation was introduced for town-dwellers and country people, etc. The structure of the state bodies was also changed in accordance with the 1936 constitution and later through amendments passed in 1946 and 1957.[17] Under these provisions, the Presidium of the USSR Supreme Soviet, the USSR Council of Ministers and the Supreme Court were reorganised to include the officials of the Union Republics (presidents of the Presidiums of the Supreme Soviets of the Union Republics, chairmen of their Councils of Ministers, etc.). These principles are now enshrined in the 1977 constitution. The state apparatus which operates along Leninist principles of close links with the population, people's control, democratic centralism, socialist legality, etc., has made further progress in the state of all the people.

Secondly, the national-territorial and administrative-territorial organisation of the state of all the people has been considerably modified. Until 1936, most of the Union Republics (the Russian Federation, the Ukraine, Byelorussia, etc.) were direct members of the Soviet Union, while the three Transcaucasian Republics (Azerbaijan, Armenia and Georgia) were members of the Union through the Transcaucasian Federation. In the state of the entire people, all the republics have the same legal status as members of the USSR and their number has increased from 4 when the Union was formed in 1922, to 15. Many formerly backward peoples have attained their own statehood. New autonomous republics, regions and areas have come into being and a new administrative territorial division based on economic zoning has been introduced.

Thirdly, the state regime has also undergone basic changes. The regime of proletarian socialist democracy gave way to the socialist democracy of all the people, as a result of the changes in the class structure of the society and the relations between the classes. The advancement of socialist democracy was marked by a further expansion of the material, political and legal rights of Soviet citizens, reflected first in the 1936 constitution, and later even more fully in the 1977 constitution.

At present, the USSR is the only example of the socialist state of all the people. But the state of all the people is a necessary stage of development in other socialist countries too, although its forms will have specific features of their own.

Notes

1   For details see V.E. Chirkin, *Forms of Socialist State*. Moscow, 1973, pp. 7–8, 18–23 (in Russian).

2   *The State Law of the Capitalist Countries and Countries that have Freed Themselves from Colonial Dependence*. Moscow, 1979, p. 168 (Russian).

3   M. Gulcynsky, T. Twinski and W. Lamentowicz, *Instytucje polityczne współczesnego kapitalizmu*. Warsaw, 1978, p. 8.

4   G.N. Manov, 'On the Notion of the Form of the State', *Transactions of Tajik State University*, vol. 9, *Transactions of the School of Law*, N 4, 1956, p. 7 (in Russian).

5   V. Tsonev, *The Form and Contents of the State*. Sofia, Pravna Misl, 1969, no. 3, p. 82 (in Bulgarian).

6   The need to distinguish the notions of the 'political regime' and the 'state regime' is supported by the Czechoslovak political scientist J. Blahoz, 'The Development of Views on Forms of Government in the Present Day World', paper submitted to the Eleventh World Congress of the International Political Science Association, Moscow, 1979, p. 5.

7   The Czechoslovak political scientist E. Kučera underlines the need to take into account both direct and feedback connections in characterising an element of the state form, i.e. the form of government. E. Kučera, *Obecné teorie statu a práva*. Prague, Dil. I, p. 113 (in Czech).

8   V.I. Lenin, *Collected Works*, Moscow, vol. 26, p. 415.

9   F. Giese, *Staatsrecht*. Wiesbaden, 1956, p. 13.

10 H. Nawiasky, *Staatstypen der Gegenwart*. St Gallen, 1934, p. 198.

11 M. Imboden, *Die Staatsformen*, Basel, 1959, p. 45.

12 P.H. Odegard, R.K. Carr, M.N. Bernstein and D.H. Morrison, *American Government*, New York, 1961, pp. 19–27. At the same time it should be noted that in recent years certain Western scholars have been using the notion of the socio-political system in their studies on the

typology of the state. P.F. Gonidec observes that the use of the concept of social system, of two contemporary types of state, can be distinguished: the capitalist state and the socialist state: cf. P.F. Gonidec, *Relations internationales*, Paris, 1977, p. 133.

13   *The Achievements of the Soviet Government over 40 Years in Figures.* Moscow, 1957, p. 14 (in Russian).
14   *World Marxist Review*, no. 12, 1977, p. 4.
15   *The Achievements of the Soviet Government over 40 Years*, p. 11.
16   L. Brezhnev, 'A Historic Stage on the Road to Communism', *World Marxist Review*, no. 12, 1977, p. 5.
17   *The Records of the USSR Supreme Soviet*, no. 11, 1957.

14 The theory of the state and the Third World

Marcos Kaplan

The historical context

Any comparative study of the state in Third World countries requires a distinction between the situation in Latin America and that in Africa and Asia.

In the vast majority of Latin American countries the classic colonial period came to an end more than a century and a half ago, to be followed by the gradual development of the nation-state. In most African and Asian countries (with exceptions such as China, Japan and possibly India), a similar process did not begin until the mid-twentieth century. In addition to differences in the international context at the formative and initial development stage, there are also differences in the diversity of structures, the intermingling of systems, the types and degrees of development of classes within the nation and in their interrelations and links with the main actors in the international system. These are all reflected in different forms, stages of development, apparatuses and actions of the state.

The development of the theory of the state in contemporary Latin America is part and parcel of a process of change governed by a new pattern of incorporation into the international system characterised by asymmetrical interdependence, the concentration of world power and the new international division of labour.[1] This is reflected domestically in the establishment and progression of late or peripheral neo-capitalist growth,[2] the appearance of organic and endemic political

276

crisis, state interventionism and, in certain countries of the sub-continent, neo-fascism.

The great variety of classes and groups is aggravated by a proliferation and medley of ideologies. Political parties settle down into a routine, become hidebound and cease to reflect change, classes and groups, institutions and systems. More and more obstacles arise to rational forms of political action and to agreement on the ends and means of development. Irreconcilable differences, inconsistencies, disastrous imbalances between classes, institutions and parties, and periods of paralysis become increasingly commonplace.[3]

On the one hand, neo-capitalist growth breaks down the conditions and structures of oligarchic domination and of the traditional state, establishes the conditions for its own existence and perpetuation, restructures and mobilises populations, and encourages them to increase their needs, expectations and demands for wider participation. On the other hand, late neo-capitalism is powered by a driving force which marginalises populations and increases tension, conflict and antagonism. The social and power structure transfers centres of political decision-making and action into the hands of the new oligarchical élite and its associated institutions, in particular the armed forces. The accumulation process and profitability of large enterprises makes for a centralised authoritarian power requiring obedience from the masses. The oligarchical élite and its domestic and foreign supporters find it increasingly difficult to ensure the perpetuation and development of neo-capitalism; they split into opposing factions; they do not succeed in halting the mobilisation of the masses, indeed they intensify and speed it up. Tension and conflict, the levelling of criticism and attacks cause or reinforce the entropy of the system. This is expressed in social conflicts, political instability, the weakening of legitimacy, the collapse of consensus, the failure of traditional forms of coercion, power vacuums and crises of hegemony.

For the most part, with the exception of Cuba, the foundations and constituents of the traditional mode of domination are not destroyed, but the result is both to prevent the continued existence of the old oligarchical system of domination and its rebirth in a different form and with different instruments, as well as the establishment and effective functioning of a more broadly-based participatory democracy. There is an increasingly marked contradiction between the requirements of the neo-capitalist model and the forms and consequences of the political crisis.

Against this background of political crisis, growing state autonomy and intervention, authoritarianism and neo-fascism (phenomena to which we will return later), social scientists have been trying to elaborate a theory of the state. For historical and structural reasons which we have analysed in greater detail elsewhere,[4] Latin American social scientists as a rule display ambivalence in their thinking, values, attitudes and behaviour, and also in their activities and the results produced. Standards of rigour and efficiency, idealism, social rationality and innovation exist alongside feelings of frustration, dissatisfaction, criticism, opposition and a readiness to act as potential agents of change — but also alongside the desire for social advancement, reputation, increased income, a higher standard of living, greater influence and a preoccupation with politics and government administration as a means of achieving individual and group fulfilment.

The theory of the state and Latin American Marxism

Research into the state has had well-known Latin American precursors in the nineteenth century and the early twentieth century,[5] their work consisting primarily of analyses motivated by their attitudes to political conflicts, historical research into the development of the nation and the state, and constitutional law studies.[6]

The second phase comprises the period between the early twentieth century and the end of the Second World War. This saw the introduction and development of various types of Marxist, anarchist and positivist socialist thought, and the first signs of emergent populist nationalism and developmentalism, all reflecting a wide range of party-political, intellectual and professional interests, not always referring exclusively to the state, but including it in the scope of the problem studied. In some cases the concerns and activities dealt with go beyond the framework of institutionalised schools of thought, or verge towards the political field. They reveal the influence of foreign scholars, often living in virtual exile, and of isolated compatriots who, while pursuing an independent line, are nevertheless influenced by the former.[7]

The third stage, from 1945 to the present day, covers first the arrival and development of the social sciences from the United States and Western Europe, and second the beginning of the work of international governmental organisations and its results. During this period, Marxist currents of thought progressed in various doctrinal forms; they become respectable and influential in academic and political circles and in international bodies, but were at the same time critically affected by new Latin American and world phenomena, the emergence of heterodox views and attempts at improvement on various lines.

The Marxism which took root in the region from the end of the nineteenth century onwards lacked a well-developed and systematic theory of the state. It was adversely affected by the supremacy of post-Marxian dialectical materialism, setbacks in the publication of Marx's works and the predominance of reductionist, mechanistic and evolutionist trends, all perpetuated and reinforced after 1917 by the triumph of Stalinist theory and policy.[8]

Stalinism imposed a version of Marxism characterised by dogmatism, scholasticism, party and state authoritarianism, reductionism and mechanistic determinism. In sociology and political science, this manifests itself in the analysis of the relationship between *infrastructure* and *superstructure*, which are split up, linked as outwardly static entities ranked in such a way that one governs and determines the other. No account is taken of the role of mediations or of the practical autonomy and inherent effectiveness of different levels and aspects of society and their interdependent constituent parts.[9]

Reductionism takes two forms, the *structuralist* and the *instrumentalist*, partly overlapping and partly in contradiction with each other. With both of them emphasis is laid on productive forces and relations of production, class conflict, and the existence of a ruling class as being in essence creative, providing a generative principle and a key to the understanding of all that is superstructural, conceived as a collection of derived phenomena, with no specific or independent character of their own. Consequently, culture and ideology, politics and political systems, the state and the law cannot be made individual subjects of sociology or political science, having their own theoretical bases and susceptible to empirical investigation. Deprived of their own reality and logic, of their autonomy and feedback capacity of their functions in helping to produce and reproduce or change the economy, of their class system and general infrastructure, politics and affairs of state become identified with a single form of domination, with a single type of problem and conflict, processes and objectives, resources and achievements. The lack of analysis, criticism and creativity makes itself felt both negatively and positively, both in scientific practice and in social and political activity.

First, there is a tendency to do away with history, all that is novel and unforeseen, chance and contingency, creativity; there is an inclination towards fatalistic optimism and passivity in thought and deed.

Second, there is an essentialistic conception of classes, a unique principle used to explain politics and the state. Classes are seen as entities pre-established once and for all, defined by relations of production, beyond the scope of any structuring, restructuring or redefinition process, however complex. No account is taken of different structures, forms of expression, trends, attitudes and behaviour, projects and strategies. The class criterion is the prime source and connective principle of all characteristics, trends and conduct of an ideological or political nature. The class system is the fundamental socio-historical subject and the only important field of conflict.

Third, thinking on power and politics becomes ambivalent. These are regarded, on the one hand, as a reflection and instrument of authority, subordinated to its use, and on the other, as subject to manipulation in the light of any alternative project put forward. No thought is given either to the phenomena of the alienation of politics (its autonomy and separation from society and class, the specialisation and professionalisation of politicians each with their own interests) or to the possibility that the political sphere might bring together actors, activities, structures and processes by and through which societies, groups and individuals would assume responsibility for themselves, directing and organising power structures and their content, making changes as necessary, and examining and adopting their own choice of policies.

Attitudes towards the state oscillate between two viewpoints. The first presents it as an apparatus that is a reflection, or instrument, the sole function of which is conservation and repression: a closed system in which the majority of social actors have no chance of participating or striving to control or modify it. The second attitude, characterised by a kind of fetishism and worshipping of the state, presents it as a remedy for all ills, to be instituted by means of reform or revolution, with a view to controlling and making use of it as it is, not replacing it with new forms of political organisation.

Lastly, identification of the socialist alternative with 'socialism as it actually exists' precludes the possibility of applying to socialist countries the Marxist method and categories of analysis and assessment which are applied to the capitalist world. This epistemological schizophrenia hampers progress towards a sociology and political science having universal bases and scope.

Crises and reactions

The course of recent events in Latin America and the world has caused certain adjustments to be made to the various forms of Marxist doctrine. Events have not been in accordance with forecasts and expectations. Classes, groups, institutions, political parties and states have developed a wide variety of forms and trends, and produced different results. The Latin American dominated classes have not necessarily joined self-proclaimed revolutionary parties, but on the contrary have sometimes given their support to populist-nationalist, developmentalist or liberal-democratic movements and regimes.

Classes and coalitions identified with the system of domination have shown a frequently underestimated gift for self-defence and counter-attack.

The reductionist view of politics as an instrument of class domination by means of manipulation and coercion extends to include the putting forward of alternatives with emphasis on violent revolution as the only effective means of solving conflicts and achieving structural changes. This approach sets little store by and indeed rejects important aspects of political life such as negotiation, compromise, agreement, alliances and reforms. Democracy is ignored or disparaged as the political expression of liberal capitalism, spurious and unattainable before the socialist revolution and irrelevant or superfluous once it has taken place.

Lastly, the world crisis in orthodox Marxist doctrine contests the notion of a Marxist Mecca representing an ideal system, theory and method. The claims of pluralism, polycentrism and specific local and historical circumstances are being reasserted. Emphasis is being placed on the value of theory, methodology, the techniques of empirical investigation, sociological imagination and political creativity. In addition to solitary precursors such as José Carlos Mariátegui, new figures emerged in the 1940s and there was increased interest in research. In the following two decades this trend developed and expanded with the work of new researchers and/or militants who, while affiliated to Marxism to a greater or lesser degree, were freer and more critical, and sought approaches in keeping with the political challenges of the time.

Dogmatism is losing ground and being undermined, but it is still resisting and regaining force, surviving or re-emerging in new forms. The theory of state monopoly capitalism, although it admits the importance of political factors in the analysis of capitalist production and the anti-establishment struggle, is still marked by economicism and continues to deny that the state, its functionaries and its policies possess their own reality, logic and driving force, differentiated and autonomous interests.[10]

The influence of Louis Althusser and his neo-Marxist approach makes itself felt as an ideology presented as a science. An attempt is made to rediscover ontological orthodoxy through an academic analysis of Marxist texts which leads to his thought becoming closed in on itself and repetitive. Intellectually and politically, Althusser's philosophy represents a strategic withdrawal, a hidden recuperation of official dogmas. This, together with a limited historical frame of reference and rejection of empirical investigation and active participation in social and political affairs, means that Althusser's contribution to the development of a theory of the state in Latin America can ultimately be regarded as negligible.[11]

A more complex, stimulating influence is that of Nicos Poulantzas in his persistent, if incomplete, attempt to combat economic reductionism, reinstate the importance of political factors and analyse the concept of the capitalist state and its degree of relative autonomy.[12]

The Berlin 'Logical School of Capital' attempts to view the state as a phenomenon which is both superstructural and infrastructural, a bridge between the economic and the political spheres. Its Latin American contribution has been limited, due in part to the difficulties inherent in its approach (recourse to deduction based on linked categories, a tendency to switch from the abstract to the empirical, the failure to demonstrate the possibility of and need for a differentiated and autonomous state), and in part to its use in the region mainly in order to strengthen arguments on the limits of state intervention.[13]

The contribution from 'the Fiscal Crisis of the State' school of thought is its insistence on the need to introduce political and cultural-ideological forms of mediation into the infrastructure and operation of the system (organisations, the activities and struggles of classes and groups, political crises). It lacks however a structural theory of the place of politics and the state in capitalism, pre-capitalist societies and post-revolutionary regimes.[14]

Gramsci, with the differing reception given to his ideas both inside and outside communist parties, has helped to reinstate the superstructure, hegemony, politics and the state as the articulatory elements of the historical block. This applies particularly to problems relating to forms of power and domination; political practice and hegemonic processes; the wide range of contradictions, conflicts, antagonisms and problematic areas; the falsity of polarised alternatives (reform or revolution, Stalinist communism or neo-capitalist social democracy), and possible new forms of political life, the state and society.[15] This positive influence has been curbed in Latin America by the seal set on doctrinal orthodoxy and support for its reinstatement.

Western inputs and international bodies

The influence of Western social science has made itself felt in two ways. The earlier of the two, the more direct, represents a juridico-political view of the state, with emphasis on constitutional and administrative law and the philosophy of law. The other form, more recent and indirect, influenced by United States social science, has served as a vehicle for introducing into Latin America the ideas of the 'Machiavellians' (Pareto, Mosca, Michels, Burnham) and of Max Weber. The influence of the former has acted as a corrective to economic reductionism, but only to fall into political and élitist reductionism. Weber's emphasis on power relations and processes and the sociology of domination and the state has had an impact in Latin America in view of its experience of government intervention, including populist-nationalist, developmentalist and didactorial movements or regimes.[16]

Major social science trends in the English-speaking world have for long ignored the state, though recently there has been some partial recognition of its existence. The dominant tendencies, which combine Weberianism, strutural-functionalism, systems theory and cybernetics, represent the convergence of two basic approaches, namely hyperfactual empiricism and abstract theorising.

In particular, the theory of political development presents a model drawn from United States and Western European experience as a paradigm for all political systems. The same frame of reference provides concepts, categories and proposals for the specific political development of Third World countries, putting forward structures and systems which would maximise desirable patterns of organisation and behaviour.

According to some theories of political development there is inevitably correspondence between the stages of political development and those of economic growth, the former being dependent on the latter. The political system and form of government are not regarded as an essential variable of change, and the role of the state in the Third World is ignored or underestimated.

The streams of Latin American sociology and political science which reflect the above-mentioned approaches display omissions and gaps in their treatment of the state. The state may be presented as one group among many, as one power within a plurality of powers and micropowers. Or it may be absorbed within the vague concept of a centralised political system, which in turn is presented as inherent in all societies at all times. Through its identification with government or, more obliquely, as a result of being seen in terms of the people involved in politics, it may be reduced to the idea of bureaucracy, elections, constitutional systems or diplomacy.

In another school of thought the state appears as a special higher entity, beyond and above social context, historical process and political conflict. A tendency which has recently come to the fore places the state once again in an organic and evolutionary context identified with the sociology of modernisation. This views the state as both a product and an aspect, either final or temporary, of the growth process (endogenous, uniform, ongoing or completed) of nations which are in transition from a traditional to a modern society. Modernisation, which is equated with industrialisation and advances in the division of labour, is seen as an inevitable linear process in which the structures of society become differentiated, autonomous and universal, and in which the processes resulting from and influencing change become institutionalised. Differentiation is an independent variable which seeks to provide an explanation on universally rational grounds. The reorganisation and redistribution which arise from the structures of domination provide each society with a political centre and co-ordinating structures, and extend the field of political activity. The state is born and develops from and through the transfer of powers previously held by the political structures which coexisted autonomously in pre-state societies. In all societies and in all periods the state is the necessary result of and a priori solution to conflicts and crises arising from the differentiation of internal structures. As a neutral and independent arbiter, the state reconciles conflicting interests; it is a functional substitute for community solidarity and spontaneous consensus. The state shapes and sponsors the cultural and political unification of the nation, giving full recognition to the complete differentiation between political and public, as well as between social and private life. As the product and superstructure of growth, industrialisation and social rationalisation, the only possible form of political modernisation transcending cultural diversities and historical praxis, the state becomes a universal category and a unique model of political organization.[17]

Currents of thought originating in the United States have influenced Latin American theories of the state. Concepts such as bureaucratic authoritarianism are concerned with examining the regime rather than the theory and practice of the state; they have not yet succeeded in producing a full and satisfactory conceptual approach to the problem of the state in Latin America.[18]

Inter-governmental organisations located in the region, especially the Economic Commission for Latin America (ECLA), have recently begun to include this problem among their concerns, although only gradually and partially. Their almost exclusive initial concern with theoretical questions and with the search for conditions conducive to peripheral neo-capitalist growth in Latin America has been succeeded by a recognition not only of the obstacles thereto, and to social change, but also of its negative consequences, and this has made it necessary to seek the aid of sociologists and political scientists. Such topics as power structures, planning, integration and external dependence have given rise to analyses, diagnoses and models which, although deserving of interest in themselves, possess only a limited capacity to explain and regulate the process of growth and change, and do not lend themselves to the planning or implementation of an integral development strategy. The subject of the state is barely dealt

284

with in the contributions by ECLA, and then only incidentally or indirectly.[19]

African and Asian specificities

The theory of the state in the Asian and African contexts must take as its starting point those situations which are common to the countries of both continents: frequent, large-scale state intervention; transition from traditional colonialism to neo-colonialism; the adoption by political and administrative élites of a model of the state originating in the developed industrialised countries of the West, the Soviet Union or China. This external model of the state is superimposed on forces, structures and processes which differ from the premises of the original model. The local situations present the state with particular problems, without providing the resources and means with which to deal with them effectively. The state comes into being and operates under conditions of neo-colonial dependency; levels of growth and productivity are low; there is little progress towards the social division of labour; classes hardly exist, and if they do, they are fluid and weak; civil society and a properly organised and functioning political community are missing. The embryonic native élites are not sufficiently numerous to take on the task of constructing and administering the state, but they take advantage of their limited numbers to form themselves into and act as a governing bureaucracy which enjoys a monopoly of power. They face an intractable contradiction between the policies based on participation which confer legitimacy upon government and were imposed as a result of independence, and the policies which concentrate wealth, income and power in the hands of national and foreign minorities, which are imposed by the weight of neo-colonialism and peripheral neo-capitalism.[20]

In the ex-colonial countries of Africa and Asia, the state acquires crucial importance and state intervention is far more frequent and extensive than in the developed capitalist countries. This is reflected in the nationalisation of firms, the steady increase in the functions, powers and resources of the state and of the governing élite, the tendency towards autonomisation and the frequent occurrence of military risings and authoritarian rule. It can also be seen in the different development strategies (neo-colonialist, national-populist, collectivist-authoritarian), which reflect alliances of classes and of ethnic and regional groups. Through its strategies and policies, the state conditions or determines the formation and structure of classes and groups, their evolution and their successes and failures.

The political and governing élites which constitute, embody and

285

manage the state take measures to further their own growth and expansion and to defend their interests, powers and privileges; autonomisation and political authoritarianism find favour with them. They combine repression with the encouragement of consensus (a one-party system, patronage, corporativism) and they tend to convert themselves into the dominant class, either exclusively or in alliance with private groups, national and foreign. The state and the governing élite oscillate between action to reject and oppose foreign firms, the renegotiation of dependency and attempts at autonomy, although all these tendencies are frequently combined in varying proportions.

In the limited theoretical analysis and empirical research which has so far been carried out on the state, Marxism in its various forms has acquired a certain ascendancy.

Certain Marxist schools of thought tend to favour economic reductionism. According to one extreme version, the economically dominant class is also politically dominant both before and after independence, and the owners of capital are also the owners and masters of the state, whether in the ex-colonial power or in the ex-colony. Self-determination is unattainable without an anti-imperialist revolution. According to another strand of Marxist thought, there is a distinction between, on the one hand, the financial oligarchy which is a globally dominant class throughout the planet and which dictates the functions of the state and the movements of socio-economic forces in Asia and Africa and, on the other hand, the governing class and the higher sections of society in the individual states, which have no real power of their own.

For writers such as Issa Shivji, however, political independence is important for it creates a national state no longer directly controlled by classes wielding colonial power, although that does not automatically mean the end of domination by international capital and finance. Control of the state passes into the hands of one or more of the dominant local classes, who have their own particular interests which coincide with imperialist interests only in the last resort. The character, forms and policy of any African state stem from the interests of and contradictions between the pre-capitalist and capitalist classes and relations within the country, inter-imperialist rivalries and power struggles between different tendencies and traditions. This is reflected in constant political upheavals and realignments.

An alternative approach, which is situated at the other end of the spectrum and which in turn can be subdivided, regards the classes in Africa as shapeless and fluid, too weak to promote either capitalism or socialism, while at the same time privately financed capitalism is neither willing nor able to achieve sustained and integrated growth.[21] Only the state can achieve development. This means a transitional state of an indeterminate nature. It is established and managed by a bureaucracy drawn from the intermediate strata of society which assumes power after independence. Its ideology combines nationalist, anti-imperialist and socialist elements and it adopts a policy of state capitalism. Such a policy favours a rupture with neo-colonialism and supports growth and industrialisation, but not socialism. The pursuit of capitalist development, the outward forms of rhetoric of socialism notwithstanding, may represent an attempt to reduce dependence within a context of foreign domination, to impose the supremacy of the bureaucracy over the national bourgeoisie while continuing to protect it and sooner or later to achieve integration within the world capitalist system.

Finally, in the opinion of other political analysts, state capitalism may lead in the long term to advancement along a non-capitalist path: it may have the effect not only of obstructing the growth of the local bourgeoisie, but of destroying it and producing a form of proto-socialist development which will lead on to socialism. This line of argument refers to various African countries which other analysts have criticised as examples of bureaucratic collectivism and Third World Stalinism. Such criticism is usually accompanied by the proposal of an alternative model of socialism.[22]

Alternative approaches

Since the 1950s attempts have been made to construct a critical theory of the state in Latin America, including those of the author of the present paper. In addition to defining a theory of the state[23] and investigating the formation and development of the state in Latin America, these efforts have concentrated on the evolution of this phenomenon over the last few decades.

During the process of change referred to above, the state and the ruling groups intervene increasingly, extend their functions, their spheres of action and their activities, and increase the powers and means of action at their disposal. The state becomes a 'Creole Leviathan', divided and ambiguous, with relative autonomy in some fields, and although this autonomy is contradictory it is limited only in the final analysis.[24]

Modern neo-capitalism cannot take root and grow solely as the result of a spontaneous and self-regulating process, or the free play of market forces and of the actions of large national and foreign firms. These take no interest whatsoever in such matters as the socio-economic conditions and the regulations and guarantees which are required for activities which produce no profit and are extremely risky and long-term ventures, but which are essential for the emergence and development of a private sector, for the satisfaction of the needs of the populations and for the reproduction of the system.

The state must therefore act as guarantor for the general conditions governing the establishment and organisation and the reproduction and growth of modern neo-capitalism, mainly by the exercise of its functions of collective organisation and its socio-economic policies. The state and the public sector become the principal saver, producer, buyer and seller of goods and services, direct investor and supporter of private investment, the main employer and the guarantor of social security and of the purchasing power of large sections of society. The state and the nationalised firms assume responsibility for the public financing of part of production and for curbing the threat of over-accumulation by large national and foreign companies, applying various mechanisms to reduce the value of social capital. These have the effect of making society responsible for the risks and losses of the monopolies and they help to increase their profits and rates of accumulation by transferring the costs of their operations on to small -and medium-sized firms, the middle classes and the workers (taxes, inflation).[25]

The state does perform other functions and tasks: the institutional-isation of social relations and relationships of command — obedience as well as that of its own intervention in a variety of areas and problems; the creation and reinforcement of legitimacy and consensus for its own purposes and as regards the overall system and the growth model and, finally, legal regulation.

At the same time the state must strengthen its political and administrative control apparatus and its work of social coercion. It becomes more concentrated and centralised as an apparatus, as a moving force and as a centre of power; both its nature and its modes of operation are redefined.

The growth and centralisation of state power are achieved through the ascendancy of the executive at the expense of the other branches; through the monopoly of information and communication; through the technicalisation of politics and administration, and through the advance of the technocracy and of militarisation and repression. The state atomises and robotises the society, converting it into an amorphous body without organs of expression, participation or self-defence.

Through its subsystems of control and its other functions, the state sets itself up as an arbitral authority over classes, groups and institutions; it regulates their relationships and conflicts, and imposes compromises. The state provides the facilities and mechanisms for the political unification of the various factions of the dominant class and

288

for solutions to the crises of hegemony. It regulates the partial rise and incorporation of subordinate, dominated groups, restricts their effective participation and creates feelings of national loyalty with a view to the attainment of internal integration and the management of external relations.

The state's international functions lead it to play a central role in the establishment of external dependency and of peripheral neo-capitalism, although it is not the mere tool of foreign interests. It mediates and arbitrates between internal and external groups, between the nation and the ex-colonial powers and between autonomy and dependency. Although vacillating and erratic, its nationalist policies channel towards the exterior forces presenting a threat to the system and provide a means of mobilising support which will strengthen its hand when dealing with states and corporations in the developed world. Nationalism and the demands for a new international order simultaneously seek the renegotiation of dependency, favourable treatment within the present world system and the strengthening of the autonomy of the state.[26]

The growth of state control is closely linked with the strengthening and autonomisation of political and administrative personnel and of the civil and military technocracy. The administrative bureaucracy performs the role of mediator between and regulator of the various classes and groups, which it makes dependent on itself or on the state for their existence and advancement. A section of the middle and lower classes finds in public service a means of existence and advancement. They concentrate their attention on their own classes and on the groups from which they originate, and organise, control and manipulate them so as to place them in a dependent position and use them as a power base. Both within the bureaucracy itself and outside it, there grow up subsystems of power and constellations of interest which reinforce its autonomisation.

The armed forces are an extreme example of this tendency: they become politicised, tend to convert themselves into a technocratic élite making common cause with the civil technocracy, and assume responsibility for guiding the nation, acting as an autonomous decision-making centre with its own interests to protect.

The democratisation of political recruitment brings into play certain mechanisms for the social advancement of individuals and groups. This opens the state up to politicians and officials from the middle and upper strata of society, reinforces the influence and negotiating strength of these strata and the introduction of measures which benefit them, and also contributes to the further autonomisation of the state itself.

In general terms, decisions by the state tend to be taken in accordance with a scale of priorities which favours: (1) the ruling élite; (2) the overall rationality of the system; (3) the most influential factions within the dominant class; (4) the dominant class as a whole; (5) organised factions and groups belonging to the subordinate and dominated classes; and (6) certain specific *ad hoc* combinations of some of the previous elements.

Notes

1   M. Kaplan, 'La concentración del poder político a escala mundial' in *El trimestre económico*, Mexico, no. 161, January–March 1974; 'Lo viejo y lo neuvo en el orden político mundial' in Jorge Castaneda (ed.), *Derecho económico internacional*, Mexico, Fondo de Cultura Económica, 1976.

2   Antonio García, *Atraso y dependencia en América Latina. Hacia una teoría latinoamericana del desarrollo*, Buenos Aires, El Ateneo, 1972; Jorge Graciarena, *Poder y clases sociales en el desarrollo de América Latina*, Buenos Aires, Paidos, 1967.

3   On the impact of the various ideologies, see M. Kaplan, '50 años de historia argentina (1925–1975): El laberinto de la frustración' in Pablo González Casanova (co-ordinator), *América Latina: Historia de medio siglo. 1.–América del Sur*, Mexico, Siglo XXI Editores, 1977; M. Kaplan, *Estado, cultura y ciencia en América Latina*, Tokyo, The United Nations University, 1981. On the political crisis there are earlier studies by Silvio Frondizi, *La crisis política argentina. Ensayo de interpretación ideológica*, Buenos Aires, ADI, 1946, and *La crisis de la democracia*, 2nd edn, Buenos Aires, Praxis, 1952; Gino Germani, *Política y sociedad en una época de transición — De la sociedad tradicional a la sociedad de masas*, Buenos Aires, Editorial Paidos, 1962.

4   M. Kaplan, *La ciencia política latinoamericana en la encrucijada*, Santiago de Chile, 1st edn, Editorial Universitaria, 1969; M. Kaplan, *La investigación latinoamericana en ciancias sociales*, Mexico, Jornadas 74, El Colegio de México, 1973.

5   See José Luis Romero, *Las ideas políticas en Argentina*, 1st edn, Mexico, Fondo de Cultura Económica, 1946; M. Kaplan, *Formación del Estado Nacional en América Latina*, 1st edition, Santiago de Chile, Editorial Universitaria, 1969, 2nd edition, Buenos Aires, Amorrortu Editores, 1976.

6   See Romero, op. cit.; Myron Burgin, *Economic Aspects of Argentine Federalism*, Cambridge, Mass., Harvard University Press, 1946.

7   In connection with Argentina alone, mention should be made of the importance and influence of Rodolfo Mondolfo. his research and teaching on political philosophy and theory, especiallyy *Marx y el marxismo*, Mexico, Fondo de Cultura Economica, 1960; Felix Weil, joint founder and organiser of the Frankfurt School, who lived in

Argentina in the 1960s, author of *The Argentine Riddle*, New York, The John Day Co., 1944; Myron Burgin, op. cit., partly prepared during his stay in Argentina; Silvio Frondizi, *El estado moderno*, Buenos Aires, Editorial Losada, 1944, and *La realidad argentina — ensayo de interpretación sociológica*, two vols, Buenos Aires, Ediciones Praxis, 1955 and 1957; Sergio Bagú, *Economía de la sociedad colonial*, Buenos Aires, El Ateneo, 1949, and *Estructura social de la colonia*, Buenos Aires, El Ateneo, 1952.

8   For a critical analysis of the main views of the left in Latin America at various times in its history, see: Silvio Frondizi, *La realidad argentina*, Vol. II: La revolución socialista; M. Kaplan, *Política y vida cotidiana*, Buenos Aires, Colección Liberación, 1960; Teodoro Petkoff, *Proceso a la izquierda*, Barcelona, Editorial Planeta, 2nd edn, 1976.

9   I have developed this critical approach in M. Kaplan, *Estado y sociedad*, Mexico, UNAM, 1978; see also Cornelius Castoriadis, *L'Institution imaginaire de la société*, Paris, Seuil, 1976; David Gold, Clarence Y.H. Lo, Erik Olin Wright, 'Recent Developments in Marxist Theory of the Capitalist State', *Monthly Review*, October 1975, pp. 2–43 and November 1975, pp. 36–51.

10   Criticisms of the theory of monopoly state capitalism which have influenced theorists and politicians in the Third World include J.M. Vincent *et al.*, 'L'Etat contemporain et le marxisme' in *Critiques de l'économie politique*, Paris, Maspero, 1975; Jacques Valier, *Le parti communiste français et le capitalisme monopoliste d'Etat*, Paris, Maspero, 1976.

11   Important criticisms of the work of L. Althusser include Henri Lefebvre, *Au-delà du structuralisme*, Paris, Anthropos, 1971; Raymond Aron, *Marxismes imaginaires*, Paris, Gallimard, 1970; J.M. Vincent *et al.*, *Contre Althusser*, Paris, Coll. 10/18, 1974; George Lichtheim, 'A New Twist in the Dialectic' in *From Marx to Hegel*, New York, Herder and Herder, 1971.

12   The influence of Poulantzas can be examined in 'Préliminaires à l'étude de l'hégémonie dans l'Etat', *Les Temps modernes*, no. 234, November 1965; *Pouvoir politique et classes sociales de l'Etat capitaliste*, Paris, Maspero, 1968; 'Les Transformations actuelles de l'Etat, la crise politique et la crise de l'Etat' in N. Poulantzas (ed.), *La crise de l'Etat*, Paris, PUF, 1976.

13   Vincent *et al.*, *L'Etat contemporain;* J. Holloway and Sol Picciotto (eds.), *State and Capital — A Marxist Debate*, London, Edward Arnold, 1978; Tilman Evers, *El Estado en la periferia capitalista*, Mexico, Siglo XXI Editores, 1979; Ernesto Laclaum, 'Teorías marxistas del estado: debates y perspectivas' in N. Lechner (ed.), *Estado y política en América Latina*, Mexico, Siglo XXI Editores, 1981.

14   J. O'Connor, *The Fiscal Crisis of the State*, New York, St Martin's Press, 1973, and *The Corporations and the State*, New York, Harper and Row, 1974.

15   In addition to Gramsci himself and commentators on his work, see Giorgio Napolitano, *La alternativa eurocomunista*, Barcelona, Editorial

Blume, 1977; Wolfgang Leonhard, *Euro-Kommunismus — Herausforderung für Ost und West*, Munich, C. Bertelsmann Verlag, 1978.

16 M. Kaplan, *La ciencia política* and *Estado y sociedad*.

17 Bertrand Badie and Pierre Birnbaum, *Sociologie de l'état*, Paris, Grasset, 1979, especially the second part.

18 The first approach is principally represented by Gino Germani, *Política ya sociedad*, and *Sociología de la modernización*, Buenos Aires, Paidos, 1971; and by Helio Jaguaribe, *Sociedad, cambio y sistema político; Jaguaribe, Desarrollo político: sentido y condiciones;* and *Crisis y alternativas de América Latina: reforma o revolución*, Buenos Aires, Paidos, 1972. On the second approach, see David Callier (ed.), *The New Authoritarianism in Latin America*, Princeton, NJ, Princeton University Press, 1979.

19 Economic Commission for Latin America (ECLA/CEPAL), *El desarrollo social de América Latina en la posguerra*, Buenos Aires, Solar/Hachette, 1963; *El pensamiento de la CEPAL*, Santiago de Chile, Editorial Universitaria, 1969; CEPAL, *El cambio social y la política de desarrollo social en América Latina*, New York, United Nations, 1969; Raul Prebisch, *Capitalismo periférico — Crisis y transformación*, Mexico, Fondo de Cultura Económica, 1981.

20 See, on the theoretical and political debate on the state in Africa and Asia, Richard Sandbrook, *The Politics of Basic Needs — Urban Aspects of Assaulting Poverty in Africa*, Toronto-Buffalo, University of Toronto Press, 1982, especially Chapter 4; Issa G. Shivji, 'The State in the Dominated Social Formations of Africa: Some Theoretical Issues', *International Social Science Journal*, vol. 32, no. 4, 1980; Yash Ghai (ed.), *Law in the Political Economy of Public Enterprise — African Perspectives*, see especially Yash Ghai, 'Control and Management of the Economy: Research Perspectives on Public Enterprise' and Björn Beckman, 'Public Enterprise and State Capitalism' both in Ghai, op. cit.; Hamza Alavi, 'The State in Postcolonial Societies: Pakistan and Bangladesh', in *New Left Review*, no. 74, July–August 1974, pp. 145–73.

21 James F. Petras, 'State Capitalism and the Third World', *Journal of Contemporary Asia*, vol. 6, no. 4, 1976, and an examination of his analysis in Beckman, op. cit.

22 Sandbrook, op. cit., chap. 7.

23 M. Kaplan, *Estado y Sociedad*.

24 M. Kaplan, 'El Leviathan criollo', *Revista Mexicana de Sociología*, vol. 40, no. 3, July–September 1978, and 'Estado acumulación de capital y distribución del ingreso en América Latina', *Comercio Exterior*, Mexico, vol. 29, no. 4, April 1979.

25 M. Kaplan, *El Estado en el Desarrollo y la Integración de América Latina*, Caracas, Monte Avila Editores, 1969.

26 M. Kaplan, *Problemas del Desarrollo y de la Integración de América Latina*, Caracas, Monte Avila Editores, 1968; and 'Corporaciones Públicas Multinacionales para el Desarrollo y la Integración de América Latina', *Comercio Exterior*, Mexico, August–September 1970.

Index